EQUESTRIAN STUDIES

The Salem College Guide to
Sources in English, 1950–1980

MYRON J. SMITH, Jr.

The Scarecrow Press, Inc.
Metuchen, N.J., & London
1981

Library of Congress Cataloging in Publication Data

Smith, Myron J.
  Equestrian studies.

  Includes index.
  1. Horses--Bibliography. 2. Horsemanship--
Bibliography. I. Salem College (Salem, W. Va.)
II. Title.
Z6240.S58   [SF285]   016.6361   81-2002
ISBN 0-8108-1423-4   AACR2

for

Marion O. Smith

iii

FOREWORD

Through history we have used the horse, pony, and donkey to fulfill our needs; transportation, war, food, entertainment, friendship; a platform of honor--a symbol of success.

In the good times we have taught them to play our games. In the hard times, they shared our work. In the sad times, some carried our dead. All of these things and more they did with honor. Centuries of common needs, shared tasks and deep friendships are expressed in the equestrian literature of almost every culture.

The desire to study and thereby know and use these honored servants better, especially the horse, has up to now been complicated by the lack of methodical training programs--programs which explain the current applications of the knowledge accumulated by centuries of horsemen and horsewomen.

At Salem College we have simplified the search for real equestrian knowledge by assembling programs which provide theoretical and practical avenues of study. These programs have as their core a group of specialized professionals whose dedication is to the logical presentation of pertinent, usable information.

This guide to the literature of equestrian studies, by the noted bibliographer Myron J. Smith, Jr., is an outstanding example of quality, accuracy and relevance which we hope will become the industry standard.

As a student of horses, an instructor, or a fancier, this is the first book you need. It will help you select the others and many additional forms of material, print and non-print, as well.

Ronald W. Meredith, Director
Meredith Manor
Waverly, WV
July 1980

Opposite: Kay Meredith on her Swedish Warm-Blood, Domino. Photo by Becky Hance.

v

CONTENTS

INTRODUCTION

Background

Some 60 million years ago during that geological period
called Tertiary, great and strange mammals inhabited the earth's
surface. Among these were fierce carnivores such as the Sabre-
Toothed Tiger and a variety of herbivores ranging in size from the
Woolly Mammoth to the little, many-toed Eohippus.

A small creature which sought its leafy food in the safety of
the forest, the Eohippus was no larger than a fox. More advanced
refinements followed this "Dawn Horse" in the millions of years
that followed. These moved from the forest to the plain, consumed
grass instead of ferns and boughs, and developed hoofs. Through
evolution, little Eohippus became Phiohippus, true ancestor of the
present horse/ass/zebra family.

When early man appeared, he found the horse family an excellent source of food. Later as he settled the land and began to
farm, the horse was domesticated. In the millennia since, the horse
has patiently served man in a host of different ways, in agriculture,
warfare, transportation, communication, exploration, and entertainment. A partner in the everyday life of man, the horse and members of the horse family have appeared in literature, art, and re-
ligion.

In a never-ending quest to improve his lot, man became a
creature of invention. Some of the developments were destined to
alter his ages-old relationship with the horse. The first major
change was the steam engine; later, gasoline and diesel engines con-
tributed to a mechanization which all but removed the horse as a
serious economic contributor in many parts of the world. Two or
three generations ago in America, it was common to see the horse
pulling a wagon or before the plough; today, few working horses remain except on the ranch or on the occasional Amish farm.

The decline of the working horse in America and in other in-
dustrialized nations in the years following World War I brought with
it a certain corresponding decline in that breeding/management/
use/care collectively known as the horse industry. As fewer animals were required in an industrialized-mechanized economy, the
horse industry moved in a new direction. By 1950, pleasure or
light horses had come to the fore. Increased emphasis was placed

1

on the competitive aspects of horsemanship; breeding to win received increased attention. Yearly, races, horse shows, rodeos, and mounted games increased in number and in popularity. The appeal of riding, present through the centuries, grew in all segments of the population. As a result, the horse industry today is not only alive--it is thriving.

Man's quest for knowledge about the horse and its employment is ancient. Graeco-Roman writers such as Xenophon and Virgil wrote about horsemanship. Important treatises appeared during the Renaissance and Romantic periods. Early in this century, Italian Federico Caprilli began a riding revolution with his description of a "forward seat." While much has been written about the equestrian art over the years, much more information was oral, passed on by trainers, breeders, and others of experience from one generation to the next.

A small number of colleges and universities in America today are adding equestrian studies to their curricula. These studies are designed to bring the student into contact with different programs and the finest information available from all resources. A pioneer in this area is the Salem College-Meredith Manor joint venture in West Virginia.

Found in 1888, Salem College is a private, career-oriented institution committed to engaging students in a life-long process of learning and career development. Meredith Manor, founded by Ronald and Kay Meredith in 1963, directs its efforts toward a combination of technical training and realistic innovation in a manner calculated to introduce the challenge of horsemanship as a discipline. Joining forces in 1973, Salem College and Meredith Manor, through a close dialogue between career and liberal education, have created a dynamic union of academics necessary in a college education with the practical application of preparing students to serve the changing needs of their profession.

In 1980, Salem College and Meredith Manor are teaching perhaps the most complete equestrian studies program available anywhere. Not only do many students earn a Bachelor of Science in Equestrian Studies degree but, if qualified, they may study for the fully-accredited Master of Arts, with specialization in Equestrian Studies. Both degrees provide the student with keen insight and the skills necessary for success in the modern horse industry.

Objectives

Following the "revival" of the horse industry in America after World War II, the literature of horsemanship grew to a point where it is currently much more extensive than most would imagine. Some four to nine thousand book titles are believed to exist in Western European languages, and nearly 700 periodical titles are being published worldwide. Bibliographic control has been attempted, but remains inadequate. Fully annotated guides cannot list many titles; those attempting comprehensiveness must, because of publishing costs, omit annotations.

This work was originally undertaken to provide a limited in-house aid for students examining the literature of equestrian studies in the Benedum Learning Resources Center of Salem College. Later, it was expanded to serve as a major resource for graduate students preparing for the thesis component of the Master of Arts degree. The current edition, the first to be commercially published, is intended as a working bibliography of English-language sources on horses and horsemanship issued worldwide during the years 1950-1980. While still aimed primarily at students, teachers, and librarians, it should also prove useful to general readers, journalists, and those in the horse industry. It may also prove interesting to that category of specialized student known as the "horse enthusiast."

This bibliography is not definitive, but it attempts comprehensiveness in that virtually all factors concerning the equestrian art are covered. As a reference tool, it enables the user to determine quickly much of what material is available and helps to establish a basis for further research. In general, the items cited are those the user might reasonably expect to find in large university, public, or government libraries or in the possession of those institutions offering equestrian programs. Should you be unable to turn up a given reference in your area, almost every citation is available through interlibrary loan, details of which service can be obtained at your nearest library.

Although this is my first bibliography devoted to a subject outside of the social sciences, it is not the first with which I have been associated. The criteria for selection in this compilation are the same as those employed in, among others, my American Naval Bibliography Series (5 vols.; Metuchen, N. J.: The Scarecrow Press, 1972-1974), Air War Southeast Asia, 1961-1973 (Metuchen, N. J.: The Scarecrow Press, 1979), and The Secret Wars (3 vols.; Santa Barbara, CA: ABC/Clio, 1980-1981). The following types of published material are represented: books and monographs, scholarly papers, periodical and journal articles not indexed in The Readers' Guide to Periodical Literature; government documents; doctoral dissertations and master's theses; and a fully-annotated guide to 16mm educational motion pictures. A list of journals consulted will be found in the Appendix.

Although much has been included, it was necessary to draw a line somewhere, to omit certain kinds of information and be extremely selective with others. Excluded materials include newspaper articles (unless reprinted), poetry, and book reviews. Limited materials include children's works (identified where cited by the symbol "juv."), fiction anthologies, and novels (fully annotated when cited).

The content, context, and emphasis of English language

sources on horses and horsemanship vary. Certain publishers such as A. S. Barnes, Arco, Farnam, and J. A. Allen specialize in equestrian titles. Many books from Britain and Australia offer a different slant from what may be found in U. S. titles on similar topics, e. g., flat racing. As the output of equestrian literature continues to grow, the user will find it necessary to consult continuously the indexes noted in Part I.

Arrangement

The first eleven main sections in the table of contents, with their subsections, form a classified subject index to the bibliography of printed sources. Each reference has an entry number and no references are repeated. The entry numbers run consecutively throughout. An author index keyed to entry numbers is provided for printed sources only. Annotations of a non-critical nature are provided occasionally, basically in order to clarify title content. Titles sometimes include bracketed notes to the same end. No effort is made to identify "best" titles, a task better left to the individual user.

Acknowledgments

For their advice, assistance, or encouragement in the formulation, research, and completion of this endeavor, the following persons and libraries are gratefully acknowledged:

W. H. Longenecker, Reference Branch, U. S. National Agricultural Library, Beltsville, MD.
Linda Romeika, Practical Horseman Magazine.
V. J. Sapp, Librarian, Ohio Agricultural Research and Development Center Library, Wooster.
Georgine Winslett, American Horse Council, Washington, D. C.
Karen E. Goff, Reference Librarian, West Virginia Library Commission, Charleston.
Antoinette Powell, Reference Librarian, Agriculture Library, University of Kentucky, Lexington.
James M. Simms, Co-operative Extension Service, West Virginia University, Morgantown.
Coleea Moore, Secretary, Green Mountain Horse Association, Inc.
William Slaymaker, President, Eastern Saddle Horse Breeders Association, Inc.
Jean LeMaster, International Arabian Horse Association.
Kentucky Department of Library and Archives, Frankfort.
West Virginia University Library, Morgantown.
Library of Congress, Washington, D. C.

Special appreciation is reserved for colleagues and students at Salem College-Meredith Manor, without whose backing and aid this project would still be in file boxes. President James C. Stam, Dean Ronald O. Champagne, and Dean of Graduate Studies Gary

McAllister provided continuous support and the encouragement to proceed. Margaret Allen, Jacqueline Isaacs, Sara Casey, and Stu Godfrey of the Benedum Learning Resources Center staff and Becky Hance, Meredith Manor Librarian, provided bibliographic and inter-library loan assistance. Kay Meredith and Elliot Abhau, Dean of Students, at Meredith Manor were major sources of inspiration and information. Salem College graduate and undergraduate equestrian studies students, especially Judi Matthews and Anona Van Zant, were helpful with mailings and research.

Finally, hearty thanks is due to Ronald W. Meredith, founder and director of Meredith Manor, for his splendid foreword and un-selfish cooperation and inspiration.

Myron J. Smith, Jr.
Salem, West Virginia
July 1980

THE EXPERTS:

Their Favorite Books*

Horsemen and women at the top of their
fields describe the books that were most
influential in shaping their performance
and technique.

Jimmy Williams, Show Hunter Trainer

How do you judge your show hunter's pace between fences?
How do you judge distance? Jimmy Williams, one of the most successful instructors and trainers on the West Coast for 35 years,
whose students have included USET members Mary Mairs Chapot
and Robert Ridland, says the best book to answer these questions
and all others on training your show hunter is A. L. D'Endrody's
Give Your Horse a Chance (2466).

"One of the hardest things to learn is the relationship of
speed to the distances between fences. This book has a formula
that absolutely sets it up. It's my bible. I take it to all the shows."
D'Endrody interprets course distances into miles per hour and feet
per stride and, according to Williams, "his figures work."

The reader learns training techniques from scratch; right
and left lateral reflexes, turns on the forehand, haunches, the importance of the half halt. The author explains the importance of
riding on the correct diagonals and why the rider's legs should be
in a certain place.

"Most trainers," says Williams, "hurry their horses. You
have to lower your IQ to the level of your horse and only bring him
along at the speed he can manage. This book gives the horse time
to think. You just don't spoil a horse if you follow what D'Endrody
says.

"I underline certain things and then I tape those sections and
send the tapes home with my students for them to play while they

*Reprinted by permission from Practical Horseman (October 1977),
pp. 26-30. Bibliographic details for items cited in this article are
given in the entries numbered in parentheses following the titles.

7

sleep. Then I test them and I've found the tape really helps. If you can't get in the front door, use the back door or the window or the chimney or anything. I have my own index in the back of the book where I make notes about my pupils and what particular information they need from the chapters. "

D'Endrody starts with the basics and takes you right into the ring, all the way to Grand Prix and Olympic levels of riding. "If you could only have one book in your whole life this is it. It will give you a challenge if you care. "

Mrs. Dorothy Galbreath, Breeder

You want to breed a derby winner? We asked Mrs. Dorothy Galbreath, owner and breeder of Sanhedrin, one of this year's leading three-year-olds, for her selection of the best how-to book on breeding.

Mrs. Galbreath and her husband John W. Galbreath own Darby Dan Farm in Lexington, Kentucky which has produced two Kentucky Derby and Belmont Stakes winners and winners of the Preakness, English Derby and many other stakes races, including such famous horses as Summer Tan, His Majesty, Prince Thou Art and True Knight.

"The best book I've ever read on breeding is Frederico Tesio's Breeding the Racehorse (546). We've passed it around so much that it's very dog-eared now. "

Tesio bred Ribot in 1952. His book details that great horse's breeding and describes what type of breeding stock should be used. Tesio began with a few mares and bred them to better and better stallions, constantly upgrading them.

"I have followed Tesio's advice in planning breeding programs. If you want to breed a classic stakes winner which must run over a distance, choose the best classic sire possible, one that could stay a mile and a quarter and with top lineage as far back as possible.

"The mare must also have good blood and hopefully have been a winner but she need not have gone the distance. Tesio stresses the importance of avoiding horses which have been overraced. A mare may use herself up, exhaust a good deal of that indefinable quality within her which sets her progeny apart from others. There is a happy medium. I don't like to breed a mare that hasn't raced at all but I've never raced a mare past four years old. If you race them too long they are frequently hard to get in foal.

"A stallion is different. Nine times out of ten he is raced until he shows signs of deteriorating. That is one reason why the same stud horse should not be used too often in the same breeding line. I avoid line breeding closer than three generations and I use outside stallions for fresh outcrosses. "

Tesio describes in detail the ideal conformation for a race-horse and provides all kinds of biological explanations including the various genes for successful unions.

"He says you want to breed a big, fast, sound horse with a good shoulder and straight legs, not legs that turn out or in, are too close together or cow hocked. I share his preference for good disposition and I believe an intelligent head indicates an awful lot about a horse. A sulking horse is bad and a sulking mare will pro-duce a sulking foal. If you have a highly strung mare you must be careful what kind of stallion you breed to.

Melanie Smith, Winning Grand Prix Rider

How do you create and maintain your show jumper's impul-sion for today's big Grand Prix courses and keep him sufficiently supple and obedient for the final jump-off? We asked Melanie Smith, who piloted Radnor II to be leading money winner on the 1976 Grand Prix circuit, for the show jumping book she has found most useful in her career.

"I go back to Training Hunters, Jumpers and Hacks by Harry D. Chamberlin (2104) again and again because he explains all the im-portant suppling movements you need so clearly that they are easy to understand. Much of what he says is basic dressage but he shows you its relationship to jumping and tells you exactly how to ride each movement."

Chamberlin meticulously lays out the elements of obedience: 1. suppleness; 2. relaxation; 3. balance; 4. agility; 5. lengthening the stride at all gaits. He defines each one and tells how to achieve it. To improve balance and obedience, he prescribes a carefully described series of exercises calling for transitions from halt through extended trot. As the horse becomes more proficient intermediate paces are gradually eliminated.

Line drawings demonstrate the sequence of more complex suppling movements including turns and half-turns and shoulders-in on a straight line and on an angle.

"Those are very important loosening and suppling exercises," says Melanie. "I do them for five or ten minutes before a class to warm up my horse, make him pliant and attentive to my aids."

In a step-by-step section on jumping, Chamberlin explains how to teach your horse to jump, from leading him over poles and longeing over fences to riding competition courses. He tells you how to maintain your horse's confidence, courage and form and pro-vides guidelines for the amount of jumping to be done. He segments the jumping effort into the approach, clearing the obstacle, and landing and tells you how to ride each section.

Bruce Davidson, World Champion Eventer

How do you condition your horse for a one-day event? Bring him and yourself to peak fitness for major three-day competition? World Champion Bruce Davidson, a member of the Gold Medal winning Olympic and Burghley three-day teams, says Eventing--The Book of the 3-Day Event by Caroline Silver, Advisor Lucinda Prior-Palmer (3394) gives complete coverage of the sport.

"It is an educational and appealing book," says Davidson, "whether you ride on weekends for fun or you're a professional competitor seeking to sharpen your skills."

The author provides fundamental guidance on the kind of horse to buy for each level of competition, the best way to plan your fitness program and differentiates between the demands of the three phases--dressage, cross country and jumping.

The book's most valuable contribution, says Davidson, is its emphasis on the need for a training schedule, a written log kept in your stable by which you plan your fitness program. "While it's possible to put some conditioning on a horse by galloping about in haphazard, incoherent spurts," he says, "you benefit in the long term from a definite program which takes into account the differing mental and physical requirements of each of the three phases. It's no good galloping a horse, for example, the day before your dressage test. This book teaches you how to maintain your horse's equanimity despite the stresses of the sport."

A section on interval training details the system of work periods interspersed with brief rests. "You put a certain amount of exertion on the heart, lungs and muscles, then you stop and start again before respiration and heart rate have returned to normal. Instead of putting a heavy stress on the horse for a long period, you give him opportunities to recover between sharp works. This system builds fitness faster while reducing injuries resulting from fatigue.

Photographs depict the do's and don'ts of riding a dressage test and the book is well rounded off with an ample section on how to keep the rider fit. The program includes jogging and gymnastics and advises on the degree of human fitness needed for each level of competition.

Davidson also recommends the U.S. Equestrian Team Book of Riding (3424). It covers every phase of riding and has very useful sections on eventing.

Buddy Brown, Equitation Finalist

Looking for a comprehensive, yet simple book on a subject as complicated as equitation? We asked Olympic jumping team member and 1973 winner of the AHSA Hunt Seat Medal for Equitation, Buddy Brown, for the text to carry you from beginner to the top.

"You won't find a more up to date and straightforward book than <u>Hunter Seat Equitation</u> by George Morris (2400) and you won't need an instructor to understand and use the advice it contains, " says Brown. "Morris is a contemporary Gordon Wright with a modern approach, clearly explained. His book has something for every rider, from beginner to advanced competitor. "

Stressing the basics, Morris offers precise descriptions of the correct positions and functions of each part of the body. "He tells you exactly where your hands and head, legs and feet should be and what they should do, " says Brown.

Beginning with mounting and dismounting, the author progresses from the basics of riding without stirrups, longeing horse and rider, the aids and the results they should produce, to jumping small and big fences.

There are detailed sections on preparing your horse for shows and what is expected of both horse and rider in the ring. "He tells you to 'keep three eyes open--one on yourself, one on the other horses in the class, and one on the judge, ' " says Brown.

He explains the best methods of riding Maclay, Medal and USET classes and gives sound advice to teachers about how to mount their students safely and how best to impart their knowledge.

"George emphasizes the elegance of riding, " says Brown, "he avoids a stiff, mechanical style. " The book contains closeup photographs showing good and bad positions for each part of the body and the correct positions for different aids. Six photographs demonstrate direct, indirect, open, pulley and bearing reins. The author analyzes each photograph explaining what should be corrected and what should be emulated.

He tells you how to stop a bolting horse and correct one that bucks, how to keep a rearing horse on the ground and move a shying animal past whatever is frightening him. "He can't anticipate every conceivable riding problem, " says Brown, "but he stresses the basics so completely that you are well prepared to deal with problems as they arise. "

Billy Turner, Triple Crown Trainer

How do you bring your horse to peak condition and keep him there? How do you ensure he receives sufficient feed for the work he's doing? What should his feed contain? Billy Turner, trainer of Triple Crown winner Seattle Slew, says the answer is two-fold.

"First you must know the machine and then you must learn how to keep it fueled. You must understand the basics of the horse's biochemistry, his anatomy, and how best to nuture him.

"George Stubbs' <u>Anatomy of the Horse</u> (4317) and <u>Feeds and</u>

Feeding (1352) by Frank B. Morrison were the two books that gave
me my basic knowledge. Feeds and Feeding is now out of print,
but The Horse by J. Warren Evans, Anthony Borton, Harold F.
Hintz and L. Dale Van Vleck (212a) has taken its place.

"There's nothing clearer than Stubbs' sketches of equine
anatomy," says Turner. "If you read Stubbs and study his diagrams
you'll be able to recognize almost immediately your own horse's
strengths and weaknesses. Then you can put together an intelligent
program of training and feeding."

The Horse contains a 100-page section detailing feeding practices and explaining inter-relationships between feed and exercise.
Hintz, a leading nutritionist from Cornell University, analyzes feeds
for their energy, mineral and vitamin value, and describes the ideal
mix for optimum protein and digestibility.

A fundamental understanding of these factors is essential to
your horse's health, "and remember, no two horses are alike,"
says Turner.

"I feed according to the type of horse and his individual
needs. I feed a big horse, one that is basically sound without other
problems, for the maximum effort. If your horse has potential
problems, you must settle for a bit less than maximum effort and
adapt your diet.

"Basic knowledge of the machine enables you to know how to
recognize a problem or a potential problem and to make intelligent
judgments on when to slow your training program and when to stop.

"When you walk the fine line between success and disaster,
you always watch for the small problems and remember that no matter how good an animal is you must constantly weigh success against
potential danger."

Hilda Gurney, Olympic Dressage Medalist

How do you start off on the road to collection and extension?
How do you know you've arrived? How do you school your horse
for the higher levels of dressage? Burning the midnight oil with
Bengt Ljungquist, Richard Watjen and Alois Podhajsky will help you
learn this art, recommends Hilda Gurney, dressage bronze medal
winner at the 1976 Olympics and trainer of Brian Sabo, leading 3-
day rider in California.

"When I was starting, I used all three books as a reference.
As I worked my horse I'd think about what I had read."

Bengt Ljungquist's volumes (3353-3354) are very current and
down to earth. Mr. Ljungquist is trainer of the USET dressage
team. "He explains what dressage is and how to school your horse,

clearly demonstrating how to do each movement correctly" says
Gurney. "His illustrations of American riders are unique, carefully
chosen and enhance his explanations a great deal. "

In Dressage Riding, Richard Watjen (3370) defines terms and
describes the aids. "He tells you how each movement should look
with a little less emphasis than Mr. Ljungquist on how to get your
horse to cooperate.

"Dressage Riding gives specific directions but recognizes
that each horse is a book unto himself which cannot conform to a
pattern. Both writers dwell in such detail on elasticity and extension that they convey the feeling of the movement to the reader. "

Ljungquist and Watjen are oriented toward competition rather
than classical dressage. Complete Training of the Horse and Rider
in the Principles of Classical Horsemanship by Alois Podhajsky and
V. D. Williams (2154) is a more theoretical book.

The authors take you through each stage of training and describe how to correct problems along the way. Their solutions may
not work with your particular horse but they provide excellent ideas
which you can adapt to your needs. They give extensive explanations
of haute ecole training of the type performed in the Spanish Riding
School.

"Used together these books reinforce each other, " says Gurney, "providing the basics and goals of dressage and the classical
roots of contemporary competition. "

Judy Richter, Horsewoman of the Year

Your young friend is in school without much time for reading
horse books but he needs one good book to balance his trainer's
practical tuition.

Judy Richter, 1974 Horsewoman of the Year and operator of
Coker Farm in Greenwich, Connecticut which has produced some of
the best young riders in the northeast, says you cannot improve on
Riding and Jumping by William Steinkraus (2361).

"I've read this book several times and learned more from it
with each reading, " says Richter. "Bill Steinkraus has a very practical approach giving intelligent, specific advice on how to prepare
horse and rider for shows. The book is sound and the details are
there, nothing is left up in the clouds.

"I particularly like his realistic attitude that the horse should
be treated as an individual. He stresses that horses are like people; they have a tremendous range of temperaments and conformation
and that riders must be sensitive to these differences. He talks
about the kind of animals the rider will be dealing with, those with
problems, not some perfect creature that doesn't exist. "

The book is good for young riders. Steinkraus describes his classic approach to riding in simple terms. He uses graphic phrases to explain a position or correction of a movement such as telling the reader to "sit over the center of gravity with your heel under your hip. " He recommends "feeling for your shirt collar with the back of your neck to correct the position of your upper body. "

His approach is patient. He spends a good deal of time explaining how to prepare the horse both at home and at the show. He meticulously describes working the horse on the flat, for obedience and suppleness. He doesn't take short cuts and he doesn't believe in using gadgets to force the horse into a required shape. For example, he advocates extensive longeing to improve balance.

"His best chapters are those on taking your horse to shows, " says Richter. "He says you should know clearly why you are at a show, whether it is to school a green horse or win a big class: you must have objectives, which I think are very important and a frequently overlooked point. " He explains how much work you should do in the preceding days at home and describes schooling over the practice course just before your class. He also devotes a very useful section to learning from observation; how to watch other people and figure out how they are doing what they are doing.

"Another valid point is that people press their horses too hard and ruin many as a result. Steinkraus says when you go to a show with a young horse you must go with the understanding that the show is just part of his education. You don't go only to win classes.

"An excellent group of photographs illustrates the major points with very specific captions. Above all the book is very readable. My riders use it a good deal and it doesn't go over their heads. "

Dr. Charles Raker, Veterinarian

How do you deal with sudden swellings? What do you do if your horse hemorrhages? How should you condition your broodmare? We asked Dr. Charles Raker, chief of surgery at the University of Pennsylvania's New Bolton Center for large animals to pick the most informative, in-depth horse care book available in bookshops.

His choice was E. C. Straiton's The Horse Owner's Vet Book (365). "This book stands out, " says Raker, "it gives the most current information in a clear fashion laymen can easily understand. "

Straiton covers all the problems horse owners face daily. There are detailed sections on wounds, diseases, worming, breeding, feeding and immunization. He describes all the common ailments organized by regions of the body.

"I thought he did a particularly good job on wound care, "
says Raker. "He tells exactly how to give treatments and indicates
when and why the owner may be in trouble. He gives direct advice
and often stipulates when to call the veterinarian. "

The approach is practical, many of the products recommended
are household items or reasonably priced. The author often gives
dosages.

Problems are clearly illustrated. Beneath the section "irri-
tation of the eye" three photographs show signs of disease, how to
clear the eye and where to apply antibiotic ointment.

"Dr. Straiton doesn't miss a question, " says Raker, "He explains the causes, symptoms, side effects, seriousness, treatment
and prevention of each ailment. He also gives valuable advice on
first aid supplies to keep in your barn and shows you different methods of restraining your horse for treatment. "

PART I REFERENCE WORKS

A BIBLIOGRAPHIES AND INDEXES

1 Access: The Supplementary Index to Periodicals. Syracuse,
    N. Y.: Gaylord, 1975--. v. 1--.

2 Agricultural Index. New York: H. W. Wilson, 1950-1964. v.
    34-48.

3 America: History and Life--a Guide to Periodical Literature.
    Santa Barbara, CA: ABC/Clio Press, 1964--. v. 1--.

4 American Book Publishing Record. New York: R. R. Bowker,
    1968--. v. 1--.

5 American Historical Association. Writings on American History,
    1950-1961. Washington, D. C. : U. S. Government Printing
    Office, 1951-1962.

6 _____. _____, 1962-1973. 4 vols. New York: Kraus
    Reprint, 1975.

7 _____. _____, 1974--. New York: Kraus Reprint,
    1976--.

8 Bibliography of Agriculture. Phoenix, AZ: Oryx Press, 1950--.
    v. 14--.

9 Biological and Agricultural Index. New York: H. W. Wilson,
    1964--. v. 1--.

10 Book Review Digest. New York: H. W. Wilson, 1950--. v.
     15--.

11 Book Review Index. New York: Gale Research, 1968--. v.
     1--.

12 Botlorff, Robert M. , ed. Popular Periodical Index. New York,
     1973--. v. 1--.

17

13 British Books in Print: The Reference Catalogue of Current Literature--Author, Title, and Subject. New York: R. R. Bowker, 1967--. v. 1--.

14 Buckley, Amelia K. Keeneland Association Library: A Guide to the Collection. Lexington, KY: University of Kentucky Press, 1958. 206p.

15 Burke, John G., ed. The Access Index to Little Magazines. Syracuse, N.Y.: Gaylord Professional Publications, 1977--. v. 1--.

16 Burkhardt, Barbara A. "A Capsule History of Breed Registries." Western Horseman, XLIV (April 1979), 146-147.

17 California News[paper] Index. Claremont, CA: Center for California Public Affairs, 1970--. v. 1--.

18 The Christian Science Monitor Index. Corvallis, OR: Helen M. Cropsey, 1960--. v. 1--.

19 The Cumulative Book Index. New York: H. W. Wilson, 1950--.

20 Davis, Bonnie. "Movies for Horsemen." Western Horseman, XLIV (December 1979), 120-128, 132.

21 "The Experts: Their Favorite Books." Practical Horseman, V (October 1977), 26-30.

22 Felton, W. Sidney. The Literature of Equitation. West Chester, PA: U.S. Pony Clubs, 1978. 36p.

23 Forthcoming Books. New York: R. R. Bowker, 1966--. v. 1--.

24 Great Britain. British Museum. Department of Printed Books. Catalog of Printed Books: Additions. London: Clowes, 1963--. v. 1--.

25 Harrah, Barbara K. Sports Books for Children: An Annotated Bibliography. Metuchen, N.J.: The Scarecrow Press, 1978. 526p.

26 Higginson, A. Henry. British and American Sporting Authors: Their Writings and Biography. London: Hutchinson, 1951. 444p.

27 "How to Buy a Horse Book Worth Reading." Horse Lover's Magazine, VII (December 1974-January 1975), 744.

28 Humanities Index. New York: H. W. Wilson, 1975--. v. 1--.

29 Huth, Frederick H. Books on Horses and Equitation: A Bib-

liographical Record of Hippology.   London: Bernard Quaritch,
1887.   439p.
    Classic and basic; available from University Microfilms,
    order no. OP 55, 681F.

30 Index to Legal Periodicals.   New York: H. W. Wilson, 1950--.
    v. 53--.

31 Index to the Contemporary Scene.   Detroit, MI: Gale Research,
    1973--.   v. 1--.

32 Index to U. S. Government Periodicals.   Chicago: Infordata In-
    ternational, 1975--.   v. 1--.

33 Jones, William E. , comp.   A Descriptive Bibliography of 1, 001
    Horse Books.   East Lansing, MI: Caballus Publications,
    1972.   103p.

34 Loder, Eileen.   Bibliography of the History and Organization of
    Horse Racing and Thoroughbred Breeding in Great Britain
    and Ireland.   London: J. A. Allen, 1978.   368p.

35 McCally, Michael, comp.   Therapeutic Horsemanship Bibliogra-
    phy.   Wilsonville, OR: North American Riding for the Handi-
    capped Association, 1978.   23p.

36 Morris Animal Foundation.   An Index of Current Equine Re-
    search.   Denver, CO., 1966.   48p.

37 The National Observer Index.   Flint, MI: Newspaper Indexing
    Center, 1970--.   v. 1--.

38 The New Periodicals Index.   Boulder, CO: Mediaworks, 1977--.
    v. 1--.

39 Newspaper Index.   Wooster, OH: Bell & Howell, 1972--.   v.
    1--.
    Covers Chicago Tribune, Washington Post, Los Angeles
    Times, and New Orleans Picayune.

40 The New York Times Index.   New York, 1950--.

41 O'Malley, Jeanne.   "Start a Horse Book Collection. "   Practical
    Horseman, VI (February-March 1978), 33-35, 64-65.

42 O'Rourke, Mrs. George W. , comp.   From the Horse's Mouth:
    A Selected Bibliography on Horses.   Frankfort, KY: Ken-
    tucky Department of Libraries and Archives, 1969.   9p.

43 _____. _____: Supplement.   Frankfort, KY: Kentucky
    Department of Libraries and Archives, 1974.   6p.

44 P. A. I. S. Bulletin.   New York: Public Affairs Information Ser-
    vice, 1950--.   v. 35--.

45 Pady, Donald S.   Horses and Horsemanship: Selected Books and
     Periodicals in the Iowa State Library--an Annotated Bibliography.
     Ames: Iowa State University Library, 1973. 226p.

46 Paperback Books in Print. New York: R. R. Bowker, 1955--.
     v. 1--.

47 Readers' Guide to Periodical Literature. New York: H. W.
     Wilson, 1950--.
         A source common to almost every library in the United
     States; periodical citations from that guide are not included in
     this bibliography.

48 Rittenhouse, Jack D.   Carriage Hundred: A Bibliography on
     Horse-Drawn Transportation. Houston, TX: Stagecoach Press,
     1961. 49p.

49 Schlebecker, John T. , comp.   Bibliography of Books and Pam-
     phlets on the History of Agriculture in the United States, 1607-
     1967. Santa Barbara, CA: Clio Books, 1969. 183p.

50 Social Sciences and Humanities Index. New York: H. W. Wil-
     son, 1950-1974.

51 Social Sciences Index. New York: H. W. Wilson, 1975--. v.
     1--.

52 Times of London. Index to the Times. London, 1950--.

53 Toole-Stott, Raymond. The Circus and Allied Arts: A World
     Bibliography. 4 vols. Derby, Eng. : Harpur & Sons, 1958-
     1971.
         See Vol. 3 for a section on circus horses.

54 Turner, Pearl, comp. Index to Outdoor Sports, Games, and
     Activities. Westwood, MA: F. W. Faxon, 1978. 409p.

55 Subject Index to Books in Print. New York: R. R. Bowker,
     1957--. v. 1--.

56 United States. Library of Congress. Library of Congress,
     Books: Subjects--a Cumulative List of Works Represented by
     Library of Congress Printed Cards. Washington, D. C. : U. S.
     Government Printing Office, 1950--.

57 Vertical File Index. New York: H. W. Wilson, 1950--. v.
     19--.

58 The Wall Street Journal Index. New York: Dow Jones, 1958--.
     v. 1--.

59 Wells, Ellen B. "Hippobibliography: A Survey." American
     Notes and Queries, VIII (February 1970), 83-86.

60 _____. Horsemanship: A Guide to Information Sources. Detroit: Gale Research, 1978. 138p.
The best annotated bibliography; covers approximately 500
titles.

61 Wilshire Movies. Wilshire Directory of Horse Films, Horse
Books, [and] Camera Equipment. Hollywood, CA, 1964. 64p.

62 Wilson, Robert A. Ben K. Green: A Descriptive Bibliography
of Writings By and About Him. Flagstaff, AZ: Northland
Press, 1977. 158p.

B DICTIONARIES AND GLOSSARIES

63 Adams, Ramon F. Western Words: A Dictionary of the American West. By Andy Adams, pseud. New ed. , rev. and enl.
Norman: University of Oklahoma Press, 1968. 355p.

64 Agricultural Terms Dictionary. Phoenix, AZ: Oryx Press,
1978. 122p.

65 Avis, Frederick C. Horses and Show Jumping Dictionary. London: J. A. Allen, 1979. 96p.

66 Baranowski, Zdzislaw. The International Horseman's Dictionary:
English, French, and German. London: Museum Press,
1955. 176p.

67 Berkebile, Don H. Carriage Terminology: An Historical Dictionary. Washington, D. C. : Smithsonian Institution Press, 1978.
488p.

68 Bloodgood, Linda F. The Horseman's Dictionary. New York:
E. P. Dutton, 1963. 214p.

69 Brander, Michael. A Dictionary of Sporting Terms. London:
Black, 1968. 224p.

70 Connell, Edward. "Cowboy Talk." Horse and Rider, XIV (April
1975), 61-63.

71 Cuddon, J. A. The International Dictionary of Sports and Games.
New York: Schocken, 1980. 800p.

72 Cummings, G. Clark. "The Language of Horse Racing." American Speech, XXX (February 1955), 17-29; XXXI (December
1956), 298-299.

73 DeKunnfy, Charles. "Some Important Dressage Terminologies."
Dressage and CT, XVII (April 1980), 14-15.

74 Devlin, C. B. Horseman's Dictionary: Medical and General.
South Brunswick, NJ: A. S. Barnes, 1974. 134p.

75 Evans, Edna H. " 'Horse' Is the Word." Western Horseman,
    XXXIX (February 1974), 115-119.

76 Fetros, John G. Dictionary of Factual and Fictional Horses and
    Their Riders. New York: Exposition Press, 1979. 200p.

77 Fleitmann, Lida L. and Piero Santini, comps. The Horseman's
    Dictionary. New York: E. P. Dutton, 1964. 214p.

78 Frommer, Harvey. Sports Lingo: A Dictionary of the Language
    of Sports. New York: Atheneum, 1979. 302p.

79 _____. Sports Roots: How Nicknames, Namesakes, Trophies,
    Competitions, and Expressions in the World of Sports Came to
    Be. New York: Atheneum, 1979. 191p.

80 Harris, Freddie S. "Unusual Horse Words." Horseman, XVI
    (July 1972), 60-65.

81 Harris, L. E. "Revised International Feed Vocabulary." Pro-
    ceedings of the American Society of Animal Science, Western
    Section, XXIX (1978), 383-386.

82 Lacombe, Allen. " 'Black Cat's' Glossary." New Orleans, XIII
    (November 1978), 52-53.

83 Lawrence, John, ed. Dictionary of the British Turf. London:
    Chancery House Publishing Company, 1961. 446p.

84 Mason, I. L. A World Dictionary of Breeds, Types, and Varie-
    ties of Livestock. Farnham Royal, Eng.: Commonwealth
    Agricultural Bureau, 1951.

85 Mueller, Hanns. The Pocket Book of Horseman's Terms. Trans-
    lated from the German. London: Country Life, 1969. 143p.

86 O'Flaherty, W. D. "Contributions to an Equine Lexicology, with
    Special Reference to Frogs." American Oriental Society Jour-
    nal, XCVIII (October 1978), 475-478.

87 Patten, John W. "The Terminology of Breeds." Rapidan River
    Farm Digest, I (Winter 1975), 232-238.

88 Potter, Edgar R. Cowboy Slang. Seattle, WA: Superior Pub-
    lishing Company, 1978. 64p.

89 Radlauer, Edward and Ruth. Horses Pix Dix: A Picture Dic-
    tionary. Glendale, CA: Bowman, 1970. [juv.]

90 Salak, John S., ed. Dictionary of American Sports. New York:
    Philosophical Library, 1961. 491p.

91 Selsam, Millicent. Questions and Answers About Horses. New
    York: Four Winds Press, 1973. 62p. [juv.]

92 Slahor, Stephanie. "Horse Breeding Language." Horseman,
    XXI (November 1977), 46-50.

93 _____. "Rodeo Definitions." Horseman, XXI (March 1977),
    36-38.

94 Stratton, Charles P. The International Horseman's Dictionary.
    London and New York: Hamlyn Publishing, 1975. 256p.

95 Turner, Allton. "Cowboy Expressions." Horseman, XXIII (April
    1979), 74-82.

96 _____. "Cow Country Expressions." Horseman, XXIV (Janu-
    ary 1980), 49-52.

97 Winburne, John N. A Dictionary of Agricultural and Allied Ter-
    minology. East Lansing, MI: Michigan State University Press,
    1962. 905p.

98 Wright, Graeme. The Rand McNally Illustrated Dictionary of
    Sports. Chicago: Rand McNally, 1978. 192p.

C ENCYCLOPEDIAS AND HANDBOOKS

99 Booth, Rintoul. The Horseman's Handbook to End All Horse-
    men's Handbooks. London: Wolfe Publishing Company, 1975.
    159p.

100 Brander, Michael. The Complete Guide to Horsemanship. New
    York: Scribner, 1972. 444p.

101 Coggins, Jack. The Horseman's Bible. Garden City, NY:
    Doubleday, 1966. 187p.

102 Cooper, Marcia S. The Horseman's Etiquette Book. New York:
    Scribner, 1976. 144p.

103 Disston, Harry. Horse and Rider: 4,000 Questions and Answers
    for Horsemen. South Brunswick, NJ: A. S. Barnes, 1964.
    226p.

104 _____. Know About Horses: A Ready Reference Guide to
    Horses, Horse People, and Horse Sports. Chicago: Devin-
    Adair, 1961. 216p.

105 Edwards, E. Hartley. The Horseman's Guide. London: Country
    Life, 1969. 256p.

106 _____. The Larousse Guide to Horses and Ponies of the
    World. New York: Larousse and Company, 1979. 238p.

107 Ensminger, Marion E. The Complete Encyclopedia of Horses.
    South Brunswick, NJ: A. S. Barnes, 1977. 487p.

108 _____. The Stockman's Handbook. 5th ed. Danville, IL: Interstate Printers and Publishers, 1978. 1,192p.

109 Galloping Off in All Directions: An Anthology for Horse Lovers. New York: St. Martin's Press, 1978. 186p.

110 Geddes, Candida, ed. The Horse: The Complete Book of Horses and Horsemanship. London: Octopus Books, 1978. 400p.

111 Hope, Charles E. G. A to Z of Horses: All You Need to Know About Buying, Conformation, Diseases, Feeding, Foaling, Gaits, Jumping, Training, etc. Toronto, Ont.: Clarke, Irwin and Company, 1960. 128p.

112 _____ and G. N. Jackson, eds. The Encyclopedia of the Horse. New York: Viking Press, 1973. 336p.

113 Kidd, Jane, et al. The Complete Horse Encyclopedia. London and New York: Hamlyn Publishing, 1976. 256p.

114 _____. The Salamander Horse and Pony Manual: A Comprehensive Guide to Caring For, Training, and Riding Your Horse. London: Salamander Books, 1977. 209p.

115 McClure, Robert, ed. Every Horse Owner's 'Cyclopedia. Huntsville, TX: I-Tex Publishing Company, 1970. 582p. Reprint of the 1871 Porter and Coates (Philadelphia) edition.

116 McKibbin, Lloyd S. and Al Sugarman. Horse Owner's Handbook. London: Saunders, 1977. 420p.

117 McTaggart, Maxwell F. Handbook for Horse Owners. 5th rev. ed. London: Methuen, 1951. 150p.

118 Menke, Frank G. The Encyclopedia of Sports. 6th rev. ed. South Brunswick, NJ: A. S. Barnes, 1978. 1,132p.

119 Money, Keith. The Equestrian World. New York: Watts, 1963. 190p.

120 Murray, William H. H. The Perfect Horse: How to Know Him, How to Breed Him, How to Train Him, How to Shoe Him, How to Drive Him. Rev. ed. New York: Vantage Press, 1966. 342p.

121 Newman, Gerald, ed. The Concise Encyclopedia of Sports. 2nd rev. ed. New York: Watts, 1979. 218p.

122 Norback, Craig T. The Horseman's Catalog. New York: McGraw-Hill, 1979. 520p.

123 Price, Steven D., et al., eds. The Whole Horse Catalog. New York: Simon and Schuster, 1977. 246p.

124 Roberts, Estelle, et al. , eds. The Horse World Catalog. Phil-
     adelphia: Lippincott, 1977. 159p.

125 Self, Margaret C. The Horseman's Almanac and Handbook.
     New York: Watts, 1965. 235p.

126 _____. Horseman's Encyclopedia. New York: A. S. Barnes,
     1946. 519p.
     A classic.

127 _____. _____. New and rev. ed. New York: A. S.
     Barnes, 1963. 428p.

128 Seth-Smith, Michael, ed. The Horse. New York: Mayflower
     Books, 1980. 479p.

129 Skelton, Elizabeth C. Rand McNally Pictorial Encyclopedia of
     Horses and Riding. Chicago: Rand McNally, 1978. 216p.

130 Smith, Norman L. Sports and Games Almanac. New York:
     Facts on File, Inc. , 1979. 400p.

131 The Spectator's Guide to Sports. New York: New American
     Library, 1976. 192p.

132 Steffan, Randy. Horseman's Scrapbook. 3 vols. Colorado
     Springs, CO: Western Horseman, 1970-1972.

133 Summerhays, Reginald S. Summerhays' Encyclopedia for Horse-
     men, 6th ed. , rev. London and New York: Warner, 1975.
     419p.

134 Talbot-Ponsonby, John A. , ed. The Horseman's Bedside Book.
     Westminster, MD: J. W. Eckenrode, 1965. 224p.

135 Taylor, Louis. Harper's Encyclopedia for Horsemen: The Com-
     plete Book of the Horse. New York: Harper & Row, 1973.
     558p.

136 Tickner, John. Tickner's Horse Encyclopedia. London: Put-
     nam, 1960. 95p.

137 Van Tuyl, Barbara. The Horseman's Book: A Modern Encyclo-
     pedia of Matters Pertaining to Horses and Horsemanship.
     Englewood Cliffs, NJ: Prentice-Hall, 1973. 262p.

138 Williams, Dorian, ed. The Horseman's Companion. 2nd ed.
     London: Eyre and Spottiswoode, 1978. 566p.

D GENERAL ANNUALS AND YEARBOOKS

139 Ammann, Max E. , ed. L'Année Hippique: The Equestrian Year,
     1978--. Bern, Switzerland: Buechler & Co. , 1978--. v. 31--.

140 Horse and Pony Annual Illustrated. London: Guilford Press,
     1950--.

141 The Horseman's Year. London: Collins, 1950--. v. 4--.

142 L'Année Hippique: The Equestrian Year, 1950-1973. Lausaunne,
     Switzerland: Bridel and Cornay, 1950-1973. v. 7-30.

143 The Old Horseman's Almanak. Beverly, MA: T. R. T. Pub-
     lications, 1974--. v. 1--.

144 The Pony Club Annual. London: Naldretl, 1950--. v. 1--.

145 Pony Magazine Annual. London: Parrish, 1960--. v. 1--.

E   STATISTICAL REPORTS

146 Chisholm, Oliver. The Professional Touch: An Encyclopedia
     of Turf Statistics. London: Wolfe Publications, 1969. 478p.

147 Cohn, David. "Characteristics of a Normal Equine Population
     of Delaware and Chester Counties, Pennsylvania, 1968-1969."
     American Journal of Veterinary Research, XXXIII (June 1972),
     1285-1295.

148 Fisher, George, comp. The Guinness Book of Turf Records.
     London: Guinness Superlatives, 1964. 68p.

149 Hines, Charles A. and Charles L. Ruckman. Michigan Equine
     Survey, August 1971. Lansing: Michigan Crop Reporting
     Survey, 1972. 26p.

150 Kentucky Horse Council. Kentucky Equine Survey. Frankfort,
     1977.

151 McWhirter, Norris D. and A. Ross, eds. The Guinness Book
     of Olympic Records. Rev. ed. New York: Bantam Books,
     1979.

152 _____. The Guinness Sports Record Book. New York:
     Sterling Publishing Company, 1972--. v. 1--.

153 Neft, David S. , et al. Grosset and Dunlap's All Sports World
     Record Book. New York: Grosset and Dunlap, 1976. 320p.

154 New York. Crop Reporting Service. New York Equine Survey.
     Albany, 1978.

155 Stark, B. G. "Changes in Horse Numbers as Related to Farm
     Mechanization, Recreation, and Sport." Unpublished MS
     Thesis, Washington State University, 1960.

156 Williams, Dorian. Equestrianism. London: Guinness Super-
    latives, 1980. 237p.

F COLLECTIVE BIOGRAPHY

1 General Works

157 Berke, Art, ed. The Lincoln Library of Sports Champions.
    20 vols. Columbus, OH: Sports Resources Company, 1971.

158 Biography Index. New York: H. W. Wilson, 1950--. v. 3--.

159 Birmingham, Nan. "The Horse People: Who They Are and
    Where They Are." Town and Country, CXXXI (March 1977),
    28+.

160 Bowmar, Dan M. Giants of the Turf: The Alexanders, the
    Belmonts, James R. Keene, the Whitneys. Lexington, KY:
    The Blood-Horse, 1960. 224p.

161 Campbell, Judith. Royalty on Horseback. Garden City, NY:
    Doubleday, 1975. 141p.

162 Cathcart, Helen. The Queen [Elizabeth II] and the Turf. Lon-
    don: S. Paul, 1959. 200p.

163 Current Biography. New York: H. W. Wilson, 1950--. v.
    10--.

164 Dictionary of International Biography. London, 1964--. v. 1--.

165 Engelhard, Jack. The Horsemen. Chicago: Regnery, 1974.
    222p.

166 Facts on File, Editors of. Obituaries on File [1940-1978]. 2
    vols. New York: Facts on File, Inc., 1979.

167 Ferguson, Bob. Who's Who in Canadian Sport. Englewood
    Cliffs, NJ: Prentice-Hall, 1977. 310p.

168 Harvison, Clifford W. The Horsemen. London: Macmillan,
    1968. 271p.

169 Hickok, Ralph. Who Was Who in American Sports. New York:
    Hawthorn Books, 1971. 338p.

170 The Horseman's Directory. Danville, NY: Owen, 1950--. v.
    4--.

171 The International Who's Who. London: Europa Publications,
    1950--. v. 15--.

172 Livingston, Bernard. Their Turf: America's Horsey Set and Its Princely Dynasties. New Rochelle, NY: Arbor House, 1973. 302p.

173 Money, Keith. Salute the Horse: Personalities of Today's Horse World. New Rochelle, NY: Sportshelf, 1960. 144p.

174 Mortimer, Roger, el al. Biographical Encyclopedia of British Flat Racing. London: Macdonald and Jane's, 1978. 699p.

175 New York Times Obituary Index, 1858-1968. New York: New York Times Company, 1970. 1,136p.

176 Phillips, Lance. Folks I Knowed and Horses They Rode. Ashland, VA: Plantation Press, 1975. 223p.

177 Porter, Willard H. 13 Flat: Tales of Thirty Famous Rodeo Ropers and Their Great Horses. South Brunswick, NJ: A. S. Barnes, 1967. 256p.

178 Ransom, James H. , comp. Who's Who in Horsedom: The 400 of the Sport of Kings. Lexington, KY: 1963. 100p.

179 Times of London. Obituaries from the Times, 1961-1970. Reading Eng. : Newspaper Archive Developments, 1976. 952p.

180 U. S. Dressage Federation. Dressage Directory: Instructors, Clinicians, and Officials. Lincoln, NE: 1973--. v. 1--.

181 Wasson, Bryan. Horses and Horsemen. Abilene, TX: Cowboy Book Store, 1965. 122p.

182 Who's Who and Where in Horsedom: The Directory of Horsemen. Princeton, IL: Ransom Agency, 1950--. v. 2--.

183 Who's Who in Thoroughbred Racing. Washington, D. C. , 1950--. v. 4--.

Further References: See also Parts V: A; VI: A and F; VII: G; VIII; IX: D; X: B and C; XI: B below.

2 Women and Horsemanship

184 Adler, Larry. Young Women in the World of Race Horses. New York: David McKay, 1978. 56p. [juv.]

185 Australian Information Service. "Horseback Policewomen." Western Horseman, XL (July 1975), 113.

186 Beker, Anna. Woman on a Horse. Translated from the German. London: Kimber, 1956. 204p.

187 Campbell, Judith. The Queen [Elizabeth II] Rides. New York:
     Viking Press, 1965. 95p.

188 Coleman, Alix. "Aching Saddles." Women Sports, II (March
     1975), 38-47.

189 Cosner, Sharon. American Cowgirls: Yesterday and Today.
     New York: David McKay, 1978. 56p. [juv.]

190 Davis, Ray. "All Around Cowgirl, Jan Collier." Western
     Horseman, XXXIX (April 1974), 104-105, 131-132.

191 Dean, Frank. "Girl Trick Ropers, Then and Now." Western
     Horseman, XLI (December 1976), 30-33.

192 Dean, Sharon. "Etiquette and the Single Horsewoman." West-
     ern Horseman, XXXIX (September 1974), 150-151.

193 Foyster, Bernard. Princess Anne, Champion of Europe. Lon-
     don: Arlington Books, 1972. 116p.

194 Freeman, Chris. "Australian Girl Jockeys." Western Horse-
     man, XXXIX (July 1974), 15, 118-122.

195 Golden, Flora. Women in Sports: Horseback Riding. New
     York: Harvey House, 1978. 70p.

196 Hollander, Phyllis. 100 Greatest Women in Sports. New York:
     Grosset and Dunlap, 1977. 147p.

197 Horse and Rider, Editors of. Horse Women. Temecula, CA,
     1979. 96p.

198 Hurley, Jimmie. "Jimmie Gibbs: World Champion Cow-
     girl." Western Horseman, XLI (April 1976), 44-46,
     130-132.

199 "Ladies in Rodeo." Horse and Horseman, I (June 1973), passim.

200 "The Lady Is a Trainer: Interviews." Horse and Rider, XI
     (August 1972), 18-26.

201 Martin, Ann. The Equestrian Woman: Interviews. New York:
     Paddington House, 1979. 224p.

202 Peck, William K. "What Is This Thing with Girls and Horses?"
     Horseman, XV (July 1971), 58-68.

203 Phillips, Louis. Women in Sports. New York: Harcourt
     Brace, 1979.

204 Pitts, P. "Advice to Cowgirls: Don't Marry Your Farrier."
     Western Horseman, XXXIX (August 1974), 52+.

205 Ramsden, Caroline. Ladies in Racing: Sixteenth Century to the Present Day. London: S. Paul, 1973. 192p.

206 Remley, M. L. "From Sidesaddle to Rodeo." Journal of the West, XVII (July 1978), 44-52.

207 Roach, Joyce G. The Cowgirls. Houston, TX: Cordovan Corporation, 1979. 232p.

208 _____. "Leather Skirts and Satin Bloomers." Horseman, XVI (October 1971), 38-50.

209 Rue, Bonnie. "Tanya Tucker--Singing and Horses." Western Horseman, XLI (December 1976), 81-82.

PART II EQUINE MAKEUP, HEALTH, AND REPRODUCTION

A GENERAL WORKS

210 DeBeaumont, Marguerite. Horses and Ponies: Their Breeding,
     Feeding, and Management. London: J. A. Allen, 1976.
     144p.

211 Ensminger, Marion E. , ed. Horse Science Handbook. 3 vols.
     Clovis, CA: Agriservices Foundation, 1963-1966.

212 _____. Horsemanship and Horse Care. Agricultural Hand-
     book, no. 357. Washington, D. C. : U. S. Government Print-
     ing Office, 1972. 50p.

212a Evans, J. Warren, et al. The Horse. San Francisco, CA:
      W. H. Freeman, 1977. 766p.

213 Hayes, Matthew H. Points of the Horse: A Treatise on the
     Conformation, Movements, Breeds, and Evolution of the
     Horse. 7th rev. ed. New York: Arco, 1969. 541p.

214 Kays, Donald J. The Horse: Judging, Breeding, Feeding,
     Management, Selling. Rev. ed. South Brunswick, NJ:
     A. S. Barnes, 1970. 439p.

215 Thomas, Heather S. Horses: Their Breeding, Care, and
     Training. South Brunswick, NJ: A. S. Barnes, 1974. 559p.

216 Vischer, Peter, ed. An Anthology of Articles and Pictures
     from the Magazine [Horse and Horseman]. New York: Van
     Nostrand, 1967. 272p.

217 _____. Horse and Horseman: An Anthology of Arts and
     Pictures from America's Most Celebrated Horse Magazine.
     New York: Arco, 1975. 272p.

218 Walraven, Louise E. Horses and Horsemanship. South Bruns-
     wick, NJ: A. S. Barnes, 1970. 312p.

219 Willis, Malcolm B. The Horse. San Francisco, CA: Freeman,
     1977. 766p.

B   EQUINE MAKEUP

1   Anatomy and Conformation

220   American Association of Equine Practitioners.   Guide for De-
       termining the Age of the Horse.   Golden, CO: 1966. 35p.

221   Beeman, Marvin.   "Conformation: The Relationship of Form of
       Function. "   Quarter Horse Journal, XXV (Fall 1972), 82+.

222   Blazer, Don.   "Ideal Conformation of the Western Horse. "
       Horse and Horseman, VII (November 1979), 23-29.

223   Bone, Jesse F.   Animal Anatomy and Physiology.   Reston, VA:
       Reston Publishing Company, 1979.   560p.

224   Close, Pat.   "Jack Denton's Rules of Thumb for Balance and
       Height. "   Western Horseman, XLIV (May 1979), 66-67.

225   Decker, J. Arthur.   "Your Horse's Eyes. "   Horse Illustrated,
       X (January-February 1979), 16-18.

226   Dial, Scott.   "What Made 'Secretariat' Great. "   Horseman, XXI
       (February 1977), 50-55.

227   Edwards, Gladys B.   Anatomy and Conformation of the Horse.
       Croton-on-Hudson, NY: Dreenan Press, 1973.   218p.

228   Frandson, R. D.   Anatomy and Physiology of Farm Animals.
       2nd ed.   Philadelphia: Lea and Febiger, 1974.   494p.

229   Goody, Peter C.   Horse Anatomy: A Pictorial Approach to
       Equine Structure.   London: J. A. Allen, 1976.   71p.

230   Green, Ben K.   Horse Conformation as to Soundness and Per-
       formance.   Rev. ed.   Flagstaff, AZ: Northland Press,
       1975.   80p.

231   Hamilton, Samantha.   "Conformation: Athletic and Aesthetic. "
       Equus, no. 30 (April 1980), 22-28, 78-79.

232   Harper, Frederick.   "Your Horse's Digestive System. "   West-
       ern Horseman, XLIV (February 1979), 31-32.

233   Hurley, Jimmie.   "What's a Good Horse?"   Horse and Rider,
       XIV (May 1975), 56-62.

234   Jones, Dave.   "How Horses Function. " Horse and Horseman,
       VII (March-May 1979), 52-53, 54-55, 56-57.

235   Jones, William E. , ed.   The Teeth of the Horse.   Ft. Collins,
       CO: Caballus Publications, 1973.   79p.

236 Know the Anatomy of the Horse. Omaha, NE: Farnam Horse
     Library, 1977. 64p.

237 Kovacs, Gyula. The Equine Tarsus. Translated from the Hun-
     garian. Budapest, Hungary: Akademiai Kiado, 1963. 146p.

238 Leitch, Midge. "Your Horse's Stifle." Practical Horseman,
     VI (July 1978), 35-41.
     Hind leg to laymen.

239 Luard, Lowes D. Anatomy and Action of the Horse. Wood-
     stock, VT: Countryman Press, 1958. 122p.

240 Mackay, Anne. "Conformation and Its Faults." Agricultural
     Technology, VIII (November 1977), 26-28.

241 Meredith, Kay. "Conformation, Disposition and Capability."
     Horse and Rider, XVII (November 1979), 38-44.

242 Moxley, H. F. "The Sound Horse." Michigan Agricultural Ex-
     tension Bulletin, no. 330 (1955), 1-40.

243 Rooney, James R. Rooney's Guide to the Dissection of the
     Horse. Ithaca, NY: Veterinary Textbooks, 1977. 245p.

244 _____, et al. Guide to the Dissection of the Horse. Rev.
     ed. New York: J. W. Edwards, 1967. 216p.

245 Sedito, Elaine. "Your Horse's Back." Practical Horseman,
     VI (November 1978), 54-60.

246 Shebitz, Horst. Atlas of Radiographic Anatomy of the Horse.
     Translated from the German. 3rd ed. San Francisco, CA:
     W. B. Saunders, 1978. 100p.

247 Smith, A. F. "The Teeth of the Horse." Unpublished paper,
     Southwest Planning Conference of Livestockmen, Waco, Texas,
     1973.

248 Smythe, Reginald H. The Horse: Structure and Movement.
     Rev. ed. London: J. A. Allen, 1972. 184p.

249 _____. What Makes a Good Horse: Its Structure and Per-
     formance. London: Country Life, 1957. 125p.

250 Snow, D. H. "The Structure and Biochemistry of Equine Muscle."
     Proceedings of the Annual Convention of the American Asso-
     ciation of Equine Practitioners. XXII (1977), 199-210.

251 Swenson, Melvin J., ed. Dukes' Physiology of Domestic Ani-
     mals. Ithaca, NY: Cornell University Press, 1970.
     1,463p.

252 Thomas, Heather S. "How to Judge Conformation." Horse and
     Horseman, III (October 1975), 20-22, 42, 64-65.

253 Way, Robert F. and Donald G. Lee. The Anatomy of the Horse:
     A Pictorial Approach. Philadelphia: Lippincott, 1965. 214p.

2 Behavior and Psychology

254 Ainslie, Tom and Bonnie Ledbetter. The Body Language of
     Horses. New York: Morrow, 1980. 224p.

255 Amaral, Anthony. "The Importance of Disposition." Western
     Horseman, XXXIX (April 1974), 45, 150-152.

256 Blake, Henry. Talking with Horses: A Study of Communication
     Between Man and Horse. New York: E. P. Dutton, 1976.
     172p.

257 _____. Thinking with Horses. London: Souvenir Press,
     1977. 199p.

258 DeBeaumont, Marguerite. Way of a Horse. New York: Mc-
     Graw-Hill, 1953. 191p.

259 Dorrance, Tom. "Does Your Horse Have a 'People Problem?' "
     Horseman, XVI (February 1971), 30-49.

260 Fiske, Jeanna C. "Discrimination Reversed Learning in Yearling
     Horses." Journal of Animal Science, XLIX (August 1979),
     583-588.

261 _____. "A Guide to Horse Mentality." Practical Horseman,
     VI (July 1978), 20-25.

262 _____. How Horses Learn: Equine Psychology Applied to
     Training. Brattleboro, VT: Stephen Greene Press, 1979.
     148p.

263 _____. "How Your Horse Learns." Practical Horseman,
     VII (October 1979), 40-46.

264 Fraser, Andrew F. Farm Animal Behavior. London: B. Tind-
     all, 1974. 196p.

265 Grzimek, Bernhard. "On the Psychology of the Horse." In:
     Heinz Friedrich, ed. Man and Animal: Studies in Behavior.
     Translated from the German. New York: St. Martin's Press,
     1972. pp. 37-45.

266 Haley, Neale. Understanding Your Horse: Equine Character
     and Psychology. South Brunswick, NJ: A. S. Barnes, 1973.
     204p.

267 Hamilton, Samantha. "Untangling the Intricate Switchboard Sys-
       tem That Is the Horse's Brain." Equus, no. 23 (September
       1979), 26-32, 84.

268 Hatch, Eric. What Goes on in Horses' Heads. New York:
       G. P. Putnam, 1970. 123p.

269 Heird, James C. "Effect of Early Experience on the Learning
       Ability of Yearling Horses." Unpublished Ph. D. Disserta-
       tion, Texas Tech University, 1978.

270 Kiley-Worthington, M. Behavioral Problems in Farm Animals.
       London: Oriel Press, 1977. 134p.

271 Mackintosh, Nicholas J. The Psychology of Animal Learning.
       London and New York: Academic Press, 1974. 730p.

272 Miller, Robert V. Horse Behavior and Training. Bozeman,
       MT: Montana State University Bookstore, 1974. 300p.

273 _____. "Horse Psychology." Western Horseman, XLIV
       (January-March 1979), 34-37, 54-60, 8-12.

274 _____. Western Horse Behavior and Training. Garden City,
       NY: Doubleday, 1975. 305p.

275 Mizwa, Tad. "Getting into Your Colt's Mind." Horseman, XXII
       (September 1978), 22-34.

276 Mullen, Gary. "Hoss Psychology." Horse and Rider, XVI
       (February 1977), 32-34.

277 "Psychology and Your Horse." Horse and Rider, VIII (July
       1969), passim.

278 Rossdale, Peter D. "Abnormal Perinatal Behaviour in the
       Thoroughbred Horse." British Veterinary Journal, CXXIV
       (1968), 540+.

279 _____. "Perinatal Behaviour in the Thoroughbred Horse."
       British Veterinary Journal, CXXVI (1970), 656+.

280 Schäfer, Michael. The Language of the Horse: Habits and
       Forms of Expression. Translated from the German. New
       York: Arco, 1975. 186p.

281 Self, Margaret C. The Nature of the Horse. New York: Arco,
       1974. 217p.

282 Shaw, C. J. "Out-Thinking the Horse." Horseman, XXII (April
       1978), 72-74, 77.

283 Smythe, Reginald H. The Mind of the Horse. Brattleboro, VT:
       Stephen Greene Press, 1965. 123p.

284   Understanding Horse Psychology. Omaha, NE: Farnam Horse
        Library, 1976.   64p.

285   Vavra, Robert J.   Such Is the Real Nature of the Horse.   New
        York: Morrow, 1979.   238p.

286   Williams, Moyra.   A Breed of Horses.   Oxford and New York:
        Pergamon Press, 1971.   196p.

287   _____.   Horse Psychology.   Hollywood, CA: Wilshire Books,
        1973.   194p.

288   Williamson, Marion B.   Applied Horse Psychology.   Houston,
        TX: Horseman Books, 1979.   64p.

289   Wonnell, Jeff.   "Does Your Horse Know What You're Trying to
        Accomplish?"   Horseman, XV (November 1970), 37-50.

3   Gaits

290   Alexander, R. M. , ed.   Mechanics and Energetics of Animal
        Locomotion.   New York: Halsted Press, 1977.   346p.

291   Bartel, D. L. , et al.   "Locomotion in the Horse."   American
        Veterinary Research, XXXIX (November 1978), 1721-1733.

292   Brandl, Albert.   Modern Riding: Walk, Trot, Canter, Gallop.
        London: E. P. Group, 1973.   142p.

293   Gaines, David.   "Science of Stride and Stress."   Horseman,
        XXII (June 1978), 30-40.

294   Gambaryan, P. P.   How Mammals Run: Anatomical Adaptations.
        Translated from the Russian.   New York: John Wiley, 1974.
        367p.

295   Grogan, J. W.   "Gaits of Horses."   American Veterinary Medi-
        cine Association Journal, CXIX (August 1951), 112-117.

296   Howell, Alfred B.   Speed in Animals: Their Specialization for
        Running and Leaping.   New York: Hafner, 1965.   277p.
        Reprint of 1944 edition.

297   McCall, Jim.   "The Trot."   Horseman, XXIV (March 1980),
        26-30.

298   Madlener, Elizabeth.   "The Rising Trot."   Practical Horseman.
        VII (May 1979), 60-70.

299   Meredith, Kay.   "The Walk--Retaining or Retraining?"   Dres-
        sage & CT, XV (December 1978), 28.

300   Mizwa, Tad S. "The Science of Horse Movement." Horseman,
      XXII (March 1978), 68-72.

301   Muybridge, Eadweard. Muybridge's Complete Human and Animal
      Locomotion: All 781 Plates from the 1887 "Animal Locomo-
      tion." 3 vols. New York: Dover, 1979.

302   Pratt, George. "How Your Horse Gallops." Practical Horse-
      man, VI (June 1978), 38-48.

303   Smythe, Reginald H. Horses in Action. London: Country Life,
      1963. 148p.

304   Tavares, Nancee. "Arriving at the Seventh Departure." Horse
      and Rider, XVII (January 1978), 14-18.

305   Wynmalen, Henry and Michael Lyne. The Horse in Action.
      New York: Arco, 1973. 58p.

                    C HEALTH AND DISEASE

1 General Works

306   Albert, Waco. Foot and Health Care of Horses. Agricul-
      tural Extension Circular, no. 1103. Springfield: Illinois
      Agricultural Extension Serivce, 1974. 15p.

307   Altman, Robert B. and James R. Coffman, eds. Symposia on
      Cage Birds and Equine Medicine. Veterinary Clinics of North
      America, v. 3, no. 2. Philadelphia: Saunders, 1972. 317p.

308   American Association of Equine Practitioners. Proceedings of
      the Annual Convention. N. p. , 1954--. v. 1--.

309   Bailey, Nevajec. The Save Your Horse Handbook. Omaha, NE:
      Farnam Horse Library, 1978. 64p.

310   Beaver, Bonnie V. G. Your Horse's Health: A Handbook for
      Owners and Trainers. South Brunswick, NJ: A. S. Barnes,
      1980. 89p.

311   Beeman, G. Marvin. "First Aid for Horses." Western Horse-
      man, XXXVI (September 1971), 38-42.

312   _____. Know First Aid for Your Horse. Omaha, NE: Far-
      nam Horse Library, 1978. 64p.

313   Belschner, Herman G. Horse Diseases. Sydney, Aust. : Angus
      and Robertson, 1969. 258p.

314   Bierschwal, C. J. and C. H. Debois. The Techniques of Feto-

tomy in Large Animals. Bonner Springs, KA: Veterinary
Medicine Publishing Company, 1972. 50p.

315 Blood, Douglas C. Veterinary Medicine: A Textbook of the
Diseases of Cattle, Sheep, Pigs, and Horses. 5th ed. Philadelphia: Lea and Febiger, 1979. 1,135p.

316 Blue Cross Veterinary Products. Pottie's Horse [Disease] Dictionary. 6th rev. ed. Melbourne, Aust.: Hicks Smith and
Sons, 1958. 125p.

317 Bone, Jesse F., et al., eds. Equine Medicine and Surgery:
A Text and Reference Work. Santa Barbara, CA: American
Veterinary Publications, 1963. 815p.

318 Catcott, Earl J., ed. Progress in Equine Practice. Modern
Veterinary Reference Series, no. 1. Wheaton, IL: American
Veterinary Publications, 1966. 595p.

319 Cernik, Sheridan L. Preventative Medicine and Management for
the Horse. South Brunswick, NJ: A. S. Barnes, 1978.
234p.

320 Codrington, William S. Know Your Horse: A Guide to Selection
and Care in Health and Disease. Rev. ed. London: J. A.
Allen, 1974. 220p.

321 Davidson, Joseph B. Horsemen's Veterinary Advisor. New
York: Arco, 1973. 256p.

322 _____. Keep Your Horse Healthy. Rexdale, Ont.: Coles
Publications, 1978. 256p.
A reprint of the above citation.

323 Dunn, Angus M. Veterinary Helminthology. Philadelphia: Lea
and Febiger, 1969. 302p.

324 Dykstra, R. R. Animal Sanitation and Disease Control. Danville, IL: Interstate Printers and Publishers, 1961. 858p.

325 Ensminger, Marion E. "Basics of First Aid for Horses."
Horse and Rider, IX (March 1970), 74-75.

326 Equine Research Publications. An Illustrated Veterinary Encyclopedia for Horsemen. Grapevine, TX: 1975. 702p.

327 Equus Medical Library. 9 vols. Gaithersburg, MD: Fleet
Street Publications, 1979.

328 Foley, C. W., et al. Abnormalities of Companion Animals:
Analysis of Herbitability. Ames: Iowa State University
Press, 1979. 270p.

329 Hamilton, Samantha. "Body Language: The Equine Alphabet in
    Sickness and in Health." Equus, no. 20 (June 1979), 26-32,
    78.

330 Hanauer, Elsie V. No Foot, No Horse. Fort Collins, CO:
    Caballus Publications, 1974. 125p.

331 Harvey, K. "First Aid: Do It Right!" Horseman, XXXI (Feb-
    ruary 1978), 30-34, 37.

332 Hayes, Matthew H. Veterinary Notes for Horse Owners: a
    Manual of Horse Medicine and Surgery. 15th rev. ed. New
    York: Arco, 1964. 656p.

333 How to Recognize Horse Health Problems. Omaha, NE: Farnam
    Horse Library, 1977. 64p.

334 Jones, Dave. "What to Do Until the Vet Arrives." Horse and
    Horseman, VI (November 1978), 22-25.

335 Kester, Wayne O. "The Emergency Situation." Horse and
    Horseman, VII (September 1979), 48-49.

336 "Equine Diseases: The Big Picture." Horse and Horseman,
    I (January 1974), 18, 63.

337 _____. "Veterinary Responsibilities of Horse Ownership."
    Horse and Horseman, VI (August 1978), 12-14.

338 King, Patricia A. "Barometer for Horse Health." Horse and
    Rider, VIII (December 1969), 52-53.

339 Kirk, Robert W. Handbook of Veterinarian Procedures and
    Emergency Treatment. 2nd ed. Philadelphia: Saunders,
    1975. 716p.

340 Lyons, William E. First Aid Hints for the Horse Owner: A
    Veterinary Notebook. 2nd ed. London: Collins, 1978. 151p.

341 Mackay-Smith, Matthew. "The Picture of Health: How to Know
    a Well Horse When You See One." Equus, no. 28 (February
    1980), 34-40.

342 Marlin, Herb and Sam Savitt. How to Take Care of Your Horse
    Until the Vet Comes: A Horse Health and First Aid Guide.
    New York: Dodd, Mead, 1975. 96p.

343 Martin, M. T. "Don't Vacillate, Vaccinate." Horseman, XXII
    (April 1978), 31-35.

344 Miller, Robert M. Health Problems of the Horse. Colorado
    Springs, CO: Western Horseman, 1971. 48p.

345 _____. "How to Reduce Your Veterinary Bills." Western
 Horseman, XLIII (December 1978), 47, 85.

346 Naviaux, James L. Horses: In Health and Disease. New York:
 Arco, 1974. 256p.

347 Oehme, Frederick W. and James E. Prier. Textbook of Large
 Animal Surgery. Baltimore, MD: Williams and Wilkins,
 1974. 608p.

348 Olsen, Richard G. Immunology and Immunopathology of Domestic Animals. Springfield, IL.: C. C. Thomas, 1979. 309p.

349 Pippi, Ney L. "Pain Model and Analgesic Drug Tests in Horses."
 Unpublished Ph. D. Dissertation, Colorado State University,
 1978.

350 Rooney, James R. Clinical Neurology of the Horse. Kennett
 Square, PA: KNA Press, 1971. 104p.

351 _____. The Sick Horse: Causes, Symptoms, and Treatment.
 South Brunswick, NJ: A. S. Barnes, 1977. 170p.

352 Rossdale, Peter D. Horse Ailments Explained. New York:
 Arco, 1979. 96p.

353 _____. Seeing Equine Practice. London: Heinemann, 1976.
 160p.

354 _____ and S. W. Ricketts. The Practice of Equine Stud
 Medicine. London: Baillière Publications, 1974. 421p.

355 _____ and S. M. Wreford. The Horse's Health from A to
 Z: An Equine Dictionary. London: David and Charles,
 1974. 433p.

356 "Scheduling Your Horse's Health." Practical Horseman, VIII
 (June 1980), 63-69.

357 Seiden, Rudolph. Livestock Health Encyclopedia. 2nd ed. New
 York: Springer Publishing Company, 1961. 628p.

358 Self, Charles, Jr. Winning Tips on Health and Grooming.
 Omaha, NE: Farnam Horse Library, 1978. 64p.

359 Sevelius, Fritz, et al. Keeping Your Horse Healthy: The Prevention and Cure of Illness. Translated from the German.
 London: David and Charles, 1978. 176p.

360 Siegmund, Otto H. , ed. The Merck Veterinary Manual: A
 Handbook of Diagnosis and Therapy for the Veterinarian. 5th
 ed. Rahway, NJ: Merck Publications, 1979. 1,630p.

361 Simmons, Hoyt H. Horseman's Veterinary Guide. Colorado
    Springs, CO: Western Horseman, 1963. 48p.

362 Slahor, Stephanie. The Layman's Guide to Horse Health Care.
    Houston, TX: Cordovan Corp., 1978. 236p.

363 Spaulding, C. E. A. A Veterinary Guide for Animal Owners.
    Emmaus, PA: Rodale Press, 1976. 420p.

364 Sporting Life, Editors of. Your Horse: A Veterinary Book.
    London: Sporting Life, 1967. 149p.

365 Straiton, Edward C. The Horse Owner's Vet Book. Rev. ed.
    Philadelphia: Lippincott, 1979. 199p.

366 _____. The T. V. Vet Horse Book: Recognition and Treat-
    ment of Common Horse and Pony Ailments. By T. V. Vet,
    pseud. 2nd ed. Ipswich, Eng.: Farming Press, 1973.
    196p.

367 Veterinary Annual. London: Wright-Scientechnica, 1960--. v.
    1--.

368 Vincent, S. G. "First Aid for Horsemen." Horseman, XXIII
    (February 1979), 74-77.

369 Whitney, Leon F. Animal Doctor: The History and Practice of
    Veterinary Medicine. New York: David McKay, 1973. 104p.

370 _____. The Farm Veterinarian. Springfield, IL: C. C.
    Thomas, 1964. 720p.

371 Your Horse's Health: A Handbook for Owners and Trainers.
    South Brunswick, NJ: A. S. Barnes, 1979.

2 Veterinarians

372 American Association of Equine Practitioners. Guide for Veter-
    inary Service and Judging of Equestrian Events. 2nd ed.
    Golden, CO:, 1976. 74p.

373 Dayton, Jay. "Patients and Fortitude." Horse and Rider, XI
    (July 1972), 36-41.

374 Evans, C. R. "Selecting a Veterinarian." Equus, no. 12
    (October 1978), 46-51, 70.

375 Farrier, Denis. Country Vet. New York: Taplinger, 1972.
    196p.

376 Green, Ben K. The Village Horse Doctor: West of the Pecos.
    New York: Alfred A. Knopf, 1971. 306p.

377 Herriot, James. All Creatures Great and Small. New York:
     St. Martin's Press, 1972. 442p.

378 _____. All Things Bright and Beautiful. New York: St.
     Martin's Press, 1974. 378p.

379 _____. All Things Wise and Wonderful. 2 vols. New York:
     St. Martin's Press, 1977.

380 Jamieson, Ann. "Vets--Your Horse Isn't the Only Patient He's
     Got." American Horseman, VIII (October 1978), 20-28.

381 Learn, Charles R. "A Day in the Life of a Vet: On Call."
     Horse and Rider, X (March 1971), 34-37, 54.

382 Logue, Jeanne. The Wonder of It All. New York: Harper and
     Row, 1979. 207p.

383 McPhee, Richard B. Rounds With a Country Vet. New York:
     Dodd, Mead, 1977. 74p.

384 Markus, Kurt. "Bill Throgmorton, D. V. M.: An Interview."
     Western Horseman, XLII (June 1977), 38-43.

385 Roberts, S. J. "Problems in Pleasure Horse Practice." Cor-
     nell Veterinarian, LXVIII (January 1978), 31-40.

386 Yates, Elizabeth. Is There a Doctor in the Barn?: A Day in
     the Life of Forrest F. Tenney, D. V. M. New York: E.
     P. Dutton, 1966. 207p.

3 Specific Diseases/Treatments

387 Adams, O. R. Lameness in Horses. 3rd ed. Philadelphia:
     Lea and Febiger, 1972. 570p.

388 Bourassa, Jean. "Bad Bots." Horse and Rider, XI (March
     1972), 52-55.

389 Bryans, J. T., ed. Equine Infections Diseases: Proceedings
     of an International Conference. Basel, Switzerland: Karger,
     1970. 335p.

390 Coggins, Leroy. "Equine Infectious Anemia." Rapidan River
     Farm Digest, I (Winter 1975), 187-190.

391 Cotchin, Edward. "A General Survey of Tumours in the Horse."
     Equine Veterinary Journal, IX (January 1977), 16-21.

392 Drudge, J. H. "The Control of Internal Parasites." Rapidan
     River Farm Digest, I (Winter 1975), 248-254.

393   Gaines, David. "Colic: Death Penalty for Stalled Horses."
       Horseman, XXIII (June 1979). 44-48.

394   Garcia, Marolo C. "Regulation of Luteinizing Hormone in the
       Mare." Unpublished Ph. D. Dissertation, University of Wis-
       consin at Madison, 1976.

395   Guy, P. S. "The Effect of Training and Detraining on Muscle
       Composition in the Horse." Journal of Physiology, CCLXIX
       (July 1977), 33-51.

396   Hall, R. F. Horse Worms and Their Treatment. Moscow:
       Cooperative Extension Service, University of Idaho. 1975.
       2p.

397   Hoeppner, Gabby. "Parasites and the Horse." Horse and Horse-
       man, V (April 1977), 38-42.

398   Hooper, Freia I. "Oh, His Aching Back." Horse and Rider,
       XVIII (April 1979), 38-43.

399   Humphries, James P. "Equine Infectious Diseases." Western
       Horseman, XLIV (April 1979), 50-58.

400   Ingram, J. B. "Lameness in the Horse." The Washington
       Horse, XXX (June 1976), 934-938.

401   Ivens, Virginia R. Principal Parasites of Domestic Animals in
       the United States: Biological and Diagnostic Information.
       Champagne: College of Agriculture, University of Illinois,
       1978. 270p.

402   Jackson, Terry A. "Equine Herpesvirus-1: Infection of Horses."
       Unpublished Ph. D. Dissertation, University of California at
       Davis, 1974.

403   James, Ruth. "Back Problems: Causes and Cures." Western
       Horseman, XLI (November 1976), 152-157.

404   Kaufman, Gary. "Splints." Western Horseman, XLV (March
       1980), 35-38.

405   Krook, Lennart and J. E. Lowe. Nutritional Secondary Hyper-
       parathyroidism in the Horse. White Plains, NY: Albert J.
       Phiebig Books, 1964. 98p.

406   Lockart, Royce A. "Studies on Factors Influencing the Inter-
       action of Western Equine Encephalomyelitis Virus and Selected
       Cells." Unpublished Ph. D. Dissertation, University of Wash-
       ington, 1958.

407   Mackay-Smith, Matthew. "Facing a Fracture: What Are the Odds
       for Recovery?" Equus, no. 30 (April 1980), 32-38, 81.

408   Magnuson, Nancy S. "Metabolic Studies on Lymphocytes and Erythrocytes from Hores with Combined Immunodeficiency." Unpublished Ph. D. Dissertation, Washington State University, 1978.

409   Mayhew, Ian G. "Spinal Cord Disease in the Horse." Unpublished Ph. D. Dissertation, Cornell University, 1978.

410   Miller, Robert M. "Common Causes of Lameness." Western Horseman, XL (February 1975), 7.

411   Moyer, William. "Lameness Caused by Improper Shoeing." American Veterinary Medical Association Journal, CLXVI (January 1, 1975), 47-52.

412   Pipers, Frank S. "Echocardiography in the Horse." Unpublished Ph. D. Dissertation, Ohio State University, 1978.

413   Rhodes, Bob. "Understanding the Lame Horse." Horse and Rider, XII (September 1973), 64-67.

414   Roberts, J. E. "The Common External Parasites of Horses." Program/Proceedings of the National Horseman's Seminar, II (1977), 37-44.

415   Rooney, James R. Biomechanics of Lameness in Horses. Huntington, NY: Krieger, 1977. 259p.

416   _____. Lameness: A Horse Owner's Guide. Huntington, NY: Krieger, 1979. 260p.

417   Schroeder, W. G. "Suggestions for Handling Horses Exposed to Rabies." American Veterinary Medical Association Journal, CLV (December 15, 1968), 1842-1843.

418   Serth, Geoffrey W. The Horse Owner's Guide to Common Ailments. London: Pelham Books, 1977. 97p.

419   Sippel, William L. "Rabies in Horses." Western Horseman, XXXIX (January 1974), 20, 114.

420   Srihakim, Somchai. "A Study of Pathology and Pathogenesis of 'Parascaris Equorum' Infection in Parasite-Free Pony Foals." Unpublished Ph. D. Dissertation, University of Kentucky, 1977.

421   Strong, Charles L. Horses Injuries: Common-Sense Therapy of Muscles and Joints for the Layman. New York: Arco, 1973. 118p.

422   Thiffault, Mark. "Do's and Don'ts of Colic." Horse and Horseman, VII (September 1979), 44-46.

423   _____. "New Hope for the Lame Horse." Horse and Horseman, III (September 1975), 44-47.

424 Thompson, Diana. "They Kill While You Wait: Plotting an Offensive Strategy Against Parasites." Equus, no. 23 (September 1979), 35-42.

425 Turner, Diane E. Understanding Your Horse's Lameness. New York: Arco, 1979. 96p.

426 United States. Department of Agriculture. Agricultural Research Service. Entomology Research Division. Horse Bots: How to Control Them. Leaflet, no. 450. Washington, D. C.: U. S. Government Printing Office, 1970. 8p.

427 _____. National Cancer Institute. Epijootiology Section. Standard Nomenclature of Veterinary Diseases and Operations. Washington, D. C.: U. S. Government Printing Office, 1966. 622p.

428 Usenik, Edward A. "Sympathetic Innervation of the Head and Neck of the Horse: Neuropharmacological Studies of Sweating in the Horse." Unpublished Ph. D. Dissertation, University of Minnesota, 1958.

D REPRODUCTION

1 Breeding: General Works

429 Allen, W. R. Some Recent Studies Upon Reproduction in the Mare. London: Henderson Group One, 1972. 16p.

430 Anderson, C. William. Tomorrow's Champion. New York: Macmillan, 1951. 84p.

431 Arnold, Jobie. "Syndicating the Studs." Town and Country, CXXX (July 1976), 72+.

432 Bearden, H. Joe and John Fuquay. Applied Animal Reproduction. Englewood Cliffs, NJ: Prentice-Hall, 1980. 352p.

433 Breeding Management and Foal Development. Tyler, TX: Equine Research, Inc., 1980.

434 Buck, Susan. "To Breed or Not to Breed: That Is the Question." Western Horseman, XLI (March 1976), 6, 78-79.

435 Coffey, Joel. "Planned Parenthood." Horse and Rider, XII (March 1973), 24-30, 76.

436 Connor, Jack T. "Breeding at Rapidan River Farm." Rapidan River Farm Digest, I (Winter 1975), 112-115.

437 Cunha, Tony J. "Time to Breed." Horse and Rider, X (April 1971), 36-37.

438   Doll, E. R. "Breeding Problems." In: U. S. Department of
       Agriculture. Agriculture Yearbook, 1956. Washington,
       D. C. : U. S. Government Printing Office, 1956. pp. 536-541.

439   Dougall, Neil. "U. S. Training Pays Off in Britain." Western
       Horseman, XXXVIII (June 1973), 100-101, 176-177.
       American breeding "superiority."

440   Ensminger, Marion E. Breeding and Raising Horses. Agricul-
       tural Handbook, no. 394. Washington, D. C. : U. S. Govern-
       ment Printing Office, 1972. 79p.

441   _____. Horse Husbandry. Danville, IL: Interstate Printers
       and Publishers, 1951. 336p.

442   _____. "Pregnancy Signs and Tests." Horse and Rider, X
       (March 1971), 58-59.

443   _____. Stud Manager's Handbook. Clovis, CA: Agriservices
       Foundation, 1971. 186p.

444   Farrington, Merry. "Stallion Syndication." Chronicle of the
       Horse, XLIII (March 28, 1980), 56-57.

445   Finney, Humphrey S. Stud Farm Diary. Middleburg, VA:
       American Racing Publications, Inc. , 1959. 135p.

446   Forbes, Joanne. "The Quality of Mothering in Brood Mares."
       Western Horseman, XXXVIII (March 1973), 24, 120+.

447   Gaines, David. "Problem Mares Lose Money." Horseman,
       XXIII (April 1979), 16-20, 22.

448   _____. "Why Half-Blood Registries." Horseman, XXII
       (April 1978), 78-83.

449   Gomez, Al V. The Foundation Stock. New York: Vantage
       Press, 1976. 173p.

450   Graham, Charles. "When in Doubt, Breed Her." Horse and
       Rider, XVIII (April 1979), 17-21.

451   Great Britain. Committee on National Stud Policy. Report.
       London: H. M. Stationery Office, 1955. 12p.

452   _____. Parliament. Horse Breeding Act. London: H. M.
       Stationery Office, 1958. 12p.

453   Gribble, Philip. Off the Cuff. London: Phoenix House, 1964.
       190p.

454   Hafez, E. S. E. , ed. Reproduction in Farm Animals. 2nd ed.
       Philadelphia: Lea and Febiger, 1968. 440p.

455 Hardmann, Ann C. L. The Amateur Horse Breeder. South Brunswick, NJ: A. S. Barnes, 1971. 155p.

456 Haynes, Glynn W. "How to Read a Pedigree." Horse and Horseman, VIII (July 1980), 16-21.

457 Hutton, C. A. "Reproductive Efficiency on Fourteen Horse Farms." Journal of Animal Science, XXVII (March 1968), 434-438.

458 Hyde, Gavin. "Vigil of Vay Is Mere." Westways, LXX (April 1978), 22-25.

459 Ireland, Republic of. Department of Agriculture and Fisheries. Report of the Survey Team on the Horse Breeding Industry. Dublin: Government Stationary Office, 1966. 52p.

460 James, Ruth V. "Choosing the Broodmare." Western Horseman, XLV (January 1980), 16-20.

461 _____. "Getting the Mare Ready for Breeding." Western Horseman, XLV (February 1980), 37-40.

462 Jones, Arlene. "The Breeding Contract." Horse of Course, IX (February 1979), 20-24.

463 Jones, Dave. "That Mating Game." Horse and Rider, XVII (February 1978), 28-31.

464 Jones, William E. "Breeding Under Control." Horse and Rider, XIX (January 1980), 36-39.

465 _____, ed. Care and Breeding of Horses. Fort Collins, CO: Caballus Publications, 1974. 113p.

466 Kays, John M. Some Horse Breeding Problems. Bulletin, no. 590. Columbia: Agricultural Experimental Station, University of Missouri, 1953. 12p.

467 Kimberley, C. J. "A Guide to Horses, Including Breeding." Journal of Agriculture (Melbourne), LXXVI (November 1978), 381-392.

468 Know Practical Horse Breeding. Omaha, NE: Farnam Horse Library, 1977. 64p.

469 Kreuz, K. "Horse Breeding in the Union of South Africa." South African Agricultural Department Bulletin, no. 353 (1957), 1-26.

470 Lindsay, Peter. "Horse Breeding on a Mixed Farm." Journal of the Ministry of Agriculture, LXX (October 1963), 483-486.

471 Lose, M. Phyllis. Blessed are the Brood Mares. New York:
Macmillan, 1978. 224p.

472 Loy, Robert G. "The Reproductive Cycle of the Mare." Rapidan
River Farm Digest, I (Winter 1975), 135-144.

473 Mackay-Smith, Matthew. "Breeding Your Horse: What Are the
Options." Equus, no. 27 (January 1980), 28-32, 76-81.

474 McPherson, Mary. "Breeding Free." Horse and Rider, XVIII
(January 1979), 12-17, 64.

475 Mahaffey, Leo W., ed. "Stud and Stable" Veterinary Handbook,
1962-1969. London: Stud and Stable, 1970. 216p.

476 Maule, Tex. "Will the Real [Thomas Porter] Whitney Stand
Up?" Classic, III (December 1977-January 1978), 106-111.

477 Miller, William C. Practical Essentials in the Care and Management of Horses on Thoroughbred Studs. London: Thoroughbred Breeders' Association, 1965.

478 Napier, Miles. Blood Will Tell: Orthodox Breeding Theories
Explained. London: J. A. Allen, 1977. 160p.

479 "Needed: Responsible Breeders." Horseman, XXIV (May 1980),
72-76.

480 Nelson, Mary J. "Retiring a Horse to Stud." American Horseman, VIII (October 1978), 36-40.

481 Orchard, Vincent. The Stud Farm. London: S. Paul, 1964.
149p.

482 "Pasture Breeding." Horse and Rider, IX (September 1970),
passim.

483 Pattie, Jane. "Breeding the King Ranch Way." Horse and
Rider, XIX (March-April 1980), 16-20, 34-38.

484 _____. "Give Him a Hand, Folks." Horse and Rider, XVIII
(February 1979), 14-19.

485 _____. "The Light of Their Life." Horse and Rider, XVII
(February 1978), 16-21.

486 Rossdale, Peter D. The Horse, From Conception to Maturity.
London: J. A. Allen, 1975. 224p.

487 Rule, Fred. "Breeding Soundness in Stallions." Quarter Horse
Journal, XXIV (Fall 1971), 53+.

488 Sager, Floyd C. "Care of Broodmares." Rapidan River Farm
Digest, I (Winter 1975), 123-134.

489 Schuessler, Raymond. "From Basic Breeding Techniques."
     Horse and Rider, XI (March 1972), 28-33.

490 Sebrey, Mary A. "Family Planning: 1984?" Horse and Rider,
     XVI (January 1976), 34-36.

491 Silk, George and Daphne Hurford. "It's All in the Family."
     Life, II (February 1979), 44-48.

492 Sorensen, Antom M. Animal Reproduction: Principles and
     Practices. New York: McGraw-Hill, 1979. 496p.

493 Sossamon, George. "Confessions of a Stallion Man." Horse
     and Rider, XIII (March 1974), 18-25.

494 Stewart, Dwight. "I Prefer to Pasture Breed." Horse and
     Rider, IX (April 1970), 16-21, 44.

495 Stud Manager's Handbook. Clovis, CA: Agriservices Founda-
     tion, 1965--. v. 1--.

496 Tottenham, Katherine. Horse and Pony Breeding Explained.
     New York: Arco, 1979. 96p.

497 Ulmer, Donald E. and Elwood M. Jurgensen. Approved Prac-
     tices in Raising and Handling Horses. Danville, IL: Inter-
     state Printers and Publishers, 1974. 331p.

498 Wall, John F. A Horseman's Handbook on Practical Breeding.
     3rd ed., rev. Camden, SC: Thoroughbred Bloodlines, 1950.
     412p.

499 Warwick, Everett J. Breeding and Improvement of Farm Ani-
     mals. 7th ed. New York: McGraw-Hill, 1979. 624p.

500 Washington Horse Breeders' Association. Horseman's Short
     Course: Proceedings. Seattle, 1968.

501 Wentworth, Judith A. D. Horses in the Making. London: J. A. Al-
     len, 1951. 155p.

502 Willis, Larryanne C. The Horse Breeding Farm. Rev. ed.
     South Brunswick, NJ: A. S. Barnes, 1977. 426p.

503 Worthington, William. "Care of Stallions." Rapidan River
     Farm Digest, I (Winter 1975), 116-122.

504 Wynmalen, Henry. Horse Breeding and Stud Management. 2nd
     ed. London: J. A. Allen, 1971. 176p.

2 Equine Genetics

505 Equine Genetics and Selection Procedures. Tyler, TX: Equine

Research, Inc. , 1980.

506   Jones, William E.   "Genetics That Kill."   Horseman, XXII
        (September 1978), 46, 72.

507   _____ and Ralph Bogart.   Genetics of the Horse.   East
        Lansing, MI: Caballus Publishers, 1971.   356p.

508   Lasley, John F.   Genetic Principles in Horse Breeding.   Hous-
        ton, TX: Horseman Books, 1979.   64p.

509   Nishikawa, Yoshimasa.   Studies on Reproduction in Horses:
        Singularity and Aritfical Control in Reproductive Phenomena.
        Tokyo, Japan: Japan Racing Association, 1959.   340p.

510   Rhodes, Bob.   "Genetics for Better Results."   Horse and Rider,
        XIV (January 1975), 33-36, 42-43.

3   Breeding: Specific Animals

511   American Horse Council.   Thoroughbred Breeders Incentive Pro-
        grams, by State.   Washington, D. C. , 1979.   21p.

512   American Quarter Horse Association.   Breeder's Reference
        Guide.   Rev. ed.   Amarillo, TX, 1980.   32p.

513   Bishop, S. E.   "Raising Race Horses."   Extension Service Re-
        view, XXIX (August 1958), 168+.

514   Bochnak, Stephen.   "Thoroughbred Breeding: New York's 'New
        Industry.' "   Empire State Report, VI (January 28-February
        4, 1980), 29+, 37+.

515   British Bloodstock Agency.   Bloodstock Breeders' Review: An
        Illustrated Annual Devoted to the British Thoroughbred.   Lon-
        don: J. A. Allen, 1950--.   v. 39--.

516   Craig, Dennis.   Breeding Racehorses From Cluster Mares.
        London: J. A. Allen, 1964.   183p.

517   Dayton, Jay.   "The Four-Horse Man [Clark Thompson] of the
        Appaloosas."   Horse and Rider, XI (February 1972), 22-26.

518   DeBiase, Achille.   The Development of the Successful Thorough-
        bred Sire Lines in England and France.   London: J. A.
        Allen, 1961.   270p.

519   Dixon, William S.   The Influence of Racing and the Thorough-
        bred Horse on Light Horse Breeding.   London: Hurst and
        Blackett, 1925.   247p.
           A classic.

520 Dougall, Neil. The Management and Handling of Stallions. London: J. A. Allen, 1972. 112p.

521 Eversfield, Martin E. , et al. Thoroughbred Breeding of the World. Translated from the German. Dorheim: Published for the Directorate of Thoroughbred Breeding and Horseracing, Cologne, by Podzun-Verlag, 1970. 635p.

522 Fenwick-Palmer, Roderic. Out of the Ruck: National Hunt Breeding and Training. 2nd ed. London: J. A. Allen, 1966. 192p.

523 Florida. Department of Agriculture. Thoroughbred Horse Breeding in Florida. Bulletin, no. 182. Tallahassee, 1959. 57p.

524 Gill, James. Bloodstock: Breeding Winners in Europe and America. New York: Arco, 1977. 319p.

525 Hampton, H. D. C. First Scientific Principles of Thoroughbred Breeding. Auckland, New Zealand: Scientific Breeding and Racing Publications, 1954. 40p.

526 Hardman, Ann C. L. Stallion Management: A Practical Guide for Stud Owners. London: Pelham Books, 1974. 157p.

527 Harris, Freddie S. "How the Using Horse Evolved in Early Texas: Thoroughbred with Mustang." Horseman, XXIII (February 1979), 34-41.

528 Hislop, John. Breeding for Racing. London: Secker and Warburg, 1976. 192p.

529 Hudson, R. S. , et al. "Breeding Arabian and Thoroughbred Stallions to Light and Heavyweight Percheron Mares." Michigan Agricultural Experimental Service Bulletin, no. 375 (1951), 1-22.

530 Leicester, Charles B. W. Bloodstock Breeding. Rev. ed. London: J. A. Allen, 1965. 482p.

531 Llewellyn, Rhys. Breeding to Race. London: J. A. Allen, 1965. 78p.

532 Lowe, C. Bruce, comp. Breeding Racehorses by the Figure System. 2nd ed. London: The Field and Queen, 1913. 262p.
       A classic.

533 Miller, William C. Practical Essentials in the Care and Management of Horses on Thoroughbred Studs. London: Thoroughbred Breeders' Association, 1965. 128p.

52 / Equestrian Studies

534 Napier, Miles. Blood Will Tell. London: J. A. Allen, 1979.
160p.

535 Nathan, Herm. "Russell Deen: Texas Paso Breeder." Western Horseman, XLIV (October 1979), 122, 168.

536 Pieper, Jim and Jeanne. California Mule Raiser [George Cham-
berlain]." Western Horseman, XLI (March 1976), 64, 126-
127.

537 Reese, Herbert H. Arabian Horse Breeding. Los Angeles,
CA: Borden Publishing Company, 1953. 160p.

538 Robbins, Sonia. "Trottingbred Horses for Fun (But No Profit)."
Vermont Life, XXXII (Summer 1978), 72-75.

539 Rooney, James R. "Problems in Crossbreeding the Thoroughbred." Western Horseman, XLI (March 1976), 86.

540 Sager, Floyd C. "Breeding Problems of Thoroughbreds." U.S.
Live Stock Sanitary Association Proceedings, (1952), 52-60.

541 Santa Ynez Valley Arabian Horse Breeders' Association. Valley
of the Arabian Horse. Santa Ynez, CA, 1974. Unpaged.

542 Sasse, F. H. Theme on a Pipe Dream: A Formula for Buying,
Breeding, and Backing the Derby Winner. London: J. A.
Allen, 1969. 32p.

543 Skorkowski, E. Arab Breeding in Poland. Columbus, WI:
Your Pony, 1969.

544 _____. "Streaming Pureblood Arab Breeding." World Review of Animal Production, XIV (January-March 1978), 63-
69.

545 Smythe, Patricia. Bred to Jump. London: Cassell, 1965.
184p.

546 Tesio, Frederico. Breeding the Racehorse. Translated from
the Italian. London: J. A. Allen, 1959. 130p.

547 Treadwell, Sandy. "Body Beautiful [Steve Reeves] Builds New
[Morgan] Bodies." Classic, II (August-September 1977),
134-138.

548 _____. "Going Like the Wind at Tara [Farm, Georgia]."
Classic, IV (February-March 1979), 86-94.
Breeding Morgan horses.

549 Wakeman, Donald L. Light Horse Production in Florida. Bulletin, no. 188. Tallahassee: Florida Department of Agriculture, 1965. 215p.

550 Witte, Randy. "Raising Mules at Windy Valley Ranch [California]." Western Horseman, XLIV (April 1979), 8-10.

4 Foals and Their Development

551 Andrist, Friedrich. Mares, Foals, and Foaling: A Handbook for the Small Breeder. Translated from the German. London: J. A. Allen, 1966. 57p.

552 Beeman, G. Marvin. "The Broodmare and Her Foal." Western Horseman, XLI (January 1976), 50-51, 119-121.

553 Black, Leonard. "Objective: Live Foals." Horse and Rider, XVI (February 1977), 36-40.

554 Calhoun, Jim. "Nature and Your Foal." Horse and Rider, IX (February 1970), 28-32.

555 Cash, C. K. "Foaling." Horseman, XXI (January 1977), 26-34.

556 Coen, Sue. Between Mare and Foal. Omaha, NE: Farnam Horse Library, 1978. 64p.

557 Cornwell, John C. "Endocrine Status of the Periparturient Mare and Induction of Estrus After Foal Heat with Prostaglandin F2a." Unpublished Ph. D. Dissertation, Louisiana State University, 1976.

558 Craft, Buck. "Broodmare and Foal Care at the Pitchfork [Ranch]." Horse and Rider, X (February 1971), 16-23.

559 Gemming, Elizabeth and Klaus. Born in a Barn: Farm Animals and Their Young. New York: Coward, McCann, 1974. 46p. [juv.]

560 Goodman, Pat. "Tragedy to Triumph: A Foaling Story." Chronicle of the Horse, XLIII (April 4, 1980), 14-16, 23.

561 Griffith, Frank B. The Fun of Raising a Colt. South Brunswick, NJ: A. S. Barnes, 1970. 173p.

562 Guide to the Care and Feeding of Orphan and Early-Weaned Foals. Norfolk VA: Chemical Division, Borden Company, 1972. 39p.

563 Hamilton, Samantha. "Mare and Foal." Equus, no. 29 (March 1980), 55-58, 77.

564 "How Your Horse Grows and What You Can Do About It." Practical Horseman, V (December 1977), 40-50.

565 Howell, Jane. <u>Rearing a Foal.</u> London: Nelson, 1970. 92p.

566 "An Illustrated Guide to Foaling." <u>Practical Horseman</u>, VII (January 1979), 19-26.

567 Isenbart, Hans-Heinrich. <u>A Foal Is Born.</u> Translated from the German. New York: G. P. Putnam, 1976. 42p. [juv.]

568 Jones, William E. "Genesis of a Foal." <u>Horse and Rider</u>, XVIII (January 1980), 24-26.

569 Knappenberger, R. F. "Equine Pediatrics." <u>Rapidan River Farm Digest</u>, I (Winter 1975), 164-173.

570 McGee, William. "Care of Newborn Foals." <u>Rapidan River Farm Digest</u>, I (Winter 1975), 152-163.

571 Mackay, Anne. "The Care of the Mare and Newly-Born Foal." <u>Agricultural Technology</u>, VIII (November 1977), 24-25.

572 Miller, Robert M. "Gelding: When and Why." <u>Western Horseman</u>, XLII (July 1977), 66, 146-148.

573 "A Moment of Truth and Beauty." <u>Horse and Rider</u>, XVI (February 1977), 12-17.

574 Nelson, Mary J. "From Conception to Weaning." <u>Horse and Horseman</u>, I (January 1974), 58-62.

575 Ommert, William. "Help Mother Nature Increase Your Live Foal Rate." <u>Horseman</u>, XVII (July 1973), 14-23.

576 Pattie, Jane. "Foaling Around." <u>Horse and Rider</u>, XIV (April 1975), 24-25.

577 Pittenger, Peggy J. <u>The Backyard Foal.</u> New York: Arco, 1973. 189p.

578 _____. <u>How to Raise a Foal.</u> Omaha, NE: Farnam Horse Library, 1979. 64p.

579 _____. "Weaning Time." <u>Western Horseman</u>, XXXV (September 1970), 47.

580 <u>Practical Horseman</u>, Editors of. <u>An Illustrated Guide to Foaling.</u> West Chester, PA, 1979. 8p.

581 _____. <u>From Breeding to Weaning: A Guide for the Mare Owner.</u> West Chester, PA, 1979. 8p.

582 Rabinowitz, Sandy. <u>What's Happening to Daisey?</u> New York: Harper & Row, 1977. [juv.]

Makeup, Health, Reproduction / 55

583　Rich, Ray. "A Chief Off the Old Block." Horse and Rider, XVII (February 1978), 32-37.

584　_____. "An Eye for Action." Horse and Rider, XIII (January 1974), 44-49.

585　_____. "The Time of Your Life." Horse and Rider, XVIII (March 1979), 26-30.

586　Richards, Rusty. "Don't Fool With Foals." Horse and Horseman, I (August 1973), 16-23.

587　Robertson, Junior. "From Foaling to First Show." Horse and Rider, X (September 1971), 16-21.

588　Sain, L. C. "Helping Your Mare to Foal." Horse Lover's National Magazine, XLIII (April 1978), 13-18.

589　Swager, Peggy. "Labor-Saving Labor." Horse and Rider, XVI (January 1977), 24-26.

590　Vavra, Robert J. Equus: The Creation of a Horse. New York: Morrow, 1979. 224p.

5　Identification, Color, and Markings

591　Abeles, Hetty M. S. "A Coat of Many Colors: The Horse and How He Got His Paint Job." Equus, no. 17 (March 1979), 30-38.

592　Armstrong, Kathleen. "Where There's Smoke, There's Branding." Horse and Rider, XIII (April 1974), 74-76.

593　Arnold, Oren and John P. Hale. Hot Irons: Heraldry of the Range. New York: Cooper Square Publications, 1972. 242p.

594　Benson and Hedges. The Benson and Hedges Book of Racing Colours. London: Jockeys' Association of Great Britain, 1973. 320p.

595　Bogart, Ralph. "Color Inheritance in Horses." Western Horseman, XXXIX (September 1974), 14-15+.

596　Castle, W. E. "Coat Color Inheritance in Horses and Other Mammals." Genetics, XXXIX (January 1954), 35-44.

597　Close, Pat. "How to Brand a Horse." Western Horseman, XLII (February 1977), 54-56.

598　Green, Ben K. "The Color of Horses." Arizona Highways, LI (January 1975), 2-9.

599 _____. The Color of Horses: The Scientific and Authorita-
tive Identification of the Color of the Horse. Flagstaff, AZ:
Northland Press, 1974. 127p.

600 Hart, Ed. "Breeding for Colour--Fancy or Function?" Heavy
Horse Driving, II (Spring 1978), 36-37.

601 Hewitt, B. "Look at Brand Inspection in the West." Western
Horseman, XXXVII (January-February 1972), 74-75+, 52-54.

602 Holden, Gene. "Don't Color Me Ugly." Horse and Rider, XIV
(July 1975), 46-49.

603 James, Ruth B. "A Horse's Color." Western Horseman, XLIV
(May 1979), 50-52.

604 Lewis, Jack. "Coded for Color." Horse and Rider, VIII (December 1969), 22-26.

605 Searle, Anthony G. Comparative Genetics of Coat Colour in
Mammals. London: Logos Press, 1968. 308p.

606 Smith, Jean F. D. Horse Markings and Coloration. South
Brunswick, NJ: A. S. Barnes, 1977. 101p.

607 Wolfenstine, Manfred R. The Manual of Brands and Marks.
Norman: University of Oklahoma Press, 1970. 434p.

Further References: See also Parts IV and V below.

PART III   HORSE BREEDS

A   GENERAL WORKS/ANNUALS

608   Alcock, Anne. The Love of Horses. London: Octopus Books,
        1973. 104p.

609   Alexander, David. The History and Romance of the Horse.
        New York: Cooper Square Publishers, 1963. 128p.

610   All About Horses. London: Orbis Books, 1976. 143p.

611   Anderson, C. William. Smashers. New York: Harper & Row,
        1954. 100p.

612   Balch, Glenn. The Book of Horses. New York: Four Winds
        Press, 1967. 96p. [juv.]

613   _____. Horses. Sportsman Series, no. M-130. New York:
        MACO Magazine Association, 1965. 80p.

614   Berg, William A. Mysterious Horses of Western North Amer-
        ica. New York: Pageant Press, 1960. 298p.

615   Brady, Irene. America's Horses and Ponies. Boston: Hough-
        ton Mifflin, 1976. 202p.

616   Campbell, Judith. The World of Horses. London and New
        York: Hamlyn Publishing, 1969. 140p.

617   Chandoha, Walter. Book of Foals and Horses. New York:
        Crown, 1971. 224p.

618   Churchill, Peter. All Colour World of Horses. London: Octo-
        pus Books, 1978. 104p.

619   Clarke, Margaret I. Australian Horses. Waterloo, Aust. :
        Rigby, 1974. 30p.

620   Coakes, Marion. Marion Coakes' Book of Horses. London:
        Pelham Books, 1968. 120p.

621 Colbeby, Patricia. Introducing Horses Everywhere. London and New York: Hamlyn Publishing, 1964. 80p.

622 Crowell, Pers. Cavalcade of American Horses. Garden City, NY: Garden City Publishing Co. , 1954. 317p.

623 Denhardt, Robert M. The Horse of the Americas. New ed. , rev. and enl. Norman: University of Oklahoma Press, 1975. 343p.

624 Dossenbach, Monique. Irish Horses. London: Hart-Davis, 1977. 192p.

625 Dougall, Neil. Horses and Ponies. London: Smith and Son, 1976. 192p.

626 Duggan, Moira. Horses. New York: Golden Press, 1972. 160p. [juv.]

627 Edwards, Elwyn H. The Horseman's Guide. London: Country Life, 1969. 256p.

628 Edwards, Lionel D. R. Thy Servant the Horse. London: Country Life, 1953. 118p.

629 Geddes, Candida, ed. The Concise Book of the Horse. New York: Arco, 1976. 166p.

630 Glyn, Richard H. , ed. The World's Finest Horses and Ponies. London: Harrap, 1971. 128p.

631 Goodall, Daphne M. Horses and Their World. New York: Maxon/Charter, 1976. 168p.

632 _____. Horses of the World: An Illustrated Survey. New and rev. ed. New York: Macmillan, 1973. 272p.

633 The Great Book of Australian Horses. Waterloo, Aust. : Rigby, 1976. 304p.

634 Groves, Colin P. Horses, Asses, and Zebras in the World. Newton Abbot, Eng. : David and Charles, 1974. 192p.

635 Hamilton, Samantha. "The View From Out There: A Nonequestrian Takes a Boggled Look at the World of Horses. " Equus, no. 31 (May 1980), 50-54, 77.

636 Henry, Marguerite. All About Horses. New York: Random House, 1967. 129p.

637 _____. Dear Readers and Riders. Chicago: Rand McNally, 1969. 223p.

638 Hogner, Dorothy C. The Horse Family. New York: Walck, 1953. 70p. [juv.]

639 Hope, Charles E. G. Beauty of Horses. London: Parrish, 1959. 128p.

640 _____. The Horse-Lover's Book. Chicago: Regnery, 1970. 254p.

641 _____. Horses and Ponies Pictorial, 1960. London: Barrie and Rockliff, 1959. 60p.

642 Horses. London and New York: Hamlyn Publishing, 1962. 160p.

643 Johnson, Elizabeth. All Colour Book of Horses. London: Octopus Books, 1972. 160p.

644 Johnson, Patricia H. Horse Fever: A Guide for Horse-Lovers and Riders. New York: Grosset and Dunlap, 1961. 92p.

645 _____. Horse Talk. New York: Funk and Wagnalls, 1967. 130p.

646 _____. Meet the Horse. New York: Grosset and Dunlap, 1967. 144p.

647 Lange, Harald and Kurt Jeschko. The Horse Today and Tomorrow. Translated from the German. New York: Arco, 1972. Unpaged.

648 Lavine, Sigmund A. and Brigid Casey. Wonders of the World of Horses. New York: Dodd, Mead, 1972. 80p. [juv.]

649 Lewis, Howard J. Complete Book of Horses. New York: Random House, 1957. 144p.

650 Long, Matthew. The Wonderful World of Horses. London: Octopus Books, 1976. 96p.

651 Mackay-Smith, Alexander. "Stallions: The Breeds." Practical Horseman, V (December 1977), 50-57.

652 McMillan, George. The Golden Book of Horses. New York: Golden Press, 1968. 105p. [juv.]

653 Magee, Robert. The Classic World of Horses. New York: Arco, 1974. 143p.

654 Molesworth, Roger. Knowing Horses. New York: Arco, 1962. 219p.

655 Mullins, Barbara G. and Julia. Horses and Ponies in Australia:

An Outline of the History of Distinctive Australian Breeds.
Wellington, New Zealand: A. H. and A. W. Reed, 1978.
33p.

656 Nagler, Barney. The American Horse. New York: Macmillan,
1966. 182p.

657 Nockels, David. Know About Horses. London: Young World
Productions, 1968. 94p. [juv.]

658 Nowas, Cate and Vic. The Beauty of the Horse. New York:
Viking Press, 1972. Unpaged.

659 Osborne, Walter D. and Patricia H. Johnson. The Treasury of
Horses. New York: Golden Press, 1966. 251p. [juv.]

660 Otto, Margaret and Otto. Horse and Pony Book. New York:
Morrow, 1953. 62p. [juv.]

661 Phillips, Greta M. Horses in Our Blood: A History of Horses
and Ponies of the British Isles and Their Uses. London:
Turf Newspapers, 1974. 311p.

662 Pistorius, Anna. What Horse Is It? Chicago: Follett Publishing Company, 1968. 25p. [juv.]

663 Pluckrose, Henry, ed. Horses. New York: Watts, 1979. 28p.
[juv.]

664 Posell, Elsa Z. The True Book of Horses. Chicago: Childrens Press, 1961. 47p. [juv.]

665 Price, Steven D. Panorama of American Horses. Richmond,
VA: Westover Publishing Company, 1972. 240p.

666 Rachlis, Eugene. Horses. New York: Golden Press, 1965.
62p. [juv.]

667 Ransford, Sandy. The Beaver Horse and Pony Quiz Book. London and New York: Hamlyn Publishing, 1979. 109p. [juv.]

668 Reddick, Kate. Horses. New York: Bantam Books, 1976.
159p.

669 Reese, Herbert H. Horses of Today: Their History, Breeds,
and Qualifications. Pasadena, CA: Wood and Jones, 1956.
144p.

670 Reich, Hanns. Horses. New York: Hill and Wang, 1968. 71p.
[juv.]

671 Rendel, John. The Horse Book. New York: Arco, 1960.
143p.

672 Roberts, Peter. Horses and Ponies. London: Longacre Press, 1960. 120p.

673 Rudofsky, Hubert. Young Horses. Croton-on-Hudson, NY: Dreenan Press, 1977. 75p.

674 Savitt, Sam. Around the World With Horses. New York: Dial Press, 1962.

675 Self, Margaret C. The Complete Book of Horses and Ponies. New York: McGraw-Hill, 1963. 316p.

676 _____. Horses of Today: Arabian, Thoroughbred, Saddle Horse, Standardbred, Western, Pony. New York: Duell, Sloan and Pearce, 1964. 143p.

677 _____. The How and Why Wonder Book of Horses. New York: Grosset and Dunlap, 1961. 48p. [juv.]

678 Sherman, Jane. The Real Book of Horses. By Jay Sherman, pseud. Rev. ed. London: Dennis Dobson, 1959. 190p. [juv.]

679 Shuttleworth, Dorothy E. The Story of Horses. Garden City, NY: Doubleday, 1960. 57p. [juv.]

680 Sidney, Samuel. The Book of the Horse. 2nd ed. Hollywood, CA: Wilshire Books, 1977. 608p.

681 Silver, Caroline. Guide to the Horses of the World. Oxford, Eng.: Phaidon Press, 1976. 223p.

682 Slaughter, Jean. Horses 'Round the World. Philadelphia: Lippincott, 1955. 87p. [juv.]

683 Smythe, Patricia. Book of Horses. London: Cassell, 1955. 119p.

684 Summerhays, Reginald S. The Young Rider's Guide to the Horse World. London: Warne, 1961. 256p.

685 Taylor, Louis. The Story of America's Horses. Cleveland, OH: World Publishing Company, 1968. 128p. [juv.]

686 Thorson, Juli S. "Enduring Types." Horse and Rider, XVII (April 1978), 44-49.

687 Thwaites, Jeanne. Horses of the West. South Brunswick, NJ: A. S. Barnes, 1968. 183p.

688 Trench, Charles C., et al. The Treasury of Horses. London: Octopus Books, 1972. 136p.

689 Walford, Bonny. Champion Horses of the Americas. New
      York: Galahad Books, 1975. 252p.

690 Walker, Stella A. , comp. Long Live the Horse: An Anthology.
      London: Country Life, 1955. 156p.

691 Weatherman, Lynn. A Chronological History of the American
      Saddle Horse. Louisville, KY: American Saddle Horse
      Breeders' Association, n. d. 2p.

692 Webber, Toni. Know Your Horses. Chicago: Rand McNally,
      1977. 49p. [juv.]

693 Whitbread and Company, Ltd. Book of Horses. New York:
      Arco, 1963. 127p.

694 Williams, Dorian. The Book of Horses. Philadelphia: Lippin-
      cott, 1971.

695 _____ and Jennifer, eds. The Girl's Book of Horses and
      Riding. 3rd ed. London: Burke Publishing Company, 1968.
      127p. [juv.]

696 Willoughby, David P. The Empire of Equus. South Brunswick,
      NJ: A. S. Barnes, 1973. 475p.

B LIGHT HORSES

1 General Works

697 American Saddle Horse Breeders' Association. The All Ameri-
      can Horse: The American Saddle Horse. Louisville, KY,
      1978. 18p.

698 _____ . Get to Know the American Saddlebred. Louisville,
      KY, n. d. 13p.

699 _____ . Register. Louisville, KY, 1950--. v. 59--.

700 _____ . The Saddlebred: The All American Horse. Louis-
      ville, KY, n. d. 15p.

701 Arnold, Jobie. "The Saddlebred Horse." Town and Country,
      CXXXIII (June 1979), 106-107.

702 Barton, Frank T. Light Horses and Light Horse Keeping. 3rd
      ed. London: Jarrolds, 1951. 256p.

703 Broadhead, W. S. Hoof Prints Over America: The Illustrated
      Story of the Light Horse in America. New York: Scribners,
      1951. 96p.

704 Canada. Department of Agriculture. The Saddle Horse. Pub-
     lication, no. 1462. Ottawa, Ont., 1972. 46p.

705 Churchill, Peter. The Sporting Horse. London: Marshall
     Cavendish, 1976. 120p.

706 Conley, Harlan L. 4-H Light Horses. Des Moines: Iowa
     Horse and Mule Breeders' Association, 1954. 60p.

707 Ensminger, Marion E. "Light Horses." Farmer's Bulletin,
     no. 2127 (1958), 1-48.

708 _____. Light Horses. Rev. ed. Washington, D.C.: Pre-
     pared in Cooperation with the Department of Animal Science,
     Washington State University, by the Animal Husbandry Re-
     search Division, Agricultural Research Service, U.S. Depart-
     ment of Agriculture, 1962. 56p.

709 Hurley, Jimmie. "Jim Rodriguez, Jr., Describes the Ideal
     Heading Horse." Western Horseman, XXXIX (June 1974),
     56-57+.

710 Lee, Hollis. The Pleasure Horse. Barrington, IL: Country-
     side Books, 1978. Unpaged.

711 Orcutt, Harry P. America's Riding Horses: A Guide to All
     Breeds for the Amateur. Princeton, NJ: Van Nostrand,
     1958. 280p.

712 Patten, John W. The Light Horse Breeds: Their Origin, Char-
     acteristics, and Principal Uses. New York: A. S. Barnes,
     1960. 262p.

713 Pattie, Jane. "John Cratty Discusses the Raw Materials for
     Making a Pleasure Horse." Western Horseman, XXXVII
     (April 1972), 40-41, 140-142.

714 "The Pleasure Horse." New Hampshire Agricultural Extension
     Bulletin, no. 146 (1958), 1-35.

715 Ransom, James H. History of the American Saddle Horse.
     Lexington, KY, 1962. 398p.

716 Rosel, Mike. "The Australian Stock Horse: A Brief History."
     Western Horseman, XLIII (July 1978), 38-44, 104.

717 Scharf, Emily E. "The Origin and Development of the American
     Saddle Horse." Rapidan River Farm Digest, I (Winter 1975),
     35-39.

718 Sundahl, Ivan. Light Horse Project: 4-H Members' Guide.
     Morgantown: Cooperative Extension Service, Center for Ex-

tension and Continuing Education, West Virginia University, 1963. 22p. Rpr. 1977.

2 Specific Breeds

American Paso Fino

719 American Paso Fino Horse Association. The Paso Fino Horse. 3rd ed. Pittsburgh, PA, 1976. 31p.

720 Anderson, M. M. "Paso Fino." Horseman, XXIII (February 1979), 72-74.

721 Hirsch, Maurice L., Jr. "The American Paso Fino." Western Horseman, XXXVIII (November 1973), 62, 166.

722 LaHood, George J., Jr. and Rosalie MacWilliam. The American Paso Fino. Columbus, NC: Friendship Enterprises, 1976. 102p.

Andalusian

723 Adkins, Becky S. "The Andalusian." Western Horseman, XXXVI (November 1971), 48.

724 Christopher, Renny. "The Andalusian: Renaissance Horse." Horse Lover's National Magazine, XLIII (May 1978), 42-43, 59-60.

725 Engemann, Barbara. "Magnificos Caballos." Horse and Rider, XVI (April 1976), 36-38.

726 Woodcock, Chris. The First Horse of the Americas. Silver City, NM: American Andalusian Horse Association, 1972. 16p.

Appaloosa

727 Appaloosa. East Lansing, MI: The Horse Book Publisher, n.d. 103p.

728 Appaloosa Data, Inc. Appaloosa Champions, 1948-1976. Pryor, OK, 1977. 201p.

729 "Appaloosa Horse Talk." Horse and Rider, IX (July 1970), passim.

730 The Appaloosa Yearbook. San Jose, CA: R. C. Logan Publishing Company, 1973--. v. 1--.

731 Arlandson, Lee. Know the Appaloosa Horse. Omaha, NE: Farnam Horse Library, 1979. 64p.

732 Balch, Glenn. Spotted Horse. New York: T. Y. Crowell, 1961. 176p. [juv.]

733 Barnard, Patty. "Appaloosa: The Special Breed." The Spot-Lighter, (January 1976), 18-26.

734 Fitzgerald, O. A. "Appaloosa, Pride of the Rough Country." Farm Journal, LXXVIII (February 1954), 52+.

735 Haddle, Jan. The Complete Book of the Appaloosa. South Brunswick, NJ: A. S. Barnes, 1976. 371p.

736 Haines, Frances. Appaloosa: The Spotted Horse in Art and History. Austin: Published for the Amon Carter Museum of Western Art, Ft. Worth, by the University of Texas, 1963. 103p.

737 _____, et al. The Appaloosa Horse. Lewiston, ID: R. C. Bailey, 1957. 512p.

738 Treadwell, Sandy. "The No-Nonsense Nonagenarian [Tom Clay] from Nowhere Nevada." Classic, II (December 1976-January 1977), 116-122.

739 _____. "Plain Billy [Williams] and His Spotted Gold Mine." Classic, II (October-November 1977), 94-100.

740 Walker, Don. "The Appaloosa." Country Gentleman, CXXVI (Fall 1976), 49+.

741 _____. _____. Western Horseman, XLIV (October 1979), 38-40.

The Arabian

742 Arab Horse Society. The Arab Horse in Great Britain and Ire-land. London: J. A. Allen, 1964. 102p.

743 _____. Stud Book. Growborough, Eng., 1950--. v. 6--.

744 Arabian Horse Association International. Purebred Arabian Horse Yearbook. Seal Beach, CA, 1953--. v. 1--.

745 Arabian Horse Registry of America. Arabian Stud Book. Den-ver, CO, 1950--. v. 41--.

746 Arquette, Carol. "Desert Bred." Horse Illustrated, XII (May-June 1979), 8-10.

747 The Blue Arabian Horse Catalog. Newport, VT: Pine Hill Farm, 1961--. v. 1--.

748 Bond, Marian. "Choosing the Best Arabian." Horseman, XXIII
     (January 1979), 44-50.

749 Borden, Spencer. The Arab Horse. New York: Doubleday,
     1906. 130p.
     A classic.

750 Boucaut, James. The Arab, Horse of the Future. London:
     Gay and Bird, 1905. 249p.
     Another early title.

751 Brock, Paul. "Arabians of the Desert." Western Horseman,
     XLII (August 1977), 70-74.

752 Brown, William R. The Horse of the Desert. New York:
     Derrydale Press, 1924. 218p.

753 Carroll, Jackson. "Arabs Ain't English." Horse and Rider, XII
     (February 1973), 28-33, 78.

754 Close, Pat. "The Arabian." Western Horseman, XLIV (October
     1979), 70-73.

755 Conn, George H. The Arabian Horse in America. New and
     rev. ed. South Brunswick, NJ: A. S. Barnes, 1972. 321p.

756 _____., ed. Arabian Horse in Fact, Fantasy, and Fiction.
     New York: A. S. Barnes, 1959. 384p.

757 Cotterman, Dan. "Kellogg's Legacy." Horse and Rider, XIII
     (April-May, 1974), 26-32, 50-57.

758 Daumas, Melchior J. E. The Horses of the Sahara. Trans-
     lated from the French. 9th ed., rev. Austin: University
     of Texas Press, 1968. 256p.

759 Davenport, Homer. Arab Horses and the Crabbet Stud. Ft.
     Collins, CO: Caballus Publications, 1973. 186p.

760 _____. Davenport's Arabians. Ft. Collins, CO: Caballus
     Publications, 1973. 331p.
     First published in 1909 as My Quest of the Arab Horse.

761 Edwards, Gladys B. "Arabian Action." Horse and Rider, XVI
     (January 1976), 38-45.

762 _____. "The Arabian Connection." Horse and Rider, XII
     (September-October 1973), 44-48, 55-62.

763 _____. "The Arabian Racehorse." Horse and Rider, X
     (May 1971), 46-58.

764 _____. The Arabian: War Horse to Show Horse. 2nd ed.
     Covina, CA: Gallant Library, 1972. 300p.

765 _____. "History of the Arabian." Rapidan River Farm Digest, I (Winter 1975), 39-49.

766 _____. Know the Arabian Horse. Omaha, NE: Farnam Horse Library, 1977. 64p.

767 _____. "Mare Power." Horse and Rider, XI (August 1972), 46-52.

768 _____. "Roots of the Family Tree." Horse and Rider, XI (January 1972), 63-67, 72.

769 Forbis, Judith E. The Classic Arabian Horse. New York: W. W. Norton, 1976. 431p.

770 _____. "The Desert Dancer." Horse and Rider, XIII (January 1974), 60-63.

771 Foss, John. "The Future of the Arabian." American Horseman, IV (October 1974), 16-18, 42.

772 Galbreath, Jim W. "A Report on the Arabian." Western Horseman, XXXIX (November 1974), 32, 138-140.

773 Gazder, Pesi J. Arab Horse Families: An Introduction and Guide to Stud Book. 2nd rev. ed. Cranbrook, Eng.: Arab Horse Society, 1976. 143p.

774 _____. "Genetic History of the Arabian Horse in the United States." Journal of Heredity, XLV (March 1954), 95-98.

775 Gleason, Linda. "The Arabians Come to Town." New Mexico Magazine, LVII (October 1979), 12+.

776 Greely, Margaret. Arabian Exodus [Into Europe]. London: J. A. Allen, 1975. 231p.

777 Harris, Albert W. The History of the Arabian Horse Club Registry of America, Inc. Chicago: Arabian Horse Club Registry of America, Inc., 1950. 64p.

778 International Arabian Horse Association. The Arabian Horse. Burbank, CA, n.d. 5p.

779 _____. The Half-Arabian and Anglo-Arabian. Burbank, CA, n.d. 5p.

780 _____. Handbook. Burbank, CA, 1967--. v. 1--.

781 Jones, William E. "Desert Gems." Horse and Rider, XVII (August 1978), 62-65.

782 Kullman, Joe. "The Day of the Arabians." Phoenix, IV (August 1979), 92-94.

783 Markatos, Kathie C. "Arabians: The Proud Breed." <u>Classic,</u> III (October-November 1978), 123-139.

784 Maule, Tex. "Boom Time in Arabian Country [Scottsdale, Arizona]." <u>Classic</u>, III (December 1977-January 1978), 124-129.

785 Mulder, Carol W., ed. <u>Imported Foundation Stock of North American Arabian Horses.</u> Alhambra, CA: Borden Publishing Company, 1969--. v. 1--.

786 Raswan, Carl R. <u>The Arab and His Horse.</u> Oakland, CA, 1955. 148p.

787 _____. <u>Drinkers of the Wind.</u> New York: Farrar, Straus, 1961. 160p. [juv.]

788 _____. <u>My Life Among the Bedouins.</u> Ft. Collins, CO: Printed Horse, 1975. 256p. Reprint of 1936 edition.

789 _____. <u>The Raswon Index and Handbook for Arabian Breeders.</u> Mexico, D.F.: Editorial Authority, 1957. Unpaged.

790 Reese, Herbert H. and Gladys B. Edwards. <u>Kellogg Arabians: Their Background and Influence.</u> Los Angeles, CA: Borden Publishing Company, 1958. 222p.

791 Rosenvold, Lloyd and Doris. <u>Tales of the King's Horses.</u> Montrose, CO, 1958. 182p.

792 Ryan, Dixie. <u>Stories of Champions and the National Arabian Shows.</u> Ft. Collins, CO: Printed Horse, 1975. 300p.

793 Schiele, Erika. <u>The Arab Horse in Europe: History and Present Breeding of the Pure Arab.</u> Translated from the German. Alhambra, CA: Borden Publishing Company, 1970. 319p.

794 Selby, Roger A., comp. <u>Arabian Horses.</u> Barnesville, MD: Arabian Horse Owners' Foundation, 1968. 104p.

795 Simmons, Diane C. "Desert Legacy." <u>Horse Lover's National Magazine</u>, XLIV (September 1979), 32-39.

796 Summerhays, Reginald S. <u>The Arabian Horse.</u> South Brunswick, NJ: A. S. Barnes, 1970. 103p.

797 _____. <u>The Arabian Horse in Great Britain.</u> London: Country Life, 1967. 103p.

798 Tweedie, William. <u>The Arabian Horse: His Country and His People.</u> London: Blackwoods, 1894. 433p. A classic.

799 Wentworth, Judith A. D. W. The Authentic Arabian Horse and His Descendants. New York: Crown, 1963. 367p.

800 _____. Crabbet Arabian Stud. London: J. A. Allen, 1957. 69p.

801 _____. The World's Best Horse. London: J. A. Allen, 1958. 252p.

802 Wrangel, Varnon A. The Arabian in Arabia. London: J. A. Allen, 1962. 96p.

803 Young, John R. Arabian Cow Horse. Chicago: Wilcox and Follett, 1953. 256p.

Buckskin

804 American Buckskin Registry Association. Official Handbook. Anderson, CA, 1962--. v. 1--.

Cleveland Bay

805 Cleveland Bay Society of America. Cleveland Bay [Annual] Magazine. Hopewell, NJ, 1950--. v. 65--.

806 Dent, Anthony A. Cleveland Bay Horses. London: J. A. Allen,

Creole

807 DeBroen-Foote, Elly. "The Creole Horses of South America." Western Horseman, XXXVIII (August 1973), 96-97, 126-128.

Curly Horse

808 Martin, Sunny. "The Curly Horses." Western Horseman, XXXVIII (November 1973), 112-114.

Galiceno

809 Stubblefield, Helen J. "The Galiceno." Western Horseman, XXXVII (October 1972), 69, 172.

Gotland

810 Lee, Pepper. "The Gotland." Western Horseman. XXXVIII (October 1973), 18, 126.

Holstein

811 Mann, Gerhard. Holstein Horses. Croton-on-Hudson, NY:
Dreenan Press, 1977.

Lipizzaner

812 Podhajsky, Alois. The Lipizzaners. Garden City, NY: Doubleday, 1969. 140p.

813 _____. The White Stallions of Vienna. New York: E. P.
Dutton, 1963. 201p.

814 Quick, Kenneth. Immortal Henry: The Story of a Lipizzaner
Stallion. London: Elek, 1977. 142p.

815 Trotter, Patricia. "Lipizzans: A Day at Temple Farms [Illi-
nois]." Western Horseman, XLIII (July 1978), 56-60, 137-
140.

Lusitanian

816 Mackay-Smith, Alexander. "The Lusitanian." Western Horseman, XLV (April 1980), 98-110.

Morgan

817 Dana, C. "Keeping an American Legacy Alive." Horseman,
XXII (April 1978) , 36-38, 40-42.

818 Elam, Margaret. "Morgans: Those Park Ranger Horses."
Western Horseman, XLIV (March 1979), 45-46.

819 Ford, Linda L. The Morgan Horse World of Frank Wellington
Wall. Fountain Valley, CA, 1977. 113p.

820 Freeman, Pam. "The Morgan." Western Horseman, XLIV
(October 1979) , 12-15.

821 Jex, H. S. "The Morgan Horse." Nature Magazine, XLVII
(February 1954), 75-77.

822 Linsley, D. C. Morgan Horses. New York: C. M. Saxton
and Company, 1857. 340p.
The classic.

823 Mellin, Jeanne. The Morgan Horse. Rev. ed. Brattleboro,
VT: Stephen Greene Press, 1980. 256p.

824 Owen, Mabel. "History of the Morgan." Rapidan River Farm
Digest, I (Winter 1975), 17-20.

825 Parker, R. H. "Morgan Horses in Georgia." Western Horseman, XXXVII (January 1972), 16-17+.

826 Pittenger, Peggy J. Morgan Horses. South Brunswick, NJ:
A. S. Barnes, 1967. 287p.

827 _____. "Morgan Jumpers." Western Horseman, XXXVII
(June 1972), 64-65.

828 Reese, Monte. "The Morgan Horse." Western Horseman, XLI
(November 1978), 86-87.

829 Self, Margaret C. The Morgan Horse in Pictures. Chicago:
Macrae Smith, 1967. 149p.

830 Simmons, Diane C. "Morgans for the Mountains." Horseman,
XXIII (January 1979), 18-24.

831 Tyler, Chuck. "The Morgan Manner." Horse and Rider, VIII
(December 1969), 38-43.

Morocco Spotted Horse

832 Rott, Lowell H. "The Morocco Spotted Horse." Western Horseman, XXXVI (November 1971), 22, 134.

Paints

833 American Paint Horse Association. Paints. Ft. Worth, TX,
n. d. 20p.

834 _____. Stud Book and Registry. Ft. Worth, TX, 1962--.
v. 1--.

835 Haynes, Glynn W. The American Paint Horse. Norman: University of Oklahoma Press, 1976. 351p.

836 King, Henry. "The Paint Horse." Western Horseman, XLIV
(October 1979), 54-56.

837 Spencer, Dick, 3rd. "Paint or Pinto?" Western Horseman,
XXXVI (December 1971), 6, 92.

Palomino

838 Castle, W. E. "The Palomino Horse." Genetics, XLVI (September 1961), 1143-1150.

839 Lewis, Jack. "Palominos on Parade." Horse and Rider, IX
(November 1970), 22-26.

840   Palomino Horse Breeders of America, Inc.   Official Stud Book
      and Registry.   Mineral Wells, TX, 1950--.   v.   8--.

841   Shiflet, Robert J.   "The Golden Palomino."   Horse Illustrated,
      IV (July 1980), 20-22.

842   Smith, Lewis.   "Palomino Pal o' Mine."   Horse and Rider,
      XIII (September 1974), 24-28.

Peruvian Paso

843   Albright, Verne.   "The Great Paso Caper."   Horse and Rider,
      IX (November 1970), 28-34.

844   _____.   The Peruvian Paso and His Classic Equitation.   Ft.
      Collins, CO: Printed Horse, 1975.   122p.

845   Curry, Henry F., Jr.   "The Peruvian Paso."   Western Horse-
      man, XXXVIII (October 1973), 46, 134.

846   Daniels, Rick.   "Paso Misconceptions."   Horse and Rider, X
      (May 1971), 54-57.

847   Konauth, Percy.   "Pace Setters with Panache."   Classic, IV
      (April-May 1979), 44-48.

848   "The Peruvian Paso."   Horse and Rider, VII (December 1968),
      passim.

849   Sanderson, Nancy.   "Chalan Logistics."   Horse and Rider, XVII
      (April 1978), 22-26.

850   Thiffault, Mark.   "Peruvian Paso: Hoofbeats in History."   Horse
      and Horseman, III (October 1975), 52-56.

Pinto

851   Buske, Randy.   "The Painted Desertbred."   Horse and Rider,
      XIII (August 1974), 49-52.

852   Dines, Glen.   Indian Pony: The Tough, Hardy Little Horse of
      the Far-Roving Red Man.   New York: Macmillan, 1963.
      48p.   [juv.]

853   Greene, Roxanne D., ed.   A World of Pinto Horses.   San Diego,
      CA: Pinto Horse Association of America, 1970.   172p.

854   Maule, Tex.   "Plumbing the Depths of the Pinto Line."   Classic,
      II (October-November 1977), 122-129.

855   Milby, Verna L.   "The Pinto Horse."   Western Horseman, XLIV
      (October 1979), 62-64.

856 Perkins, Charles E. The Pinto Horse. Santa Barbara, CA: Fisher and Schofield, 1937. 76p. Rpr. 1960.

857 Pinto Horse Association of America. Pinto Horse Register. San Jose, CA, 1972--. v. 1--.

Przevalsky

858 Bökönyl, Sandor. The Przevalsky Horse. Translated from the Hungarian. London: Souvenir Press, 1974. 140p.

Quarter Horse

859 Adams, Ramon F. "Horses." In: James Monaghan, ed. The Book of the American West. New York: Julian Messner, 1963. pp. 356-364.

860 American Quarter Horse Association. "History of the Quarter Horse." Rapidan River Farm Digest, I (Winter 1975), 53-55.

861 _____. Official Handbook. Amarillo, TX, 1951--. v. 1--.

862 _____. Quarter Horse Yearbook. Berkeley, CA, 1963--. v. 1--.

863 _____. Ride American Quarter Horses. Amarillo, TX, 1980. 32p.

864 _____. Selecting, Training, and Feeding American Quarter Horses. Amarillo, TX, 1976. 33p.

865 Bond, Marian. "Training Youth Champion Quarter Horses." Horse and Rider, XVI (November 1976), 12-16.

866 Cunningham, K. A Study of Growth and Development in the Quarter Horse. Bulletin, no. 546. Baton Rouge: Agricultural Experimental Station, Louisiana State University, 1961. 23p.

867 Dams of Quarter Racing Stakes. Horses, 1949-1976. Tucson, AZ: R. H. Smelker Publications, 1977. 415p. A stud book.

868 Davis, Deering. The American Cow Pony: The Background, Training, Equipment and Use of the Western Horse. Princeton, NJ: Van Nostrand, 1962. 166p.

869 Denhardt, Robert M. Foundation Sires of the American Quarter Horse. Norman: Published in Association with the American Quarter Horse Association, by the University of Oklahoma Press, 1976. 269p.

870 _____. The King Ranch Quarter Horses. Norman: University of Oklahoma Press, 1970. 256p.

871 _____. Quarter Horses: A Story of Two Centuries. Norman: University of Oklahoma Press, 1967. 192p.

872 _____. The Quarter Running Horse: America's Oldest Breed. Norman: University of Oklahoma Press, 1979. 302p.

873 James, Byrne. "My Life with Quarter Horses." Western Horseman, XLIV (September 1979), 26-30.

874 Jank, Lyn. That Special Breed: The American Quarter Horse. Ft. Worth, TX: Branch-Smith, 1977. 357p.

875 Kenoyer, Natlee. The Western Horse: A Handbook. New York: Duell, Sloan, and Pearce, 1962. 111p.

876 Know the American Quarter Horse. Omaha, NE: Farnam Horse Library, 1977. 64p.

877 Laune, Paul. America's Quarter Horses. Garden City, NY: Doubleday, 1973. 558p.

878 Lindeman, M. H., ed. The Quarter Horse Breeder: Basic Text and References on the American Quarter Horse. Wichita Falls, TX: Quarter Horse Breeders Publishing Company, 1960. 216p.

879 Morgan, Bill. "From Dusters to Husters." Horse and Rider, XVI (April 1977), 24-28.

880 Muse, Barbara. The Grand Twenty. N.p., 1971. 254p.

881 Nye, Nelson C. The Complete Book of the Quarter Horse: A Breeder's Guide and Turfman's Reference. New York: A. S. Barnes, 1964. 471p.

882 Osborne, Walter D. The Quarter Horse. New York: Grosset and Dunlap, 1967. 128p.

883 Phillips, Betty L. The American Quarter Horse. New York: David McKay, 1979. 150p.

884 Porter, Willard H. How to Enjoy the Quarter Horse. South Brunswick, NJ: A. S. Barnes, 1973. 200p.

885 Quarter Horse Reference. Grapevine, TX, 1972--. v. 1--.

886 Reynolds, Franklin. King Was Not a Quarter Horse. Canyon, TX, 1960. 44p.

887 Robertson, Anna. "The Making of a Great Working Horse." Horse and Rider, XIV (March 1975), 17-25.

888 Self, Margaret C. _The American Quarter Horse in Pictures._
     New York: Macrae Smith, 1969. 159p.

889 Sikes, L. N. and Bob Gray. _Using the American Quarter Horse._
     Houston, TX: Saddlerock Corp. of Houston, 1958. 159p.

890 Sutherland, Robert Q. _The Quarter Horse as I See Him._ Kan-
     sas City, MO, 1953. 96p.

891 Tippin, Jackie. "The American Quarter Horse." _Western
     Horseman_, XLIV (October 1979), 6-8.

892 Widmer, Jack. _The American Quarter Horse._ New York:
     Scribners, 1959. 127p.

Rangerbred

893 Knisley, Vera. "Rangerbreds Go Royal." _Western Horseman_,
     XLIV (November 1979), 80-81.

Spanish Barb

894 Cash, Peg. _The Spanish Barb._ Colorado Springs, CO: Spanish
     Barb Breeders' Association, 1978. 29p.

Standardbred

895 Berry, Barbara J. _The Standardbreds._ South Brunswick, NJ:
     A. S. Barnes, 1979. 174p.

896 Hintz, R. L. "Factors Influencing Racing Performance of the
     Standardbred Pacer." _Journal of Animal Science_, XLVI (Jan-
     uary 1978), 60-68.

897 McCarr, Ken. _The Kentucky Harness Horse._ Lexington, KY:
     University of Kentucky Press, 1978. 129p.

898 United States Trotting Association. "A History of the Standard-
     bred." _Rapidan River Farm Digest_, I (Winter 1975), 30-35.

899 _____. _Hoofbeats: The Fun of Owning Standardbreds._ Col-
     umbus, OH, 1978. 13p.

900 _____. _Sires and Dams._ Columbus, OH, 1950--. v. 1--.

Tennessee Walking Horse

901 Abbott, Peter. "Hoof Beats from Nashville." _Horse and Rider_,
     XVIII (July 1979), 46-47.

902   Crouter, Sylvia W.   "Tennessee Walkers."   Western Horseman,
       XLIII (September 1978), 25-27.

903   Green, Ben A.   Biography of the Tennessee Walking Horse.
       Nashville, TN: Parthenon Press, 1960.   236p.

904   Middleton, Marie.   "The Tennessee Walking Horse."   Horse
       Lover's National Magazine, XLIV (July 1979), 60-61, 64.

905   Simmons, Diane C.   "Walking Horse Fever."   Horse and Rider,
       XVIII (May 1980), 32-37, 54.

906   Tennessee Walking Horse Breeders' and Exhibitors' Association.
       Horsemanship: Walking Seat and Stock Seat Equitation.
       Lewisburg, TN, n. d.   14p.

907   _____.   Register. Lewisburg, TN, 1950--. v. 11--.

908   Twitty, Harold.   "A Walk on the Mild Side."   Classic, IV (Au-
       gust-September 1979), 38-43.

909   United States.   Congress.   House.   Committee on Interstate and
       Foreign Commerce.   Subcommittee on Public Health and Wel-
       fare.   Horse Protection Act of 1970: Hearings.   91st Cong. ,
       2nd sess.   Washington, D. C. : U. S. Government Printing
       Office, 1970.   143p.

910   _____.   _____. Senate.   Committee on Commerce.   Sub-
       committee on Energy, Natural Resources, and the Environ-
       ment.   Horse Protection Act of 1969: Hearings.   91st Cong. ,
       1st sess.   Washington, D. C. : U. S. Government Printing
       Office, 1969.   146p.

911   _____.   _____.   _____.   _____.   Horse Pro-
       tection Act of 1970: Hearings.   93rd Cong. , 1st sess.   Wash-
       ington, D. C. : U. S. Government Printing Office, 1974.   68p.

912   Webb, Joe.   Care and Training of the Tennessee Walker. Searcy,
       AR, 1962.   120p.

Thoroughbred

913   American Race Horses.   New York: A. S. Barnes, 1950--.
       v. 15--.

914   Anderson, James D.   Making the American Thoroughbred, Es-
       pecially in Tennessee, 1800-1845.   Norwood, MA: Plimpton
       Press, 1916.   300p.
       A classic.

915   Australian Jockey Club.   The Australian Stud Book, Containing
       Petigrees of Racehorses.   Melbourne, 1950--. v. 72--.

916 Barrie, Douglas M. Australian Bloodhorse. Sydney: Angus and Robertson, 1956. 503p.

917 Berry, Barbara J. The Thoroughbreds. Indianapolis, IN: Bobbs-Merrill, 1974. 149p.

918 Birch, Franklin E., comp. Pedigrees of Leading Winners, 1912-1959. London: Thoroughbred Breeders Association, 1960. 147p.

919 _____ Pedigrees of Leading Winners, 1947-1953. London: J. A. Allen, 1954. 51p.

920 The Blood Horse. Stallion Register and Mating Book. Lexington, KY, 1954--. v. 1--.

921 _____. Thoroughbred Sires and Dams. Lexington, KY, 1950--. v. 9--.

922 Ciechanowska, Paola. The French Thoroughbred: English and French Text. London: J. A. Allen, 1969. 128p.

923 Close, Pat. "The Thoroughbred." Western Horseman, XLIV (October 1979), 46-50.

924 Estes, J. A. and Joe H. Palmer. "History of the Thoroughbred." Rapidan River Farm Digest, I (Winter 1975), 20-29.

925 The General Stud Book, Containing Pedigrees of Race Horses, etc., etc., from the Earliest Accounts to the Year Inclusive. London: Weatherby and Sons, 1950--. v. 147--.

926 Hartigan, Joe. To Own a Race Horse. London: J. A. Allen, 1975. 104p.

927 Hewitt, Abram S. Sire Lines. Lexington, KY: Blood Horse Library, 1977. 595p.

928 Hollingworth, Kent. The Kentucky Thoroughbred. Lexington, KY: University of Kentucky Press, 1976. 155p.

929 Hosley, C. "In Defense of the Thoroughbred as a Stock Horse." Western Horseman, XXXVI (November 1971), 4-5, 178-179.

930 Jerdein, Charles and F. R. Kaye. British Bloodlines. London: J. A. Allen, 1955. 352p.

931 "Jockey Club Registration Made Easier." Practical Horseman, V (July 1977), 49-53.

932 McFadden, W. J. Thoroughbred Families of Australia and New Zealand. Sydney, Aust.: Angus and Robertson, 1969. 462p.

933 Montgomery, Edward S. The Thoroughbred. South Brunswick, NJ: A.S. Barnes, 1972. 582p.

934 Napier, Miles. Thoroughbred Pedigrees Simplified. London: J. A. Allen, 1973. 76p.

935 Osborne, Walter D. The Thoroughbred World. Cleveland, OH: World Publishing Company, 1972. 181p.

936 Prior, C. M. Stud Book Lore. Bletchley, Eng.: F. M. Prior, 1951. 284p.

937 Racehorses of ___. London: Timeform, 1950--. v. 2--.

938 Ridgeway, William. The Origin and Influence of the Thoroughbred Horse. New York: B. Blom, 1972. 538p. Reprint of the 1905 edition.

939 S. D. Warren Company. The Thoroughbred Idea. Boston, MA, 1978. 23p.

940 Seth-Smith, Michael. Bred for the Purple. London: Frewin, 1969. 287p.

941 _____. International Stallions and Studs. New York: Dial Press, 1974. 160p.

942 Stanton, Mary W. "Of Elegant Form and Carriage." Horse Lover's National Magazine, XLIV (August 1979), 16-21.

943 Thayer, Bert C. The Thoroughbred: Pictorial Highlights of Breeding and Racing. New York: Duell, Sloan and Pearce, 1964.

944 Thoroughbred Breeders' Association. Statistical Record. London, 1971--. v. 1--.

945 Thoroughbred Owners and Breeders' Association. A Second Quarter Century of American Racing and Breeding, 1941 through 1965. Lexington, KY, 1967. 608p.

946 Thoroughbreds. London: Veterinary Bloodstock Agency, 1960. 84p.

947 Tourtellot, Arthur B. The History of the Race Horse. By Arthur Vernon, pseud. Detroit, MI: Gale Research Company, 1974. 525p. Reprint of the 1946 edition.

948 Willett, Peter. An Introduction to the Thoroughbred. London: S. Paul, 1966. 180p.

949 _____. The Thoroughbred. New York: G. P. Putnam, 1970. 288p.

Trakehner

950 Goodall, Daphne M. The Flight of the East Prussian Horses.
New York: Arco, 1973. 143p.

951 Guard, S. R. "Horses of Hanover." Breeder's Gazette, CXVIII
(July 1953), 5+.

952 Howard, Helen A. "Germany's Captured Superhorses." Western
Horseman, XLII (May 1977), 50-52, 146-151.

953 Rudofsky, Herbert. Trakehnen Horses. Croton-on-Hudson,
NY: Dreenan Press, 1977.

954 Thompson, Vivian. "Trakehners Go West." Western Horseman,
XLIV (August 1979), 118-120.

955 Thurber, Sarah A. "Homeland of the Trakehners." Dressage
and CT, XVI (December 1979), 22-26.

C DRAFT HORSES

1 General Works

956 Anderson, M. M. "Work Horses: Heroes of Early Butte [Mon-
tana]." Western Horseman, XXXIX (June 1974), 61-62+.

957 Brusha, Mary A. "Draft Horses in Oregon." Western Horseman, XXXVII (April 1972), 12, 116.

958 Cockcroft, Barry. Princes of the Plough: The Return of the
Heavy Horse. London: J. M. Dent., 1978. 128p.

959 Dallas, K. M. Horsepower. Hobart, Aust.: Fullers Bookshop,
1968. 100p.

960 Densford, L. E. "Fuel Pinch Signals Draft Horse Return."
DVM, X (June 1979), 1, 50-52.

961 Evans, George E. Horse Power and Magic. London: Faber
and Faber, 1979. 222p.

962 _____. The Horse in the Furrow. London: Faber and
Faber, 1960. 292p.

963 Hart, Edward. The Golden Guinea Book of Heavy Horses, Past
and Present. London: David and Charles, 1976. 126p.

964 House, C. O. "Who Said Drafter's Done?" Breeders' Gazette,
CXXVII (September 1962), 22-23.

965 Jackson, Paula S. "Drafters in the Midwest." Western Horseman, XLI (March 1976), 66-67, 121-123.

966 Jepsen, Stanley M. The Coach Horse: Servant With Style.
     South Brunswick, NJ: A. S. Barnes, 1977. 133p.

967 _____. The Gentle Giants: The Story of Draft Horses.
     South Brunswick, NJ: A. S. Barnes, 1971. 143p.

968 Kramer, Mary. "Hard-at-Work Draft Horses." Western Horse-
     man, XLIII (February 1978), 48-50.

969 Lessiter, Frank. Horse Power. Milwaukee, Wisc.: Reiman
     Publications, 1977. 255p.

970 Miller, Robyn. "Draft Horses: A Big Fair Attraction." West-
     ern Horseman, XXXV (September 1970), 91.

971 "Ressurection of the Draft: Is The Draft Horse Coming Back
     Over the Horizon?" Equus, no. 13 (November 1978), 42-49,
     66.

972 Richards, E. D. "The Draft Horse." Western Horseman, XLIV
     (October 1979) , 16-17.

973 Rider, Bevan. Horses in Harness Today. London: Kaye and
     Ward, 1977. 128p.

974 Sebrey, Mary A. "The Draft Horse Comeback." Horse Illus-
     trated, IV (June 1980), 40-42.

975 Spellman, S. R. "Breeds of Draft Horses." Farmer's Bulletin,
     no. 619 (1954), 1-16.

976 Spiesschaert, Mae. "Oregon: Draft Horse Country." Western
     Horseman, XL (March 1975) , 50-52, 132-134.

977 Street, David. Horses: A Working Tradition. New York:
     McGraw-Hill, 1977. 160p.

978 Telleen, Maurice. The Draft Horse Primer: A Guide to the
     Care and Use of Work Horses and Mules. Emmaus, PA:
     Rodale Press, 1977. 386p.

979 Villers, Guy. The British Heavy Horse. London: Barrie and
     Jenkins, 1976. 96p.

980 Watney, Marylian and Sanders. Horse Power. London and New
     York: Hamlyn Publishing, 1975. 96p.

981 Weber, Philip and Stanley M. Jepsen. Heroes in Harness: A
     Pictorial Tribute to the Workhorse. South Brunswick, NJ:
     A. S. Barnes, 1979. 159p.

2 Specific Breeds

Belgian

982 Belgian Draft Horse Corporation of America. Belgian Review.
     Wabash, IN, 1950--. v. 63--.

Clydesdale

983 Bemis, C. C. "The Day the Clydesdales Went Through the
     Ice." Yankee, XLIII (March 1979), 182+.

984 Close, Pat. "The Budweiser Clydesdales." Western Horseman,
     XLII (January 1977), 44-45.

985 Clydesdale Horse Society of Great Britain and Ireland. The
     Clydesdale Stud Book. Perth, Eng. , 1950-1967. v. 64-81.

986 Jacobs, Beth. "Lou Silva and His Clydesdales." Western
     Horseman, XLII (June 1977), 34, 132-136.

987 Probert, Alan. "Heretic Horses: The Introduction of the Clydes-
     dale Breed Into Mexico." American West, IX (October 1970),
     519-536.

Haflinger

988 Osmer, Virginia T. "Elmer [Briggs] and the Haflingers."
     Western Horseman, XXXIX (February 1974), 54-56, 108-109.

Percheron

989 Nelson, Edna C. The Magnificant Percheron. Los Angeles,
     CA: Borden Publishing Company, 1963. 55p.

990 Percheron Horse Association of America. Percheron Notes.
     Belmont, OH, 1952--. v. 1--.

Shire

991 Cole, G. R. "The Shire and the Ardennes Differ Like the Jobs
     They Were Bred to Do." Heavy Horse Driving, II (Spring
     1978), 29-30.

992 Dean, Sandy. "The Berkshire Horse." Western Horseman,
     XLII (October 1977), 104.

993 Oaksey, John. Pride of the Shires: The Story of the Whitbread
     Horses. London: Hutchinson, 1979. 64p.

Suffolk

994 Thompson, M. "In Praise of the Versatile Suffolk." Heavy Horse Driving, II (Spring 1978), 23.

D PONIES

1 General Works

995 Blake, Neil F. The Pony Club World. Garden City, NY: Doubleday, 1970. 171p.

996 The Book of Ponies and Riding. New York: St. Martin's Press, 1972. 318p.

997 Bullen, Anne. Ponycraft. Rev. ed. London: Blandford, 1963. 64p.

998 Burns, Ursula. Ponies. Princeton, NJ: Van Nostrand, 1961. 97p. [juv.]

999 Campbell, Judith. The World of Ponies. London and New York: Hamlyn Publishing, 1970. 141p.

1000 Dent, Anthony A. and Daphne M. Goodall. The Foals of Epona: A History of British Ponies from the Bronze Age to Yesterday. London: Gallery Press, 1962. 305p.

1001 Goodall, Daphne M. British Native Ponies. London: Country Life, 1963. 111p.

1002 _____. Know Your Pony. South Brunswick, NJ: A. S. Barnes, 1972. 123p.

1003 _____. Ponies. South Brunswick, NJ: A. S. Barnes, 1967. 111p.
        American edition of the author's British Native Ponies.

1004 Healey, Pepper M. You and Your Pony. South Brunswick, NJ: A. S. Barnes, 1977. 276p.

1005 Heath, Veronica. Ponies and Pony Management. New York: Arco, 1966. 114p.

1006 Hope, Charles E. G. The Perfect Pony Owner. New Rochelle, NY: Sportshelf, 1968. 128p.

1007 _____. The Pony Owner's Encyclopedia. London: Pelham Books, 1965. 239p.

1008 LeRoi, David. Ponies and Donkeys. New Rochelle, NY: Sportshelf, 1976. 96p.

1009 Macgregor-Morris, Pamela. Look at Ponies. London: Hamilton, 1960. 95p.

1010 Mitchell, Ehrman B. Ponies for Young People. Princeton, NJ: Van Nostrand, 1960. 151p.

1011 Murphy, Genevieve. The Young Pony Rider's Companion: A Complete Guide to the Riding, Training, and Ownership of Ponies. New Rochelle, NY: Sportshelf, 1962. 125p.

1012 Pullein-Thompson, Josephine. I Had Two Ponies. London: Collins, 1974. 158p.

1013 _____. Ponies in Color. New York: Studio Publications, 1962. 70p.

1014 _____, ed. Pony Parade. London: Dragon Books, 1978. 141p.

1015 Russell, Valerie. New Forest Ponies. London: David and Charles, 1976. 136p.

1016 Thurow, Robert C. Pony Tracks and Reflections. LeSueur, MN, 1979. 94p.

1017 The Vanguard Book of Ponies and Riding. London: Collins, 1966. 318p.

1018 Wiederhold, Hermann. Your Pony Book. Brattleboro, VT: Stephen Greene Press, 1958. 135p.

1019 Wilding, Suzanne. The Book of Ponies. New York: St. Martin's Press, 1965. 60p. [juv.]

1020 Woodhouse, Barbara. The Book of Ponies. New ed. Campions, Eng., 1970. 95p.

2 Specific Breeds

Appaloosa Pony

1021 Born, Marjorie. "The National Appaloosa Pony." Western Horseman, XXXVIII (November 1973), 174-175.

Connemara Pony

1022 American Connemara Pony Society. Stud Book. Goshen, CT, 1956--. v. 1--.

1023 Burns, Ursula. Connemara. Translated from the German. London: Harrap, 1971. 40p.

1024 Lyons, Dorothy. "The Connemara." Western Horseman,
      XXXIX (February 1979), 76-77, 120.

Exmoor Pony

1025 Dent, Anthony A. The Pure Breed Exmoor Pony. Dulverton,
      Eng.: Exmoor Press, 1970. 48p.

Hackney Pony

1026 American Hackney Horse Association. "History of the Hackney
      Pony." Rapidan River Farm Digest, I (Winter 1975), 51-
      53.

1027 Davis, Ray. "John Shea Training the Hackney Pony." Western
      Horseman, XL (October 1975), 20-23, 117-119.

Pony of the Americas

1028 Fairbanks, Jean. "Pony of the Americas." Western Horse-
      man, XLIV (October 1979), 76-78.

1029 Pony of the Americas Club. Official Stud Book. Mason City,
      IA, 1961--. v. 1--.

1030 _____. Yearbook. Mason City, IA, 1961--. v. 1--.

Shetland Pony

1031 American Shetland Pony Club. Stud Book. Fowler, IN, 1950--.
      v. 43--.

1032 Barbalace, Roberta C. "Tiny Horse, Big Praise." Western
      Horseman, XLII (September 1977), 82.

1033 Bedell, L. Frank. Shetland Pony. Ames: Iowa State Univer-
      sity Press, 1959. 334p.

1034 Cox, Maurice C. The Shetland Pony. London: A. and C.
      Black, 1965. 158p.

1035 Hess, Lilo. Shetland Ponies. New York: Crowell, 1964.
      57p. [juv.]

1036 Kays, John M. Shetland Pony Handbook. West Lafayette, IN:
      American Shetland Pony Club, n.d. 47p.

Walking Pony

1037   McKay, Anne. "The American Walking Pony." Western Horse-
       man, XXXVIII (November 1973), 180.

Welsh Pony

1038   Carlisle, John W. "Welsh Ponies Are for Kids." Western
       Horseman, XLII (December 1977), 32-33.

1039   Elliston, Mary E. "Showing Welsh Ponies." Horse Illustrated,
       IX (September-October 1978), 50-52.

1040   Howlett, Lorna. "Little Critters Down Under [in Australia]."
       Horse and Rider, XVI (May 1977), 38-40.

1041   Welsh Pony and Cob Society of America. National Welsh Pony
       Stud Book. White Post, VA, 1959--. v. 1--.

1042   _____. National Welsh Pony Yearbook. White Post, VA,
       1959--. v. 1--.

1043   _____. The Welsh Pony. White Post, VA, n. d. 10p.

E   DONKEYS AND MULES

1044   Barnes, Sisley. "More About the Mule." Western Horseman,
       XLIV (March 1979), 90-94.

1045   Boles, Chris. "There's More to a Mule Than Ears." West-
       ern Horseman, XLIII (February 1978), 30-31.

1046   Borwick, Robin. People With Long Ears: A Practical Guide
       to Donkey Keeping. New Rochelle, NY: Sportshelf, 1966.
       180p.

1047   Brookshire, Frank. The Burro. Norman: University of Okla-
       homa Press, 1974. 370p.

1048   Dent, Anthony A. Donkey: The Story of the Ass from East
       to West. London: Harrap, 1972. 175p.

1049   DeWesselow, Mary R. P. Donkeys: A Practical Guide to
       Their Management. Fontwell, Eng.: Centaur Press, 1967.
       144p.

1050   Dunkels, Marjorie. Donkey Wrinkles and Tales. London:
       J. A. Allen, 1977. 80p.

1051   _____. Training Your Donkey. London: J. A. Allen, 1973.
       52p.

1052 Holder, Gene. "Jacks I Have Known and Played With." Horse and Rider, X (April 1971), 46-50.

1053 Hudgins, Sam. "Mules' Paradise." Horse and Rider, XIII (May 1974), 36-37.

1054 Hutchins, Paul and Betsey. Donkeys. Denton, TX: American Donkey and Mule Association, 1979. 120p.

1055 _____. The Modern Mule. Denton, TX: Hee Haw Book Service, 1978. 148p.

1056 Kania, Alan J. "Get Your Ass to the Pass: Gold Fever Lives on in Burro Racing's Triple Crown." Equus, no. 31 (May 1980), 28-32.

1057 Lamb, Robert B. The Mule in Southern Agriculture. Publications in Geography, no. 15. Berkeley: University of California Press, 1963. 99p.

1058 Mason, Michael H. Wild Ass Free. London: Murray, 1959. 180p.

1059 Miller, Robert M. "Reconsider the Mule." Western Horseman, XLIII (September 1978), 112-119.

1060 Mills, Frank C. History of America Jacks and Mules. Hutchinson, KA: Hutch-Line, 1971. 255p.

1061 Pitts, Don. "The Ears Have It." Horse and Rider, XVI (September 1976), 66-69.

1062 Rickell, Walt. The Misunderstood Mule. Los Angeles, CA: Reproductions West, 1978. 64p.

1063 _____. "The Mule Is a Mazzard." Horse and Rider, XVII (May 1978) , 22-27.

1064 Riley, Harvey. The Mule. Denton, TX: Hee Haw Book Service, 1973. 107p.
      Reprint of the 1867 edition.

1065 Sternberg, Monica. My Wishes Were Donkeys. London: Pelham Books, 1972. 127p.

1066 Stewart, Miller J. "The Followers of the Bell." Western Horseman, XXXIX (April 1974), 28, 170-175.

1067 Stothard, Robin. Donkeys. New York: Arco, 1973. 63p.

1068 Summerhays, Reginald S. The Donkey Owner's Guide. London: Nelson, 1970. 102p.

1069   Swinfen, Averil E.   Donkeys Galore.   North Pomfret, VT:
       David and Charles, 1976.   136p.

1070   Tanner, Jean.   "Mule Days."   Horse and Rider, XVIII (May
       1980), 44-47.

1071   Thoene, Bodie.   "Mules Ain't Dumb."   Western Horseman,
       XLIII (February 1978), 104-108.

1072   White, Joyce.   "The Making of a Mule Fan."   Western Horse-
       man, XLI (November 1976), 50, 108-109.

       F   WILD HORSES, PONIES, DONKEYS, AND MUSTANGS

1073   "Abandoned Horses on the Federal Range."   American Cattle
       Producer, XL (November 1958), 20-21.

1074   Amaral, Anthony A.   "The Last Machismo in the West."
       Nevada Magazine, XXXVIII (January-March 1978), 18-
       21.

1075   _____.   Mustang: Life and Legends of Nevada's Wild Horses.
       Reno: University of Nevada Press, 1977.   156p.

1076   American Mustang Association.   Breeder's Listing.   Yucaipa,
       CA, 1962--.   v.   1--.

1077   Barber, Ted.   "Wild Horses on Welfare."   Western Horseman,
       XXXIX (April 1974), 80-83, 161-163.

1078   Bearcroft, Norma.   Wild Horses of Canada.   London: J. A.
       Allen, 1966.   89p.

1079   Beebe, Burdetta F. and J. R. Johnson.   American Wild Horses.
       New York: David McKay, 1964.   180p.

1080   Blumenstock, Kathy.   "The Storybook Ponies [of Chincoteague]."
       Classic, III (April-May 1978), 78-79.

1081   Cook, C. Wayne.   "Wild Horses and Burros: A New Manage-
       ment Problem."   Rangeman's Journal, II (Spring 1975),
       19-21.

1082   Devereaux, Linda E.   "Philip Nolan and His 'Wild Horses.'"
       Texana, XII (Spring 1974), 88-100.

1083   Dobie, J. Frank.   The Mustangs.   Boston: Little, Brown,
       1964.   376p.

1084   _____.   "Wild and Free Mustangs."   Country Gentleman,
       CXXII (October 1952), 34-35+.

1085 Green, Ben K. A Thousand Miles of Mustangin'. Flagstaff, AZ: Northland Press, 1972. 145p.

1086 Grosvenor, Donna K. The Wild Ponies of Assateague Island. Washington, D. C.: National Geographic Society, 1975. 30p. [juv.]

1087 Henry, Marguerite. Mustang, Wild Spirit of the West. Chicago: Rand McNally, 1971. 222p.

1088 Hopf, Alice L. Wild Cousins of the Horse. New York: G. P. Putnam, 1977. 127p.

1089 Johnston, Velma. "You Can Save This Horse." Women Sports, II (March 1975), 35-38+.

1090 Kidd, Raena. "Rodeo Broncs: Where Do They Come From?" Western Horseman, XLIII (April 1978), 32-36.

1091 King, Chuck. "A Realistic Look at the Mustang-Wild Horse Situation." Western Horseman, XXXVI (May 1971), 44-45, 156-158.

1092 Laune, Paul. Mustang Roundup. New York: Holt, 1964. 154p. [juv.]

1093 McArthur, J. Wayne. "The Wild Horse: An Asset or a Liability?" Western Horseman, XXXVIII (June 1973), 16-17, 140-144.

1094 McGuire, Jerry. "The Mustangers." Argosy, CCCLXXXIV (August 1976), 42+.

1095 Mays, Buddy. "Roundup for the [New Mexico] Desert Mustangs." Desert, XXXVIII (February 1975), 26-30.

1096 Mohr, Erma. The Asiatic Wild Horse. Translated from the German. London: J. A. Allen, 1971. 124p.

1097 National Advisory Board for Wild Free-Roaming Horses and Burros. Proceedings [of a Meeting], Rock Springs, Wyoming, September 4-5, 1975. Washington, D. C.: U. S. Forest Service, 1975. 58p.

1098 Peterson, C. O. "Desert Horses of the 1920's." Western Horseman, XLI (December 1976), 34, 135-139.

1099 Pine, Kay. "Wild Horses [of Assateague] by the Ocean." Western Horseman, XLIII (August 1978), 16-17.

1100 "The Real World of Island Living [Chincoteague]." Equus, no. 10 (August 1978), 36-42.

1101　Reiss, Bob. "Wild Horses: Our Runaway Heritage." Equus, no. 20 (June 1979), 44-53, 72.

1102　Rickell, Walt. "Where Have the Wild Horses Gone?" Horse and Rider, XVII (June 1978), 28-32.

1103　Rideout, Leana. "The Spanish Mustang." Western Horseman, XXXVIII (November 1973), 181-182.

1104　Robertson, Alden. The Wild Horse Gatherers. New York: Scribners, 1978. 95p.

1105　Roever, J. M. and Wilfried. The Mustangs. Austin, TX: Steck-Vaughn, 1971. 30p. [juv.]

1106　Rood, Ronald N. Hundred Acre Welcome: The Story of a Chincoteague Pony. Brattleboro, VT: Stephen Greene Press, 1967. 132p.

1107　Rounds, Glen. Wild Horses of the Red Desert. New York: Holiday House, 1969. Unpaged. [juv.]

1108　Ryden, Hope. America's Last Wild Horses. Rev. ed. New York: E. P. Dutton, 1978. 320p.

1109　————. Mustangs: A Return to the Wild. New York: Viking Press, 1972. 111p.

1110　————. The Wild Colt: The Life of a Young Mustang. New York: Coward, McCann, 1972. 64p. [juv.]

1111　Salomon, Lothar L. Investigation of Deaths of Horses at Orr Springs: Final Report. Dugway Proving Grounds, UT: U.S. Army, 1976. 297p.

1112　Satchell, Michael. "Can We Save the Burros?" Parade Magazine, (April 27, 1980), 4-5.

1113　Schoenfeld, F. J. Wild Horse Losses Orr Spring Area, Dugway Proving Ground, Utah. Salt Lake City, UT: Veterinary Services Division, U.S. Department of Agriculture, 1976. 56p.

1114　Sherlock, Patti. "Are Wild Horses Really Wild?" Horse Illustrated, IX (September-October 1978), 34-37.

1115　Smith, Bradley. The Horse in the West. Cleveland, OH: World Publishing Company, 1969. 255p.

1116　Spies, Joseph R. Wild Ponies of Chincoteague. Cambridge, MD: Tidewater Publications, 1978. 13p.

1117 Thomas, Heather. "Living Free." Horse Illustrated, X (January-February 1979), 53-56.

1118 _____. The Wild Horse Controversy. South Brunswick, NJ: A. S. Barnes, 1979.

1119 Thrall, Ellen J. "The Tarpan." Western Horseman, XXXVI (November 1971), 96.

1120 United States. Congress. House. Committee on Interior and Insular Affairs. Subcommittee on Public Lands. Protection of Wild Horses on Public Lands: Hearings. 92nd Cong., 1st sess. Washington, D.C.: U.S. Government Printing Office, 1971. 200p.

1121 _____. _____. _____. _____. _____. Wild and Free-Roaming Horses and Burros Act Amendments: Hearings. 94th Cong., 1st and 2nd sess. Washington, D.C.: U. S. Government Printing Office, 1976. 286p.

1122 _____. _____. Senate. Committee on Interior and Insular Affairs. Wild Free-Roaming Horse and Burro Act of 1971: Hearings. 93rd Cong., 2nd sess. Washington, D. C.: U. S. Government Printing Office, 1974. 140p.

1123 _____. _____. _____. _____. Subcommittee on Public Lands. Protection of Wild Horses and Burros on Public Lands: Hearings. 92nd Cong., 1st sess. Washington, D. C.: U. S. Government Printing Office, 1971. 192p.

1124 _____. Department of the Interior. A Report to Congress by the Secretary of Interior and the Secretary of Agriculture on Administration of the Wild Free-Roaming Horse and Burro Act, Public Law 92-195. Washington, D. C.: U. S. Government Printing Office, 1974. 58p.

1125 Varley, Ed. "Chincoteague--Pony from the Island." Horse and Horseman, V (October 1977), 48-50.

1126 Venn, May E. The American Mustang. By Genevieve Vaughan-Jackson, pseud. New York: Hastings House, 1964. 61p. [juv.]

1127 Warwick, Chad. "So You'd Like to Adopt a Wild Horse or Burro." Horse Illustrated, XI (June 1980), 59-61.

1128 Wayne, Mel. Wild Horse Kingdom. London: Collins, 1960. 255p.

1129 Webb, Harry. "G. S. Garcia and His Mustang Trap." Nevada Magazine, XXXIX (Spring 1979), 20+.

1130 Weiss, Ann E. Save the Mustangs: How a Federal Law Is Passed. New York: Julian Messner, 1974. 96p.

1131 Wilcher, Talmage. King of Assateague. New York: Vantage
     Press, 1964. 64p. [juv.]

1132 "Wild Horse and Wild Burro Numbers Are Increasing." West-
     ern Horseman, XXXIX (November 1974), 9.

1133 Worcester, Donald E. "Wild Horses West: Fact and Fancy."
     Arizona and the West, II (Summer 1960), 140-147.

1134 Wyman, Walter D. The Wild Horse of the West. Omaha:
     University of Nebraska Press, 1962. 348p.

                    G FAMOUS HORSES

1 Collective Works

1135 Aiscan, John. Important Winners in 1970. London: British
     Racehorse, 1970. 36p.

1136 Berman, Lucy. Famous Horses. New York: Golden Press,
     1972. 117p. [juv.]

1137 The Blood Horse. Stakes Winners. Lexington, KY, 1950--.
     v. 21--.

1138 Campbell, Judith. The Champions: Great Racehorses and Show
     Jumpers of Our Time. London: Barker, 1973. 168p.

1139 Carroll, Theodus. Firsts Under the Wire: The World's Fast-
     est Horses, 1900-1950. New York: C. P. I., 1978. 47p.

1140 Costello, John B. Galloping Greats. Auckland, New Zealand:
     Moa Publications, 1973. 223p.

1141 Davidson, Margaret. Five True Horse Stories. New York:
     Scholastic Book Services, 1979. 64p. [juv.]
        Justin Morgan, Pacing White Mustang, Misty, Clever
     Hans, and Brighty the Donkey.

1142 Devereux, Frederick L. Famous American Horses: 21 Steep-
     lechasers, Trotters, Cowponies, Hunters, Flat Racers,
     Show Horses, and Battle Mounts That Have Made History.
     New York: Devin-Adair, 1975. 117p.

1143 Downey, Fairfax D. Famous Horses of the Civil War. Apple-
     ton, WI: Nelson, 1959. 128p. [juv.]

1144 Drager, Marvin. The Most Glorious Crown: The Story of
     American Triple Crown Thoroughbreds, from Sir Barton
     to Secretariat. New York: Scribner, 1975. 216p.

1145 Evans, Edna H. Famous Horses and Their People. Brattle-
     boro, VT: Stephen Greene Press, 1975. 168p.

1146 Frayne, Trent G. Northern Dancer and Friends. New York:
      Funk and Wagnalls, 1969. 152p.

1147 Fritz, John H. Champion Horses and Riders of North America.
      Philadelphia: Lippincott, 1975. 176p.

1148 Great Horses of the Year. London: MacGibbon, 1950--. v.
      1--.

1149 Harris, Freddie S. "General [Ulysses S.] Grant's Favorite
      Horses." Western Horseman, XLII (September 1977), 56-
      57.

1150 Jenkins, Ron. Great Trotters. Wellington, New Zealand:
      Reed, 1974. 380p.

1151 Klimo, Kate. Heroic Horses and Their Riders. New York:
      Platt and Munk, 1974. 91p. [juv.]

1152 LeNoir, John M. Famous Thoroughbreds I Have Known. Los
      Angeles, CA: Borden Publishing Company, 1953. 242p.

1153 Lowery, Thurm. "Great Roping Horses: Past and Present."
      Horse and Horseman, III (October-November 1975), 32-35,
      47-57.

1154 Mortimer, Roger. Twenty Great Horses of the British Turf.
      South Brunswick, NJ: A. S. Barnes, 1968. 172p.

1155 _____. and Peter Willett. Great Racehorses of the World.
      New York: St. Martin's Press, 1970. 240p.

1156 _____. More Great Racehorses of the World. London:
      Joseph, 1972. 263p.

1157 Muse, Richard. "The Ten Best." Spur, XVI (May-June 1980),
      55-58.

1158 One Hundred Jumpers to Follow. London: Racehorse, 1963--.
      v. 1--.

1159 One Hundred Winners. London: Racehorse, 1963--. v. 1--.

1160 Pattie, Jane. "Pine Johnsen Discusses What Makes a Great
      Horse." Horse and Rider, X (March 1971), 16-23.

1161 Reeves, Richard S. and Patrick Robinson. Classic Lines: a
      Gallery of the Great Thoroughbreds. Birmingham, AL:
      Oxmoor House, 1975. 179p.

1162 Seth-Smith, Michael. International Stallions and Studs. Slough,
      Eng.: Foulsham, 1974. 160p.

1163 Steinkraus, William and Sam Savitt. Great Horses of the United States Equestrian Team. New York: Dodd, Mead, 1977. 96p.

1164 Stoneridge, M. A. Great Horses of Our Time. Garden City, NY: Doubleday, 1972. 543p.

1165 "The Top Hunters and Jumpers of 1979." Practical Horseman, VIII (April 1980), 20-33.

1166 Walford, Bonny. Best of Breed: The Champion Horses of the American Continent. South Brunswick, NJ: A. S. Barnes, 1971. 252p.

1167 Walker, Stella A. Horses of Renown. London: Country Life, 1954. 144p.

1168 Weatherley, Lee. Great Horses of Britain. Royal Parade, Eng.: Saiga Publications, 1978. 269p.

1169 Wilding, Suzanne and Anthony DelBalso. The Triple Crown Winners: The Story of America's Nine Superstar Race Horses. New York: Parents Magazine Press, 1975. 182p. [juv.]

1170 Winners for 19--. London: Good Betts, 1950--. v. 6--.

2 Individual Animals

Adios

1171 Hill, Marie. Adios, the Big Daddy of Harness Racing. South Brunswick, NJ: A. S. Barnes, 1971. 204p.

Albatross

1172 Evans, Donald P. Super Bird: The Story of Albatross. South Brunswick, NJ: A. S. Barnes, 1975. 246p.

Arkle

1173 Herbert, Ivor. Arkle: The Story of a Champion. London: Pelham Books, 1966. 187p.

1174 Richmond, John. Arkel, the Wonder Horse. London: Pictorial Presentations, 1968. 40p.

1175 Wright, Howard. Arkle, a Pictorial Record of a Great Horse. Halifax, Nova Scotia: Portway Press, 1968. 32p.

Baulking Green

1176 Liddiard, Ron. Baulking Green: Champion Hunter-Chaser. London: J. A. Allen, 1971. 140p.

Black Gold

1177 Henry, Marguerite. Black Gold. Chicago: Rand McNally, 1957. 172p.

Black Jack

1178 Richard, Marjorie. " 'Black Jack': The Army's Living Tradition." Western Horseman, XXXIX (July 1974), 179-182.

Bold Forbes

1179 Irwin, Barry. "Bold Forbes." The Thoroughbred of California, LXIII (July 1976), 26-32.

Bret Hanover

1180 Evans, Donald P. Big Bum: The Story of Bret Hanover. South Brunswick, NJ: A. S. Barnes, 1969. 220p.

The Brigadier

1181 Hislop, John. The Brigadier. London: Secker and Warburg, 1973. 212p.

Cardigan Bay

1182 Bisman, Ron. Cardigan Bay: The Horse That Won a Million Dollars. New York: Arco, 1972.

Cicero

1183 Drummond, James. Cicero: The Queen's Drum Horse. Edinburgh, Scotland: Homes, McDougall, 1972. 36p.

Classic Lives

1184 Silver, Caroline. Classic Lives: The Education of a Racehorse. New York: Harcourt Brace, 1973. 250p.

Commanche

1185 Amaral, Anthony A. Commanche: The Horse That Survived the Custer Massacre. Los Angeles, CA: Westernlore Press, 1961. 86p.

1186 Dary, David A. "Commanche, a Century Later." Frontier and True West, LI (August-September 1977), 18-23. 51.

Expensive Hobby

1187 Close, Pat. " 'Expensive Hobby': An Extraordinary Reining
Horse." Western Horseman, XLIV (March 1979), 50-57.

Forego

1188 Kweskin, Steve. "The 'Forego' Era." Western Horseman,
XXXIX (July 1974), 39, 145-146.

1189 _____. "One for the History Books." Classic, II (December 1976-January 1977), 46-51.

1190 Tower, Whitney. "This Is No Foregone Conclusion." Classic,
III (December 1977-January 1978), 80-85.

Freddie

1191 Smith, Vivian. A Horse Called Freddie. London: S. Paul,
1967. 144p.

Gaudenzia

1192 Henry, Marguerite. Gaudenzia: Price of the Palio. Chicago:
Rand McNally, 1960. 237p.

Golden Miller

1193 Blaxland, Gregory. Golden Miller. London: Constable, 1972.
240p.

Grundy

1194 Fitzgeorge-Parker, Tim. Grundy: The Making of a Derby
Winner. London: J. A. Allen, 1976. 196p.

Hyperion

1195 Graham, Clive, ed. Hyperion. London: J. A. Allen, 1967.
202p.

Justin Morgan

1196 Felton, Harold W. A Horse Named Justin Morgan. New York:
Dodd, Mead, 1962. 160p. [juv.]

1197 Selman, Charles and Sharon. " 'Justin Morgan': A Founding
Father." Western Horseman, XXXIX (July 1974), 72-74,
162-164.

Kelso

1198 Johnson, Pat. A Horse Named Kelso. New York: Funk and
Wagnalls, 1970. 96p.

Lord Winsalot

1199   Alwan, Dick. " 'Lord Winsalot': A $5,000 Bargain." <u>Western Horseman</u>, XLI (September 1976), 72-73.

Man-o'-War

1200   Anderson, Clarence W. <u>Horse of the Century: Man-o'-War.</u> New York: Macmillan, 1970. 4p. Captioned illustrations.

1201   Farley, Walter. <u>Man-o'-War.</u> New York: Random House, 1962. 326p.

Maxwell G

1202   Schorsch, L. M. "<u>Maxwell G, "The Racehorse's Racehorse.</u>" Des Plaines, IL: Common Sense, Ltd. , 1978. 107p.

Nevele Pride

1203   Evans, Donald P. <u>Nevele Pride: Speed 'n Spirit.</u> South Brunswick, NJ: A. S. Barnes, 1972. 230p.

Nijinsky

1204   Baerlein, Richard. <u>Nijinsky, Triple Crown Winner.</u> London: Pelham Books, 1971. 158p.

Persian War

1205   Barnes, Sid and Henry Alper. <u>The Persian War Story.</u> London: Pelham Books, 1971. 227p.

Phar Lap

1206   Carter, Isabel R. <u>Phar Lap: The Story of a Big Horse.</u> Melbourne, Aust. : Lansdowne, 1965. 166p.

Pin Ears

1207   Squire, Reuben. "The Notorious Bucking Horse 'Pin Ears.' " <u>Western Horseman</u>, XLIII (June 1978), 156-180.

Red Rum

1208   Herbert, Ivor. <u>Red Rum: The Full and Extraordinary Story of a Horse of Courage.</u> New York: Hippocrene Books, 1975. 272p.

1209   _____. "When the One Good Horse Came Along." <u>Classic</u>, III (December 1977-January 1978), 86-99.

Rising Fast

1210 Spring, Leicester R. Racing with Rising Fast. Auckland,
New Zealand: Hodder and Stoughton, 1971. 171p.

Ruffian

1211 Claflin, Edward. Ruffian, Queen of the Fillies. New Canaan,
CT: Scrambling Press, 1975. 104p.

1212 Kester, Wayne O. "Ruffian: What Really Happened?" California Horse Review, XII (September 1975), 147-153.

Saba Sam

1213 Larter, Chris. Around the World for a Horse. Wellington,
New Zealand: A. C. and A. W. Reed, 1970. 162p.

Seabiscuit

1214 Eck, Frank. "Seabiscuit." Horse Illustrated, XI (March-April
1979), 52-53.

Seattle Slew

1215 Bayless, Skip. "Seattle Slew." Horse Illustrated, IX (September-October 1978), 22-24.

1216 Cady, Steve and Barton Silverman. Seattle Slew. Baltimore,
MD: Penguin Books, 1977. 142p.

1217 Howell, Julie. "True Slew." Spur, XIV (November-December
1978), 40-45.

1218 Kweskin, Steve. " 'Seattle Slew': Triple Crown Winner."
Western Horseman, XLII (August 1977), 52.

1219 Tower, Whitney. "Good, Fine, Great!" Classic, II (August-
September 1977), 52-57.

Secretariat

1220 Edwards, Gladys E. "The Big Red Machine." Horse and
Rider, XII (November 1973), 49-58.

1221 Kweskin, Steve. "Secretariat: Triple Crown Winner." Western Horseman, XXXVIII (August 1973), 20-21, 146-151.

1222 Nack, William. Big Red of Meadow Stable: Secretariat, the
Making of a Champion. New York: A. Fields, 1975. 341p.

1223 Woolfe, Raymond G., Jr. and Elizabeth Jahab. Secretariat.
Philadelphia: Chilton, 1974. 187p.

Single G

1224 Hill, Marie. Single G: The Horse That Time Forgot. South Brunswick, NJ: A. S. Barnes, 1968. 147p.

Snowman

1225 Montgomery, Rutherford G. Snowman. New York: Duell, Sloan and Pearce, 1962. 131p.

Squealer

1226 Akers, Trey. " 'Squealer': He's a Kicker." Western Horseman, XXXVIII (August 1973), 60-61, 158-160.

Stormy Weather

1227 Gregory, Bern. " 'Stormy Weather': Baddest Bareback Bronc." Western Horseman, XLI (September 1976), 62, 100.

Tipperary

1228 Smith, Beatrice S. The Proudest Horse on the Prairie. Minneapolis, MN: Lerner, 1971. 48p. [juv.]

Traveller

1229 Hinsdale, Harriet. Confederate Gray: The Story of Traveller, General Robert E. Lee's Favorite Horse. Peterborough, NH: R. R. Smith, 1963. 102p.

Trigger

1230 Bird, Allen. "Trigger." Horseman, XXII (May 1978), 39-49.

Whirlaway

1231 Thayer, Bert C. Whirlaway: The Life and Times of a Great Racer. New York: Abercrombie and Fitch, 1966. 103p.

Witez II

1232 Smith, Linell. And Miles to Go: The Biography of a Great Arabian Horse, Witez II. Boston: Little, Brown, 1967. 237p.

Workboy

1233 Blacker, Cecil H. The Story of Workboy. London: Collins, 1960. 192p.

Zantanon

1234 Gray, Bob. "Zantanon: Man-o'-War of Mexico." In: Bob

Gray, ed. Western Rider's Yearbook and Buyer's Guide
for 1970. Houston, TX: Cordovan Corp. , 1969.   pp. 24-
28.

Further References: See also Parts V; VI: G; VII; VIII: E; and X:
A below.

PART IV EQUINE CARE AND THE HORSE BUSINESS

A EQUINE CARE

1 General Works

1235 Allen, Luther. "A Close Look at Horse Care." Horseman,
      XXII (February 1978), 14-15, 19.

1236 Baird, Eric. Horse Care. New York: Winchester Press,
      1979. 146p.

1237 Carnation-Alberts Company. Horses: A Complete Management
      Program. Kansas City, MO, n. d. 93p.

1238 Carne, Barbara and Bruce Mills. A Basic Guide to Horse Care
      and Management. New York: Arco, 1979. 293p.

1239 Carson, Gerald. Men, Beasts, and Gods: A History of Cruelty
      and Kindness to Animals. New York: Scribners, 1974.
      268p.

1240 Clarke, Margaret I. Care of the Australian Horse and Pony.
      San Francisco, CA: Tri-Ocean Books, 1966. 144p.

1241 Cooper, Marcia S. Take Care of Your Horse: A Guide to the
      Essentials for Everyone Who Rides, Owns, or Hopes to Own
      a Horse. New York: Scribners, 1974. 132p.

1242 Davis, Lloyd. "Keeping a Horse in the Suburbs." Country
      Gentleman, CXXVII (Winter 1977), 42+.

1243 Dougall, Neil. Horses and Ponies in Small Areas. London:
      J. A. Allen, 1976. 22p.

1244 Gorman, John A. Horses: Their Care and Training. Helena:
      Wyoming Agricultural Extension Service, 1963. 33p.

1245 Gregory, Diana. Owning a Horse: A Pictorial Guide. New
      York: Harper & Row, 1977. 208p.

1246 Griffith, Frank B. How to Live with a Horse. South Bruns-
      wick, NJ: A. S. Barnes, 1967. 119p.

1247 Hanauer, Elsie V. Horse Owner's Concise Guide. South
      Brunswick, NJ: A. S. Barnes, 1969. 102p.

1248 Hapgood, Ruth K. First Horse: Basic Horse Care Illustrated.
      San Francisco, CA: Chronicle Books, 1972. 158p.

1249 Harper, Frederick. Top Form Book of Horse Care. New
      York: Popular Library, 1966. 191p.

1250 Harris, Catherine A. Practical Pony Keeping. New York:
      Arco, 1978. 128p.

1251 Harrison, James C. , et al. Care and Training of the Trotter
      and Pacer, with a Special Section on Nutrition. Columbus,
      OH: United States Trotting Association, 1968. 1,054p.

1252 Holmes, Edward. Horse and Pony Care in Pictures. New
      York: Arco, 1977. 223p.

1253 Horse and Rider, Editors of. Horse Care. Temecula, CA,
      1980. 96p.

1254 Howell, Jane. Rearing a Foal. London: Nelson, 1970. 92p.

1255 Hurley, Jimmie. "The Care and Feeding of a Barrel Horse."
      Western Horseman, XXXIX (April 1974), 86-88, 148-149.

1256 _____. "The Care and Feeding of a Steer Wrestling Horse."
      Western Horseman, XXXIX (December 1974) , 56-60.

1257 Jacobson, Patricia and Marcia Hayes. A Horse Around the
      House. New York: Crown, 1972. 308p.

1258 Kauffman, Sandra. Kauffman's Manual of Riding Safety. New
      York: Clarkson N. Potter, 1978. 152p.

1259 Kays, John M. The Care of Light Horses. Circular, no. 353.
      Columbus, MO: Agricultural Experimental Station, University
      of Missouri, 1950.

1260 Kearley, Bernard L. You and Your Horse: How to Buy, Train,
      and Enjoy Owning a Horse. London: Country Life, 1965.
      124p.

1261 LeBlanc, John. "You Can Kill Your Horse with Kindness."
      Western Horseman, XLI (December 1976), 66, 100.

1262 Leech, Jay. How to Care for Your Horse. South Brunswick,
      NJ: A. S. Barnes, 1979. 133p.

1263 Leonard, M. C. "The Care of the Horse." New Zealand
      Journal of Agriculture, CXXVI (September 1978), 25-29.

1264 Loomis, Joyce. "It Pays to Take Care." Horse and Rider,
      XIII (November 1974), 17-22.

1265 Morse, Mel. Ordeal of the Animals. Englewood Cliffs, NJ:
      Prentice-Hall, 1968. 212p.

1266 Murray, Robbie. Common Sense Horse Care. Norwood, Aust.:
      Rigby, 1979. 94p.

1267 Phillips, Greta M. You and the Horse. London: J. A. Allen,
      1966. 266p.

1268 Posey, Jeanne K. The Horse Keeper's Handbook. New York:
      Winchester Press, 1974. 282p.

1269 Pullein-Thompson, Josephine, comp. Horses and Their Owners.
      London: Nelson, 1970. 208p.

1270 Rogers, Tex. Mare Owner's Handbook. Houston, TX: Cor-
      dovan Corp., 1971. Unpaged.

1271 Shell Chemical Company. Three Ways You Can Improve Your
      Horse Care Program. San Ramon, CA, 1976. 6p.

1272 Slaughter, Jean. Pony Care. New York: Alfred A. Knopf,
      1961. 115p.

1273 Smith, Heather. A Horse in Your Life: A Guide for the New
      Owner. South Brunswick, NJ: A. S. Barnes, 1966. 208p.

1274 Tait, Margaret E. Horses and Ponies: Their Care and Manage-
      ment for Owners and Riders. London: Published for the
      Royal Society for the Prevention of Cruelty to Animals, by
      Blandford, 1972. 112p.

1275 Tankersley, H. C. and Edward Duren. Horse Sense and Safety
      for Beginners. Bulletin, no. 492. Boise: Idaho Agricul-
      tural Extension Service, 1968. 28p.

1276 Thomas, Heather S. Your Horse and You. South Brunswick,
      NJ: A. S. Barnes, 1970. 215p.

1277 Tuke, Diana R. Horse by Horse: A Guide to Equine Care.
      London: J. A. Allen, 1973. 202p.

1278 Van Tuyl, Barbara. Select, Buy, Train, Care for Your Own
      Horse. New York: Grosset and Dunlap, 1969. 125p.

1279 Walter, William H. Horse Keeper's Encyclopedia. New York:
      Arc Books, 1979. 182p.

1280 Webber, Toni. The Pony-Lover's Handbook. London: Pelham Books, 1973. 199p.

1281 West, Geoffrey P., ed. Encyclopedia of Animal Care. 12th ed. Baltimore, MD: Williams and Wilkins, 1977. 867.

1282 Wheatley, George. Keep Your Own Pony. 6th ed. London: S. Paul, 1977. 256p.

1283 Widmer, Jack. Practical Guide for Horse Owners. New York: Scribners, 1958. 162p.

2 Feeding and Nutrition

1284 Albert, Waco W. Feeding Suggestions for Horses. Circular, no. 1034. Rev. ed. Springfield: Illinois Agricultural Extension Service, 1972. 20p.

1285 Allman, M. S. "Building Superior Pastures." Horseman, XXI (September 1977), 22-25.

1286 Blazer, Don. "How to Feed Your Horse." Horse and Horseman, VI (August 1978), 20-25.

1287 Bradbury, Peggy and Steve Werk. Horse Nutrition Handbook. Houston, TX: Cordovan Corp., 1974. 114p.

1288 Breuer, Les H., Jr. "Elements of Broodmare Feeding Management." Western Horseman, XXXVIII (August 1973), 15, 144-146.

1289 _____. "Feeding After Breeding." Horse and Horseman, I (August 1973), 30-31.

1290 Bullard, T. L. "Nutrition--Some Basic Thoughts on Horse Feeding." Unpublished paper, Southwestern Planning Conference for Livestockmen, Waco, Texas, 1973.

1291 "Buying Hay Right." Practical Horseman, VI (October 1978), 54-62.

1292 Caley, Homer K. Equine Feeding Tips. Manhattan: Cooperative Extension Service, Kansas State University, 1976. 4p.

1293 Cash, C. K. "Feeding Practices." Horseman, XXI (September 1977), 34-42.

1294 Cassard, Daniel W., et al. Approved Practices in Feeds and Feeding. 5th ed. Danville, IL: Interstate Printers and Publishers, 1977. 445p.

1295 Caswell, L. F. Feeding Light Horses and Ponies. Blacksburg: Cooperative Extension Division, Virginia Polytechnic Institute and State University, 1973. 12p.

1296 "Choosing a Commercial Feed." Practical Horseman, VI (August 1978), 22-29.

1297 Common Sense Horse Nutrition. LaSalle, CO: John Ewing Co., 1971. 20p.

1298 Conser, Diana. "Thoughts on Buying Hay." Western Horseman, XLIII (August 1978), 67-68.

1299 Crampton, E. W. and L. E. Harris. Applied Animal Nutrition. 2nd ed. San Francisco, CA: W. H. Freeman, 1969. 753p.

1300 Cullison, Arthur E. Feeds and Feeding. 2nd ed. Englewood Cliffs, NJ: Prentice-Hall, 1979. 595p.

1301 Cunha, Tony J. "The Art and Science of Feeding Horses." Horse and Rider, XVI (June 1977), 33.

1302 _____. "Avoid Myths on Horse Feeding." Horse and Rider, XVII (January 1978), 23.

1303 _____. "Digestion of Feeds." Horse and Rider, XVIII (July 1979), 22.

1304 _____. "Hints on Feeding." Horse and Rider, IX (September 1970), 82-83.

1305 _____. "Hints on Using Grains for Horses." Horse and Rider, XVI (August 1977), 33.

1306 _____. "Horse Feeding and Nutrition." Feedstuffs, XLI (July 12, 1969), 19+.

1307 _____. "Nutrition and the Performance Horse." Horse and Rider, XVI (September 1976), 59.

1308 _____. "Pasture Management Hints." Horse and Rider, XVIII (May 1979), 22.

1309 _____. "Ration of Hay to Concentrates." Horses and Rider, XVI (February 1977), 41.

1310 _____. "Suggested Nutrient Levels for the Horse." Feedstuffs, XXXVIII (August 20, 1966), 62-64+.

1311 _____. "Suggestions for Feeding By-Products to Horses." Horse and Rider, XVI (October 1977), 21.

1312 _____. "Vitamins and Minerals for Horses." Feedstuffs, XXXVIII (1966), 62-66.

1313 _____. "Water for Horses." Horse and Rider, X (February 1971), 26.

1314 _____. "Water Needs of the Horse." Horse and Rider, XVIII (April 1979), 22.

1315 Dunham, Don. "Feeding to Win." Horse Illustrated, XII (June 1980), 15-17.

1316 ElShorafa, Waleed M. "Effect of Vitamin D and Sunlight on Growth and Bone Development of Young Ponies." Unpublished Ph. D. Dissertation, University of Florida, 1978.

1317 Ensminger, Marion E. and Charles G. Olentine, Jr. Feeds and Nutrition. Clovis, CA: Ensminger Publishing Co., 1977. 1,400p.

1318 "Forum: How Do You Put Weight on a Horse?" Practical Horseman, V (March 1977), 22-31.

1319 Gallagher, James. Horse Feeding and Nutrition. Circular, no. 209. Harrisburg: Pennsylvania Agricultural Extension Service, 1975. 11p.

1320 Gerken, H. J., Jr. "Basic Horse Nutrition." Rapidan River Farm Digest, I (Winter 1975), 105-111.

1321 Guenthner, H. R. Horse Pastures. Reno: Cooperative Extension Service, University of Nevada, 1974. 4p.

1322 Guthrie, Helen A. Introductory Nutrition. St. Louis, MO: C. V. Mosby, 1971. 511p.

1323 Hafez, E. S. E., ed. Animal Growth and Nutrition. Philadelphia: Lea and Febiger, 1969. 402p.

1324 Hale, Frank. "Basic Principles of Feeding Horses." Texas Agricultural Experimental Service, Texas Feed Service Report, XXII (December 1961), 8-9.

1325 Hanauer, Elsie V. The Science of Equine Feeding: A Feeding Guide. South Brunswick, NJ: A. S. Barnes, 1973. 78p.

1326 Hansen, R. M. "Foods of Free-Roaming Horses in Southern New Mexico." Journal of Range Management, XXIX (July 1976), 347+.

1327 _____. "Foods of Wild Horses, Deer, and Cattle in the Douglas Mountain Area, Colorado." Journal of Range Management, XXX (March 1977), 116-118.

1328 Hardman, Ann C. L. A Guide to Feeding Horses and Ponies. London: Pelham Books, 1977. 163p.

1329 Hardy, T. K. "Toward Simpler Horse Feeding." Horseman, XXIV (March 1980), 18-25.

1330 Harper, Frederick. "The Art of Feeding Horses." Horse Illustrated, XI (May-June 1979), 19-23.

1331 Herrick, J. B. "Vitamin Nutrition of the Horse." Veterinary Medicine, LXVII (June 1972), 688-690+.

1332 Heusner, Gary L. "Energy Requirements and Management of the Growing Equine." Unpublished Ph. D. Dissertation, University of Illinois at Urbana-Champagne, 1977.

1333 Hintz, Harald F. "Feeding Performance Horses." Program/ Proceedings of the National Horsemen's Seminar, II (1977), 118-121.

1334 "If You Use One Yardstick, Make It Protein." Practical Horseman, VI (December 1978), 50-54, 62.

1335 James, Ruth V. "The Nuts and Bolts of Horse Feeding." Western Horseman, XLV (April 1980), 46-51.

1336 Jennings, Joseph B. Feeding, Digestion, and Assimilation in Animals. 2nd ed. New York: St. Martin's Press, 1973. 244p.

1337 Jordan, R. M. Horse Nutrition and Feeding. Bulletin, no. 348. Minneapolis: Agricultural Extension Service, University of Minnesota, 1977. 11p.

1338 _____. Reducing Horse Feeding Costs. Minneapolis: Agricultural Extension Service, University of Minnesota, 1976. 4p.

1339 Jurgens, Marshall H. Animal Feeding and Nutrition. 4th ed. Dubuque, IA: Kendall/Hunt, 1978. 448p.

1340 Kamstra, Leslie. Nutrition of Farm Animals. Dubuque, IA: Kendall/Hunt, 1975. 207p.

1341 Keith, T. B. and John P. Baker. Feed Formulation Manual. 2nd ed. Danville, IL: Interstate Printers and Publishers, 1976. 93p.

1342 Kern, Dona L. "Studies on the Utilization of Manure as a Feedstuff for Rabbits and Ponies." Unpublished Ph. D. Dissertation, University of Maryland, 1976.

1343 Kiesner, Richard E. "Feeding Alfalfa." Western Horseman, XXXVII (October 1972), 60, 196-197.

1344 Leighton-Hardman, Ann C. A Guide to Feeding Horses and Ponies. London: Pelham Books, 1977. 163p.

1345 Lloyd, W. E. "Feeding the Horse." Veterinary Medicine, LX (June 1965), 616-622+.

1346 McCaulley, LeMoyne. "Hey!: Is Your Alfalfa Fit to Feed?" Horseman, XXII (May 1978), 60-63.

1347 McVickar, Malcolm H. Approved Practices in Pasture Management. 3rd ed. Danville, IL: Interstate Printers and Publishers, 1974. 400p.

1348 "Making the Most of Your Pasture." Practical Horseman, VII (April 1979), 91-97.

1349 Maynard, Leonard A. , et al. Animal Nutrition. 7th ed. New York: McGraw-Hill, 1979. 602p.

1350 Miller, Robert M. "Grass Founder." Western Horseman, XLI (April 1976), 78-79.

1351 Miller, William C. Feeding Ponies. London: J. A. Allen, 1968. 60p.

1352 Morrison, Frank B. Feeds and Feeding. 22nd ed. Clinton, IA, 1959. 1,165p.

1353 National Research Council. Subcommittee on Horse Nutrition. Nutritional Requirements of Horses. Nutrient Requirements of Domestic Animals, no. 6. 4th rev. ed. Washington, D. C.: National Academy of Sciences, 1978. 33p.

1354 Nelson, Robert H. Introduction to Feeding Farm Livestock. 2nd ed. New York and London: Pergamon Press, 1979. 112p.

1355 "Nutritional Horse Sense." Breeder's Gazette, CXXVII (November 1962), 24-25.

1356 Olsen, F. W. "Food Relations of Wild Free-Roaming Horses to Livestock and Big Game, Red Desert, Wyoming." Journal of Range Management, XXX (January 1977), 17-20.

1357 Ott, E. A. "Nutrition for the Breeding Farm Horse." Program/Proceedings of the National Horsemen's Seminar, II (1977), 51-59.

1358 Patton, Wesley R. , Daniel W. Cassard, and Elwood M. Juergenson. Approved Practices in Feeds and Feeding. 5th ed. Danville, IL: Interstate Printers and Publishers, 1977. 444p.

1359 Perry, Tilden W. Feed Formulations. 2nd ed. Danville, IL: Interstate Printers and Publishers, 1975. 272p.

108 / Equestrian Studies

1360 Potter, Gary D. Horse Feeding Management. Renner, TX: Research Center, Texas Agricultural Extension Service, 1973. 10p.

1361 _____. "Simplified Nutrition." Horse and Rider, XVIII (September 1979), 42-45.

1362 Practical Horseman, Editors of. The Complete Guide to Feeding Your Horse. West Chester, PA, 1979. Unpaged.

1363 Randall, Ronald P. "Some Psychophysiological Aspects of Taste and Eating Rate in Cattle, Sheep, and Horses." Unpublished Ph.D. Dissertation, Oregon State University, 1974.

1364 Rhulen Agency. "Feeding Problems." Quarter Horse World, VII (February 1979), 52-54.

1365 Robinson, D. W. "The Current Status of Knowledge on the Nutrition of Equines." Journal of Animal Science, XXXIX (December 1974), 1045-1066.

1366 Schryver, H. F. Feeding Horses. Ithaca: New York State College of Agriculture and Life Sciences, n.d. 19p.

1367 Seiden, Rudolph. The Handbook of Feedstuffs. New York: Springer, 1957. 591p.

1368 Slade, L. M. "Protein Needs of Equine Athletes." Utah Science, XL (March 1979), 10-13.

1369 Sodano, Charles S. Animal Feeds and Pet Foods: Recent Developments. Food Technology Review, no. 50. Park Ridge, NJ: Noyes Data Corp., 1979. 258p.

1370 Squibb, Robert L. "Fifty Years of Research in America on the Nutrition of the Horse." Journal of Animal Science, XVII (November 1958), 1007-1014.

1371 "Suggestions on Horse Feeds Offered." Feedstuffs, XXXVIII (May 7, 1966), 123-123+.

1372 "To Greener Pastures: Starting and Maintaining the Equine Buffet--Anywhere." Equus, no. 18 (April 1979), 26-32.

1373 Ullrey, D. E. Feeding Horses. East Lansing: Animal Husbandry Department, Michigan State University, 1971. 20p.

1374 "Vitamin-Mineral Supplements: When Do They Pay?" Practical Horseman, VII (June 1979), 68-76.

1375 Wagoner, Don M., ed. Feeding to Win. Dallas, TX: Equine Research Publications, 1973. 314p.

1376 Waymack, Lester B. and Albert M. Lane. Feeding the Arizona
     Horse: A Nutrition Guide for the Horseowner in Arizona and
     the Southwest. Tucson: Cooperative Extension Service,
     University of Arizona, 1975. 12p.

1377 Weikel, Bill, ed. Know Practical Horse Feeding. Omaha,
     NE: Farnam Horse Library, 1971. 64p.

1378 White, H. E. "Establishing and Managing Horse Pastures."
     Program/ Proceedings of the National Horsemen's Seminar,
     II (1977), 32-36.

1379 _____. "Producing and Buying Hay for Horses." Program/
     Proceedings of the National Horsemen's Seminar, II (1977),
     79-80.

1380 Willard, John C. "Digestible Energy Requirement of Horses
     at Maintenance and at Two Levels of Work." Unpublished
     Ph. D. Dissertation, University of Kentucky, 1978.

1381 Willard, Judith G. "Feeding Behavior in the Equine Feed Con-
     centrate Versus Roughage Diets." Unpublished Ph. D. Dis-
     sertation, University of Kentucky, 1975.

1382 Willoughby, David P. Growth and Nutrition in Horses. South
     Brunswick, NJ: A. S. Barnes, 1975. 194p.

3 Safety

1383 Bagley, Kathryn N. "Safety Factors." Western Horseman,
     XLIII (March 1978), 96, 116.

1384 Blazer, Don. "Show Safely and Win." Horse and Horseman,
     VII (May 1979), 34-37.

1385 Bradbury, Peggy. "Horse Safety." Horseman, XXI (October
     1977), 70-77.

1386 Kohler, June. "If It's Worth Doing With a Horse, It's Worth
     Doing Safely." Western Horseman, XLIV (February 1979),
     46, 109-116.

1387 Mahaley, M. S., Jr. Accident and Safety Considerations of
     Horseback Riding. 2 pts. Durham, NC: Department of
     Surgery, Duke University Medical Center, 1976.

1388 National Horse and Pony Youth Activity Council. Horse Safety
     Guidelines. New York, 1979. 9p.

1389 Pitts, Jim and Jane Pattie. Twenty Rules for Riding Safety.
     Houston, TX: Horseman, 1968. 32p.

1390 Swanson, Elaine. "Horse Booby Traps." Western Horseman, XXXVIII (December 1973), 34-36, 159-161.

1391 United States. Department of Agriculture. Extension Service. Horse Safety Guidelines. Washington, D.C.: U. S. Government Printing Office, 1973. 16p.

1392 Vincent, S. G. "Horse Wreck: The Dangerous Side of Riding." Horseman, XXII (June 1978), 50-54.

4 Grooming

1393 Bloom, Lynda. "Braiding Tales." Western Horseman, XLIII (August 1978), 84-85.

1394 Burks, Katherine S. "Show Biz Grooms." Horse and Rider, XVII (May 1978), 62-65.

1395 Burt, Don. "Grooming: An Aid to Winning." Horse and Rider, XI (September 1972), 70-71.

1396 Grantz, Sherry. "Half of the Battle...." Horse and Rider, XVIII (May 1979), 38-41.

1397 Griffith, Perry B. "Tail Braiding Made Easy." Horse and Horseman, VII (July 1979), 56-57.

1398 _____. "Three Styles of Braiding Manes." Horse and Horseman, VII (June 1979), 50-53.

1399 Haley, Neale. Grooming Your Horse. South Brunswick, NJ: A. S. Barnes, 1974. 197p.

1400 Harris, Susan E. Grooming to Win: How to Groom, Trim, Braid, and Prepare Your Horse for Show. New York: Scribners, 1977. 191p.

1401 _____. "Step-by-Step Grooming Your Horse." Practical Horseman, VIII (April-June 1980), 42-50, 22-50, 72-80.

1402 Imlay, Clark. "Braiding." Horseman, XXI (November 1977), 68-75.

1403 Jones, William E. "Grooming for Beginners." Horse and Rider, XVIII (June 1979), 44-47.

1404 Klein, Helen. "Braiding for a Showy Edge." Classic, IV (August-September 1979), 80-83.

1405 McCord, Branch. "Good Grooming Habits." Horse Illustrated, XII (July 1980), 15-20.

1406 McNabb, Bill, Jr. "Elbow Grease." Horse and Rider, IX
      (November 1970), 38-42.

1407 McNair, Tom. "No-Hassle Grooming." Horse and Rider,
      XVIII (April 1979), 30-33, 47.

1408 Moon, Vicki. "Doing Up at Hill Top." Practical Horseman,
      VI (May 1978), 22-24.

1409 Perry, Laurie M. Braiding for the Show Ring." Practical
      Horseman, V (May 1977), 134-138.

1410 Sayles, Martha O. "How to Groom Your Horse to Stay in the
      Winner's Circle." Horseman, XVII (May 1973), 18-32.

1411 Silling, Rose M. "How to Braid Your Hunter." Horse Lover's
      Magazine, XXXIX (June-July 1974), 41-43.

1412 Smith, Annette. "Conditioning Is Grooming." Horse and Rider,
      XVI (May 1976), 26-33.

1413 Swartzbaugh, Christine. "Mane Braiding and Bandaging Legs."
      Horse and Rider, XVIII (May 1979), 32-36.

5 Housing and Transportation

1414 Barnes, P. K. "The Potomac Horse Center." Western Horse-
      man, XXXVI (June 1971), 47, 115-116.

1415 Bloom, Lynda. "Hints for Hauling Scramblers." Western
      Horseman, XLIV (November 1979), 22-25.

1416 Brann, Donald R. How to Build a Stable and a Red Barn Tool
      House. Briarcliff Manor, NY: Directions Simplified, 1972.
      178p.

1417 _____. How to Build a One-Car Garage, Carport, and Con-
      vert a Garage Into a Stable. Rev. ed. Briarcliff Manor,
      NY: Directions Simplified, 1972. 146p.

1418 Chandler, Arlene. "Stable Plans for Rusty's Stable [Califor-
      nia]." Western Horseman, XLI (September 1976), 60-61.

1419 Chandler, Geoffrey. The Construction and Maintenance of an
      Outdoor Menage. Chislehurst, Eng., 1974. 8p.

1420 Close, Pat. "What to Do in Case of a Horse Trailer Accident."
      Western Horseman, XLIV (December 1979), 62-66.

1421 Creiger, S. E. "A Horse Trailer Designed for Horses."
      Horseman, XXI (May 1978), 70-74, 76.

1422 Cuckler Building Systems. Horse Housing. Farm Building Library. Monticello, IA, 1971. 32p.

1423 Davis, Ray. "Building Fence." Western Horseman, XLIV (June 1979), 8-12.

1424 Equus 2: Stables, Farms, and Equipment. Gaithersburg, MD: Fleet Street Corp., 1980. 23p.

1425 "From the Ground Up." Equus, no. 25 (November 1979), 38-43.

1426 Grennell, Dean A. "Trailoring Tips." Horse and Rider, X (March 1971), 74-76.

1427 Harris, Freddie S. "Horse Trailer History." Horseman, XXI (July 1977), 34-41.

1428 Hoeppner, Gabrielle L. "Trailoring: Safe and Sane Hauling." Horse Lover's Magazine, XXXIX (June-July 1974), 48-51.

1429 Holland, Patricia N. "Trailor Pulling Tips." Western Horseman, XLIII (March 1978), 54-55.

1430 "Horse Trailors." Western Horseman, XXXIX (May 1974), 86-91.

1431 "Horse Trailors to Give a Champ a Lift." Western Horseman, XXXVII (May 1972), 104-109.

1432 Hurley, Jimmie. "Let's Get Loaded, Gloria." Horse and Rider, XVI (July 1977), 23-28.

1433 Jackson, Cappy. "Streamlined System for a Hunting Stable." Practical Horseman, VIII (May 1980), 27-32.

1434 Jackson, Howard E. "Ever See a Horse Fly?" Horse and Rider, XI (March 1972), 40-45.

1435 Jacobson, Patricia and Marcia Hayes. A Horse Around the House. New, rev. and enl. ed. New York: Crown, 1978. 401p.

1436 Knowles, Ralph. Guide to Interstate Health Requirements. Washington, D.C.: American Horse Council, 1980. 2p.

1437 Loomis, Joyce. "Hauling for the World." Horse and Rider, XIII (December 1974), 20-24.

1438 Midwest Planning Service. Horse Housing and Equipment Guide. Ames, IA: Iowa State University, 1971. 60p.

1439 Miller, Robert M. "The Box Stall: A Mixed Blessing." Western Horseman, XLII (June 1977), 94-95.

1440 Mizwa, Tad. "Planning a Better Barn." Horseman, XXIII (November 1979), 44-52.

1441 Munn, Marilyn E. "Buying Tow Vehicles, Hitches, and Trailers." Horse and Horseman, VI (February 1979), 42-45.

1442 _____. "Hauling: Putting It All Together." Horse and Horseman, VII (May 1979), 20-23.

1443 _____. "How to Build Your Own Barn." Horse and Horseman, V (September 1977), 48-51.

1444 _____. "How to Pull a Trailor." Horse and Horseman, VIII (May 1980), 32-36.

1445 Scallan, Lenore. "Shipping Your Horse." Practical Horseman, V (November 1977), 49-53.

1446 Serfass, Ralph. "Stable Plans: Large-Scale Horse Keeping on Tiny Acreage." Practical Horseman, VII (November 1979), 70-76.

1447 Smith, Peter C. The Design and Construction of Stables and Ancillary Buildings. London: J. A. Allen, 1967. 98p.

1448 "Stable Plans: Al Lease's Barn." Western Horseman, XLI (August 1976), 38-39.

1449 "Stable Plans: The Convertible Barn." Practical Horseman, VI (May 1979), 15-21.

1450 "Stable Plans: Four-Part Facility Under One Roof." Practical Horseman, VI (August 1978), 55-60.

1451 "Stable Plans: Luxury Upstairs, Luxury Downstairs." Practical Horseman, VI (May 1978), 52-55.

1452 "Stable Plans: Maurer Stable." Western Horseman, XLI (April 1976), 54-55.

1453 "Stable Plans: An Old Barn Works Like New." Practical Horseman, VI (October 1978), 39-45.

1454 Strum, Nancy. "Trailer for a Horseshoer." Western Horseman, VI (October 1978), 39-45.

1455 Teague, S. "Reflections on Pulling a Horse Trailor." Western Horseman, XXXIX (March 1974), 68+.

1456 Trent, L. A. "The Science of Hauling a Horse." Western Horseman: XXXVII (May 1972), 9+.

1457 Walker, Hoot. "Long Distance Horse Hauling." Western Horseman, XLIII (December 1978), 48-53.

1458 White, Joyce. "Old Time Corrals." Western Horseman,
      XXXVIII (January 1973), 56-57.

1459 Witte, Randy. "Horse Trailor Maintenance." Western Horse-
      man, XLIII (May 1978), 17-18.

6   Farriery

1460 Banner, Susan. "Handling Your Horse for the Shoer." West-
      ern Horseman, XXXVIII (August 1973), 70-72, 165.

1461 Bealer, Alex W. The Art of Blacksmithing. New York: Funk
      and Wagnalls, 1970. 425p.

1462 Beaston, Bud. Bud Beaston's 'The Master Farrier': Manual
      of Problem Horseshoeing. Sperry, OK: Oklahoma Farrier's
      College, 1976. 50p.

1463 Brown, Bud. "Shoeing for Pavement." Western Horseman,
      XLIV (November 1979), 76-78.

1464 Butler, Doug. The Principles of Horseshoeing: A Manual for
      Horseshoers. Ithaca, NY, 1974. 428p.

1465 _____. "Some Principles of Horseshoeing." California
      Horse Review, XVI (May 1979), 178-180.

1466 Camardo, Dave. "If the Shoe Fits...." Horse and Rider, VII
      (August 1968), 34-37.

1467 Canfield, D. M. Elements of Farrier Science. Murfreesboro,
      TN: Agriservice Foundation, Middle Tennessee State Uni-
      versity, 1970.

1468 "Care of the Horse's Feet." Breeder's Gazette, CXXVII (No-
      vember 1962), 19+.

1469 Churchill, Frank G. Practical and Scientific Horseshoeing.
      Wheaton, IL: Kjellberg, 1972. 127p.
      Reprint of the 1912 edition.

1470 Close, Pat. "Tips for Shoeing When You Ride 'em and Slide
      'em." Western Horseman, XLV (April 1980), 22-26.

1471 "Corrective Shoeing." Horse and Rider, VIII (April 1969),
      passim.

1472 Cromwell, Ken, et al. "Hoof and Leg Care." Horse and
      Rider, XVI (February 1977), 19-26.

1473 Darling, R. "Farrier Facts for New Owners." Horseman,
      XXII (May 1978), 64-68.

1474 Davenport, Colin. The Foot and Shoeing. Woodbury, NY: Barron's Educational Service, 1977. 49p.

1475 Dayton, Jay. "Tricks of the Tread." Horse and Rider, XI (January 1972), 54-58.

1476 DeHaven, William. Horseshoeing Technology. New York: Harbor House Publishers, 1978.

1477 Emery, Leslie, et al. Horseshoeing Theory and Hoof Care. Philadelphia: Lea and Febiger, 1977. 271p.

1478 Ensminger, Marion E. "How to Recognize Good or Shoddy Shoeing." Horse and Rider, X (May 1971), 60-61.

1479 Fisher, Leonard E. The Blacksmiths. New York: Watts, 1976. 47p. [juv.]

1480 Freeze, Gene. "What the Shoes Say About the Horse." Practical Horseman, VIII (July 1980), 51-56.

1481 "Further on Shoeing, with a Distaff Ferrier." Horse and Horseman, I (August 1973), passim.

1482 Greeley, R. Gordon. The Art and Science of Horseshoeing. Philadelphia: Lippincott, 1970. 176p.

1483 Gretz, A. L. and B. Sandrey. Shoe Your Own Horse. New York: Arco, 1977.

1484 Gunston, David. "Farriery Yesterday and Today." Journal of the Ministry of Agriculture, LXI (July 1954), 172-175.

1485 Harris, Freddie S. "The Wheelwright's Work." Western Horseman, XXXVIII (December 1973), 56-57, 108-118.

1486 Hewitt, Bob. "Horseshoe History." Western Horseman, XXXVII (October 1972), 44-45, 156-157.

1487 Hickman, John. Farriery: A Complete Illustrated Guide. Canaan, NY: Sporting Books Center, 1977. 240p.

1488 Hogg, Garry. Hammer and Tongs: Blacksmithing Down the Ages. Chester Springs, PA: Dufour Editions, 1964. 160p.

1489 Holmstrom, John G. Drake's Modern Blacksmithing and Horseshoeing. New York: Drake Publishers, 1971. 111p.

1490 "How and When to Shoe." Horse and Horseman, I (March 1973), passim.

1491 "How to Shoe a Horse." Horse and Rider, VII (August 1968), passim.

116 / Equestrian Studies

1492 Jobe, Barbara. "Young Man [William Baird]--Old Trade."
Western Horseman, XXXVI (November 1971), 46, 150-151.

1493 Johnson, Eugene M. "Trimming a Jenny." Western Horseman,
XXXIX (July 1974), 58, 160.

1494 Jones, Dave. "The Brutal Farrier." Horse and Horseman,
VI (April 1978), 22-27.

1495 _____. "The Causes of Horse Abuse." American Farriers
Journal, IV (June 1978), 35, 51.

1496 _____. "Humane Horse Handling." American Farriers Journal, IV (September 1978), 74-75.

1497 Jones, William E. , ed. Horseshoeing. Ft. Collins, CO:
Printed Horse, 1973. Unpaged.

1498 Layton, E. W. "Care of the Horse's Feet from a Farrier's
Point of View." Veterinary Medicine, LX (March 1965),
248-257+.

1499 Lungwitz, Anton. A Textbook of Horseshoeing for Horseshoers
and Veterinarians. 11th ed. Eugene: University of Oregon
Press, 1967.

1500 McArthur, P. "Beware of Corrective Shoes." Horseman, XXIII
(April 1979), 26-28, 31.

1501 Maeder, Marla. "Farrier Tales." Horse and Rider, XVIII
(August 1979), 36-37.

1502 _____. "They Shoe Horses." Horse and Rider, XVIII (May
1979), 42-43.

1503 Manweill, Marion C. How to Shoe a Horse. South Brunswick,
NJ: A. S. Barnes, 1968. 109p.

1504 Megow, Larry. "Can You Beat That [Anvil]?" Horse and
Rider, XIII (July 1974), 61-62.

1505 Miller, Robert M. "Corrective Horseshoeing." Western Horseman, XXXVI (August 1971), 130+.

1506 Moyer, William. "You and the Shoe." Equus, no. 10 (August
1978), 30-34.

1507 Murray, Barry. "Evils of the Anvil." Horse and Rider, XII
(May 1973) , 36-39.

1508 Nedrow, Al. "Teaching a Horse to Stand for Shoeing." Western Horseman, XLIII (June 1978), 80-81.

1509 Neuens, David. "Horseshoeing." American Cattle Producer, LIII (October 1962), 41+.

1510 Pitts, Don. "Hoof Care." American Horseman, IV (October 1974), 20, 52-53.

1511 Serafin, Terri R. "The Trials of a Beginning Farrier." Western Horseman, XLIII (June 1978), 88-90.

1512 Shields, Mitchell J. "Georgia's Blacksmiths." Brown's Guide, VII (June 1979), 22-31.

1513 Simons, M. A. P. "The Future of Farriery." Veterinary Record, XCVIII (January 24, 1976), 72-73.

1514 Simpson, Scott. How to Build Horseshoeing Tools and Equipment. Belgrade, MT, 1978. Unpaged.

1515 _____. "Shoeing the Problem Horse." California Horse Review, XVI (May 1979), 172-173.

1516 _____. "Tips for Winter Shoeing." Western Horseman, XLII (January 1977), 78.

1517 Springhall, John. Elements of Horseshoeing. Brisbane, Aust.: University of Queensland Press, 1964. 44p.

1518 Stewart, Miller J. "Fearless Farriers: Frightful Cures." Horseman, XVII (March 1973), 56-62.

1519 Sutherland, S. "Horseshoeing for the Non-Tradesman." Agricultural Technology, VIII (November 1977), 29-31.

1520 Tallman, Anne S. "The Fair [C. J. Desrosiers] Farrier." Horse and Horseman, I (August 1973), 72-77, 88.

1521 Thiffault, Mark. "History of a Horseshoe." Horse and Horseman, I (January 1974), 44-50, 70.

1522 Tollefson, Randi. "Beauty for the Beast." Horse and Rider, XI (June 1972), 46-52.

1523 Trahan, Ronald. "Garth Bodkin: Farrier." Horse of Course, VIII (January 1979), 16-19.

1524 United States. War Department. Office of the Chief of Cavalry. A Practical Guide to Horseshoeing. TM 2-220. North Hollywood, CA: Wilshire Books, 1972. 117p.
         Reprint of the 1941 edition.

1525 Urschel, William, Jr. "Shoeing Basics." Western Horseman, XLIII (October 1978), 26-28.

1526 Western Horseman, Editors of. Horseshoeing and Hoof Care.
Colorado Springs, CO, 1971. 36p.

1527 Wheeler, Linette L. "Today's Farrier." Horse Illustrated,
X (January-February 1979), 48-49.

1528 Wiseman, Robert F. The Complete Horseshoeing Guide. Norman: University of Oklahoma Press, 1968. 238p.

1529 _____. How to Shoe Your Horse. Omaha, NE: Farnam
Horse Library, 1977. 64p.

1530 Worcester, Thomas K. "Tips from a Horseshoer." Western
Horseman, XLV (February 1980), 18-19.

1531 Young, John R. "Keep Your Good Farrier Happy." Horseman,
XXIV (February 1980), 30-36.

7 Tackle, Equipment and Attire

a General Works/Catalogs

1532 Adams, Ramon F. "Cowboy Equipment." In: James Monaghan, ed. The Book of the American West. New York:
Julian Messner, 1963. pp. 338-348.

1533 Carroll, Jack. "A Bag of Tricks." Horse and Rider, XVII
(February 1978), 38-43.

1534 Dean, Frank. "Knots to Hold Your Horse." Western Horseman, XLIII (January 1978), 44-46.

1535 Dulaney, George. Know All About Tack. Omaha, NE: Farnam Horse Library, 1978. 64p.

1536 Ensminger, Marion E. Horses and Tack. Boston: Houghton
Mifflin, 1977. 446p.

1537 _____. Tack, Tack, Tack. Clovis, CA: Agriservices
Foundation, 1965.

1538 "Equipment for Stable, Tack Room, and Corral." Western
Horseman, XXXIX (May 1974), 54-56+.

1539 "Forum: What Is the Best Way to Care for Tack and Saddlery?"
Practical Horseman, I (June 1971), passim.

1540 Green, Carol. Tack Explained: A Horseman's Handbook.
New York: Arco, 1978. 96p.

1541 Griffith, Perry B. "Basic Tack for Horsemen." Horse and
Horseman, VI (August 1978), 60-62.

1542 _____. "How to Buy the Right Accessories." Horse and Horseman, V (July 1977), 50-53.

1543 Hasluck, Paul N., ed. Saddlery and Harness Making. London: J. A. Allen, 1973. 160p.

1544 "Horse Equipment Miscellany." Western Horseman, XXXIX (May 1974), 22-26.

1545 Jones, Dave, ed. Equus 2: Saddlery, Tack and Accessories. Gaithersburg, MD: Fleet Street Corp., 1980. 24p.

1546 Juergenson, Elwood M. Handbook of Livestock Equipment. 2nd ed. Danville, IL: Interstate Printers and Publishers, 1979. 371p.

1547 Miller's Catalog for Horsemen. New York, 1950--. v. 82--.

1548 Moldauer, Anne. The Selection of Tack Suitable for You and Your Horse. Napierville, IL: The Napierville Sun, 1973. 30p.

1549 Moseman and Brother. Moseman's Illustrated Guide for Purchasers of Horse Furnishing Goods, Novelties, and Stable Appointments, Imported and Domestic. New York: Arco, 1976. 303p.
      Reprint of the 1894 edition.

1550 Norback, Craig T. Horseman's Catalog. New York: McGraw-Hill, 1979. 520p.

1551 Osmer, Virginia T. "Proper Fitting for Competition." Horse and Rider, XIII (July 1974), 53-56.

1552 Ray, Phil. "The Western Pelham." Horse and Rider, XVIII (October 1979), 24-27.

1553 Rickey, Donald, Jr. $10 Horse, $40 Saddle: Cowboy Clothing, Arms, Tools, and Horse Gear of the 1880's. Ft. Collins, CO: Old Army Press, 1976. 135p.

1554 Thiffault, Mark. "Tips on Buying Tack." Horse and Horseman, V (November 1977), 30-33.

1555 Vocational Education Productions. The Illustrated Glossary of Horse Equipment. New York: Arco, 1976. 63p.

1556 Woodworth, R. A. "Leather Care for the Horseman." Western Horseman, XLIV (May 1979), 18-26.

b Attire

1557 Burt, Don. "Dressing: Fit to Win." Horse and Rider, X (May 1971), 28-32.

1558 Close, Pat. "The Cowboy's Hat." Western Horseman, XLIII
(May 1978), 24-26.

1559 _____. "Making Equitation Suits." Western Horseman, XLIII
(May 1978), 46-52.

1560 Equus 2: Apparel. Gaithersburg, MD: Fleet Street Corp.,
1980. 24p.

1561 Griffith, Perry B. "How to Buy the Right Togs." Horse and
Horseman, V (June 1977), 18-22.

1562 House, Mary J. "Western Wear." Horseman, XXI (September
1977), 58-63.

1563 Klein, Helen. "Loose Fits With a Feminine Flair." Classic,
II (October-November 1977), 152-155.

1564 Kroll, Lois A. Arabian Costumes. N.p., 1963. 47p.

1565 Kuller, Doris. "Warming Up to High Country Fashion." Denver, VII (January 1979), 39-41.

1566 Meek, Nanette. "Fashion in the Field." Horse Lover's National Magazine, XLIII (December 1978), 38-40.

1567 Mizwa, Tad. "Chaps That Fit." Horseman, XXV (July 1980),
32-40.

1568 Nelson, Todd. "Area Wear." Horseman, XXI (May 1977), 20-23.

1569 Ringel, Eleanor. "Riding Wardroves." Classic, II (December
1976-January 1977), 34+.

1570 Vorhes, Corliss. "How to Make Your Own Work Chaps."
Western Horseman, XLIV (March 1979), 34-36.

1571 Wilkinson-Latham, Robert and Christopher. Cavalry Uniforms,
Including Other Mounted Troops of Britain and the Commonwealth. New York: Macmillan, 1969. 215p.

c Boots and Spurs

1572 Bish, Tommy L. "Rowels That Growl, and Tines That Charm."
Horse and Rider, VII (August 1968), 44-48.

1573 Carroll, Jack. "Working Spurs." Horse and Rider, XVII (September 1978), 28-31.

1574 Delaney, Pat. " '79-'79: Bootmaking--a 100-Year Tradition
[Justin Boot Co.]." Horse and Rider, XVIII (February
1979), 45-46.

1575 Gardner-Baker, Sandra. "How to Break and Train Your Riding Boots." Horse Lover's National Magazine, XLIII (September 1978), 34-36.

1576 Hewitt, Bob. "High-Heeled Boot Tracks." Western Horseman, XXXVII (June 1972), 4-6, 124-126.

1577 Holder, Gene. "Spurs and Straps Forever." Horse and Rider, XI (September 1972), 22-25.

1578 Huber, Dwight. "Spurs: An Illustrated History." Western Horseman, XLIV (January-February 1979), 14-20, 15-17.

1579 "Justin's 100 Years: A Story in Boots." Horseman, XXIII (June 1979), 27-33.

1580 Nelson, Mary J. "What's in a Boot Besides Your Foot?" American Horseman, IV (October 1974), 36-37, 59.

1581 Rickell, Walt. "The Cowboy Spur." Horse and Rider, XIV (June 1975), 44.

1582 _____. "Frontier Bootmaker [H. J. Justin]." Horse and Rider, XI (March 1972), 60-63.

1583 Rogers, Ben. "How to Make Your Own Spurs." Western Horseman, XLIII (July 1978), 102-103.

1584 Roming, John. "Comfort in Cowboy Boots." Western Horseman, XXXVII (September 1972), 16, 165-166.

1585 Schipman, Henry, Jr. "Mexican Cowboy Boots." Western Horseman, XLI (November 1978), 78-82.

1586 Thomas, Jack. "A History of the Texas Spur." Western Horseman, XXXVIII (August-September 1973), 86-88, 166-170, 4-6, 60-61.

1587 Tollefson, Randi. "Spurs: From Aid to Pain." Horse and Rider, IX (July 1970), 50-52.

1588 "Your Riding Boots." Practical Horseman, VI (October 1978), 52-53.

d Bits and Bridles

1589 Babcock, Gil and Frank Hildenbrand. Bridle-Bits of the West. San Luis Obispo, CA: Bridle Bits, 1972. 102p.

1590 The Bible of Bridal Bits. Valley Falls, KA, 1975. Unpaged.

1591 "Bits and Their Purpose." Horse and Horseman, I (June 1973), passim.

1592 Bloom, Lynda. "Into the Bridle." Horse of Course, V (October 1976), 22-27.

1593 Bond, Marian. "Snaffles--Not Just for Kindergarten." Horseman, XXIII (October 1979), 18-27.

1594 Carroll, Jack. "A Bit of Class." Horse and Rider, XVII (January 1978), 20-22.

1595 _____. "To Bit or Not to Bit." Western Horseman, XXXVIII (July 1973), 27, 169-171.

1596 _____. "Two Ways to Train." Horse and Rider, XIV (July 1975), 25-28, 66.
        Snaffle and hackamore bits.

1597 _____. "Understanding the Hackamore [Bit]." Horse and Rider, X (October-November 1971), 16-21, 36-40.

1598 Christopher, Renny. "A Bit of History." Horse Lover's National Magazine, XLIII (July 1978), 12-14.

1599 Close, Pat. "The Snaffle Bit Futurity." Western Horseman, XLI (December 1976), 22-27.

1600 Connell, Ed. "Fitting the Mecate [Bridle]." Horse and Rider, XVI (September 1976), 34-36.

1601 _____. "The Hackamore: Fit to Be Tied." Horse and Rider, XVI (April 1976), 24-26.

1602 _____. Reinsmen of the West. Livermore, CA: Connell Publications, 1976. Unpaged.

1603 "Famous Riders and Trainers on Bits." Practical Horseman, VIII (March 1980), 69-77.

1604 Franklyn, Beve. "Bits, Bitting, and Behavior." Horse and Rider, XIV (May 1975), 65-67.

1605 Johnson, Pine and Jane Pattie. "Is Your Bit Fit to Use?" Horse and Rider, XVIII (June 1979), 16-19.

1606 Jones, Dave. "Bits and the Three R's." Horse and Horseman, VII (September 1979), 18-21, 64-65.

1607 _____. "Bits I Like--and Loathe." Horse and Horseman, VI (May 1978), 26-30.

1608 _____. "The Hackamore." Horse and Rider, XVII (September-December 1978), 32-35, 32-37, 16-20, 14-19.

1609 King, Chuck. "Snaffle Training." Western Horseman, XLV (January 1980), 24-25, 66.

1610 Kissman, Annette. "The War Bridle: Its Uses and Pitfalls." Horse of Course, VII (November 1978), 38-42.

1611 Leshnik, L. S. "Some Early Indian Horse-Bits and Other Bridle Equipment." American Journal of Archaeology, LXXV (April 1971), 141-150.

1612 Lieberman, Bobbie. "The Bit-Buyer's Challenge." Equus, no. 29 (March 1980), 44-50, 74.

1613 Malm, Gerhard A. Treasury of Bits. Valley Falls, KA: V. F. Vindicator, 1967. 52p.

1614 Meredith, Byron. "Bits." Horseman, XXI (June 1977), 59-65.

1615 Meredith, Kay. "On the Bit--Again." Dressage and CT, XII (February 1977), 18.

1616 Necer, George. "History of the Hackamore." Horse and Rider, XII (June 1973), 36-40.

1617 _____. "The Vanishing Chileno [Bit]." Horse and Rider, XVI (October 1977), 22-26.

1618 Pattie, Jane. "Snaffle, Hackamore, or Both?" Horse and Rider, XVI (May-June 1977), 16-21, 12-19.

1619 Rickell, Walt. "Cowboy Bridles." Horse and Rider, XVI (May 1976), 40.

1620 _____. "The Hackamore." Horse and Rider, XVI (January 1976), 69.

1621 _____. "The Ring Bit." Horse and Rider, XIV (August 1975), 28.

1622 _____. "A Vicious [Ring Bit] Circle?" Horse and Rider, XII (March 1973), 54-56.

1623 Roberts, Tom. Horse Control and the Bit. 2nd ed. Richmond, S. Aust.: T. A. and P. R. Roberts, 1973. 129p.

1624 Roder, Art and Sheri. "Martingale." Horse and Rider, IX (March 1970), 28-32, 72.

1625 Smith, Fred and Lynda Bloom. "Cosmic Bitting." Horse and Rider, XVII (June-July 1978), 16-21, 34-39.

1626 Tollefson, Randi. "Bits of Knowledge." Horse and Rider, X (February-March 1971), 42-45, 38-44.

1627 _____. "Uses and Misuses of the Mechanical Hackamore." Horse and Rider, X (December 1971), 54-57.

1628 Tuke, Diana. Bit-by-Bit: A Guide to Equine Bits. 2nd ed. New York: Arco, 1978. 73p.

1629 Tutton, Jane S. "Bits for Beginners." American Horseman, VIII (October 1978), 50-56.

1630 Vasiloff, Mary J. "Snaffle Bits Can Be Instruments of Torture." Horse of Course, II (October 1973), 17-19.

1631 Ward, Fay E. "Hackamore Gimmicks." Western Horseman, XXXVIII (December 1973), 7.

1632 Young, John R. "Making a Good Mouth." Horseman, XXIII (January 1979), 30-37.

e Saddles and Harness

1633 Anderson, G. Kent. "From Hispanola to Paniolo." Horse and Rider, XIII (December 1974), 50-51. Hawaiian saddles.

1634 "Buyer's Guide: Saddles." Practical Horseman, VI (November 1978), 21-28.

1635 Carroll, Jack. "Back and the Saddle." Horse and Rider, XII (December 1973), 28-32.

1636 _____. "Custom Saddles: Who Needs 'Em?" Horse and Rider, XI (June 1972), 36-41.

1637 _____. "Saddle-Saving Savvy." Horse and Rider, XIII (November 1974), 28-31.

1638 Connell, Ed. "A Saddlemaker Looks at the Forward Seat." Horse and Rider, X (January 1971), 36-41.

1639 Davis, Ray. "Dennis Reiners Discusses Bronc Saddles." Western Horseman, XXXVIII (September 1973), 26-28, 123-126.

1640 DeCamp, L. S. "Before Stirrups." Isis, LI (June 1960), 159-160; LIII (March 1961), 97.

1641 Edwards, E. Hartley. Saddlery: Modern Equipment for Horse and Stable. London: J. A. Allen, 1963. 200p.

1642 Fellows, Fred. "Illustrated History of Western Saddles." Montana Magazine of Western History, XVI (January 1966), 57-83.

1643 Grant, Bruce. How to Make Cowboy Harness and Gear. Ithaca, NY: Cornell Maritime Press, 1953. 108p.

1644 Hamilton, Samantha. "Before You Saddle Up: Be Sure It Doesn't Come Between You and Your Horse." Equus, no. 11 (September 1978), 36-42.

1645 Hohn, Otto. "The Argentine Cowboy and His Saddle." Western Horseman, XL (February 1975), 44-45.

1646 Johnson, Pine. "Is Your Saddle Fit to Use?" Horse and Rider, XVIII (June 1979), 20-28.

1647 Jones, Dave. "Saddles." Horseman, XXI (February-March 1977), 63-70, 61-68.

1648 Jones, J. L. "Horse Collar Making." Journal of the Ministry of Agriculture, LXIV (August 1957), 238-239.

1649 Keegan, Terry. The Heavy Horse: Its Harness and Harness Decoration. South Brunswick, NJ: A. S. Barnes, 1974. 217p.

1650 King, Chuck. "Saddle Trees." Western Horseman, XLIII (April-May 1978), 22-24, 102-104, 28-30, 138-140.

1651 Littauer, M. A. "Elements of Egyptian Horse Harness." Antiquity, XLVIII (December 1974), 293-295.

1652 Livingston, Phil. "A Brief History of Saddles." Horse and Rider, X (May 1971), 24-25.

1653 _____. "Rudy Gaertner, Saddle Designer." Western Horseman, XXXVIII (April 1973), 98-99, 170-172.

1654 Messineo, John. "Under the Spreading Saddle Tree...." Horse and Rider, XI (April 1972), 28-31.

1655 "The Million Mile [McClellan] Saddle." Horse Lover's National Magazine. (May 1978), 35, 56.

1656 Necer, George. "The Evolution of the Stock Saddle." Horse and Rider, XIV (March-May, 1975), 32-35, 58-59, 35-39, 36-38.

1657 Pattie, Jane. "Cinch 'em up Right, Not Tight." Horse and Rider, X (May 1971), 16-22.

1658 Perry, Bruce. "How a Custom Saddle Is Made." Horse and Horseman, III (September 1975), 64-68.

1659 Propert, Alan. "Cruciform Stirrups." Western Horseman, XLI (December 1976), 130-132.

1660 Rice, Lee. "A Bit About Old Saddles." Western Horseman, XXXIX (February 1974), 38-40, 138-142.

1661 Rickell, Walt. "The California Saddle." Horse and Rider, XVI (June 1976), 83.

1662 _____. "The Cowboy Saddle." Horse and Rider, XVI (April 1976), 46.

1663 _____. "Free Swingin' Leather." Horse and Rider, XVII (December 1978), 30-33.

1664 Rodriguez, Joe. "Long-Tipped Taps." Western Horseman, XLIV (December 1979), 22-23.
     Stirrup coverings.

1665 Rossi, P. A. "The Western Stock Saddle." American West, III (Summer 1966), 22-25.

1666 Sabin, Sam W. "Western Saddles: Structure and Construction." Quarter Horse World, VII (March 1979), 40-43.

1667 "Saddle Buyer's Roundup." Horse and Rider, X (May 1971), 40-45.

1668 "Saddle Pads." Practical Horseman, VII (October 1979), 76-85.

1669 Sherer, Richard L. Buyer's Guide to Western Saddles. Houston, TX: Cardovan Corp., 1977. 45p.

1670 Smith, Lewis. "Celebrity Saddles." Horse and Rider, XVI (November 1976). 28-31.

1671 Steffen, Randy. "The American Sidesaddle." Western Horseman, XXXVIII (June-July 1973), 81-84, 171, 74-76, 144-145.

1672 _____. "The American Stock Saddle." Western Horseman, XXXVI (May-June 1971), 40-42, 169-170, 88-92, 142-145.

1673 _____. "United States Military Saddles." Western Horseman, XXXVI (November-December 1971), 30-31+, 12-13+; XXXVII (January-April 1972), 54-56, 70+, 43+, 38-39+.

1674 _____. United States Military Saddles, 1812-1943. Norman: University of Oklahoma Press, 1973. 158p.

1675 Tuke, Diana. By Stitch: A Guide to Equine Saddles. London: J. A. Allen, 1970. 108p.

1676 Woodworth, R. A. "The Versatile McClellan Saddle." Western Horseman, XLIV (March 1979), 62-64.

1677 Young, John R. "How Saddles Affect Your Seat." Horseman, XXII (November 1978), 34-38.

B   THE HORSE BUSINESS

1   General Works

1678   Coldsmith, Don.   "Can the Backyard Breeder Compete with the
Big Boys?"   Horseman, XIV (December 1969), 30-43.

1679   Cole, H. H. , ed.   Animal Agriculture: The Biology of Domestic Animals and Their Use by Man.   San Francisco, CA:
W. H. Freeman, 1974.   788p.

1680   Conner, Jack.   "The Farm Manager of Today."   Rapidan River
Farm Digest, I (Winter 1975), 99-102.

1681   Dimmick, Barbara J.   "A Matter of Record: Organizing--and
Keeping Up With--Facts You May Need Later."   Equus, no.
30 (April 1980), 53-56, 79.

1682   Dyke, Bill and Bill Jones.   The Horse Business: An Investor's
Guide.   Ft. Collins, Co: Printed Horse, 1974.   Unpaged.

1683   Erwin, Bill and Jean.   "The Breeding Business."   Horseman,
XXI (February 1977), 59-63.

1684   Gardiner, Margaret.   Losing Less Money Raising Horses.
Hampden Highlands, ME: Highland Press, 1969.   111p.

1685   Harris, Freddie S.   "The Horse Business 100 Years Ago."
Western Horseman, XLII (May 1977), 110-112.

1686   "Hazards in the Horse Explosion."   Horse World, I (Fall 1980),
16-18.

1687   "The Horse as Big Business."   Horse and Horseman.   I (July
1973), passim.

1688   "Joys and Financial Pitfalls of Owning a Racehorse."   Canadian
Business Management, LIII (January 1980), 85-86.

1689   "The Kentucky Animal Industry: Horses and Much More."
Animal Industry Today, I (November 1978), 16-18.

1690   Kiernan, Thomas.   The Secretariat Factor: The Story of a
Multi-Million Dollar Breeding Industry.   Garden City, NY:
Doubleday, 1979.   204p.

1691   Kline, Doyle.   "New Mexico's Race Horse Industry."   New
Mexico Magazine, LVII (September 1979), 22-28.

1692   Knowles, Ralph C.   "The Role of the U. S. D. A. in the Protec-
tion of the American Horse Industry."   Preceedings of the
Annual Convention of the American Association of Equine
Pracitioners.   XXIII (1978), 203-210.

1693 Lawrence, Robert G. Maryland's Racing Industry: Its Parti-
      cipants, Organization, and Economic Impact. College Park:
      Cooperative Extension Service, University of Maryland,
      1972. 52p.

1694 Lorscheider, Low. "Equine Equity: Should You Invest in Mor-
      tality Insurance for Your Horse?" Equus, no. 33 (July
      1980), 51-54, 76.

1695 McCurdy, D. R. "A Study of the Nature of Private Horseback
      Riding Enterprises in Illinois." In: U. S. Department of
      Agriculture. McIntire-Stennis Cooperative Forestry Re-
      search Program. Carbondale: Cooperative State Research
      Service, Southern Illinois University, 1968. p. 68+.

1696 McHam, Dedi. "Memories of Our Barn." Western Horseman,
      XLIV (May 1979), 112-123.
      On owning a riding stable.

1697 McReynolds, Jack. "What It Takes to Run a Successful Breed-
      ing Operation." Horseman, XVII (January 1973), 10-23.

1698 Moncrief, L. W. , et al. Michigan's Commercial Horse Indus-
      try. Report no. 323. East Lansing: Agricultural Experi-
      mental Station, Michigan State University, 1976. 11p.

1699 Moore, B. H. "Bookkeeping for the Small Breeder." Western
      Horseman, XLII (September 1977), 38-39.

1700 Murray, William. "Last Year, Oil Leases: This Year, Race
      Horses." Los Angeles, XXI (April 1976), 112+.

1701 National Horse and Pony Youth Activity Council. Horses and
      Land Use: Planning Guidelines. New York, 1979. 16p.

1702 Nelson, Mary J. "Managing the Cold-Weather Breeding Farm."
      Horse and Horseman, III (November 1975), 52-55.

1703 New York. Temporary State Commission to Study and Investi-
      gate the Thoroughbred Industry in New York State. Report.
      Albany, 1977. 98p.

1704 Oppenheimer, Harold L. Cowboy Economics. 3rd ed. Dan-
      ville, IL: Interstate Printers and Publishers, 1976. 346p.

1705 Rhodes, Bob. "Horses Go Boom." Horse of Course, VIII
      (January 1979), 40-45.

1706 Rhulen, Peter. "Liability [Insurance] in Respect to the Horse
      Business." Program/Proceedings of the National Horse-
      men's Seminar, II (1977), 131-132.

1707 Rolapp, R. Richards. "The American Horse Council: Unity, Di-
      versity, Action." Rapidan River Farm Digest, I (Winter

1975), 93-98.

1708 _____. "Effective Government Action for Horse Owners."
Program/Proceedings of the National Horsemen's Seminar,
II (1977), 24-27.

1709 _____. "Your Horse: Hobby or Business?" Western Horseman, XLI (September 1976), 16-17.

1710 Sims, John A. and Leslie E. Johnson. Animals in the American
Economy. Ames: Iowa State University Press, 1972. 288p.

1711 Snider, Buri. "The Byzantine Business of Horse Breeding."
Cosmopolitan, CLXXXVI (January 1979), 180+.

1712 Tyler, George. "For Love of Money." Horse and Rider, XI
(September 1973), 28-32.

1713 _____. and Bob Gray. Making Money With Western Horses:
A Guide to the Economics of the Western Horse Business.
Houston, TX: Cordovan Corp., 1964. 92p.

1714 Virginia Horse Council. Virginia Horse Industry Yearbook.
Riner, VA, 1976--. v. 1--.

1715 Wilding, Suzanne. "The Horse Boom." Town and Country,
CXXIX (November 1975), 173-175.

1716 Wood, Kenneth A. The Business of Horses: A Handbook for the
California Horseman on the Economics, Business, and Legal
Aspects of Dealing with Horses. Chula Vista, CA, 1973. 268p.

2 Purchasing, Trading, Selling

1717 Abbott, Peter. "Under the Big Top." Horse and Rider, XIII
(July 1974), 70-73.
Horse auctions.

1718 Abbott, Richard D. "Seller Beware." Practical Horseman, V
(July 1977), 23-28.

1719 Albaugh, Reuben. Selecting a Light Horse. Leaflet, no. 2807.
Sacramento: California Agricultural Extension Service,
1975. 8p.

1720 _____. "Tools to Select Your Top Horse." Horse Lover's
Magazine, XXXIX (June-July 1974), 22-23.

1721 Arnold, Jobie. "How to Buy a Winning Race Horse." Town
and Country, CXXXII (August 1979), 122+.

1722 Bond, Marian. "Distaff Dealers." Horse and Rider, XII (October 1973), 24-27.

1723   Bower, A. How to Buy a Race Horse. Lexington, KY: Crom-
       well Bookstock Agency, 1968. Unpaged.

1724   Bradbury, Peggy. "Buying Hints for Beginning Horsemen."
       Horseman, XVII (July 1973) , 38-43.

1725   British Horse Society and Pony Club. A Guide to the Purchase
       of Childrens Ponies. Woodbury, NY: Barron's Educational
       Service, 1979.

1726   Chance, Mary. "The Horse Trader." Western Horseman, XLV
       (July 1980), 92-100.

1727   Close, Pat. "Buying a Registered Horse--and Getting the Pa-
       pers." Western Horseman, XXXVIII (July 1973), 86-89,
       135-136.

1728   _____. "Buying Your First Horse." Western Horseman,
       XXXIX (April 1974), 95-96, 144-146.

1729   Conant, Nance. "Selling Your Horse." Western Horseman,
       XLIV (June 1979), 52-53.

1730   Conn, George H. How to Get a Horse and Live With It. South
       Brunswick, NJ: A. S. Barnes, 1969. 262p.

1731   Conner, Jack. "Developing a Program of Sales." Program/
       Proceedings of the National Horsemen's Seminar, II (1977) ,
       48-50.

1732   Darling, John E. Yearlings at Auction. Beltsville, MD: Tho-
       ranal Publications, 1969. Unpaged.

1733   Edwards, Elwyn H. Owning a Pony: Buying, Riding, Manage-
       ment. London: Pelham Books, 1977. 148p.

1734   Ferguson, Tom. "Buying the Rope Horse." Horse and Horse-
       man, VII (September 1979), 54.

1735   Finney, Humphrey S. , with Raleigh Burroughs. Fair Exchange:
       Recollections of a Life with Horses. New York: Scribners,
       1974. 175p.

1736   Garbett, G. H. , ed. Come to Britain for Bloodstock. London:
       Anglo-Irish Agency, 1951. 48p.

1737   Green, Ben K. Some More Horse Tradin'. New York: Alfred
       A. Knopf, 1972. 255p.

1738   Griffith, Perry B. "Buying the Pleasure Horse." Horse and
       Horseman, VI (July 1978), 54-57.

1739   _____. "Selecting the Triple-Threat Horse." Horse and
       Horseman, VII (April 1979), 46-49.

1740 Hartigan, Joe. To Own a Racehorse. Orange, NJ: Albert
      Saifer, Publisher, 1976.

1741 Havemann, Ernest. "You, Too, Can Own a Race Horse." In:
      Life, Editors of. Great Readings from Life. New York:
      Harper & Row, 1960. pp. 141-149.

1742 "How Not to Conduct a Sale." Horse and Horseman, I (Novem-
      ber 1973), passim.

1743 Humphreys, Alfred G. "Peg-Leg Smith: A Horse-Trader on
      the Oregon Trail." Idaho Yesterdays, X (Summer 1966),
      28-32.

1744 Jones, Dave. "Tips on Buying a Horse." Horse Illustrated,
      XI (March-April 1979), 34-35.

1745 Jordan, R. M. Selecting Your Horse. Bulletin, no. 351. Rev.
      ed. Minneapolis: Agricultural Extension Service, Univer-
      sity of Minnesota, 1978. 16p.

1746 Josey, Martha. "Selecting a Barrel Racing Prospect." The
      Paint Horse Journal, X (July 1976), 16-24.

1747 [No entry]

1748 Kelly, J. F. Dealing with Horses. Rev. ed. London: S.
      Paul, 1972. 159p.

1749 King, Larry. "You Can't Trade Horses or Keep Bees Without
      Getting Stung." Classic, II (December 1976-January 1977),
      146-154.

1750 Lee, Jimmy. "Hints for Selling Horses." Practical Horseman,
      VII (May 1979), 8-13.

1751 Lieberman, Bobbie. "The Wary Shopper: The Careful Approach
      Will Avoid Later Headaches." Equus, no. 10 (November
      1978), 37-39, 58-59, 68.

1752 Main, Jeremy. "Ponying Up for a Backyard Horse." Money,
      IV (September 1975), 46+.

1753 Mather, Helen. Light Horsekeeping: How to Get a Horse and
      Keep It. New York: E. P. Dutton, 1970. 192p.

1754 Matson, E. "Is This Horse Right for You?" Horseman, XXII
      (December 1978), 56-60.

1755 Melcher, Carol R. The Beginner's Guide to Horses: Buying,
      Equipping, and Stabling. South Brunswick, NJ: A. S.
      Barnes, 1974. 149p.

1756 Murray, Barry G. I Want a Horse: Horse Buyer's Guide and

Soundness Evaluation Check List. Stevenson, WA: Adventure Publications, 1977. 68p.

1757 Nelson, Mary J. "Buying Yearlings." Horse and Horseman, VII (July-August 1979), 40-49, 26-29.

1758 Nordby, Julius E. and H. E. Lattig. Selecting, Fitting, and Showing Horses. Danville, IL: Interstate Printers and Publishers, 1963. 138p.

1759 Parsons, Derrick. Do You Own a Horse? Canaan, NY: Sporting Book Center, 1977. 95p.

1760 Piazza, Marj. "Buying Your First Horse." Western Horseman, XLV (June 1980), 14-16.

1761 "A Poor Woman's Guide to Horsebuying." Horse and Horseman, I (April 1973), passim.

1762 Posey, Jeanne K. The Horse Buyer's Guide. South Brunswick, NJ: A. S. Barnes, 1973. 146p.

1763 _____. How to Buy a Better Horse and Sell the One You Own. North Hollywood, CA: Wilshire Books, 1974. 146p.

1764 Ream, Joy. "How to Sell a Horse." Horse and Rider, XII (October 1973), 60-63.

1765 Reese, Herbert H. How to Select a Sound Horse. Farmer's Bulletin, no. 779. Washington, D.C.: U.S. Government Printing Office, 1950.

1766 Reese, Presley. "Rolling Out the Barrel Horses." Horse and Rider, XIV (April 1975), 86-87.

1767 Reich, Cindy. "Judging Tips for Beginners." Western Horseman, XLIV (July 1979), 46-51.
What to look for before purchasing a horse.

1768 Rich, Ray and Bill Thomas. "The High Cost of Auctions." Horse and Rider, VIII (December 1969), 68-69, 72-73.

1769 Rogers, Anne. "Fast Action at the Running W [Auction]." Horse and Rider, XI (February 1972), 28-31, 54.

1770 Sanderson, I. "How Should You Market Your Horses?" Horseman, XXII (September 1978), 68-70.

1771 Saunders, George C. Your Horse: His Selections, Stabling and Care. 2nd ed. Princeton, NJ: Van Nostrand, 1966. 207p.

1772 Self, Margaret C. Horses: Their Selection, Care, and Hand-

ling. New York: A. S. Barnes, 1943. 170p.
A classic from an important author.

1773 _____. How To Buy the Right Horse. Omaha, NE: Farnam Horse Library, 1977. 64p.

1774 Spencer, Dick, 3rd. "Horse Auction." Western Horseman,
XL (March 1975), 34, 126-128.

1775 "Stallions: To Buy or Not to Buy." Horse and Horseman, I
(August 1973), passim.

1776 Stoneridge, M. A. A Horse of Your Own. Garden City, NY:
Doubleday, 1963. 480p.

1777 Thomas, Heather S. "Buy the Right First Horse for Your
Child." Horse of Course, II (October 1973), 30-32, 60-64.

1778 Tutton, Jane S. "Selling Your Horse." American Horseman,
IV (October 1974), 26, 52.

1779 Waltenspiel, Ruth. "One Way to Buy a Winner." Western
Horseman, XLII (September 1977), 66-67.

1780 Weaver, Sue A. "Selling Your Horse at Auction." Western
Horseman, XLV (January 1980), 31-32.

1781 Willett, Pat. "Anatomy of an Auction." Horse and Rider,
XIV (June 1975), 47-49.

1782 Wisecamp, Hank. "What You Should Know About Buying a
Horse at Auction." Horseman, XVII (July 1973), 18-29.

1783 Wright, W. "Selection of the Saddle Horse." Agricultural
Technology, VIII (November 1977), 15-21.

1784 Zoll, Don. How to Buy a Horse. New York: David McKay,
1980.

3 Stable Management

1785 Bell, Glenys. Our Own Riding Stables. Wellington, New Zealand: A. H. and A. W. Reed, 1975. 168p.

1786 Bergen, Chan. "Some Ideas from the B-Bar-B." Western
Horseman, XXXIX (November 1974), 72-74.

1787 Brooke, Geoffrey F. H. Introduction to Riding and Stablecraft.
London: Seeley, 1953. 160p.

1788 Davis, Ray. "Management at Gleannlock Farms." Western
Horseman, XXXIX (August 1974), 58-60+.

1789 _____. "Management at Oklahoma Stud." Western Horseman, XLII (July 1977), 94-96.

1790 Garland, James A. The Private Stable: Its Establishment,
Management, and Appointments. Croton-on-Hudson, NY:
North River Press, 1976. 631p.

1791 Green, Carol. Stable Management Explained. London: Ward,
Lock, 1977. 96p.

1792 Hayes, Matthew H. Stable Management and Exercise: a Book
for Horse Owners and Students. 6th ed. New York: Arco,
1969. 369p.

1793 Howe, Theresa. The Owner-Groom: A Guide to Horse Management by Amateurs. 3rd ed. London: Country Life,
1960. 158p.

1794 Jackson, R. S. "Management Opportunities for Equine Practitioners." American Journal of Veterinary Medicine, CLVII
(December 1, 1970), 1595-1598.

1795 Langer, Lawrence. Know Stable Design and Management.
Omaha, NE: Farnam Horse Library, 1979. 64p.

1796 Melcher, Carol R. Elements of Stable Management: An Illustrated Guide. South Brunswick, NJ: A. S. Barnes, 1975.
165p.

1797 Molison, Sylvia. Stable Studies: Characters Good and Bad.
London: Hollis and Carter, 1959. 177p.

1798 Shackleton, N. A. Stable Management in Canada. Ottawa,
Ont.: Canadian Horse Council, 1976. 291p.

1799 "Stable Record Keeping." Practical Horseman, V (October
1977), 36-43.

1800 "Stable Supplies." Practical Horseman, VI (September 1978),
44-45.

1801 Walter, W. H. Horse Keeper's Encyclopedia. New York:
Arco, 1979. 182p.

1802 Wheatley, George. Stable Management for the Owner-Groom.
London: Cassell, 1966. 262p.

1803 Young, John R. "How Stable Management Affects Training."
Horseman, XXIV (March 1980), 36-42.

4 Business, Taxes, and the Law

1804 Abbott, Richard D., et al. "Hey Mister, Is This Your Horse?"

Practical Horseman, VI (December 1978), 24-29.

1805 Allen, Rex. "Death, Taxes, and Ol' Paint." Horse and Horse-
      man, I (January 1974), 14-15.

1806 _____. "Death, Taxes, and the Differences." Horse and
      Horseman, I (August 1973), 12.

1807 Battersby, M. E. "Horses and Taxes." Western Horseman,
      XXXVII (January 1972), 4-5+.

1808 Christenfeld, Loren B. "Horsemen and Tax Laws." Western
      Horseman, XLIII (January 1978), 66-71.

1809 _____. "Tax Deductions for Pleasure Horse Losses." West-
      ern Horseman, XLIII (February 1978), 32-33.

1810 Davis, Thomas A. Horse Owners and Breeders Tax Manual:
      A Comprehensive Tax Guide. Washington, D.C.: American
      Horse Council, 1969--. v. 1--.

1811 Dobbyn, John. "The Law On and Off Horses." Horse of
      Course, IX (June 1980), 54-62.

1812 Greene, Edward H. The Law and Your Horse. New York:
      Arco, 1971.

1813 Hannah, Harold W. and Donald F. Storm. Law for the Veter-
      inarian and Live-Stock Owner. 3rd ed. Danville, IL:
      Interstate Printers and Publishers, 1974. 262p.

1814 Loring, Murray. "Horses and Law." Horseman, XXI (Janu-
      ary 1977), 35-42.

1815 _____. "Your Horse and the Law." Program/Proceedings
      of the National Horsemen's Seminar, II (1977), 108-112.

1816 National Horse and Pony Youth Activity Council. Horsemen
      and Their Communities: Zoning Guidelines. New York,
      1979. 5p.

1817 Sophian, Theodore J. A Guide to the [British] Law Relating
      to Horses, Riders, and Riding Establishments. London:
      J. A. Allen, 1964. 88p.

1818 Taylor, Joyce K. Horses in Suburbia. London: J. A. Allen,
      1966. 72p.

1819 Thompson, Diana. "Don't Zone Me Out: Preserving a Place
      for the Suburban Horse." Equus, no. 31 (May 1980), 23-
      27, 72.

1820 Tutton, Jane S. "Make Your Horse a Good Neighbor." Amer-

ican Horseman, III (May 1973), 28-30, 62.
  Zoning.

1821 Wood, Kenneth A. How to Avoid Legal Hassles Encountered
  as a Result of Owning Horses. Omaha, NE: Farnam Horse
  Library, 1978. 64p.

1822 _____. Law for the Horse Breeder. Rancho Santa Fe, CA,
  1979. Unpaged.

1823 _____. Law, Taxes, and the Horseman. 32 pts. Rancho
  Santa Fe, CA, 1975-1978.

5 Farms, Stables, and Ranches

1824 Arbuckle, Helen. "Heyday of the Palo Alto Stock Farm."
  Western Horseman, XXXVIII (March 1973), 16-17, 142.

1825 Bergen, Chan. "Vern Wagner's Cross-Slash Ranch." Western
  Horseman, XXXVIII (September 1973), 72-75, 158-160.

1826 Burns, Robert H. "The Oxford House Ranch." Western Horseman, XXXVIII (July 1973), 4-5, 148-149.

1827 Bush, Doreen. "Foolish Pleasure's Breeding Place." Country
  Gentleman, CXXV (Winter 1975-1976), 52-55.
  Waldemar Farms in Kentucky.

1828 Cannell, Margaret. "Profile of a Riding Stable [Dutch Manor,
  New York]." Practical Horseman, V (January 1977), 34-
  39.

1829 Close, Pat. "Hawn Arabian Ranch." Western Horseman,
  XXXVIII (August 1973), 26-28, 138-140.

1830 _____. "Lasma Arabian Stud." Western Horseman, XLIV
  (September 1979), 43-48.

1831 Davis, Ray. "Chaparrosa Remuda [Ranch]." Western Horseman, XXXIX (July 1974), 48-49, 153-156.

1832 Dossenbach, Monique, et al. Great Stud-Farms of the World.
  Translated from the German. London: Thames and Hudson, 1978. 288p.

1833 Dougall, Neil. "The Fall of an Arabian Empire." Horse and
  Rider, XI (March-April 1972), 46-51, 40-45.
  Crabbet Farm in England.

1834 Duke, Cordia. 6,000 Miles of Fence: Life on the XIT Ranch
  of Texas. Austin: University of Texas Press, 1961. 231p.

1835   Evans, Donald P.   Hanover [Shoe Farms]: The Greatest Name
       in Harness Racing.   South Brunswick, NJ: A. S. Barnes,
       1976.   240p.

1836   "Forum: How Do You Choose Your Boarding Stable?"   Practi-
       cal Horseman, VI (November 1978), 12-13.

1837   Hewitt, Bob.   "Mexico's Rancho Grande."   Western Horseman,
       XXXVIII (June 1973), 38-40.

1838   _____.   "Trinchera Ranch."   Western Horseman, XXXVIII
       (February 1973), 46-48.

1839   Huntley, Paul L.   "100 Years on the Switzer Ranch."   Frontier
       and True West, LI (August-September 1977), 6-14.

1840   King, Chuck.   "C-2 Cattle Company Horses."   Western Horse-
       man, XLIV (October 1979), 102-106.

1841   Koch, Charles R.   "Claiborne Farms."   Country Gentleman,
       CXXVI (Fall 1976), 58+.

1842   Lea, Tom.   The King Ranch.   Boston: Little, Brown, 1957.

1843   Markus, Kurt.   "Backarooing on the MC [Ranch]."   Western
       Horseman, XLIV (July 1979), 37-43.

1844   _____.   "Five Generations of Horsemen: The King Ranch
       Today."   Western Horseman, XLV (April-May 1980), 37-
       45, 37-45.

1845   Pattie, Jane.   "6666 Ranch."   Horse and Rider, X (January
       1971), 16-21, 26.

1846   Peck, Lydie.   "Laguna Winds Boarding Stable."   Western Horse-
       man, XXXVIII (September 1973), 52, 164-165.

1847   Rancheros Visitadores: 25th Anniversary, 1930-1955.   Santa
       Barbara, CA, 1955.   142p.

1848   Reykdal, Dorelle.   "Ranchotel Horse Center."   Western Horse-
       man, XXXIX (July 1974), 35-36, 144-145.

1849   Richard, Marjorie.   "Rapidan River Farm."   Western Horse-
       man, XLI (March 1976), 35-38, 104-106.

1850   Rickman, John.   Eight Flat-Racing Stables.   London: Heine-
       mann, 1979.   228p.

1851   Ross, J. K. M.   Boots and Saddles: The Story of the Fabu-
       lous Ross Stable in the Golden Days of Racing.   New York:
       E. P. Dutton, 1956.   272p.

1852 Smith, Bradley. The Horse and the Blue Grass Country. Rev.
      ed. Garden City, NY: Doubleday, 1968. 160p.

1853 Tower, Whitney. "Back on the Top Rung." Classic, IV (Au-
      gust-September 1979), 32-37.
      Calumet Farm and Greentree Stable.

1854 Vogt, Don. "Valley Y Ranch." Western Horseman, XXXV
      (September 1970), 16-17, 124-126.

1855 Wilding, Suzanne. "Master of Their Fetes." Classic, III
      (October-November 1978), 114-120.

1856 Winsted, Manya. "The Valley's Arabian Horse Ranches."
      Phoenix, XI (January 1976), 74+.

1857 Zwarun, Suzanne. "Canada's Stampede Ranch." Western Horse-
      man, XXXVIII (June 1973), 117-118, 169-171.

6 Careers

1858 Arnold, Oren. Aim for a Job in Cattle Ranching. New York:
      Rosen, 1971. 127p.

1859 Benson, Christopher. Careers in Animal Care. Minneapolis,
      MN: Lerner Publications, 1974. 36p.

1860 Blazer, Don. "Girls Wanted." Horse and Rider, XVI (May
      1976), 34-38.

1861 _____. "Jobs at the Racetrack." Horse and Horseman, VI
      (December 1978), 34-37.

1862 Bleby, John. Animals as a Career. London: Batsford, 1967.
      120p.

1863 Chronicle of the Horse, Editors of. "Horse Show Judging as
      a Profession." Rapidan River Farm Digest, I (Winter 1975),
      246-247.

1864 Close, Pat. "Getting Started as a Horse Trainer." Western
      Horseman, XLIV (April 1979), 87-89.

1865 Crofts, Leonard. "Careers in the Horse Biz." Horse and
      Rider, XI (June 1972), 28-34.

1866 "Do You Want to Be a Racing Official?" Practical Horseman,
      V (August 1977), 49-56.

1867 Geurin, H. B. "What Does Industry Look for in College Gradu-
      ates?" Journal of Animal Science, XXXIII (Spring 1971),
      182-191.

1868   Hartigan, Joe.   To Become a Race Horse Trainer.   Orange,
        NJ: Albert Saifer, Publisher, 1976. 143p.

1869   Henschel, Georgie.   Careers With Horses.   London: S. Paul,
        1975. 112p.

1870   Jones, Dave. "Working In and Out of the Horse Business."
        Horse and Horseman, VII (June 1979), 12-15.

1871   Kelly, Karin.   Careers With the Circus.   Minneapolis, MN:
        Lerner Publications, 1975. 64p. [juv.]

1872   Kling, Joyce. "Cowpunchers--Still Around."   Occupational Out-
        look Quarterly, XIII (Winter 1969), 16-20.

1873   Kohl, Sam and Tom Riley.   Your Career in Animal Services.
        New York: Arco, 1977. 143p.

1874   Lehrman, Steve.   Your Career in Harness Racing.   New York:
        Atheneum, 1976. 148p.

1875   McHugh, Mary.   Veterinary Medicine and Animal Care Careers.
        New York: Watts, 1977. 66p.

1876   O'Connor, Karen.   Working With Horses: A Roundup of Ca-
        reers.   New York: Dodd, Mead, 1980.

1877   Occupational Outlook Handbook.   Washington, D.C. : U.S.
        Government Printing Office, 1980.
        An annual publication.

1879   Peterson, Paul, et al.   Working in Animal Science.   New York:
        McGraw-Hill, 1978. 248p.

1880   Potter, Gary. "Careers Through College."   Horseman, XX
        (April 1976), 48-54.

1881   Stone, Archie A.   Careers in Agribusiness and Industry.   Dan-
        ville, IL: Interstate Printers and Publishers, 1970. 352p.

1882   Swope, Robert E.   Opportunities in Veterinary Medicine.   Sko-
        kie, IL: V.G.M. Career Horizons, 1978. 155p.

1883   Williams, Dorian.   Work With Horses as a Career.   London:
        Batsford, 1963. 128p.

Further References: See also Parts II above and V below.

PART V   TRAINING

A   GENERAL WORKS

1884   Abbott, Priscilla.   "Oh, My Aching Back."   Horse and Rider,
       XVI (July 1977), 38-40.

1885   Alexander, Gerald and Jane Pattie.   "The Finishing Touches."
       Horse and Rider, XIX (February 1980), 32-37.

1886   Amaral, Anthony A.   How to Train Your Horse: A Complete
       Guide to Making an Honest Horse.   New York: Winchester
       Press, 1977.   221p.

1887   Ansell, Michael P.   Soldier On: An Autobiography.   London:
       Davies, 1973.   180p.

1888   Becher, Rolf.   Schooling by the Natural Method: English Edi-
       tion.   London: J. A. Allen, 1963.   78p.

1889   Benoist-Gironiere, Yves.   Conquest of the Horse.   Translated
       from the German.   New York: Funk and Wagnalls, 1957.
       155p.

1890   Blazer, Don.   Training the Western Show Horse.   South Bruns-
       wick, NJ: A. S. Barnes, 1978.   160p.

1891   Bloom, Lynda.   "Building for Western Pleasure."   Horse and
       Rider, XVII (September-October 1978), 16-21, 28-31.

1892   _____.   "How to Start Spooky Colts."   Western Horseman,
       XLIV (October 1979), 23-26, 154.

1893   _____.   "Two-Way [English-Western] Pleasure Training."
       Horse and Rider, XVIII (November 1979), 38-43.

1894   _____.   "Working with the Young Pleasure Horse."   Western
       Horseman, XLIV (May 1979), 38-42.

1895   Bolton, Lyndon.   Training the Horse: Thoughts on Riding.
       Rev. and enl. ed.   New Rochelle, NY: Sportshelf, 1966.
       127p.

140

1896 Bond, Marian. "Mother Nurture [Sharon Harris] and Her Brood."
      Horse and Rider, XIX (April 1980), 16-21.

1897 _____. "Three Youth Trainers [Frank Craighead, Lois
      Langer, and Tim Stewart]." Horse and Rider, XIX (February 1980), 16-21.

1898 Buchanan, Buck. "Colt Training: From Birth to Saddle."
      Horse and Horseman, III (November 1975), 38-43.

1899 Carver, Sonora. A Girl and Five Brave Horses. Garden City,
      NY: Doubleday, 1961. 208p.

1900 Childs, Marilyn C. Training Your Colt to Ride and Drive. New
      York: Arco, 1972. 136p.

1901 Close, Pat. "Vern Lawrence Talks About Pleasure Horses."
      Western Horseman, XLIII (June 1978), 6-10.

1902 Cotterman, Dan. "Never Say 'Neigh.' " Horse and Rider, XVI
      (August-September 1977), 16-21, 28-31.

1903 Crossley, Anthony. Training the Young Horse: The First Two
      Years. London: S. Paul, 1978. 191p.

1904 Cubitt, C. Guy. The Aids and Their Application. 2nd ed.
      Woodbury, NY: Barron's Educational Service, 1977. 47p.

1905 Curling, Bill. The Captain: A Biography of Captain Sir Cecil
      Boyd-Rochford, Royal Trainer. London: Barrie and Jenkins, 1970. 293p.

1906 Davis, Ray. "Basic Training, with John Ballvveg." Western
      Horseman, XXXIX (December 1974), 65-68, 137-139.

1907 _____. "Ed Workman on Horse Training." Western Horseman, XXXVI (November-December 1971), 36-38, 162-164,
      14-16, 106-108.

1908 _____. "Training at the Halfords." Western Horseman,
      XLI (March 1976), 24-26, 115-118.

1909 _____. "Training the Horse, Ranch-Style." Horse and
      Rider, XVII (May 1978), 16-21.

1910 _____. "Training, with Jack Frey." Western Horseman,
      XXXVI (August 1971), 92-94+.

1911 _____. "Training, with Jack Hart." Western Horseman,
      XLI (September 1976), 66, 130-132.

1912 Day, Carmel M. "The Quiet Trainer." Horse and Rider,
      XIII (September 1974), 30-35.

1913 Dayton, Jay. "J. Kohn, Artist." Horse and Rider, XII (July 1973), 72-77.

1914 Devereux, Frederick L. , Jr. The [U. S.] Cavalry [School] Manual of Horse Management. South Brunswick, NJ: A. S. Barnes, 1979. 236p.

1915 Dickerson, Jan. Training Your Own Young Horse. Garden City, NY: Doubleday, 1978. 201p.

1916 Dickie, Lena. "Start 'em Young." Horse and Rider, XVII (April 1978), 16-20.

1917 Edwards, Elwyn H. From Paddock to Saddle. New York: Scribners, 1972. 211p.

1918 Essary, Don. Training Quarter Horses. South Brunswick, NJ: A. S. Barnes, 1980.

1919 Farshier, Robert. Riding and Training. Edited by Eugene V. Connell. New and rev. ed. Princeton, NJ: Van Nostrand, 1959. 340p.

1920 Friedberger, J. C. "Modern Horse Training Methods: What Is Justifiable?" Veterinary Record, LXXXVII (August 22 and September 5, 1970), 229-231, 299-300.

1921 Graves, Troy. Break and Train Your Own Horse: A Complete Course in the Education of the Horse, Starting with the Four-Weeks Old Colt. Goshen, NY: Bookmill, 1954. 138p.

1922 Gray, Patsey. Happiness Is a Well-Trained Horse. Omaha, NE: Farnam Horse Library, 1978. 64p.

1923 Green, Carol. Training Explained. New York: Arco, 1977. 96p.

1924 Haley, Neale. Training Your Horse to Show. South Brunswick, NJ: A. S. Barnes, 1976. 250p.

1925 Hardman, Ann C. L. Young Horse Management. London: Pelham Books, 1976. 176p.

1926 Holyoake, Janet J. Improving Your Pony: Photographic Studies. London: Faber and Faber, 1969. 83p.

1927 Hudgins, Sam. "Easy Does It." Horse and Rider, XII (July 1973), 20-26.

1928 Hunt, Ray. "Easy Handling." Horse and Rider, XVI (April 1976), 48-54.

1929 _____. Think Harmony with Horses. Fresno, CA: Pioneer Publishing Co. , 1978. 87p.

1930 Hurley, Cynthia G. "Riding the Young Horse for the First Time." Horse Illustrated, IX (September-October 1978), 58-61.

1931 "Initial Horse Training Techniques." Horse and Horseman, I (May-July 1973), passim.

1932 Johnson, Rae. "Ponying for Profit." Horse and Rider, XVIII (May 1980), 38-43.

1933 Jones, Dave. Practical Western Training. New York: Arco, 1972. 176p.

1934 _____. The Western Trainer. New York: Arco, 1976. 229p.

1935 Kennedy, Gary. "Brick Bats or Sugar Cubes?" Horse and Rider, XVI (January 1978), 50-53.

1936 The Kikkuli Text on the Training of Horses. Translated from the German. Lexington, KY: King Library Press, 1977. 47p.
A Hittite "manual," ca. 1350 B.C.

1937 King, Chuck. "One Man's [Ken Garret] Way." Western Horseman, XLI (August 1976), 100-105.

1938 _____. "Ron White's Mule Training Tips." Western Horseman, XLIV (May 1979), 56-58, 62.

1939 Littauer, Vladimir S. Common Sense Horsemanship: A Distinct Method of Riding and Schooling Horses and of Learning to Ride. 2nd ed. Princeton, NJ: Van Nostrand, 1963. 370p.

1940 _____. Schooling Your Horse. Princeton, NJ: Van Nostrand, 1956. 177p.

1941 McCrary, Emma J. Influencing Horses. Ft. Collins, CO: Printed Horse, 1973. 181p.

1942 McNair, Tom. "Bold and Beautiful." Horse and Rider, XVIII (May 1979), 16-21.

1943 McPherson, Mary. "Heads Up Horse Handling." Horse and Rider, XI (March 1972), 18-26.

1944 Mayhew, Edward. The Illustrated Horse Management. N. Hollywood, CA: Wilshire Books, 1972. 548p.

1945 Peacock, Gordon. Professional Western Training: Ranch Reining, Pleasure Roping. Aberdeen, SD: North Plains Press, 1977. 205p.

144 / Equestrian Studies

1946 Podhajsky, Alois. My Horses, My Teachers. Garden City,
NY: Doubleday, 1968. 202p.

1947 Prince, Eleanor F. and G. M. Collier. Basic Training for
Horses: English and Western. Garden City, NY: Doubleday, 1979. 427p.

1948 Pullein-Thompson, Josephine. How Horses Are Trained. London: Routledge and Kegan Paul, 1961. 138p.

1949 Reiche, Oswald. Dog, Goat, and Horse Training: A Handbook
of Tricks and Other Skills for Animals at Home, on the
Stage, on the Farm, or on the Hunt. New York: Exposition
Press, 1963. 67p.

1950 Ricci, A. James. Understanding and Training Horses. Philadelphia: Lippincott, 1964. 146p.

1951 Rickaby, Fred. Are Your Horses Trying? London: J. A.
Allen, 1967. 191p.

1952 Rogers, Tex, ed. Training the Young Horse. Houston, TX:
Cordovan Corp., 1975. 114p.

1953 Rose, Mary. The Horsemaster's Notebook. Rev. ed. London:
Harrap, 1977. 230p.

1954 _____. Training Your Own Horse. London: Harrap, 1977.
217p.

1955 Sikes, L. N., with Bob Gray. Training Tips for Western
Riders. 5 vols. Houston, TX: Horseman Books, 1960-
1974.

1956 Simmons, Diane C. "No Artificial Flavor." Horse and Rider,
XVIII (May 1980), 16-21, 46-47.

1957 Skelton, Elizabeth C. Horses and Riding. London: S. Paul,
1974. 122p.

1958 Stephenson, Red. "Give Him Room for Mistakes." Horse and
Rider, XI (June-July 1972), 19-26, 44-48.

1959 Stillwagon, Patricia. How to Deal with a Horse. New York:
Arco, 1975. 47p.

1960 Summerhays, Reginald S. Its a Good Life with Horses. London: Country Life, 1951. 144p.

1961 _____. A Lifetime with Horses. London: Kaye, 1962.
160p.

1962 Thompson, Terry and Jeanne O'Malley. Training the Performance Horse: From Western Pleasure to Reining. Philadelphia: Lippincott, 1979. 144p.

1963 "Training California Style." Horse and Rider, XIII (August 1974), 16-33.

1964 Vasiloff, Mary J. Alone with Your Horse. New York: Harper & Row, 1978. 385p.

1965 Wanklyn, Joan. Training the Young Pony. 2nd ed. London: British Horse Society, 1964. 118p.

1966 Wells, Jerry. "Do-It-Yourself Training Program." Horse and Rider, XII (June 1973), 14-23, 48.

1967 Wheatley, George. Schooling a Young Horse. South Brunswick, NJ: A. S. Barnes, 1968. 114p.

1968 Williams, Moyra. Adventures Unbridled. London: Methuen, 1960, 199p.

1969 Williams, Vivian D. S. Basic Training for Young Horses and Ponies. Woodbury, NY: Barron's Educational Service, 1977. 63p.

1970 Williamson, Charles O. Breaking and Training the Stock Horse. 6th ed. Hamilton, MT: Williamson School of Horsemanship, 1973. 125p.

1971 Young, John R. "Proper Schooling Methods." Horseman, XXIII (May 1979), 24-29.

1972 _____. Schooling of the Western Horse. Norman: University of Oklahoma Press, 1954. 322p.

B TRAINING

1 Specific Techniques

a Breaking, Starting, and Gentling

1973 Blazer, Don. "Four Faults of Faulty Leads." Horse and Horseman, VI (February 1979), 30-33.

1974 _____. "Hackamore for Starting Reschooling." Horse and Horseman, VII (March 1979), 22-25.

1975 _____. "Start Colts Right." Horse and Horseman, VII (June 1979), 34-37.

1976 Blessinger, D. "Ground Gentling a Range Bronc." Western Horseman, XXXIX (May 1974), 74+.

146 / Equestrian Studies

1977 Chamberlain, Lyle B. You Can Break Your Own Horse: A Treatise on How a Dude Can Break His Personal Mount. Cisco, TX: Longhorn Press, 1970. 62p.

1978 Close, Pat. "A Different Way to Break a Colt." Western Horseman, XLV (January 1980), 48-55.

1979 _____. "Teaching Your Horse to Ground-Tie." Western Horseman, XLI (November 1976), 46-49.

1980 Costin, Richard. "Breaking (?) or Gentling?" Horse and Rider, XVIII (October 1979), 34-37.

1981 Crotty, Dan. Colt Breaking and Training. London: J. A. Allen, 1952. 87p.

1982 Danits, Bob. "The Whip-Broke Horse." Western Horseman, XLV (July 1980), 24-28.

1983 Davis, Ray. "Dorothy Dunn, Starting Arabian Colts." Western Horseman, XL (May 1975), 62-64, 171-173.

1984 Enk, Bill. "Starting the Stock Horse." Horse and Rider, XI (April 1972), 19-24.

1985 Faudel-Phillips, Henry F. Breaking and Schooling and Other Horse Knowledge Practised and Proved. London: J. A. Allen, 1962. 136p.

1986 Fillis, James. Breaking and Riding. Ft. Collins, CO: Printed Horse, 1975. 359p.

1987 Hough, Emerson. "Man Against Bronco." In: Charles Neider, ed. Man Against Nature. New York: Harper, 1954. pp. 274-284.

1988 How to Break and Train the Western Horse. Omaha, NE: Farnam Horse Library, 1976. 64p.

1989 Jones, Dave. "The Basics of Breaking Colts." Horse and Horseman, VII (March 1979), 36-40.

1990 _____. "Be Gentle with Colts." Horse and Horseman, VI (February 1979), 22-26.

1991 Madlener, Elizabeth. "Putting Your Horse on the Bit." Practical Horseman, V (March-April, July 1979), 36-45, 36-43, 40-45.

1992 _____. _____. West Chester, PA: Practical Horseman, 1979. Unpaged.

1993 Murray, Robbie. The Gentle Art of Horse Breaking. South Brunswick, NJ: A. S. Barnes, 1979. 93p.

1994   Neilan, Harold. I Broke Horses with the Indians. Waubay,
        SD, 1976. 60p.

1995   Palethorpe, Dawn. My Horses and I. London: Country Life,
        1956. 60p.

1996   Pattie, Jane. "Breaking Them for Ranch Work." Horse and
        Rider, XVI (June 1976), 16-20, 65-66.

1997   _____. "Tom McNair Says 'Just Snap Your Fingers.'"
        Horse and Rider, XVIII (February 1979), 28-31.

1998   _____. "The Proper Lead." Horse and Rider, XIV (July
        1975), 18-23, 36.

1999   Robnett, Don. How to Break and Train a Horse in Ten Days.
        Ft. Worth, TX, 1976. 50p.

2000   Sandall, Tony. Horse Breaking. London: Whitcombe and
        Tombs, 1965. 72p.

2001   Shanklin, Bill. "Don't Let 'em Pitch." Horse and Rider, IX
        (March 1970), 16-20.

2002   Smillie, Jack. "Gentle and School." Western Horseman, XLIV
        (July 1979), 24-28.

2003   Spencer, Dick, 3rd. Horse Breaking. Colorado Springs, CO:
        Western Horseman, 1967. 36p.

                b   Conditioning, Exercise and Balance

2004   Abhau, Elliot. "Putting the Cart Before the Horse." Horse
        Lover's National Magazine, XLV (April 1980), 54-61.
            Exercise.

2005   Anderson, M. M. "Soundness Lesson of the Three-Day Event."
        Horseman, XXIII (May 1979), 66-68.

2006   Blazer, Don. "Supplying the Western Horse." Horse and
        Horseman, VI (January 1979), 22-25.

2007   Bond, Marian. "How Dressage Exercises Can Help Your Horse."
        Horseman, XXII (December 1978), 52-54.

2008   Burkhardt, Barbara. "Body-Building Exercises for Your Horse."
        Western Horseman, XLI (December 1976), 72-73.

2009   Cash, C. K. "Bareback Exercises for Fun and Better Horse-
        manship." Western Horseman, XLV (January 1980), 80-82.

2010   Close, Pat. "Richard Shrake Describes Bareback Exercises to Make You a Better Rider." Western Horseman, XLII (March 1977), 70-74.

2011 "Forum: What's the Best Way to Achieve Rider Fitness?" Practical Horseman, VIII (June 1980), 18-21.

2012 Fraser, Carol. "Proper Balance Is the Name of the Game." Horse and Rider, IX (July-August 1970), 28-32, 58-64.

2013 Griffith, Perry B. "Back Exercises for Riders." Horse and Horseman, VII (February 1980), 16-21.

2014 _____. "Supplying the English Horse." Horse and Horseman, VI (February 1979), 38-41.

2015 Hay, Cheryl. "Exercises to Improve Your Horse." American Horseman, IV (October 1974), 33, 58-59.

2016 Honk, Jerry. "Winning: On Condition." Horse and Rider, XIII (March-April 1974), 43-49, 50-55.

2017 Kester, Wayne O. "Endurance Commandments." Horse and Horseman, VII (March 1979), 14-15.

2018 McNutt, Patty. "Conditioning for Long Distance Trail Riding." Horse of Course, VII (November 1978), 12-20.

2019 McPherson, Mary. "Exercise in Training." Horse and Rider, IX (September 1970), 16-21, 62-65.

2020 Madlener, Elizabeth. "The Sitting Trot." Practical Horseman, VII (June 1979), 38-46.

2021 Meister, Betty J. "Conditioning Your Horse for the Hunting Field." Practical Horseman, V (July 1977), 34-38.

2022 Meredith, Kay. "Counter-Canter, an Exercise in Discipline." Dressage and CT, XI (December 1976), 24.

2023 _____. "Dressage Balance and Dynamics." Horse and Rider, XVII (February 1978), 46-48.

2024 Miller, Robert M. "Exercises." Western Horseman, XXXIX (November 1974), 130-131.

2025 Nesbitt, Caroline H. "Ride the Balanced Seat." Horse of Course, V (October 1976), 18-21.

2026 O'Connor, Sally. "Practical Evening: Conditioning." Dressage and CT, XIII (July 1977), 21-24.

2027 O'Malley, Jeanne. "Horseback Exercising Can Improve Your Balance." Horseman, XVII (May 1973), 40-46.

2028 Rooney, James R. "Balance." Practical Horseman, VII (January 1979), 30-37.

2029 Swope, Jane. "Mounted Exercises." Horse of Course, IX (June 1980), 66-69.

2030 Wagoner, Don M. Conditioning to Win. Dallas, TX: Equine Research Publications, 1974. 312p.

2031 Wilkinson, Tolbert S. "Proper Harnessing of the Female Dressage Rider." Dressage and CT, XIII (August-September 1977), 18, 19-20.
      Conditioning.

2032 Young, John R. "Successful Conditioning." Horseman, XXIII (June 1979), 52-56.

      c Stopping, Backing, Turning and Sidestepping

2033 Blaylock, Joe. "Schooling the Young Horse in Roll-Backs and Stops." Western Horseman, XLIV (December 1979), 24-26.

2034 Blazer, Don. "Stop Right Now." Horse and Horseman, VI (October 1978), 22-24.

2035 _____. "Teach Your Horse to Slide Stop." Horse and Horseman, III (November 1975), 26-31.

2036 _____. "Teach Your Horse to Spin." Horse and Horseman, V (October 1977), 54-58.

2037 Bloom, Lynda. "Ellen Shaw: Teaching a Morgan to Stretch." Western Horseman, XLIII (April 1978), 8-10.

2038 Bond, Marian. "California-Style Turns." Horseman, XXIV (April 1980), 20-24.

2039 Close, Pat. "Circles, Changes, Spins, and Stops, with Paul Horn." Western Horseman, XLI (April 1976), 48-51, 120-122.

2040 Connell, Ed. "Teaching the Stop and Turn." Horse and Horseman, V (January 1978), 38-41.

2041 Davis, Ray. "Training Them to Back, with Billy Steele." Western Horseman, XLI (September 1976), 56-57.

2042 Hanson, Valerie. "Leg Pressure." Horse and Rider, XI (June 1972), 32-34.

2043 _____. "Tidbits for Beginners [on Side-Stepping]." Horse and Rider, XII (February 1973), 36-39.

2044 Hooper, Freia I. "How to Restrain Your Horse." Horse and Horseman, VII (September 1979), 26-29.

2045 Hurley, Jimmie. "Ken Luman Describes the Ideal Heeling Horse." Western Horseman, XXXIX (July 1974), 18-20, 122.

2046 Langston, Steve. "Backing." Horse Lover's National Magazine, XLIII (December 1978), 56-58.

2047 Meredith, Kay. "Flying Changes." Dressage and CT, XIV (January 1978), 16-17.

2048 Meyer, Heinz and Gustav Menke. "Natural Obliqueness, Back Movers, and Leg Movers." Dressage and CT, XIV (May 1978), 12-17.

2049 Richards, Rusty. "Your Horse Can Learn to Pack" Horse and Horseman, II (April 1972), 40-43, 67-68.

2050 Russell, Shorty. "How I Teach Roll-Backs." Western Horseman, XLIV (September 1979), 24-26.

2051 Smith, Donna. "Side Stepping, Step-by-Step." Horse and Rider, IX (April 1970), 28-30.

2052 Stecken, Albert. "Pirquettes and Flying Changes." Dressage and CT, XV (October 1978), 16-17.

d Longeing

2053 Bond, Marian. "Leadin', Loadin' and Longein'." Horse and Rider, XIII (November 1974), 32-36.

2054 Chrisley, Katharine. "Longeing Principles." Horse and Horseman, VIII (April 1980), 14-17.

2055 DeKunffy, Charles. "The Development of Horse and Rider: Longeing Exercises." Dressage and CT, XVI (February 23, 1979), 7-10.

2056 Ferguson, Joe. "Schooling on the Longe." Practical Horseman, III (November-December 1974), passim; IV (January-February 1975), passim.

2057 Froissard, Jean. "Your Work on the Longe Line." Dressage and Ct, XVII (April 1980), 19-21.

2058 Inderwick, Sheila. Longeing the Horse and Rider. London: David and Charles, 1977. 91p.

2059 McCall, James P. "Step-by-Step Tackless Training." Practi-

cal Horseman, VI (September-December 1978), 37-43, 25-
30, 39-45, 39-44.

2060 _____. Tackless Training: A No-Restraint Method for
Breaking and Training Your Horse. West Chester, PA:
Practical Horseman, 1979. 25p.

2061 McHam, Dedi. "Basic Ground Work." Horse and Rider, XVIII
(June 1979), 34-38.

2062 Meredith, Kay. "Longeing Out the Kinks." Horse and Rider,
XVI (September 1976), 38-40.

2063 _____. "A Spoonful of Longeing." Dressage and CT, X
(June 1976), 19.

2064 Page, Stephen M. "Reflections on Longeing." Dressage and
CT: XIV (March 1978), 12-14.

2065 Pattie, Jane. "Start Your Horse: Ground Driving." Horse
and Rider, XIII (September 1974), 37-48.

2066 Plum, Meg. "Training Techniques on the Longe Line." Practical Horseman, V (August 1977), 6-13.

2067 Tokar, Randi. "Going in Circles." Horse and Rider, XVI
(February 1977), 28-31.

2068 Wilde, Louise M. "The Use of Longeing in Dressage." Western Horseman, XXXVI (August 1971), 26-28+.

2069 Williamson, Marion B. "Longeing in Luxury." Horseman,
XVIII (August 1973), 66-73.

2 Specific Purposes

a Racing

2070 Blazer, Don. "Retraining the Race Horse." Horse and Rider,
XIV (August 1975), 16-22.

2071 Brown, Frank A. Sport From Within. London: Hutchinson,
1952. 230p.

2072 Burch, Preston M. "Tex." "Training and Handling Race
Horses." Western Horseman, XL (October 1975), 48-50,
126-128.

2073 _____. Training Thoroughbred Horses. Rev. ed. Lexington, KY: Blood Horse, 1967. 130p.

2074 Collins, Robert W. Race Horse Training. Lexington, KY:
Thoroughbred Record Company, 1972.

2075 Coma, Anthony S. Preparing the Thoroughbred: A Trainer's Guide. South Brunswick, NJ: A. S. Barnes, 1972. 84p.

2076 Dale, Gareth. Bracken Horse. London: Lutterworth Press, 1960. 159p.

2077 Davis, Ray. "Prep Training for Racing Colts." Western Horseman, XXXVIII (February 1973), 24-26, 139-143.

2078 _____. "Training for the Track, with Jack Hughes." Western Horseman, XXXVII (March-April 1972), 54+, 30-31, 178-180.

2079 _____. "Training Racing Colts, with Eileen Coffman." Western Horseman, XXXIX (February 1974), 60-61, 122-125.

2080 Fenwick-Palmer, Roderic. Out of the Ruck: Advice to National Hunt Breeder, Owner, and Trainer. London: J. A. Allen, 1961. 192p.

2081 Fitzgeorge-Parker, Tim. Training the Racehorse. London: Pelham Books, 1973. 204p.

2082 _____. Vincent O'Brien: A Long Way from Tipperary. London: Pelham Books, 1974. 91p.

2083 Gibson, Francis. Gibby: The Memoirs of a Horsey Man. London: J. A. Allen, 1978.

2084 Harrison, James C. Care and Training of the Trotter and Pacer. Columbus, OH: United States Trotting Association, 1968. 1,054p.

2085 Herbert, Ivor. [Fred] Winter's Tale: Study of a Stable. London: Pelham Books, 1974. 186p.

2086 _____. "In His Heart He [Vincent O'Brien] Has a Hunger." Classic, III (June-July 1978), 84-93.

2087 Jarvis, Jack. They're Off. London: Joseph, 1969. 160p.

2088 Joyce, Patrick. Horse and Man. London: Odhams, 1965. 45p.

2089 Marsh, Marcus. Racing with the Gods. London: Pelham Books, 1968. 166p.

2090 Marshall, John H. Horseman: Memoirs. London: Bodley Head, 1970. 336p.

2091 Martin, Ann. The Trainers. London: S. Paul, 1972. 192p.

2092 Stewart, Patrick D. Training the Racehorse. Rev. ed. London: S. Paul, 1959. 151p.

2093 Tristram, Dennis. "Training the Candidate." Horse and Rider, XVIII (June 1979), 40-43.

2094 Williams, Dorian. Master of One: An Autobiography. London: J. M. Dent, 1978. 235p.

b Jumping

2095 Abbey, Harlan. "Seeing Red." Horse and Rider, XVIII (January 1979), 39-42.

2096 Alverson, Donna and Sandy Vaughn. "Willing Jumpers." Horse and Rider, XVII (August-September 1978), 42-46, 22-27.

2097 Baker, Jerry. "Jerry Baker's Seven-Day Training Schedule for Hunters and Jumpers." Practical Horseman, IV (July 1975), passim.

2098 _____. "Objective: The World's Best String of Show Jumpers." Practical Horseman, VII (March 1979), 6-11.

2099 _____. "Riding Grand Prix Fences: The Effort Behind the Execution." Practical Horseman, IV (May 1975), passim.

2100 Bloom, Lynda. "Jumping Self Taught." Horse of Course, II (October 1973), 24-27.

2101 Bond, Marian. "High Jumping in a Long Way." Horse and Rider, XIII (January 1974), 68-72.

2102 _____. "Jumping, with Marvin Mayfield." Western Horseman, XXXVIII (January 1973), 66-67, 100-102.

2103 _____. "The Rusty Gait." Horse and Rider, XIV (January 1975), 62-65.

2104 Chamberlin, Harry D. Training Hunters, Jumpers, and Hacks. 2nd ed. New York: Van Nostrand-Reinhold, 1970. 329p.

2105 "A Cinema-Computer Analysis of Equestrain Jumping Techniques." Horse World, I (Fall 1980), 18-23.

2106 D'Ambrosio, Anthony, with Steven D. Price. "Teaching Your Horse to Jump." Practical Horseman, VI (May-August 1978), 9-14, 63-66, 57-62, 39-42.

2107 Davis, Ray. "Jumping, with Angela Morton." Western Horseman, XXXVI (May 1971), 80-82, 186.

2108 Dayton, Jay. "One for the Money." Horse and Rider, XII (March 1973), 68-72.

2109 Diechelbohrer, Paul and Diana. "Making the Jump." Horse Lover's National Magazine, XLIV (August 1979), 43-46.

2110 Dillon, Jane M. Form Over Fences: A Pictorial Critique of Jumping for Junior Riders. New York: Arco, 1972. 132p.

2111 Douglass, Dana. "Step-by-Step Troubleshooting for Hunters and Jumpers." Practical Horseman, VIII (July 1980), 33-41.

2112 Fitch, C. G. Best Jumpers in Training. London, 1951. 20p.

2113 Fredricson, Ingvar, et al. Horses and Jumping. Translated from the Norwegian. London: Pelham Books, 1976. 118p.

2114 Froissard, Jean. Jumping: Learning and Teaching. South Brunswick, NJ: A. S. Barnes, 1971. 204p.

2115 Green, Carol. Jumping Explained. New York: Arco, 1977. 96p.

2116 Griffith, Perry B. "The Mechanics of Jumping." Horse and Horseman, VI (September-December 1978), 32-33, 51, 50-53, 46-49, 48-51.

2117 Hankins, Cynthia. "Fundamentals of Flat Work for Jumpers." Practical Horseman, V (October-December 1977), 12-15, 27-29, 25-31.

2118 Hasseman, Mary K. "Revised Hunt Seat Riding." Horse and Horseman, III (August 1975), 38-41, 45.

2119 Heuckeroth, Patty. "Teaching Your Horse to Jump Straight." Practical Horseman, VIII (April 1980), 58.

2120 Hill, Ralph. "Teaching Your Horse Cross-Country Jumping." Practical Horseman, VII (August-December 1979), 20-29, 25-28, 28-36, 44-50, 42-49.

2121 Hurley, Jimmie. "A Can of Worms." Horse and Rider, XVIII (February 1979), 32-35.

2122 Jones, Mrs. R. C. Jumps for Pennies. Tatum, N.M., 1972. 16p.

2123 Jones, Suzanne N. "Approach and Refusal." Horseman, XXIII (December 1978), 42-46.

2124 Kirschner, Michael. Forward Freely: The Forward System. South Brunswick, NJ: A. S. Barnes, 1967. 144p.

2125 Levings, H. Patricia. Training the Quarter Horse Jumper. South Brunswick, NJ: A. S. Barnes, 1968. 117p.

2126 Littauer, Vladimir. "How a Jump Begins." Practical Horseman, II (March-June 1972), passim.

2127 Monahan, Katie. "How to Find Your Distance to the Fence." Practical Horseman, VII (April 1979), 8-15.

2128 _____. "Riding Clinic." Horse and Rider, XVI (March 1976), 8-13.

2129 "Philosophy of Jumping." Horse and Rider, IX (September-October 1969), passim.

2130 "Quarter Horse Jumping." Horse and Rider, VII (June 1968), passim.

2131 Robertson, R. L. "How You Can Start Your Horse Over Fences." Western Horseman, XLI (August 1976), 12-17.

2132 Roye, Lilian W. "Training Your Jumper with Dressage." Rapidan River Farm Digest, I (Winter 1975), 81-92.

2133 Self, Margaret C. Jumping Simplified. New York: Ronald Press, 1959. 80p.

2134 Sherred, Alison P. "Releasing, Relaxing, and Learning by Mistakes." Classic, II (August-September 1977), 106-111.

2135 Stewart, Stephanie. "Training Your Western Horse to Jump." Western Horseman, XXXIX (April 1974), 74-75, 100-102.

2136 "Techniques of Jumping." Horse and Rider, VII (September 1968), passim.

2137 Watson, Brenda. "The Training of 'George.'" Practical Horseman, VIII (July 1980), 6-11.

2138 Weaver, Charlie. "The Making and Training of a Champion." Practical Horseman, VII (February 1979), 6-14.

c Dressage and Combined Training

2139 Abhau, Elliot. "What Is This Thing Called Combined Training?" Horse Lover's National Magazine, XLIII (June 1978), 25-27, 50-51.

2140 DeKunffy, Charles. "On Engagement and Daily Riding Strategies." Dressage and CT, XVI (March 23, 1979), 11-12.

2141 Gurney, Hilda. "Sequential Schooling of the Dressage Horse."

Dressage and CT, XV (September-December 1978), 21-22,
14-15, 20-21, 15-17; XVI (February 9, March 9, April 6,
May 4, and June 1, 1979), 14-16, 14-16, 8-10, 11-13.

2142 Klime, Reiner. Cavaletti: Schooling of Horse and Rider Over
Ground Rails. Translated from the German. London: J.
A. Allen, 1969. 128p.

2143 Mallorca, Jackie. "The Making (I Trust) of a Dressage Horse,
by a Non-Expert." Dressage and CT, XV (May 4-June 1,
1979), 6-8, 12-13, 6-8.

2144 Meredith, Kay. "Avenue for Advancement." Dressage and CT,
XIII (September-October 1977), 14, 28; XIV (January-April,
1978), 16, 18, 15; XV (November-December 1978), 26, 28.

2145 _____. "Direction and Flexion." Horse and Rider, XVII
(August 1978), 36-37.

2146 _____. "Dressage for Beginners." Dressage and CT, VII
(July-December 1974), 18, 42, 77, 110, 136, 167; VIII
(January-June 1975), 20, 26, 22, 16, 14, 20; IX (July-
December 1975), 16, 22, 14, 20, 22, 20; X (January-Feb-
ruary, April-May, 1976), 16, 24, 19, 20.

2147 _____. "Fear--The Greatest Obstacle of All." Dressage
and CT, XII (May 1977), 12.

2148 _____. "The Rubber Band Effect." Practical Horseman,
V (June 1977), 31-33.

2149 _____. "Stiff and Hollow Sides." Horse and Rider, XVII
(May 1978), 38-40.

2150 _____. "Work and Willingness." Horse and Rider, XVII
(July 1978), 48-49.

2151 Mikolka, Karl. "The Correct Use of the Riding Whip and the
Circle of Aids." Dressage and CT, X (March 1976), 16-19.

2152 Mizwa, Tad S. "Dressage Basics for Barrel Racing." Horseman, XXII (October 1978), 22-23.

2153 Nelson, Mary J. "Dressage: Cure for Equine Faults?" Horse
and Horseman, III (August 1975), 20-22, 35, 71.

2154 Podhajsky, Alois. The Complete Training of Horse and Rider
in the Principles of Classical Horsemanship. Garden City,
NY: Doubleday, 1967. 287p.

2155 Pohlman, Helen S. "Dressage Can Help Train Your Horse."
Western Horseman, XXXVIII (July 1978), 109-112.

2156 "Practical Dressage Training." Horse and Rider, VII (November 1968), passim.

2157 Szalla, Peter. "Work in Hand: From the Start to the First Step of Piaffe." Dressage and CT, XIV (February 1978), 14-17.

2158 Twelveponies, Mary. "Combined Training: Method Behind the Madness." Horse and Horseman, VI (March 1978), 18-21.

2159 _____. "Everyday Training (Backyard Dressage)." Horse and Horseman, V (March-December 1977, January 1978), 22-24, 64-65, 14-19, 34-37, 56-58, 54-57, 30-37, 38-43, 38-41, 38-46, 30-37.

d Three-Day Event

2160 Abhau, Elliot. "The Blessed Event." Horse Lover's National Magazine, XLIV (October 1979), 52-67.

2161 O'Connor, Sally. "Practical Evening: Moving Up to Training Level." Dressage and CT, XIV (July 1978), 24-25.

2162 Rose, Mary. "Training Your Own Event Horse: Beginner Courses for Beginner Horses." Dressage and CT, X (March 1976), 16-18.

2163 Willcox, Shelia. The Event Horse. Philadelphia: Lippincott, 1973. 145p.

e Barrel Racing

2164 Davis, Ray. "Ann Bateson: Barrel Racing Training." Western Horseman, XLII (August 1977), 10-12.

2165 _____. "Barrel Horse Trainer, Nelda Patton." Western Horseman, XXXIX (August 1974), 72-76+.

2166 _____. "Patti Prather: Barrel Racing Basics for Young Horses." Western Horseman, XLIV (November 1979), 6-12.

2167 _____. "Training and Correcting Barrel Horses, with Nita Jacobs." Western Horseman, XXXVIII (September 1973), 14-17, 110-115.

2168 _____. "Training for Pole Bending, with Valeda Tretbar." Western Horseman, XLI (August 1976), 22-26.

2169 _____. "Training, with Karen Russell." Western Horseman, XL (February 1975), 40-41, 90-91.

2170 Gayler, Allene. "Building a Barreler." Horse and Rider, XII (December 1973), 44-47.

2171 Loomis, Joyce. "Roll 'em Out." Horse and Rider, XIII (August-September 1974), 68-73, 18-23.

2172 Taylor, Louis. "Taking the Barrels: How to Start and How to Win." Horse Lover's National Magazine, XLII (August 1977), 23-27.

2173 Thurman, Sherry. "How I Train Barrel Horses." Western Horseman, XLIII (January 1978), 8-9.

2174 Youree, Dale. Training and Riding the Barrel Horse. Colorado Springs, CO: Western Horseman, 1970. 48p.

f Cutting

2175 Clevenger, Barbara. "The Basics of Cattle Cutting." Horseman, XXII (July 1978), 32-37.

2176 Close, Pat. "Leon Harrel: A Cutting Horse's Silent Partner." Western Horseman, XLIII (August 1978), 46-49.

2177 _____. "Ronnie Richards: Training a Stock Horse to Handle a Cow." Western Horseman, XXXIX (August 1974), 14-18+.

2178 Davis, Ray. "Chuck DeHaan's Cutting Horse Techniques." Western Horseman, XLI (September 1976), 22-26.

2179 _____. "Cutting Horse Trainer Jerry Reece." Western Horseman, XLI (March 1976), 30-32, 107-108.

2180 _____. "Ranch Cutting Horses, with Buddy Wheelis." Western Horseman, XXXVIII (October 1973), 89-90, 172-173.

2181 _____. "Training Cutting Horses, with Keith Barnett." Western Horseman, XL (March 1975), 66-67, 143-145.

2182 _____. "Training Cutting Horses, with Sonny Rice." Western Horseman, XXXIX (November 1974), 34-36, 150-151.

2183 Sage, Dean. Training and Riding the Cutting Horse. Colorado Springs, CO: Western Horseman, 1961. 56p.

2184 Tully, Curly. "The Early Training of a Cutting Horse." Western Horseman, XLII (December 1977), 10-14.

2185 Young, John R. Arizona Cutting Horse. Philadelphia: Westminster Press, 1956. 207p.

g Halter

2186 Blazer, Don. "Producing Halter Winners." Horse and Horse-man, VII (April 1979), 28-31.

2187 Bloom, Lynda. Fitting and Showing the Halter Horse. New York: Arco, 1979. 96p.

2188 _____. "Mannering and Showing Halter Stallions." Western Horseman, XLIV (January 1979), 46-52.

2189 _____. "Tim Kane: Preparing the Halter Horse." Western Horseman, XLIII (December 1978), 22-26.

2190 Bond, Marian. "Training the Arab at Halter." Horse and Rider, XVII (March 1978), 42-49.

2191 Gibbs, D. "Building a Champion." Horseman, XXII (April 1978), 24-30.

2192 Janssen, Alfred, 3rd. "The Donns Discuss Conditioning the Yearling for Halter." Western Horseman, XXXVIII (June 1973), 22-24, 144-148.

2193 Pattie, Jane. "Wild or Mild?" Horse and Rider, XVII (December 1979), 24-29.

2194 Tyler, George. "Halter Hints for Novice Showmen." Horse-man, XVII (June 1973), 18-32.

2195 _____. "Selecting, Fitting, and Training the Halter Horse." Western Horseman, XLII (July 1977), 12-13, 99.

h Reining

2196 Abhau, Elliot. "Learning the Alphabet." Horse Lover's National Magazine, XLIV (January 1980), 51-61.

2197 Bond, Marion. "Bill Warne Talks About Training the Reining Horse." Western Horseman, XXXVIII (November 1973), 34-36, 184-187.

2198 Close, Pat. "Billy Allen Talks About Reining Horses." Western Horseman, XXXVI (September 1971), 4-7, 162-164.

2199 Connell, Ed. Hackamore Reinsman. Cisco, TX: Longhorn Press, 1975. 76p.

2200 _____ and Jack Carroll. "Hackamore Horse." Horse and Rider, X (August 1971), 17-22.

2201 Garrison, James. "Training Reining Horses." Western Horseman, XLIII (February 1978), 14-16.

2202 Kohler, June. "Reining Basics." Horse and Rider, XVII (August 1978), 22-26.

2203 Loomis, Bob. "Runs and Reins." Horse and Rider, XI (February 1972), 16-21.

2204 McCann, Tom. How to Train the Reining Horse. Omaha, NE: Farnam Horse Library, 1979. 64p.

2205 Phinney, Peter and Jack Brainard. Training the Reining Horse. South Brunswick, NJ: A. S. Barnes, 1977. 109p.

2206 Simmons, Diane C. "Reining Training." Horse and Rider, XVIII (August 1979), 24-29.

2207 Tavares, Nancee. "The Five Rein Effects." Horse and Rider, XVI (September 1977), 16-19.

i Roping

2208 Davis, Ray. "Marvin Cantrell, Rope Horse Training." Western Horseman, XXXV (September 1970), 74-78, 190-194.

2209 _____. "Ray Wharton, Rope Horse Trainer." Western Horseman, XXXVI (January 1971), 36-38, 122-126.

2210 King, Chuck. "Dale Carroll: Philosophy of a Rope Horse Trainer." Western Horseman, XLV (January 1980), 8-10.

2211 _____. "Dan Branco Talks About Horsemanship for the Beginning Team Roper." Western Horseman, XXXIX (August 1974), 78-81.

2212 Nelson, Michael C. How to Train the Roping Horse. Omaha, NE: Farnam Horse Library, 1979. 64p.

2213 Stephens, Danny. "Training the Race Horse for Roping." Western Horseman, XLV (April 1980), 16-18.

2214 "Train Calf Roping Horses." Horse and Horseman, I (May 1973), passim.

j Steer Wrestling

2215 Davis, Ray. "Steer Wrestling Technique, with C. R. Boucher." Western Horseman, XXXVIII (April 1973), 82-83, 151-154.

2216 Hurley, Jimmie. "Roy Duvall Discusses the Ideal Steer-Wrestling Horse." Western Horseman, XXXVII (June 1972), 66-67, 119.

k Driving

2217 Conder, Allan D. Training the Driving Pony. New York: Arco, 1977. 96p.

2218 Davis, Ray. "Driving Training, with Marjorie Bain." Western Horseman, XL (February 1975), 46, 106-107.

2219 Gaines, David. "Sleigh Training." Horseman, XXII (December 1978), 24-30.

2220 Ganton, Doris L. Breaking and Training the Driving Horse: A Detailed and Comprehensive Study. N. Hollywood, CA: Wilshire Books, 1976. 81p.

2221 _____. Drive On: Training and Showing the Advanced Driving Horse. South Brunswick, NJ: A. S. Barnes, 1979.

2222 Kellogg, Charles. Driving the Horse in Harness: Training and Technique for Pleasure and Performance. Brattleboro, VT: Stephen Greene Press, 1978. 182p.

2223 Skobalski, E. "Training a Saddle Horse to Harness." Western Horseman, XXXIX (June 1974), 46+.

l Trail Riding

2224 Bond, Marian. "Billy Harris Offers Tips on Training for the Trail." Western Horseman, XXXVIII (June 1973), 30, 149.

2225 Davis, Ray. "Cecil and Ann Hurley: Training for a Bridal Path Hack." Western Horseman, XXXIX (July 1974), 106-107, 176-179.

2226 Sordillo, Darlene. Training and Showing the Western Trail Horse. New York: Arco, 1975. 175p.

2227 Trantham, Ronnie. "Training for the Trail." Horse and Rider, X (June 1971), 18-24.

C PROBLEMS OF TRAINING

2228 Bayens, Cheri. "Getting Soiled by the Spoiled." Horse and Rider, XVII (July-August 1978), 42-46, 38-41.

2229 Bloom, Lynda. "Bob Armizo on Correcting a Horse that Runs Through the Bridle." Western Horseman, XLIII (September 1978), 34-42.

2230 _____. "Tommy Sondgroth: Working with a Lazy Performance Horse." Western Horseman, XLII (July 1977), 136-139.

2231 _____. "The Urge to Kill." Horse and Rider, XVIII (October 1979), 38-43.

2232 _____. "Working with the Hot-Headed Horse." Western Horseman, XLIV (August 1979), 8-10.

2233 Davis, Ray. "Correcting a Charging Cutting Horse, with Jerry Belew." Western Horseman, XXXVIII (June 1973), 42-43, 175-176.

2234 _____. "Correcting a Charging Roping Horse, with Bryant Foster." Western Horseman, XXXIX (January 1974), 45-46, 109.

2235 _____. "Curing Barn-Sour Horses, with Matlock Rose." Western Horseman, XXXVI (June 1971), 26-27, 106-107.

2236 Dow, Betty. "Retraining Problem Horses." Practical Horseman, IV (December 1976), passim.

2237 "Forum: How Do You Cope With a Horse That Pulls?" Practical Horseman, VI (April 1978), 18-20.

2238 "Forum: How Do You Correct a Horse That Bites?" Practical Horseman, VI (May 1978), 26-27.

2239 "Forum: How Do You Deal With a Horse That Bucks?" Practical Horseman, V (September 1977), 16-18.

2240 "Forum: How Do You Deal With the Horse That Resists the Correct Canter Lead?" Practical Horseman, VI (February-March 1978), 16-18.

2241 Gayler, Anne. "The Sour Barrel Horse." Western Horseman, XLIV (April 1979), 22-26, 30.

2242 Gilchrist, Bruce. "Correcting Problems in Show Horses." Western Horseman, XLII (April 1977), 62-68.

2243 Hamilton, Samantha. "The Vice Squad: Conquering Your Horse's Behavioral Quirks." Equus, no. 32 (June 1980), 42-46, 68-70.

2244 Hanson, Valerie. "The Horse That Shies." Horse and Rider, XIV (January 1975), 20-23.

2245 Hooper, Freia. "Tame That Baby!" Horse and Rider, XVII (March 1978), 34-36.

2246 Hunt, Ray. "Problem Horses--or Problem People?" Western Horseman, XLII (October 1977), 76-79.

2247 Jones, Dave. The Book of Bad Habits. Omaha, NE: Farnam Horse Library, 1978. 64p.

2248 _____. "How to Tackle the Ten Most Common Training Problems." Horseman, XVIII (August 1973), 18-32.

2249 _____. "Solving Really Tough Problem Horses." Horse and Horseman, VIII (July 1980), 10-14.

2250 _____. "Ten Common Horse Faults." Horse and Horseman, VII (October 1979), 44-47, 59+, 64.

2251 _____. "Training Problems and the Causes." Horse and Horseman, VII (June 1979), 14-18.

2253 Kelly, J. F. Solving Your Horse and Pony Problems. London: Country Life, 1967. 143p.

2254 Lindsey, John. "How to Take the Problem Out of Problem Horses." Horseman, XV (April 1971), 26-40.

2255 Meredith, Byron. "Breaking the Bad Ones." Horse and Rider, XIV (May 1975), 28-34.

2256 Pittenger, Peggy J. Reschooling the Thoroughbred. South Brunswick, NJ: A. S. Barnes, 1966. 172p.

2257 Pitts, Don. "The Spooky Spirit." Horse and Rider, XVI (November 1976), 24-26.

2258 Reynolds, Douglas A. Persuasion, Restraint, Subjection. Reno: Cooperative Extension Service, University of Nevada, 1975. 16p.

2259 Richards, Rusty. "Kicking the Habit." Horse and Horseman, I (January 1974), 20-24, 41.

2260 Sedito, Elaine. "Your Horse Shies Because." Practical Horseman, VII (March 1979), 23-28.

2261 Self, Margaret C. The Problem Horse and the Problem Horseman. New York: Arco, 1977. 144p.

2262 Selman, Charles. "A Cure for Halter Pullers." Horse and Rider, XI (February 1972), 44-45.

2263 Sordillo, Darlene. "Correcting the Ring-Sour Horse." Horseman, XXII (August 1978), 48-51.

2264 Spencer, Dick, 3rd. "Cheeking a Bronc." Western Horseman, XLIV (September 1977), 14-16.

2265 Stabrowski, Rita. "The Spooker." Horseman, XXI (October 1977), 30-40.

2266 Summerhays, Reginald S. The Problem Horse. 2nd ed. New York: Arco, 1977. 96p.

2267 _____ and S. A. Walker. The Controversial Horse: A Conversation Piece. South Brunswick, NJ: A. S. Barnes, 1970. 224p.

2268 Sumner, W. Dayton. Breaking Your Horse's Bad Habits. South Brunswick, NJ: A. S. Barnes, 1976. 220p.

2269 Tollefson, Randi. "The Spoiled Horse." Horse and Rider, X (September 1971), 56-61.

2270 Trantham, Ronnie. "Curing Bad Habits." Horse and Rider, XIII (July 1974), 16-23.

2271 Twelveponies, Mary. "There are No Problem Horses, Only Problem Riders." Horse and Horseman, VI (January-February 1979), 26-29, 46-49; VII (March-June, September 1979), 48-52, 38-41, 38-43, 40-43, 22-25, 57.

Further References: See also Parts IV above and VII, VIII, and X below.

PART VI EQUITATION AND HORSEMANSHIP

A GENERAL WORKS

2272 Albert, Waco W. Showing, Riding, and Driving Horses and
     Ponies. Circular, no. 1114. Champagne: Cooperative
     Extension Service, University of Illinois, 1975. 16p.

2273 Anderson, Clarence W. Complete Book of Horses and Horse-
     manship. New York: Macmillan, 1964. 182p. [juv.]

2274 Baird, Eric. An Illustrated Guide to Riding. Brattleboro, VT:
     Stephen Greene Press, 1980. 176p.

2275 Ballantine, William. Horses and Their Bosses. Philadelphia:
     Lippincott, 1964. 313p.

2276 Barrett, John L. M. Practical Horsemanship. London: Weth-
     erby, 1955. 192p.

2277 Barton, Frank T. Horse Riding for Beginners. London: Foul-
     sham, 1964. 96p.

2278 Beckwith, Brainerd K. Step and Go Together: The World of
     Horses and Horsemanship. New York: Arco, 1974. 345p.

2279 Blazer, Don. Horses Don't Care About Women's Lib. San
     Diego, CA: Joyce Press, 1978. 160p.
     A collection of the author's newspaper articles.

2280 Bloodgood, Linda F. Hoofs in the Distance. Princeton, NJ:
     Van Nostrand, 1953. 131p.

2281 Bloom, Lynda. "Equitation Salvation." Horse and Rider, XVIII
     (January 1979), 31-37.

2282 Bradley, Melvin. Practical and Scientific Horsemanship. New
     York: McGraw-Hill, 1980.

2283 British Horse Society and Sports Council Steering Committee.

165

Riding for Recreation: A Digest of the Report and Recommendations. London: H. M. Stationery Office, 1971. 9p.

2283a Brooke, Geoffrey F. H. Good Company. London: Constable, 1954. 278p.

2284 _____. Horsemanship, Dressage, and Show Jumping: A Practical Book on Horsemanship. Rev. ed. London: Seeley Service, 1959. 316p.

2285 _____. Horsemanship: The Way of a Man With a Horse. Lonsdale Library, v. 1. Woodstock, VT: Countryman, 1956. 288p.

2286 Byrne, Judith M. , ed. Horse Riding the Australian Way. Melbourne, Aust.: Lansdowne Press, 1972. 128p.

2287 Cannam, Peggie. Riding. New York: Arco, 1964. 112p.

2288 Caprilli, Federico. The Caprilli Papers: Principles of Outdoor Equitation. Translated from the Italian. London: J. A. Allen, 1968. 40p.

2289 Cavendish, William, Duke of Newcastle. A General System of Horsemanship, Volume I: A Facsimile of the London Edition of 1743. New York: Winchester Press, 1970. 142p.

2290 Churchill, Peter. Progressive Steps in Riding. New York: Arco, 1966. 84p.

2291 _____. Riding. London: Macdonald and Janes, 1979. 46p.

2292 _____. Riding Dialogue. London: Blandford, 1973. 87p.

2293 _____. Riding from A to Z: A Practical Manual of Horsemanship. New York: Taplinger, 1978. 152p.

2294 Cleaver, Hylton R. They've Won Their Spurs. London: Hale, 1956. 128p.

2295 Codrington, William S. Know Your Horse. 2nd ed. London: J. A. Allen, 1963. 180p.

2296 Coffin, Bobbie. Rider or Horseman? New York: Arco, 1978. 250p.

2297 Crabtree, Helen K. Sports Illustrated Book of Gaited Riding. Philadelphia: Lippincott, 1962. 89p.

2298 Deacon, Alan. Horse Sense: A Complete Guide to Riding and Horse Management. London: Muller, 1971. 164p.

2299 Devereux, Frederick L. Jr. Horseback Riding. New York: 1976. 63p. [juv.]

2300   _____. "Horsemanship." Washington Argicultural Extension
        Bulletin, no. 536 (1962), 1-20.

2301   Ensminger, Marion E. Horses and Horsemanship. 5th ed.
        Danville, IL: Interstate Printers and Publishers, 1977.
        546p.

2302   Fawcett, William. Riding and Horsemanship. 4th ed. Lon-
        don: A. and C. Black, 1960. 175p.

2303   Felton, W. Sidney. Masters of Equitation. London: J. A.
        Allen, 1962. 112p.

2304   Galpin, Jeanette. A Horse of Your Own: A Book for Austral-
        ian and New Zealand Riders. Wellington, New Zealand:
        Reed, 1969. 162p.

2305   Greenway, Harry. Adventure in the Saddle: A Guide to Riding
        as Recreation for All. London: Pitman, 1971. 116p.

2306   Griffen, Jeff. The Book of Horses and Horsemanship. Engle-
        wood Cliffs, NJ: Prentice-Hall, 1963. 182p.

2307   Hamilton, Samantha. "Synchronizing Horse and Man." Equus,
        no. 21 (July 1979), 26-33. 72.

2308   Hance, John E. Riding Master. London: Hale, 1960. 192p.

2309   Harder, Lois, comp. Selected Riding Articles. Washington,
        D.C.: American Association for Health, Physical Education,
        and Recreation, 1964. 128p.

2310   Heyer, H. J. Reflections on the Art of Horsemanship. Lon-
        don: J. A. Allen, 1968. 120p.

2311   Hinton, Phyllis, ed. The Rider's Treasury. New York: Arco,
        1974. 356p.

2312   _____. Riding Cavalcade. London: J. A. Allen, 1967.
        128p.

2313   Holmelund, Paul. The Art of Horsemanship. New York: A.
        S. Barnes, 1962. 159p.

2314   Hope, Charles E. G. The Book of Riding. London: Barker,
        1970. 112p.

2315   _____. Horse Riding. New Rochelle, NY: Sportshelf,
        1964. 94p.

2316   _____. Horseback Riding. New York: Crowell, 1953. 120p.

2317   _____. The Horseman's Manual. New York: Scribners,
        1976. 303p.

2318 _____. Ponies and Riding in Pictures. London: Pitman, 1953. 110p.

2319 _____. Riding. New ed. London: Hodder and Stoughton, 1975. 96p.

2320 Horse and Rider, Editors of. Horse Action. Temecula, CA, 1979. 96p.

2321 Hundt, Sheila W. Horseback Riding. N. Hollywood, CA: Wilshire Books, 1975. 124p.

2322 Jackson, Noel. Effective Horsemanship for Dressage, Three-Day Event, Jumping and Polo. Princeton, NJ: Van Nostrand, 1968. 328p.

2323 Jasper, Mrs. A. W. Horsemanship. New Brunswick, NJ: Boy Scouts of America, 1963. 59p.

2324 Kearnley, Bernard L. Riding Made Easy. London: Country Life, 1960. 125p.

2325 Kellock, Elizabeth M. The Story of Riding. New York: St. Martin's Press, 1975. 216p.

2326 Kelly, J. F. Pony Riding. New Rochelle, NY: Sportshelf, 1965. 142p.

2327 Kidd, Jane and John. Reins in Our Hands. London: Country Life, 1963. 111p.

2328 Kulesza, Severyn R. Modern Riding. South Brunswick, NJ: A. S. Barnes, 1966. 202p.

2329 Lamont, John W. F. Essentials of Horsemanship. London: Constable, 1955. 147p.

2330 Langston, Steve. "Win the Horsemanship Class." Horseman, XXIII (August 1979), 60-65.

2331 Lees, John and Joan Gray. Guide to Pony Club Tests: Horsemastership for Beginners. 5th rev. ed. London: Crosby, Lockwood and Son, 1958.

2332 Lewis, Benjamin. Riding. New York: Grosset and Dunlap, 1958. 141p.

2333 Littauer, Vladimir S. Be a Better Horseman: An Illustrated Guide to the Enjoyment of Modern Riding. New York: Essential Books, 1946. 251p.

2334 _____. Horseman's Progress: The Development of Modern Riding. Princeton, NJ: Van Nostrand, 1962. 316p.

2335 Lyons, William E. Balance and the Horse: A Book for Be-
      ginners. New York: Scribners, 1953. 128p.

2336 Martin, Desmond. Australia Astride. Sydney, Aust.: Angus
      and Robertson, 1959. 196p.

2337 Mellin, Jeanne. Ride a Horse. New York: Sterling, 1970.
      128p. [juv.]

2338 Mohan, Beverly and M. A. Riding: A Guide to Horsemanship.
      New York: Follett, 1971. 128p. [juv.]

2339 Moore, Elaine T. Winning Your Spurs. Boston: Little, Brown,
      1954. 123p. [juv.]

2340 Oliver, Alan. Book of Horsemanship. London: Muller, 1960.
      127p.

2341 Orr, Jennie H. A Manual of Riding. Rev. ed. Minneapolis,
      MN: Burgess, 1957. 33p. [juv.]

2342 Owen, Robert. Successful Riding and Jumping. London and
      New York: Hamlyn Publishing, 1975. 45p. [juv.]

2343 Paillard, Jean S. F. Understanding Equitation. Garden City,
      NY: Doubleday, 1974. 198p.

2344 Paust, Gil. The Complete Beginner's Guide to Horseback Rid-
      ing. Garden City, NY: Doubleday, 1977. 179p.

2345 Pinch, Dorothy H. Happy Horsemanship. New York: Arco,
      1975. 180p.

2346 Pony Club. Manual of Horsemanship of the British Horse So-
      ciety and Pony Club. 4th ed. London: British Horse So-
      ciety, 1959. 200p.

2347 Posey, Jeanne K. The Rider's Handbook. New York: Arco,
      1977. 216p.

2348 Pullein-Thompson, Josephine. Ride Better and Better. London:
      Blackie and Son, 1974. 122p.

2349 Rayner, Judy, ed. The Horseman's Companion: A Guide to
      Riding and Horses. London: Croom Helm, 1974. 221p.

2350 Real, Linton M. First Steps in Horsemastership. New York:
      A. S. Barnes, 1965. 128p.

2351 Richter, Judy. Horse and Rider: From Basics to Show Com-
      petition. New York: Simon and Schuster, 1979. 146p.

2352 Ritcher, Ute. Riding in Pictures. London: Ward, Lock,
      1970. 96p.

2353 Roberts, Peter, ed. The Moss Brothers Book of Horses and
Riding. London: Nicholas Kaye, 1965. 128p.

2354 Santini, Piero. The Forward Impulse. 2nd ed. London:
Country Life, 1951. 64p.

2355 Self, Margaret C. Fun on Horseback. New ed. New York:
A. S. Barnes, 1964. 271p.

2356 Seunig, Waldemar. Horsemanship: A Comprehensive Book on
Training the Horse and Its Rider. Translated from the
German. Rev. ed. Garden City, NY: Doubleday, 1961.
352p.

2357 Shapiro, Neal and Steve Lehrman. The World of Horseback
Riding. New York: Atheneum, 1976. 99p.

2358 Slaughter, Jean. Horsemanship for Beginners: Riding, Jumping, and Schooling. New York: Alfred A. Knopf, 1952.
118p.

2359 Spooner, Glenda. Instructions in Ponymastership. Rev. ed.
London: Museum Press, 1959. 192p.

2360 _____. Riding. London: Museum Press, 1964. 119p.

2361 Steinkraus, William. Riding and Jumping. New and rev. ed.
London: Pelham Books, 1971. 125p.

2362 Stull, Sally. What You Can Do with a Horse. South Brunswick, NJ: A. S. Barnes, 1977. 150p.

2363 Summerhays, Reginald S. Elements of Riding. New ed. London: Country Life, 1962. 120p.

2364 _____. Riding on a Small Income. Rev. and enl. ed. London: J. A. Allen, 1966. 108p.

2365 Sweet, George A. Whips and Sugar Cubes: Memories of a
Favorite Horse. New York: Exposition Press, 1962. 43p.

2366 Talbot-Ponsonby, John A. Harmony in Horsemanship. New
York: A. S. Barnes, 1964. 116p.

2367 Tutton, Jane S. "Which Riding Style for You?" Horse and
Horseman, VI (August-October 1978), 54-59, 40-43, 26-31.

2368 Van Tuyle, Barbara. How to Ride and Jump Your Best. New
York: Grosset and Dunlap, 1973. 115p.

2369 Vernan, Glenn R. Man on Horseback. Omaha: University of
Nebraska Press, 1972. 436p.

2370 Von Blixen-Finecke, Hans. The Art of Riding. Translated
      from the German. London: J. A. Allen, 1977. 120p.

2371 Von Romaszkan, Gregor. Equitation in Pictures. Translated
      from the German. Garden City, NY: Doubleday, 1965.
      127p.

2372 _____. Fundamentals of Riding. Translated from the Ger-
      man. Garden City, NY: Doubleday, 1964. 154p.

2373 _____. Horse and Rider in Equilibrium. Translated from
      the German. Brattleboro, VT: Stephen Greene Press,
      1967. 127p.

2374 Von Walter, Ella W. Learn to Ride. Woodbury, NY: Barron's
      Educational Service, 1976. 93p.

2375 Waltenspiel, Ruth. "Riding Check List." Horse and Rider,
      XVI (May 1977), 36-37.

2376 Walter, William H. Right Way to Ride a Horse. Rev. ed.
      New York: Arco, 1979. 126p.

2377 Wheatley, George. Let's Start Riding. London: Cassell, 1970.
      188p.

2378 _____. The Pony Rider's Book. London: J. A. Allen,
      1969. 128p.

2379 Wilding, Suzanne and Sam Savitt. Ups and Downs: A First
      Guide to Riding and Horse Care. New York: St. Martin's
      Press, 1972. 120p. [juv.]

2380 Williams, Moyra. Riding Is My Hobby. London: Wheaton,
      1962. 180p.

2381 Wright, Gordon. Sports Illustrated Horseback Riding. Rev.
      ed. Philadelphia: Lippincott, 1971. 94p.

2382 _____. The Cavalry Manual of Horsemanship and Horse-
      mastership: The Official Manual of the U.S. Army Cavalry
      School. Garden City, NY: Doubleday, 1962. 180p.

2383 Wynmalen, Henry. Equitation. 5th ed. London: J. A. Allen,
      1971. 144p.

2384 Xenophon. The Art of Horsemanship. Translated from the
      Greek. London: J. A. Allen, 1962. 187p.

2385 Younghusband, Jimmy. Novice Riding. New Rochelle, NY:
      Sportshelf, 1966. 128p.

B HORSEMANSHIP: EAST AND WEST

1 Eastern

2386 Bloom, Lynda. "Betty Franklin: Tips for 'Switch Hitting.' "
       Western Horseman, XXXIX (December 1974), 28-32, 112.

2387 _____. "Sitting Pretty." Horse and Rider, XVII (May 1977),
       22-28.

2388 Burt, Don. "Up Right." Horse and Rider, XVI (September
       1976), 36-38.

2389 Close, Pat. "Les Corbett: Saddle Seat Equitation." Western
       Horseman, XLII (July 1977), 32-34.

2390 _____. "Stock Seat Equitation." Western Horseman, XLIV
       (June 1979), 36-41.

2391 Coen, Bruce and Sue. Know English Equitation and Training.
       Omaha, NE: Farnam Horse Library, 1978. 64p.

2392 Crabtree, Helen K. Saddle Seat Equitation. Garden City, NY:
       Doubleday, 1970. 176p.

2393 D'Ambrosio, Anthony, Jr. and Steven D. Price. Schooling to
       Show: Basics of Hunter-Jumper Training. New York:
       Viking Press, 1978. 92p.

2394 Dillon, Jane M. Riding the Show Ring Hunter. Omaha, NE:
       Farnam Horse Library, 1977. 64p.

2395 "English Training and Riding." Horse and Rider, VII (July
       1968), passim.

2396 Griffith, Perry B. "Dealer's Choice." Horse and Rider, XI
       (October 1973), 74-77.

2397 _____. "From Corral to Championship: Becoming a Win-
       ning English Rider." Horse and Horseman, I (April 1973-
       January 1974), passim.

2398 _____. "They Paid Their Dues." Horse and Rider, XI
       (February 1972), 59-63.

2399 Horse and Rider, Editors of. Horse and Rider All-English
       Yearbook. Covina, CA: Rich Publishing Co., 1973--. v.
       1--.

2400 Morris, George H. Hunter Seat Equitation. Rev. ed. Garden
       City, NY: Doubleday, 1979. 215p.

2401 Richards, Ronnie. "Stock Seat Equitation." Horse and Rider,
       IX (January 1970), 16-20.

2402 Shearer, Sherry. "Winning Hunt Seat Equitation." Horse and Horseman, V (June 1977), 48-57.

2403 Shrake, Richard. "Defining Stock Seat Equitation." Western Horseman, XXXIX (January 1974), 74-77, 96.

2404 Tollefson, Randi. "Basic English." Horse and Rider, XI (April 1972), 50-52.

2405 Vezzoli, Gary C. Superior Horsemanship: Learning and Teaching the English Hunt Seat. South Brunswick, NJ: A. S. Barnes, 1978. 309p.

2406 Winkler, Hans G., et al. Riding the International Way. South Brunswick, NJ: A. S. Barnes, 1970. 114p.

2 Western

2407 B.J.B. Horsemanship. Boulder, Co., 1974. 148p.

2408 Ball, Charles E. Saddle Up: The Farm Journal Book of Western Horsemanship. Philadelphia: Lippincott, 1970. 224p.

2409 Blazer, Donald D. Natural Western Riding. Boston: Houghton Mifflin. 1979. 135p.

2410 Bloom, Lynda. "The Western Riding Class, with Russ Franklin." Western Horseman, XLI (December 1976), 55-58.

2411 Bond, Marian. "Ronnie Richards: Through the Judge's Eyes --The Western Pleasure Class." Horse Illustrated, IX (September-October 1978), 12-15.

2412 Carden, Karen W. Western Rider's Handbook. South Brunswick, NJ: A. S. Barnes, 1976. 175p.

2413 Cash, C. K. "Western Equestrian Basics." Horse Illustrated, XII (June 1980), 11-13.

2414 Gorman, John A. Western Horse: Its Types and Training. New ed. Danville, IL: Interstate Printers and Publishers, 1959. 445p.

2415 Hauser, Rick. Suggested Requirements for Western Horsemanmanship. Fargo: Cooperative Extension Service, North Dakota State University, 1974. 16p.

2416 Horse and Rider, Editors of. Horse and Rider All-Western Yearbook. Covina, CA: Rich Publishing Co., 1972--. v. 1--.

2417 Hyland, Ann. Beginner's Guide to Western Riding. London: Pelham Books, 1971. 136p.

2418 Jones, Dave. The Western Horse: Advice and Training. Norman: University of Oklahoma Press, 1974. 175p.

2419 Jones, Suzanne N. The Art of Western Riding. N. Hollywood, CA: Wilshire Books, 1974. 162p.

2420 Matlock, Rose. Advanced Western Horsemanship. Colorado Springs, CO: Western Horseman, 1971. 37p.

2421 Nye, Nelson C. Your Western Horse: His Ways and His Rider. New York: A. S. Barnes, 1963. 147p.

2422 Richards, Ronnie. Ride and Show Your Western Horse. Encino, CA: King Publishing Co., 1972. Unpaged.

2423 Simmons, Diane C. "Western Riding." Horse and Rider, XVIII (September 1979), 24-27.

2424 Spencer, Dick, 3rd. Beginning Western Horsemanship. Colorado Springs, CO: Western Horseman, 1970. 32p.

2425 _____. Intermediate Western Horsemanship. Colorado Springs, CO: Western Horseman, 1971. 32p.

2426 Stewart, Dwight. Western Equitation, Horsemanship, and Showmanship. New York: Vantage Press, 1973. 245p.

2427 _____. Western Horsemanship and Equitation. New York: Arco, 1979. 265p.

2428 Taylor, Louis. Ride Western: A Complete Guide to Western Horsemanship. New York: Harper & Row, 1968. 228p.

2429 Thiffault, Mark and Jack P. Lewis. Western Horse and Horseman's Digest. Chicago: Follett Publishing Co., 1974. 288p.

2430 Wyland, E. E. Western Horsemanship for the Average Pleasure Rider. Denver, 1956. 224p.

2431 Zoll, Don. Western Riding: Your Self-Teaching Guide. New York: David McKay, 1979. 184p.

C THE SIDE SADDLE

2432 Christopher, Renny. "Sidesaddle Synergism." Horse and Rider, XVI (November 1976), 32-35.

2433 Fleitmann, Lida L. Saddle of Queens: The Story of the Side Saddle. London: J. A. Allen, 1959. 68p.

2434 Harper, Harriet W. Around the World in Eighty Years on a Sidesaddle. New York: Spiral Press, 1966. 30p.

2435 Horiblon, Doreen A. Side Saddle Riding. London: J. A.
      Allen, 1972. 132p.

2436 Kneeland, C. B. "The Revival of Side Saddle Riding in This
      Country." Program/Proceedings of the National Horsemen's
      Seminar, II (1977), 122-125.

2437 Lewis, Margaret. "Pain in the Side (Saddle)." Horse and
      Rider, XII (February 1973), 56-61.

2438 Lorraine, Mandy. "Ride Astride." Horse Lover's National
      Magazine, XLIII (August 1978), 51-60.

2439 MacDonald, Janet W. and Valerie Francis. Elementary Side
      Saddle. Croydon, Eng.: Les Amazones with Ladies Side
      Saddle Association, 1977. 33p.

2440 _____. Riding Side Saddle. London: Pelham Books, 1978.
      167p.

2441 _____. Showing Side Saddle. Croyden, Eng.: Les Amazones
      with Ladies Side Saddle Association, 1976. 32p.

2442 McLean, Catherine. "A Lady to Ride." Western Horseman,
      XXXIX (November 1974), 90-93.

2443 Marra, Marte. "Tips on Riding Sidesaddle." Western Horse-
      man, XLII (December 1977), 24-26.

2444 O'Malley, Jeanne. "All Jumping Aside." Horse and Rider,
      XVII (August 1977), 34-37.

2445 Spiss, Kathie. "Riding Sidesaddle." Western Horseman,
      XXXVII (April 1972), 62-64, 148-150.

D STUDY AND TEACHING

1 General Works

2446 Abbey, Harlan. "Education Today for Tomorrow's Horsemen."
      American Horseman, IV (October 1974), 22-24, 60.

2447 Abhau, Elliot. "Showdown: Out of the Darkness, Into the
      Light." Horse Lover's National Magazine, XLIII (November
      1978), 8, 57.

2448 American Horse Shows Association, Inc. "Equine Programs
      Offered." Rapidan River Farm Digest, I (Winter 1975),
      220-223.

2449 Anderson, Clarence W. Heads Up, Heels Down: A Handbook
      of Horsemanship and Riding. New York: Macmillan, 1963.
      114p.

2450   Barnett, Mike. "Bobbi Wirth: Horse Trainer Trainer."
        Horse and Horseman, VII (August 1979), 60-62.

2450a   Beaham, Charlotte L. "Rodeo Schools." Western Horseman,
        XLIII (May 1978), 88-90, 126.

2451   Bloom, Lynda. "Debbie Bugge: Teaching Bareback Equitation."
        Western Horseman, XLII (October 1977), 97-99.

2452   _____. "Just for the EQ of It." Horse and Rider, XV
        January 1976), 14-20.

2453   Boren, Jon. "A Class for Trail Riders." Western Horseman,
        XLIV (November 1979), 34-36.

2454   Brandl, Albert. Improve Your Riding: Dressage, Jumping,
        Cross Country. New York: Sterling, 1980. 116p.

2455   British Horse Society and Pony Club. The Instructor's Hand-
        book. Woodbury, NY: Barron's Educational Service, 1977.
        152p.

2456   Byford, Sharon. "Horse Show Training Clinic." Western
        Horseman, XXXVIII (January 1973), 38-40, 138-139.

2457   Casida, L. E. "Graduate Training in Animal Science: Degree
        Requirements and the Involvement of the Student in the Re-
        search Program." Journal of Animal Science, XXV (Winter
        1966), 1236-1239.

2458   Cazier-Charpentier, H. "The Analysis of Teaching." Dressage
        and CT, XVII (April 1980), 22-23, 33.

2459   Clayton, Michael and Dick Tracey. Hickstead: The First
        Twelve Years. London: Pelham Books, 1972. 208p.

2460   Close, Pat. "Teaching Tricks, with Darrel Wallin." Western
        Horseman, XLII (March-April 1977), 22-26, 54-57.

2461   Coen, Sue H. Let's Ride: An Equitation Guide for Riding In-
        structors and Beginning Students. South Brunswick, NJ:
        A. S. Barnes, 1970. 246p.

2462   Coleman, Alix. "The Sun Shines Brighter." Classic, III (Au-
        gust-September 1978), 64.

2463   "Colleges and Universities Offering Horse Courses." Horse
        and Horseman, VI (September 1978), 27-29.

2464   "Courses on Horses." Practical Horseman, V (September
        1977), 30-35.

2465   Decarpentry, Albert E. E. Academic Equitation: A Prepara-

tion for International Dressage Tests. Translated from the
French. London: J. A. Allen, 1971. 281p.

2466 D'Endrödy, Agostan L. Give Your Horse a Chance: The Training of Horse and Rider for Three-Day Events, Showing and
Jumping. J. A. Allen, 1971. 281p.

2467 Dickerson, Jan. Make the Most of Your Horse: The Practical
Application of College in All Types of Riding. Garden City,
NY: Doubleday, 1970. 225p.

2468 Dillon, Jane M. School for Young Riders. Princeton, NJ:
Van Nostrand, 1959. 235p.

2469 Finley, Ann. "Teaching Pre-Schoolers to Ride." Western
Horseman, XLIV (March 1979), 83-85.

2470 Frederiksen, Aage K. The Finer Points of Riding: A Guide
and Reference Book for Instructors. London: J. A. Allen,
1969. 86p.

2471 Froissard, Jean. Equitation: Learning and Teaching. Translated from the French. Rev. ed. New York: Arco, 1977.
357p.

2472 Froud, Bill. Better Riding: In Collaboration with the British
Horse Society. New Rochelle, NY: Sportshelf, 1972. 90p.

2473 Fry, Patricia L. Hints for the Backyard Rider. South Brunswick, NJ: A. S. Barnes, 1978. 159p.

2474 Griffith, Perry B. "Become a Better Instructor." Horse and
Horseman, VII (October 1979), 60-64.

2475 Haley, Neale. How to Teach Group Riding. New York: Arco,
1976. 285p.

2476 _____. Teach Yourself to Ride. South Brunswick, NJ:
A. S. Barnes, 1974. 248p.

2477 Haworth, Josephine. Riding from Scratch: An Adult Beginner's
Handbook. London: Eyre and Spottiswoode, 1979. 87p.

2478 Heath, Veronica. Beginner's Guide to Riding. New York:
Transatlantic Arts, 1971. 144p.

2479 Henderson, Dennis. "Tidbits for Beginners." Horse and Rider,
XI (September 1972), 17-21, 50.

2480 Hitchcock, Francis C. Saddle Up: A Guide to Equitation and
Stable Management, Including Hints to Instructors. Rev.
ed. New York: Arco, 1960. 286p.

2481 Holmelund, Paul. Ride Gently--Ride Well. South Brunswick, NJ: A. S. Barnes, 1970. 199p.

2482 Holyoake, Janet J. Improving Your Riding. Rev. ed. London: Faber and Faber, 1971. 101p.

2483 _____. Learning to Ride. 3rd ed. London: Faber and Faber, 1959. 78p.

2484 Hooper, Freia I. "Crash Course for Beginning Instructors." Western Horseman, XLIII (August 1978), 22-23.

2485 _____. "Trail Class in the Open." Western Horseman, XLIV (August 1979), 80-81.

2486 Hope, Charles E. G. Learn to Ride. London: Pelham Books, 1965. 143p.

2487 _____. Tackle Riding This Way. London: S. Paul, 1960. 125p.

2488 Huff, A. N. "Horses: Vehicle for Education." Extension Service Review, XXXVII (September 1966), 8-9.

2489 Hunley, Annette. "Teaching Means Taking Time to Learn." Horseman, XXI (June 1978), 70-78.

2490 Hurley, Cynthia G. Teach Yourself to Ride a Horse. Englewood Cliffs, NJ: Prentice-Hall, 1978. 303p.

2491 Improving Your Horsemanship. Houston, TX: Cordovan Corp., 1975. 116p.

2492 Jones, Dave. "Education." Horseman, XXI (July-August 1977), 64-69, 70-77.

2493 Kearley, Bernard L. Riding Made Easy. New Rochelle, NY: Sportshelf, 1960. 125p.

2494 Kees, Timmy. "Teaching Junior Riders." Practical Horseman, III (November 1975), passim.

2495 Kilmer, Deborah B. "I Learn to Ride." Cosmopolitan, CLXXXVI (April 1979), 198+.

2496 King, Bill. "Tidbits for Beginners." Horse and Rider, XI (October 1972), 36-41.

2497 King, Chuck. "Orme's Courses Include Horses." Western Horseman, XLV (February 1980), 71-72.

2498 Koreen, Christine C. "How to Choose a Riding Instructor." Horse and Horseman, VI (August 1978), 32-33.

2499 Laffer, F. "Thoughts on Teaching Riding." Western Horse-
      man, XXXIX (September 1974), 52+.

2500 LaValley, Michele. "Tidbits for Beginners." Horse and Rider,
      XII (March 1973), 50-53.

2501 Lewis, Anne. A Guide to Basic Riding Instruction. London:
      J. A. Allen, 1975. 86p.

2502 Licart, Jean C. A. A. Start Riding Right. Princeton, NJ:
      Van Nostrand, 1966. 125p.

2503 McArthur, J. Wayne. Training for Western Riders. Salt Lake
      City, UT: Brighton Publishing Co. , 1979.

2504 McMillan, Don. "Team Roping Schools." Western Horseman,
      XXXVI (September 1971), 50, 126-127.

2505 McTaggart, Maxwell F. The Art of Riding: A Textbook for
      Beginners and Others. New York: Arco, 1963. 127p.

2506 Maeder, Marla. "The Remuda Triangle." Horse and Rider,
      XVII (December 1978), 34-36.

2507 Massachusetts. Secretary of the Commonwealth. Regulations
      and Standards Relating to Riding School Operators, Filed
      by the Department of Agriculture. Boston, 1974. 4p.

2508 Mueseler, Wilhelm. Riding Logic. Translated from the Ger-
      man. 3rd ed. London: Methuen, 1965. 185p.

2509 Myerscough, Karen. "Driving Training." Western Horseman,
      XLII (September 1977), 12-15.

2510 Owen, Robert. My Learn to Ride Book. New York: Golden
      Press, 1975. 45p. [juv.]

2511 Pattie, Jane. "Trials and Tribulations of Learning the Horse
      Business." Horseman, XV (March 1971), 38-50.

2512 Podhajsky, Alois. The Riding Teacher: A Basic Guide to
      Correct Methods of Classical Instruction. Garden City,
      NY: Doubleday, 1973. 204p.

2513 Price, Steven D. Teaching Riding at Summer Camps. Brattle-
      boro, VT: Stephen Greene Press, 1971. 64p.

2514 Pullein-Thompson, Josephine. Learn to Ride Well. London:
      Routledge and Kegan Paul, 1966. 120p.

2515 Radlauer, Edward. Rodeo School. New York: Watts, 1976.
      47p. [juv.]

2516 Reiss, Bob. "Horse Schools." Equus, no. 24 (October 1979), 37-41, 60.

2517 "Retraining Western Riders for English." Horse and Horseman, I (March 1973), passim.

2518 Roberts, Pamela. Teaching the Child Rider: Some Practical Notes for Parents and Trainee Instructors. London: J. A. Allen, 1976. 102p.

2519 Roesch, Madelyn. "Horses to Win With, Horses to Learn On." Practical Horseman, VI (April 1978), 50-53.

2520 Rogers, Tex. "Students + Horses = Education - Opportunity." Horseman, XVIII (August 1973), 76-81.

2521 Rosenfeld, Judith S. "They've Finally Got an Edge." American Education, XV (May 1979), 20-26.

2522 Santini, Piero. Riding Instructor. London: Country Life, 1952. 161p.

2523 Self, Margaret C. Horseback Riding Simplified. 2nd ed. New York: Ronald Press, 1963. 85p.

2524 _____. Horsemastership: Methods of Training the Horse and Rider. Edited by Sarah Mason. New York: A. S. Barnes, 1952. 440p.

2525 _____. Riding with Mariles. New York: McGraw-Hill, 1960. 135p.

2526 Shannon, Elizabeth. Manual for Teaching Western Riding. Washington, D. C.: National Riding Committee, Western Division, American Association for Health, Physical Education, and Recreation, 1970. 69p.

2527 Spooner, Glenda. Instruction in Ponymastership. Rev. ed. New Rochelle, NY: Sportshelf, 1962. 192p.

2528 _____. Riding, Step-by-Step. New York: Arco, 1966. 119p.

2529 Stevens, Glenn Z. Agricultural Education. New York: Center for Applied Research in Education, 1967. 113p.

2530 Taylor Joyce K. Hyde Park for Horsemanship. By Joyce Bellamy, pseud. London: J. A. Allen, 1975. 155p.

2531 Taylor, Louis. An Expert's Guide to Horseback Riding for Beginners. N. Hollywood, CA: Wilshire Books, 1972. 269p.

2532 _____. Ride American: A Practical Guide for Western and Eastern Horsemen. New York: Harper & Row, 1963. 269p.

2533 Twelveponies, Mary. Ride and Learn. 2nd ed. Capistrano
      Beach, CA: Horse and Horseman, 1979. 64p.

2534 Vorhes, Gary. "Teacher-Trainers Discuss Stock Horses and
      Students." Western Horseman, XXXVIII (September 1973),
      90-94, 162-164.

2535 Weaver, Susan. "How to be a Backyard Horse Trainer." West-
      ern Horseman, XLIV (December 1979), 18-20.

2536 Whitaker, D. "Educational and Support Services at the Local
      Level for Horsemen and Horse Farms: What is Available,
      Where, and How to Use It." Program/Proceedings of the
      National Horsemen's Seminar, II (1977), 61-65.

2537 Williams, Dorian. Great Riding Schools of the World. New
      York: Macmillan, 1975. 320p.

2538 Williams, Jimmy. "Tips for Training Riders." Practical
      Horseman, III (September 1975), passim.

2539 Wright, Gordon. Learning to Ride, Hunt, and Show. New and
      rev. ed. Garden City, NY: Doubleday, 1966. 128p.

2540 _____. and M. R. Kelley. The Riding Instructor's Manual.
      Garden City, NY: Doubleday, 1975. 138p.

2541 Young, John R. Schooling for Young Riders: A Handbook for
      the Horsemen of Tomorrow. Norman: University of Okla-
      homa Press, 1970. 324p.

2 Specific Schools

Abbey School

2542 Bergen, Chan. "Horsemanship at Abbey School [Colorado]."
      Western Horseman, XL (February 1975), 16-17, 64-66.

Calgary Stampede Rodeo College

2543 LaRocque, Dan. "Calgary Stampede Rodeo College." Western
      Horseman, XLI (January 1976), 38, 118.

Escuela Ecuestre

2544 Black, Harold. Manual of Horsemanship: Instructions from
      Mexico's Renowned Escuela Ecuestre. New York: Dodd,
      Mead, 1974. 226p.

Findlay College

2545 Close, Pat. "Studying Horses and Books at Findlay College
      [Ohio]." Western Horseman, XLV (July 1980), 61-64.

Foxcroft School

2546 West, Christy. "A [Virginia] School for Decision." Classic, II (October-November 1977), 76-82.

Josey Ranch School

2547 Everett, Jean. "A [Texas] School Kids Beg to Attend." Western Horseman, XXXIX (July 1974), 104-105, 174-176.

Lake Erie College

2548 Durhee, Cutler. "College Courses [in Ohio] for Horses." Womensports, IV, (October 1977), 26+.

Lamar Community College

2549 Manly, Marian. "Students Teaching Students [in Colorado]." Western Horseman, XLIV (May 1979), 98-99.

2550 Witte, Randy. "College Major in Horse Training and Management." Western Horseman, XLIII (August 1978), 101-103.

Marbach Academy

2551 Muzzy, Mrs. James. "Marbach: Ye Olde German Riding School." Western Horseman, XXXV (September 1970), 31, 130-134.

Marty Wood School

2552 Vorhes, Gary. "Marty Wood Bronc Riding School." Western Horseman, XXXVI (September 1971), 30-33, 128-129.

Ohio State University

2553 Leerhsen, Charlie. "Getting a Head Start at Old Harness U." Classic, II (October-November 1977), 116-121.

2554 "A Two-Year College Alternative for Horsemen." Western Horseman, XLIV (July 1979), 87-88. OSU'S Agricultural-Technical Institute.

Oklahoma Farrier's College

2555 Byers, Marjorie. "Sole Brothers." Horse and Rider, X (May 1971), 28-33.

Ricks College

2556 Cargo, Patti S. "Majoring in Horses [in Idaho]." Western Horseman, XLII (June 1977), 64-66.

Salem College--Meredith Manor

2557 Abhau, Elliot. "Educating Horsemen: Meredith Manor [West Virginia]." Horse Lover's National Magazine, XLIII (June 1978), 40-43.

2558 Meredith, Ronald W. "A Horse Named Sam." The Morgan Horse, XXXIX (January 1979), 164.

2559 New, Michael. "A College Degree for Horse Lovers." Country Gentleman, CXXVII (Fall 1977), 70+.

2560 Price, Stephen D. "Fancy Free at M and M's Place." Classic, III (April-May 1978), 72-76.

Sheldon Grant Riding School

2561 McNabb, Bill, Jr. "Live-in Jump-Overs." Horse and Rider, X (August 1971), 46-50.

Southeastern Oklahoma State University

2562 Hibbs, Lenore. "Horses at College." Horse Action, I (October 1975), 53-55.

Spanish Riding School

2563 Handler, Hans. The Spanish Riding School [Austria]: Four Centuries of Classic Horsemanship. Translated from the German. New York: McGraw-Hill, 1972. 272p.

2564 Podhajsky, Alois. The Spanish Riding School of Vienna. Wien, W. Ger.: Kunstverlag Wolfrum, 1967. 56p.

2565 Windisch-Graetz, Mathilde. Spanish Riding School: Its Traditions and Development from the 16th Century Until Today. 2nd ed. London: Cassell, 1958. 115p.

Texas A and M University

2566 Swain, Larry. "We Believe in Experience." Western Horseman, XXXVII (April 1972), 117, 154.

University of Connecticut

2567 Cowan, W. A. "Horse Program." Western Horseman, XLII (September 1977), 150-153.

University of Missouri

2568 "Equine Center." Western Horseman, XXXVIII (April 1973), 142-143.

University of Nevada at Reno

2569 Mathis, Dave. "Learning the Horse Business for College
Credit." Western Horseman, XLII (July 1977), 130-131.

Virginia Intermont College

2570 Pitts, Don. "Degree in Horsemanship." Horse and Rider,
XVI (June 1973), 73.

William Woods College

2571 Allmart, Sue. "The Courses are Horses [in Missouri]." Western Horseman, XLIV (September 1979), 111-112.

2572 Hughes, Clifford. "The Stalls of Ivy." Horse and Rider, XI
(June 1972), 60-63.

Wilton House College

2573 D'Eisenberg, Reis. The Classical [British] Riding School: The
Wilton House College. New York: Viking Press, 1979.
55p.

E   CHILDREN AND HORSES

1   General Works

2574 American Junior Quarter Horse Association. Youth Activities
and the A. J. Q. H. A. Amarillo, TX, 1979. 18p.

2575 Brotchie, J. F. , Jr. Ways for Kids to Make Money with
Horses. Beverly, MA: T. R. T. Publications, 1979. 146p.

2576 Cash, C. K. "Teaching Children to Ride." Horse Illustrated,
XII (July 1980), 47-59.

2577 Darnell, Casey and Blair. "How We Start the Small Child on
Horseback." Horseman, XV (April 1971), 20-25.

2578 Ebelhare, Jane. "Ponies for Young Riders." Practical Horseman, IV (September 1976), passim.

2579 Fawcett, William. The Young Horseman. 4th rev. ed. London: A. and C. Black, 1964. 224p.

2580 Forbis, John T. What Parents Should Know About Horses.
Houston, TX: Cordovan Corp. , 1970. 91p.

2581 Galbraith, Thistle. Outline for the Young Rider. London:
Country Life, 1953. 96p.

2582 Hanson, Valerie. "Responsible Riding Right." Horse and Rider, XVII (June 1979), 26-29.

2583 Herman, Pauline W. The Family Horse. Princeton, NJ: Van Nostrand, 1959. 130p.

2584 Hinton, Phyllis. Country Life Picture Book for Young Riders. London: Country Life, 1962. 176p. [juv.]

2585 Holyoake, Janet J. Your Book on Keeping Ponies. New, rev. ed. London: Faber and Faber, 1968. 95p. [juv.]

2586 Hope, Charles E. G. Riding for Boys and Girls. London: English Universities Press, 1949. 120p. [juv.] Rpr. 1952.

2587 _____. So They Want to Learn Riding: A Guide for Parents Whose Children Want to Learn Riding. London: Finlayson, 1967. 88p.

2588 Hughes, Cledwyn. Ponies for Children. London: Routledge and Kegan Paul, 1962. 150p.

2589 Lyon, William E., ed. Youth in the Saddle. New York: A. S. Barnes, 1955. 255p.

2590 Macgregor-Morris, Pamela. Riding for Children. New Rochelle, NY: Sportshelf, 1961. 128p.

2591 Messemer, G. "Choosing Your Child's Trainer." Horseman, XXII (January 1978), 14-19.

2592 Mohan, Beverly M. Horseback Riding for Boys and Girls. New York: Ryerson Press, 1963. 96p. [juv.]

2593 Self, Margaret C. Susan and Jane Learn to Ride. Philadelphia: Macrae Smith, 1965. 152p. [juv.]

2594 _____. The Young Rider and His First Pony. South Brunswick, NJ: A. S. Barnes, 1969. 177p.

2595 Spaulding, Jackie. The Family Horse. Seattle, WA: Modrona Publishers, 1979. 160p.

2596 Sullivan, George. Better Horseback Riding for Boys and Girls. New York: Dodd, Mead, 1969. 64p. [juv.]

2597 Thorne, Jean W. Horse and Rider. Mankato, MN: Crestwood House, 1976. 32p. [juv.]

2598 Wall, Sheila. The Young Sportsman's Guide to Horseback Riding. New York: Nelson, 1961. 94p. [juv.]

2 Clubs and Camps

2599 Baker, F. H.   4-H Club Horse Workbook.   Circular, no. E741.
Norman: Agricultural Extension Service, University of Oklahoma, 1962.   35p.

2600 Daigh, G. L. , Jr.   Horse and Pony Manual for 4-H Club Members.   Circular, no. 803.   Springfield: Illinois Agricultural
Extension Service, 1959.   48p.

2601 Jackson, R. R.   "Horse Clinics for 4-H Groups. "   Western
Horseman, XXXIX (September 1974), 17+.

2602 Jacobsen, N. A.   Horses and Riding for 4-H Clubs.   Bulletin,
no. 295.   Helena: Montana Agricultural Extension Service,
1958.   25p.

2603 _____.   Suggestions for Judging and Showing 4-H Colts and
Horses.   Circular, no. 284.   Helena: Montana Agricultural
Extension Service, 1962.   11p.

2604 Lane, Albert M.   Your 4-H Stock Horse.   Circular, no. 255.
Phoenix: Arizona Agricultural Extension Service, 1957.   19p.

2605 Michigan.   State Department of Social Services.   Horseback
Riding Safety Standards for Childrens' Camps.   Lansing,
n. d.   4p.

2606 O'Hara, Matt.   "The Fifth H. "   Horse and Rider, IX (April
1970), 22-26, 64.

2607 Sisson, Joan.   "4-H Horse Clubs: Another Viewpoint. "   Western Horseman, XLII (May 1977), 60-62, 144-145.

2608 United States.   Department of Agriculture.   Federal Extension
Service.   4-H Horsemanship Program.   2 pts.   Washington,
D. C. : U. S. Government Printing Office, 1971.

2609 _____. _____. _____.   4-H Horse Program: Guide
for Club Leaders.   Federal Extension Service Program Aid.
Washington, D. C. : U. S. Government Printing Office, 1965.
19p.

2610 Willman, H. A.   A 4-H Handbook and Lesson Guide.   2nd ed.
Ithaca, NY: Comstock Publishing Associates, 1963.   314p.

F HORSEMANSHIP FOR THE HANDICAPPED

2611 Bauer, Joseph J.   Riding for [Handicapped] Rehabilitation.   Ottawa, Ont. : Canadian Stage and Arts Publications, Ltd. ,
1973.   127p.

2612   Campbell, Juanita. "Handicapped American of the Year Rides
        Into the Winners Circle." Disabled USA, II (October 1979),
        11-13.

2613   Clemens, Virginia. Super Animals and Their Unusual Careers.
        Philadelphia: Westminster Press, 1979. 192p. [juv.]
        Includes a look at ponies for the handicapped.

2614   Davies, John A. The Reins of Life: An Instructional and In-
        formative Manual on Riding for the Disabled. London:
        J. A. Allen, 1967. 120p.

2615   "Equestrian Therapy for the Handicapped." Synergist, III (Win-
        ter 1975), 42-43.

2616   Howard, Helen A. "Horses Help the Handicapped." Horseman,
        XXII (April 1978), 13-24.

2617   LaRocque, Daniel. "Handicapped Horseman." Western Horse-
        man, XLIV (May 1979), 105-110.

2618   Lescher, Steven. "Horses Help the Handicapped." Western
        Horseman, XXXVIII (November 1973), 18, 117-118.

2619   McCowan, L. L. "Riding for the Handicapped." Program/
        Proceedings of the National Horsemen's Seminar, II (1977),
        98-101.

2620   "Mike Aronow: Trainer on Wheels." Disabled USA, II (Sep-
        tember 1979), 16-18.

2621   Nathan, Herm. "Handicapped Barrel Racer [Karen Kimbrough]."
        Horseman, XLIV (March 1979), 88.

2622   "Riding for the Disabled: A Role for the Veterinarian." Veter-
        inary Record, XCI (October 14, 1972), 388-389.

2623   Scutt, Cheryl. "The Trainer [Ollie Underwood] Works
        from a Wheelchair." Horseman, XXIII (May 1979),
        37-40.

2624   Thompson, Diana. "Four Great Legs Beneath Them." Equus,
        no. 24 (October 1979), 52-58, 67.

2625   Vollmer, M. M. "Teaching Riding to Blind Children." West-
        ern Horseman, XXXIX (June 1974), 25-26+.

2626   Williams, Carol F. "Horses and the Handicapped." Horse
        and Horseman, V (December 1977), 18-23.

2627   Williams, Corinne. "Horsemanship for the Handicapped."
        Western Horseman, XXXVI (September 1971), 67-70.

G HORSEMANSHIP, EXCLUDING RACING,
IN SELECTED LANDS

1 General Works

2628   Coggins, Jack. Horsemen of the World.   Garden City, NY:
       Doubleday, 1963. 60p. [juv.]

2 Europe

a General Works

2629   Kidd, Jane. Horsemanship in Europe.   London: J. A. Allen,
       1977. 224p.

b France

2630   Davis, Ray. "Horsemen from France."   Western Horseman,
       XXXIX (August 1974), 31+.

2631   "Marshland Cowboys."   Horse and Rider, XVIII (March 1980),
       28-30.

2632   Silvester, Hans W.   Horses of the [Ile de la] Camargue.   Har-
       mondsworth, Eng.: Penguin Books, 1979. 100p.

c Iceland

2633   Phillips-Browne, Noel.   The Horse in Iceland.   London: Pel-
       ham Books, 1967. 242p.

2634   Sigurour, A. Magnusson.   Stallion of the North.   Nantucket,
       MA: Longship Press, 1978. 95p.

2635   Vandervelde, Marjorie. "Icelandic Ponies."   Western Horse-
       man, XXXVI (January 1971), 66, 136-138.

d Ireland

2636   Cockburn, Claud. "The Way of a Green, Moist Land."   Clas-
       sic, II (June-July 1977), 132-139.

2637   Irish Horseman Annual.   Dublin: Irish Horseman, 1971--.   v.
       1--.

2638   Mahoney, Edmund.   The Galway Blazers.   Galway, Ire.:
       Kenny Galway, Ltd., 1979. 125p.

e Poland

2639   Slaski, Witold. "Polish Horsemanship and Horses."   Dressage
       and CT. XIII (December 1977), 20-21.

f Portugal

2640 "Horses Around the World: Portugal." Practical Horseman, VI (September 1978), 21-30, 54.

g Spain

2641 Janey, Frank. "The Road Back to Spain." Equus, no. 33 (July 1980), 33-40, 76.

h Switzerland

2642 Bud Brown, F. V. "The Wild Wild West--Swiss Style." Western Horseman, XXXVIII (April 1973), 103-108, 146-148.

i U.S.S.R.

2643 Haskin, Gretchen. "Stalking the Elusive Orloo, and Other Tales of a Soviet Journey." Classic, IV (April-May 1979), 84-92.

3 The Middle East and Africa

a Jordan

2644 Campbell, Judith. Horses in the Sun. London: Pelham Books, 1966. 133p.

b Saudi Arabia

2645 Van Sickle, N. D. "Notes on a Visit to Saudi Arabia." Western Horseman, XXXIX (June 1974), 45+.

c South Africa

2646 Child, Daphne. Saga of the South African Horse. Cape Town, S. A.: Timmins, 1967. 202p.

2647 "Horses Around the World: South Africa." Practical Horseman, VII (August 1979), 6-20.

2648 Struben, Pamela, ed. Horses and Riding in Southern Africa. London: Purnell, 1966. 287p.

2649 Wright, Ernest L. C. From Start to Finish. London: Macmillan, 1974. 167p.

4 Far East and Pacific

a Australia

2650 Barker, Herbert M. Droving Days. London: Pitman, 1966. 147p.

2651 Walker, A. "Horses, Donkeys, and Mules in Australia." Western Horseman, XXXIX (September 1974), 58+.

b China

2652 Springfield, Maurice O. Hunting Opium and Other Scents.
Halesworth, Eng.: Norfolk and Suffolk Publicity, 1966.
95p.

c India

2653 Kapoor, G. R. "Top Riders of India." Western Horseman,
XXXVII (May 1972), 62-63+.

d Japan

2654 Kenrick, Vivienne. Horses in Japan. London: J. A. Allen,
1965. 196p.

2655 Spencer, Dick, 3rd. "The Horse in Japan." Western Horseman, XXXIX (April 1974), 23-25.

e New Zealand

2656 Holden, Duncan, ed. The New Zealand Horseman. Wellington,
New Zealand: A. H. and A. W. Reed, 1967. 114p.

2657 Newton, Peter. Five Hundred Horses. Wellington, New Zealand: A. H. and A. W. Reed, 1978. 139p.

2658 Tucker, Glyn L. Thoroughbreds Are My Life. Wellington,
New Zealand: A. H. and A. W. Reed, 1978. 235p.

5 North America

a Canada

2659 MacEwan, John W. G. Hoofprints and Hitchingposts. Saska-
toon, Sask.: Modern Press, 1964. 249p.

b United States--Various States

2660 Brown, Stephanie. "Connecticut Velvet." Connecticut, XLII
(September 1979), 46-51.

2661 Green Mountain Horse Association. Green Mountain Horse Association, 1926-1976: A History. South Woodstock, VT,
1976. 40p.

2662 Harville, Charlie. Sports in North Carolina. Norfolk, VA:
Donning, 1978.

2663 Lawyer, Walter. "Anything for a Horse." *Nebraskaland*, LIV (April 1976), 38+.

2664 McDonald, Susan. "Horses [in Georgia]." *Brown's Guide*, VII (April 1979), 25-33.

2665 "People and Horses: Horses and People." *Nevada Magazine*, XXXVII (July-September 1977), 6-29.

2666 Simmons, Marc. "The Horses and Horsemen of New Mexico." *New Mexico Magazine*, LIII (January 1975), 10-15.

Further References: See also Parts IV and V above.

PART VII   HORSE RACING

A   GENERAL WORKS

2667   Alexander, David.   A Sound of Horses: The World of Racing
       from Eclipse to Kelso.   Indianapolis, IN: Bobbs-Merrill,
       1966.   317p.

2668   "The Arabian Horse Pentathlon."   Horse and Rider, XVII (Au-
       gust 1978), 18-20, 48-49.

2669   Atkinson, Ted.   All the Way.   New York: Paxton Slade Pub-
       lishing Co. ,   1961.   191p.

2670   Ballantine, Derek and Alan Trengrove.   The Australasian Book
       of Thoroughbred Racing.   Melbourne, Aust. :   Stockwell
       Press, 1974.   454p.

2671   Barrie, Douglas M.   Turf Cavalcade: A Review of the 150
       Years of Horse-Racing in Australia and of the Australian
       Jockey Club's 100 Years at Randwick.   Sydney, Aust. :
       Australian Jockey Club, 1960.   191p.

2672   Blunt, Noel.   Horse Racing, the Inside Story.   London and
       New York: Hamlyn Publishing, 1977.   128p.

2673   Brennan, John.   A Light-Hearted Guide to British Racing.   By
       John Welcome, pseud.   London: Macdonald and Janes,
       1975.   146p.

2674   Campbell, Barry.   Horse Racing in Britain.   London: Joseph,
       1977.   348p.

2675   Cope, Alfred, ed.   Royal Cavalcade of the Turf: Published to
       Commemorate the Coronation of Her Majesty Queen Eliza-
       beth II.   London: Cope's Publications, 1953.   100p.

2676   Craig, Dennis.   Horse-Racing: The Breeding of Thoroughbreds
       and a Short History of the English Turf.   3rd enl. and rev.
       ed.   London: J. A. Allen, 1964.   192p.

2677 Daily Telegraph, Sports Staff of. "I Was There": Twenty
Exciting Sporting Events. London: Collins, 1966. 152p.

2678 Davidson, Joseph B. Inside Horseracing: An Invaluable Guide
for Owners or Betters. New York: Arco, 1973. 282p.

2679 Downey, Fairfax D. , ed. Races to the Swift: Great Stories
of the Turf. Garden City, NY: Doubleday, 1967. 334p.

2680 Durant, John and Otto Bettman. Pictorial History of American
Sports from Colonial Times to the Present. Rev. ed.
South Brunswick, NJ: A. S. Barnes, 1965. 312p.

2681 Fitzgeorge-Parker, Tim. The Spoilsports. London: Deutsch,
1968. 192p.

2682 Forbis, Judith E. Hoofbeats Along the Tigris: Racing Arabian
Horses in Turkey. London: J. A. Allen, 1970. 129p.

2683 Francis, Dick and John Brennan, eds. The Racing Man's Bedside Book. London: Faber and Faber, 1969. 280p.

2684 Friendlich, Dick. "Horse Racing." In: his Panorama of
Sports in America. New York: Funk and Wagnalls, 1970.
pp. 128-137.

2685 Gilbey, Quintin. Champions All: Steve to Lester. London:
Hutchinson, 1971. 228p.

2686 _____. Queen of the Turf: The Dorothy Paget Story. London: Barker, 1973. 160p.

2687 Good, Meyrick. The Lure of the Turf. London: Odhams,
1957. 224p.

2688 Gordon, Stan. New Turfmaster: Speed Ratings, Track Variants,
Speed, Form, Jockeys, Weights. New York: Frederick
Fell, 1955. 45p.

2689 Gould, Nathaniel. On and Off the Turf in Australia. Sandy
Bay, Tasmania: Libra Books, 1973. 244p.
Reprint of the 1895 edition.

2690 Gregory, Alan. Racing Roundabout. London: Planned Book-
selling, 1954. 254p.

2691 Gursten, Nat. Horse in Horseracing. Detroit, MI: Royal
Publications, 1952. 147p.

2692 Halpenny, Marion R. British Racing and Racecourses. An-
dover, Eng. : Holmes and Sons, 1971. 254p.

2693 Havemann, Ernest. "Keep Out the Wreckers." Classic, II

(June-July 1977), 44-51.
The views of Ronald Reagan on racing.

2694 Hedges, David. Horses and Courses: A Pictorial History of Racing. London: Secker and Warburg, 1972. 220p.

2695 Heimer, Melvin L. Inside Racing: An Introduction to the Sport of Kings. Princeton, NJ: Van Nostrand, 1967. 215p.

2696 Hirsch, Joe. A Treasury of Questions and Answers from the Morning Telegraph and Daily Racing Form. London: Trident Press, 1969. 257p.

2697 Hislop, John. Far from a Gentleman. London: Joseph, 1960. 304p.

2698 _____. Of Horses and Races. London: Joseph, 1961. 214p.

2699 _____. Racing Reflections. London: Hutchinson, 1955. 208p.

2700 Humphreys, John O. American Racetracks and Contemporary Racing Art. South Bend, IN: South Bend Publishing Company, 1966. 240p.

2701 International Races to Come. Dublin: The Jockey Club, 1967--. v. 1--.

2702 The Irish Racing Annual. Dublin: Portside Press, 1950--. v. 4--.

2703 The Irish Racing Calendar: Races Past. Dublin: Boylen, 1950--. v. 161--.

2704 The Irish Racing Calendar: Races to Come. Dublin: Boylen, 1950--.

2705 Jockey Club. Annual Round Table Discussion of Matters Relating to Racing. New York, 1953--. v. 1--.

2706 Kelly, Robert. Racing in America, 1937-1959. New York: The Jockey Club, 1960.

2707 Livingstone-Learmouth, David. Famous Winners of the British Turf, 1949-1955. Woodstock, VT: Countryman, 1957. 160p.

2708 Longrigg, Roger. The English Squire and His Sport. New York: St. Martin's Press, 1977. 302p.

2709 _____. The History of Horse Racing. New York: Stein and Day, 1972. 320p.

2710 _____. The Turf: Three Centuries of Horse Racing. London: Methuen, 1975. 150p.

2711 Lycan, Gilbert L. Inside Racing: Sports and Politics. New York: Pageant Press, 1961. 224p.

2712 McKnight, Bob. Straight, Place, and Showdown. New York: Pageant Press, 1953. 118p.

2713 Malloy, Michael T. Racing Today. National Observer Newsbook. New York: Dow Jones, 1968. 192p.

2714 Murray, William H. H. Horse Fever. New York: Dodd, Mead, 1976. 206p.

2715 News Chronicle Racing Annual. London: News Chronicle, 1950-1960. v. 1-11.

2716 Nolan, Maggie. "Racing, French Style." Town and Country, CXXXI (October 1977), 160+.

2717 Orchard, Vincent R. Derby Stakes: A Complete History from 1900 to 1953. London: Hutchinson, 1954. 327p.

2718 _____. Tattersalls: Two Hundred Years of Sporting History. London: Hutchinson, 1953. 312p.

2719 Osborne, Walter D. Horse Racing. PB Special, no. 10102. New York: Pocket Books, 1966. 96p.

2720 Palmer, Joseph H. This Was Racing. New York: A. S. Barnes, 1953. 270p.

2721 Pattern Races. Wellingborough, Eng.: Weatherby, 1972--. v. 1--.

2722 Pegg, Norman. Focus on Racing. London: Hale, 1963. 192p.

2723 Phipps, Herb. Bill Kyne of Bay Meadow: The Man Who Brought Horse Racing Back to California. South Brunswick, NJ: A. S. Barnes, 1978. 174p.

2724 Pitman, Richard. Good Horses Make Good Jockeys. London: Pelham Books, 1976. 134p.

2725 Plante, Rem. Australian Horse Racing and Punters' Guide. North Ryde, New South Wales, 1974. 360p.

2726 Pollard, Jack. The Pictorial History of Australian Race Horsing. Sydney and New York: Hamlyn Publishing, 1971. 320p.

2727 Pullein-Thompson, Josephine. Race Horse Holiday. London: Collins, 1977. 127p.

2728 "Race Meeting in Far Hills [New Jersey]." Town and Country, CXXIX (October 1975), 152-155.

2729 Raceform Annual. London: Raceform, Ltd., 1950--. v. 16--.

2730 The Racing Calendar: Races Past. Wellingborough, Eng.: Weatherby, 1950--.

2731 The Racing Calendar: Races to Come. Wellingborough, Eng.: Weatherby, 1950--. v. 178--.

2732 Ransden, Caroline. Racing Without Tears. New and rev. ed. London: J. A. Allen, 1976. 87p.

2733 Rickman, Eric. Come Racing With Me. London: Chatto and Windus, 1951. 260p.

2734 Rodrigo, Robert, ed. The Paddock Book: A Miscellany of the Turf. London: Macdonald and Company, 1967. 255p.

2735 Ruff's Guide to the Turf. London: Sporting Life, 1950--.

2736 Scott, Karl, et al. Turf, Tufts, and Toeweights. Christchurch, New Zealand: Carlton, 1954. 304p.

2737 Scott, Marvin B. The Racing Game. Chicago: Aldine Publishing Company, 1968. 186p.

2738 Seth-Smith, Michael and Roger Mortimer. Derby 200: The Official Story of the Blue Riband of the Turf. London: Guinness Superlatives, 1979. 123p.

2739 Snyder, W. W. "Horse Racing: Testing the Efficient Markets Model." Journal of Finance, XXXIII (September 1978), 1109-1118.

2740 Sporting Chronicle, Editors of. Racing Up-to-Date. London: Kemsley, 1950--.

2741 Sporting Life's Guide to the Turf: Annual Summary of Past Racing for the Year 19 . London: Cape, 1957--. v. 1--.

2742 Sprague, Howard B. Turf Management Handbook. 2nd ed. Danville, IL: Interstate Printers and Publishers, 1976. 258p.

2743 Stewart, Kenneth. A Background to Racing. London: J. A. Allen, 1976. 142p.

2744 _____. Racing for Pleasure and Profit. London: S. Paul, 1966. 144p.

2745 Stringer, Erich H. Stringer's Standardbred Statistics. Perth, Aust., 1971. 112p.

2746 Surface, Bill. The Track. New York: Macmillan 1976.

2747 Talmadge, Marian and Iris Gilmore. Six Great Horse Rides. New York: G. P. Putnam, 1968. 127p. [juv.]

2748 Tilley, Chuck and Gene Plowden. This Is Horse Racing. Miami, FL: E. A. Seemann Publications, 1974. 183p.

2749 The Times, Editors of. Field Sports. London: Times Publishing Company, 1961. 132p.

2750 Vamplew, Wray. The Turf: A Social and Economic History of Horse Racing. London: Allen Lane, 1976. 288p.

2751 Veeck, Bill and Edward Linn. Thirty Tons a Day. New York: Viking Press, 1972. 296p.

2752 Wade, Horace A. Tales of the Turf. New York: Vantage Press, 1956. 206p.

2753 Weatherby and Sons. Weatherby's 200 Years Service to Racing. Wellingborough, Eng., 1973. 16p.

2754 Wilkinson, Jack and Warren Grant, eds. Great Australian Turf Pictures. Melbourne, Aust.: Sun Books, 1976. 96p.

2755 William Hill Racing Yearbook. London: Queen Anne Press, 1973--. v. 1--.

2756 Woods, David F., ed. The Fireside Book of Horse Racing. New York: Simon and Schuster, 1963. 341p.

B RULES AND REPORTS

2757 Arkansas. State Racing Commission. Rules and Regulations Governing Horse Racing in Arkansas. Little Rock, 1973. 149p.

2758 California. Horse Racing Board. Annual Report. Los Angeles, 1969--. v. 1--.

2759 Delaware. Racing Commission. Rules of Racing for Delaware. Dover, 1975. 78p.

2760 Florida. Legislative Council. Committee on General Legislation. Racing and the Pari-Mutuel Industry in Florida: A Study Report. Tallahassee: Legislative Council and Legislative Reference Bureau, 1965. 42p.

2761　Great Britain. Racing Industry Committee of Inquiry. The Racing Industry: Report. London: H. M. Stationery Office, 1968. 170p.

2762　Hannah, Harold W. "Veterinarians, Horse Trainers, and Racing Boards." American Veterinary Medical Association Journal, CLXVIII (June 1, 1976), 1004+.

2763　Hong Kong. Race Courses Committee. Report. Hong Kong: S. Young, 1968. 19p.

2764　Humphreys, John O. , ed. Racing Law. 3 vols. Lexington, KY: National Association of State Racing Commissioners, 1963-1973.

2765　Idaho. State Horse Racing Commission. Annual Report. Boise, 1965--. v. 1--.

2766　Illinois. General Assembly. Legislative Investigation Commission. The Illinois Racing Board Controversy: A Report. Chicago, 1973. 104p.

2767　_____. Racing Board. Annual Report. Chicago, 1974--. v. 1--.

2768　_____. _____. Rules and Regulations of Harness Racing. Springfield, 1972. 101p.

2769　Indiana. Legislative Council. Interim Study Committee. Report on Racing. Indianapolis, 1976. 133p.

2770　Ireland, Republic of. Racing Board. Annual Report. Dublin, 1950--. v. 5--.

2771　Kentucky. State Racing Commission. Annual Report. Lexington, 1950--. v. 12--.

2772　McCulley, Jim. 25 Years After: A Quarter-Century Report on the T. R. P. B. and Its Vital Role in the Ecology of Thoroughbred Racing. Hyde Park, NY: Thoroughbred Racing Protective Bureau, 1970. 46p.

2773　Maine. Running Horse Racing Commission. Rules and Regulations of Horse Racing. Augusta, 1964. 121p.

2774　Maryland. Legislative Council. Committee on Racing. Report. Baltimore, 1960. 36p.

2775　Michigan. Governor's Committee on Racing. Report. Lansing, 1969. 30p.

2776　_____. Racing Commission. Annual Report. Detroit, 1950--. v. 2--.

2777 Miller, William S. , ed. The Racing Commissioners' Manual. Lexington, KY: National Association of State Racing Commissioners. 1966. 401p.

2778 Montana. State Horse Racing Commission. Laws, Rules, and Regulations Governing Racing in the State of Montana. Helena, 1972. 86p.

2779 New Hampshire. State Racing Commission. Annual Report. Concord, 1950--. v. 18--.

2780 New Jersey. Racing Commission. Annual Report. Trenton, 1950--. v. 1--.

2781 _____. _____. Rules and Regulations for Harness Racing. Trenton, 1965. 68p.

2782 New Mexico. State Racing Commission. Annual Report. Albuquerque, 1952--. v. 1--.

2783 New York. Department of Transportation. Division of Racing. Annual Report. New York, 1950--.

2784 _____. Legislature. Joint Committee on Quarter Horse Racing. Report. Albany, 1965. 51p.

2785 _____. State Racing and Wagering Board. Annual Report. New York, 1973--. v. 1--.

2786 New Zealand. Royal Commission on Horse Racing, Trotting, and Dog Racing in New Zealand. Report. Wellington: A. R. Shearer, 1970. 322p.

2787 Ohio. State Racing Commission. Annual Report. Columbus, 1950--. v. 32--.

2788 Pennsylvania. State Harness Racing Commission. Annual Report. Harrisburg, 1950--.

2789 Rhode Island. Racing and Athletics Commission. Annual Report. Providence, 1950--.

2790 Stewart, Kenneth. Racing Control [in Britain]. London: J. A. Allen, 1974. 108p.

2791 United States. Congress. House. Committee on Interstate and Foreign Commerce. Subcommittee on Transportation and Commerce. Interstate Horseracing Act of 1976: Hearings. 95th Cong. , 2nd sess. Washington, D. C. : U. S. Government Printing Office, 1976. 175p.

2792 _____. _____. _____. _____. _____. Interstate Horseracing Act of 1977: Hearings. 95th Cong. , 2nd sess.

Washington, D. C. : U. S. Government Printing Office, 1978. 32p.

2793 Vermont. Racing Commission. Rules and Regulations. Montpelier, 1976. 265p.

2794 West Virginia. Racing Commission. Annual Report. Charleston, 1950--.

C SPECIFIC RACECOURSES

1 United States

2795 Browne, Edwin H. C. "The Boss Man [Chick Lang] of Pimlico." American Horseman, III (May 1973), 39-41, 65.

2796 Cooke, Alistair. "The Road to Churchill Downs." In: his Talk About America. New York: Alfred A. Knopf, 1968. pp. 128-137.

2797 Duis, Perry R. and Glen E. Holt. "Derby Day at Washington Park [Racetrack, Chicago]." Chicago, XXVII (December 1978), 266+.

2798 Harness Tracks of America. Directory. Chicago, 1954--. v. 1--.

2799 Kweskin, Steve. "Oaklawn Park [Arkansas]." Western Horseman, XLI (December 1976), 46-48.

2800 McCormick, Sean. "America's Ten Greatest Racetracks." Turf and Sport Digest, LIII (August 1976), 49-59.

2801 Murray, William. "Del Mar: A Summer With the Horses." New West, I (July 5, 1976), 40+.

2802 _____. "In the Money (Room) at Santa Anita." Los Angeles, XXI (February 1976), 54-55.

2803 Smith, Gene. "The Belmont of the Berkshires." Country Journal, III (Fall 1976), 42+.
Barrington Racecourse in Massachusetts.

2804 Surface, William. The Track: A Day in the Life of Belmont Park [New York]. New York and London: Macmillan, 1976. 228p.

2805 Sweeney, Brian. "A Royal Highway [Santa Anita] to Turf Glory." Classic, III (April-May 1978), 62-70.

2806 Tower, Whitney. "The Myth of the Belmont." Classic, III (June-July 1978), 48-53.

2807   Zimmermann, Mrs. James M., ed. "The Sport of Kings: Horseracing in Cincinnati." Cincinnati Historical Society Bulletin. XXXI (Summer 1973), 105-114.

2   Great Britain

2808   Campling, Peter. The Park Courses. London: Field Sport Publications, 1959. 60p.
       Tracks in southeastern England.

2809   Curling, B. W. R. British Racecourses. London: Weatherby, 1951. 148p.

2810   Directory of the British Turf. London: Chancery House, 1961--. v. 1--.

2811   Eaton, Michael. Go Horseracing with BP: A Detailed Guide to the Racecourses of England, Scotland and Wales. London: BP Retail Market Division of Shell Mex and BP, 1972. 114p.

2812   The Epsom Story. London: N. Neave, 1965. 24p.

2813   Fairfax-Blakeborough, John. Chester Races. London: Reid-Hamilton, 1951. 20p.

2814   _____. Edinburgh Racecourse. London: Reid-Hamilton, 1953. 24p.

2815   _____. Hamilton Park Racecourse. London: Reid-Hamilton, 1953. 24p.

2816   _____. Kelso Races [Roxborough]. London: Reid-Hamilton, 1955. 32p.

2817   _____. Racecourses of Yorkshire. London: Reid-Hamilton, 1953. 68p.

2818   _____. Short History of Ayr and Bogside Races. London: Reid-Hamilton, 1953. 36p.

2819   _____. Short History of Birmingham Races. London: Reid-Hamilton, 1951. 28p.

2820   _____. Short History of Doncaster Racecourse. London: Reid-Hamilton, 1950. 36p.

2821   _____. Short History of Great Yarmouth Racecourse. London: Reid-Hamilton, 1951. 20p.

2822   _____. Short History of Lanark Races. London: Reid-Hamilton, 1953. 16p.

2823 _____. Short History of Redcar Racecourse [Cleveland, England]. London: Reid-Hamilton, 1950. 32p.

2824 _____. Short History of Thirsk Racecourse [Hambleton]. London: Reid-Hamilton, 1950. 36p.

2825 _____. Short History of Wolverhampton Races. London: Reid-Hamilton, 1950. 24p.

2826 _____. Short History of York Racecourse. London: Reid-Hamilton, 1950. 52p.

2827 _____. Weatherby Racecourse [West Yorkshire]. London: Reid-Hamilton, 1950. 24p.

2828 Gale, Joan. The Blaydon Races. Newcastle-on-Tyne, Eng.: Oriel Press, 1970. 56p.
        Track at Gateshead, England.

2829 Graham, Clive. A Short History of Cheltenham Racecourse. London: Reid-Hamilton, 1950. 28p.

2830 Greaves, Ralph. Racecourses of Scotland. London: Reid-Hamilton, 1955. 124p.

2831 _____. Racecourses of Yorkshire: Stockton. London: Reid-Hamilton, 1956. 40p.

2832 _____. Short History of Carlisle Racecourse [Cumbria]. London: Reid-Hamilton, 1955. 36p.

2833 _____. Short History of Cheltenham, Folkestone, Fontwell Park, Plimpton, Lewes, Alexandra Park. London: Field Sports Publications, 1959. 48p.

2834 _____. Short History of Haydock Park Racecourse. London: Reid-Hamilton, 1959. 24p.

2835 Hedges, Alfred A. C. Racing at Yarmouth for 257 Years. Yarmouth, Eng.: The Great Yarmouth Corporation Racecourse Committee, 1973. 18p.

2836 Hunn, David. Epsom Racecourse: Its Story and Its People. London: Davis-Paynter, 1973. 217p.

2837 Johnston, Frank, ed. Cheltenham and West Country Meetings. London: Sporting Publications, 1950. 32p.

2838 _____. History of Yorkshire Racing. London: Sporting Publications, 1950. 48p.

2839 Kirkpatrick, J. C. The Liverpool Racecourse and the Grand National. London: Reid-Hamilton, 1953. 48p.

2840 Moorhouse, Sydney. The North Western Courses. London: Field Sports Publications, 1961. 64p.

2841 Onslow, Richard. The Heath and the Turf: A History of Newmarket. London: Barker, 1971. 296p.

2842 Orchard, Vincent R. Short History of Bath Racecourse. London: Reid-Hamilton, 1953. 12p.

2843 Ramsden, Herbert. Farewell Manchester: A History of Manchester Racecourse. London: J. A. Allen, 1966. 212p.

2844 Seth-Smith, Michael. Royal Ascot. London: Pitkin Pictorials, 1971. 24p.

2845 Slater, John. Newmarket: Home of Horseracing. Lavenham, Eng.: Landmark Press, 1968. 80p.

2846 Treadwell, Sandy. "Roiling on a Blessed Plot." Classic, IV (April-May 1979), 60-63.
        England's Cartmel racecourse.

2847 Wilding, Suzanne. "All the Queen's Horses." Town and Country, CXXXII (June 1979), 34+.
        Royal Ascot.

3 France

2848 Ashland, Linda. "Deauville." Town and Country, CXXX (August 1976), 58+.

2849 Boulat, Annie. "Something Special on Subway Stops." Classic, IV (June-July 1979), 38-41.
        Auteuil racecourse.

D HARNESS RACING

1 General Works

2850 Ainslie, Tom. Ainslie's Complete Guide to Harness Racing. New York: Trident Press, 1970. 480p.

2851 Arnold, Jobie. "There's No Racing Like Sulky Racing." Town and Country, CXXX (October 1976), 209+.

2852 Bergstein, Stan. "The Best Ever in Harness." Classic, III (December 1977-January 1978), 58-65.

2853 _____. "Harness Racing: Case for Change in an Old Institution." Classic, II (December 1976-January 1977), 38.

2854 _____. "Harness Racing: Hitch Your Sulky to a Star."
Equus, no. 22 (August 1979), 55-63.

2855 Betts, John R. "Agricultural Fairs and the Rise of Harness
Racing." Agricultural History, XXVII (April 1953), 71-75.

2856 Evans, Donald P. Still Hooked on Harness Racing. South
Brunswick, NJ: A. S. Barnes, 1978. 254p.

2857 Gilbey, Walter. The Harness Horse. 5th ed., rev. Royal
Parade, Eng.: Spur Publications, 1976. 100p.

2858 Leehsen, Charlie. "Leading the New Way." Classic, IV
(June-July 1979), 32-37.

2859 Maule, Tex. "Old Favorite with New Pizzazz." Classic, III
(February-March 1978), 62-69.

2860 _____. "Sharp of Eye, Firm of Hand." Classic, IV (February-March 1979), 28-31.

2861 Murray, William. Trot, Trot to Moscow. Greenfield, OH:
Greenfield Printing and Publishing Company, 1964. 142p.

2862 Novick, David. An Economic Study of Harness Racing. Santa
Monica, CA, 1962. 148p.

2863 Pines, Philip A. The Complete Book of Harness Racing.
3rd ed., rev. and enl. New York: Arco, 1978. 331p.

2864 Properjohn, Russ. "Harness Racing Down Under." Western
Horseman, XXXVIII (July 1973), 22-24, 122-126.
Australia.

2865 Roblin, Ronald. The Better's Guide to Harness Racing. Se-
caucus, NJ: Citadel Press, 1979. 216p.

2866 Rose, Carol. "Handling Horses in Harness." Western Horseman, XLIV (August 1979), 89-90.

2867 Stanavich, Felix. Trotters-Pacers. Salem, NH, 1967. 99p.

2868 Sullivan, George. Harness Racing. London: Fleet Publications, 1964. 121p.

2869 United States Trotting Association. Annual Yearbook of Trotting and Pacing. Columbus, OH, 1950--. v. 35--.

2870 _____. Trotting and Pacing Guide. Columbus, OH, 1965--.
v. 1--.

2871 _____. Your Key to Harness Racing. Columbus, OH,
1978. 33p.

2872 Welsh, Peter C. Track and Road, the American Trotting Horse: A Pictorial Record, 1820-1900. Washington, D.C.: Smithsonian Institution Press, 1967. 174p.

2873 Wolverton, Clair C. Fifty Years with Harness Horses. Harrisburg, PA: Stackpole Books, 1957. 179p.

2 Specific Races

2874 Crane, William H. The Hambletonian Winners, 1926-1950. Harrisburg, PA: Telegraph Press, 1950. 99p.

2875 Mitchell, David P. "Long Hours of Sun, Then Snow." Classic, III (October-November 1978), 140-145. Harness racing in Denmark.

E FLAT RACING

1 General Works

2876 Ainslie, Tom. Ainslie's Complete Guide to Thoroughbred Racing. Rev. ed. New York: Simon and Schuster, 1979. 470p.

2877 American Paint Horse Association. The Paint Horse Racing Chart Book [1966-1973]. Ft. Worth, TX, 1974. 110p.

2878 American Quarter Horse Racing. Los Alamitos, CA, 1972. 40p.

2879 Ayres, Michael and Gary Newbon. Under Starter's Orders: A Guide to Racing on the Flat. London: David and Charles, 1975. 208p.

2880 Batchelor, Denzil. The Turf of Old. London: Weatherby, 1951. 208p.

2881 Bland, Ernest, ed. Flat Racing Since 1900. London: Andrew Dakers, 1950. 356p.

2882 Broun, Heywood H. "A Day at the Races." Travel and Leisure, VI (April 1976), 40-42.

2883 _____. "I Own a Racehorse." Travel and Leisure, V (October 1975), 52+.

2884 Coleridge, Georgina. That's Racing: A Dream That Happened. London: Heinemann, 1978. 143p.

2885 DeHolguin Cayzer, Bea. "International Racing." Spur, XIV (January-February 1978), 31-38.

2886 Herbert, Ivor. Spot the Winner: Inside Racing with Whit-
      bread. London: Hutchinson, 1978. 100p.

2887 Hirsch, Joe and Gene Plowden. In the Winner's Circle: The
      Jones Boys [Benjamin A. and Horace A.] of Calumet Farm.
      New York: Mason and Lipscomb, 1974. 172p.

2888 Hislop, John. From Start to Finish: First Steps to Flat-Race
      Riding. London: Hutchinson, 1958. 208p.

2889 _____. The Theory and Practice of Flat-Race Riding.
      London: British Racehorse, 1971. 28p.

2890 Kisamore, Norman D. A Primer for Eastern [U.S.] Racing.
      New York: Dodd, Mead, 1963. 262p.

2891 Kolb, Ken. "It's Pony Time." New Orleans, XI (January
      1977), 7-19.

2892 Lewis, Jack. "The Great Spotted Runaway." Horse and
      Rider, IX (April 1970), 32-36.

2893 Lloyd, Alan. "This Is the Triple Crown--USA." Spur, XIV
      (November-December 1978), 46-54.

2894 McCanliss, Irene. Weight on the Thoroughbred Horse. Ches-
      ter, MA, 1967. 326p.

2895 May, Julian. The Triple Crown of Racing. Mankato, MN:
      Creative Education, 1976. 45p. [juv.]

2896 Miles, Hugh T. Horse on Course. South Brunswick, NJ:
      A. S. Barnes, 1978. 117p.

2897 Moore, Bob. "Racing on the Grass." Spur, XIV (November-
      December 1978), 11-17.

2898 Mortimer, Roger. The Encyclopedia of Flat Racing. London:
      Hale, 1971. 444p.

2899 _____. The Flat: Flat Racing in Britain Since 1939. Lon-
      don: Allen and Unwin, 1979. 406p.

2900 Nye, Nelson C. Speed and the Quarter Horse: A Payload of
      Sprinters. Caldwell, ID: Caxton Publishing Company,
      1973. 356p.

2901 Phifer, Kate G. Track Talk: An Introduction to Thoroughbred
      Racing. Washington, D.C.: Robert B. Luce, 1978. 246p.

2902 Programmes of Flat Races. Wellingborough, Eng.: Weather-
      by, 1971--. v. 1--.

2903 Reeves, Richard S. and Patrick Robinson. Decade of Champions: The Greatest Years in the History of Thoroughbred Racing, 1970-1980. Birmingham, AL: Oxmoor House, 1980. 192p.

2904 Robertson, Anna. "The Backside of Racing." Horse and Rider, XIII (July 1974), 37-40, 45-47.

2905 Robertson, William H. P. The History of Thoroughbred Racing in America. Englewood Cliffs, NJ: Prentice-Hall, 1964. 621p.

2906 Rodrigo, Robert. The Racing Game: A History of Flat Racing. London: Phoenix House, 1958. 224p.

2907 Seth-Smith, Michael, ed. A History of Flat Racing. London: New English Library, 1978. 128p.

2908 Shoemaker, Willie and Daniel G. Smith. The Shoe: Willie Shoemaker's Illustrated Book of Racing. Chicago: Rand McNally, 1976. 208p.

2909 Sweeney, Tony. Carroll's Guide to Irish Racing. Dublin: Carroll's, 1972. 52p.

2910 Swidler, David T. All About Thoroughbred Horse Racing: Aristocrat of Sports. Miami, FL: Hialeah Guild Publications, 1967. 189p.

2911 Thoroughbred Racing Association of the United States. Directory and Record Book. New York, 1955--. v. 1--.

2912 Tower, Whitney. "The Best Ever to Race in the U.S." Classic, II (June-July 1977), 60-66.

2913 _____. "Puzzle of the Two Year Olds." Classic, IV (February-March 1979), 48-54.

2914 _____. "Steady in a Rising Market." Classic, III (February-March 1978), 70-75.
       Flat racing in Canada.

2915 Treadwell, Sandy. "Fast, Fast Growth Industry." Classic, III (October-November 1978), 48-59.
       Quarter horse racing.

2916 Wiggins, Walt. The Great American Speedhorse: A Guide to Quarter Racing. New York: Sovereign Books, 1978. 270p.

2917 Willoughby, David P. "Who's Really the Greatest?" Western Horseman, XXXVIII (November 1973), 40-42, 189.

2918 Wilson, Keith and A. S. Lussier. Off and Running: Horse

Racing in Manitoba. Winnipeg, Man. : Peguis Publications, 1978. 96p.

2919 Witte, Randy. " 'Easy Angels' Dash for Cash." Western Horseman, XLIV (November 1979), 38-42.
Quarter racing.

2 Specific Races

2920 Ainsworth, Robert G. Sports in the Nation's Capital: A Pictorial History. Norfolk, VA: Donning, 1978. 295p.

2921 Alwan, Dick. "All-American Futurity." Western Horseman, XLI (November 1976), 36, 134.

2922 Arcaro, Eddie. "The [Kentucky] Derby Ain't What It Used to Be." Spur, XVI (May-June 1980), 32-39.

2923 Betts, John. The Derby. London, 1956. 24p.

2924 Buchanan, Lamont. The Kentucky Derby Story. New York: E. P. Dutton, 1954. 157p.

2925 Cavanough, Maurice and Meurig Davies. Cup Day: The Story of the Melbourne Cup, 1861-1960. Melbourne, Aust. : F. W. Cheshire, 1960. 370p.

2926 Chew, Peter. The Kentucky Derby: The First 100 Years. Boston: Houghton Mifflin, 1974. 303p.

2927 Coldsmith, Don. "The Greatest Horse Race in History." Western Horseman, XLIV (March 1979), 74-78.
In Chadron, Nebraska, 1893.

2928 Fairfax-Blakeborough, John. Northern Turf History. 3 vols. London: J. A. Allen, 1948-1951.

2929 Foulds, Jervis. The History of the Lady Dudley Challenge Cup, 1897-1977. London: J. A. Allen, 1978. 176p.

2930 Frayne, Trent. The Queen's Plate. Toronto, Ont. : McClelland and Stewart, 1959. 108p.

2931 Gildea, William. "America's No. 1 [Washington, D. C.] International Horse Race." Town and Country, CXXXII (November 1978), 106+.

2932 Hamilton, Samantha. "Bush Racing on the Bayous [of Louisiana]." Equus, no. 22 (August 1979), 40-46, 86.

2933 Hawkins, Christopher. The Race of the Century: Grundy and Bustino at Ascot. London: Allen and Unwin, 1976. 159p.

2934 Huff, Doug. Sports in West Virginia: A Pictorial History. Virginia Beach, VA: Donning, 1979. 253p.

2935 The Irish Sweeps Derby. Dublin, 1962--. v. 1--.

2936 Irving, Robert M. and Kenneth Carley. "Horse Racing on Ice was Popular in the Twin Cities." Minnesota History, XLI (Winter 1969), 372-384.

2937 Kweskin, Steve. "The 100th Kentucky Derby." Western Horseman, XXXIX (August 1974), 12+.

2938 Levy, William V. The [Kentucky] Derby. Cleveland, OH: World Publishing Company, 1967. 150p.

2939 Linde, Martha. "In Nebraska: The 1886 Horse Race." Western Horseman, XXXVIII (August 1973), 84, 196-179.

2940 McIlvanney, Hugh. "Plebeian and Too Bloody Unique." Classic, II (June-July 1977), 94-99.
         Britain's Epsom Derby.

2941 May, Julian. The Kentucky Derby. Mankato, MN: Creative Education, 1975. 47p. [juv.]

2942 Mortimer, Roger. The History of the Derby Stakes. New ed. London: Joseph, 1973. 764p.

2943 Orchard, Vincent. The Derby Stakes: A Complete History from 1900 to 1953. London: Hutchinson, 1954. 325p.

2944 Palethorpe, Michael. "Queen's Plate Nostalgia: A Fond Look at the Inferno Years." Canadian Horse, (June 1976), 12-22.

2945 "Pimlico and the Preakness." The Backstretch, XV (April-June 1976), 12-18.

2946 Scott, Jim. "Right--Not Quite!" Horse and Rider, XIV (May 1975), 22-26.

F STEEPLECHASING AND POINT-TO-POINT

1 General Works

2947 Alcock, Anne. They're Off: The Story of the First Girl Jump Jockeys. London: J. A. Allen, 1979. 152p.

2948 Ayres, Michael and Gary Newbon. Over the Sticks: The Sport of National Hunt Racing. London: David and Charles, 1971. 216p.

2949 Barr, David. "Point-to-Point Racing in Britain." Western Horseman, XLI (November 1976), 20-22.

2950 Bauer, Dan. "Hunt Racing." Western Horseman, XLI (March 1976), 50-52, 106.

2951 Brush, Peter. The Hunter-Chaser. London: Hutchinson, 1947. 192p.

2952 The Chaseform Annual. London: Raceform, Ltd., 1950--.

2953 Cranham, Gerry, et al. The Guinness Guide to Steeplechasing. London: Guinness Superlatives, 1978. 240p.

2954 Curling, Bill. All the Queen's Horses. London: Chatto and Windus, 1978. 146p.

2955 Drage, Bert. Reminiscences. Kettering, Eng.: David Green, 1955. 78p.

2956 Eliot, Elizabeth. Portrait of a Sport: The Story of Steeple-chasing in Great Britain and the United States. Woodstock, VT: Countryman, 1958. 141p.

2957 Herbert, Ivor. The Queen Mother's Horses. London: Pelham Books, 1967. 244p.

2958 _____ and Patricia Smiley. The Winter Kings. London: Pelham Books, 1968. 187p.

2959 Hislop, John. Steeplechasing. London: J. A. Allen, 1973. 250p.

2960 _____. _____. New York: E. P. Dutton, 1952. 255p.

2961 Lofting, Colin M. "Meanwhile Back East, It's Steeplechasing." Western Horseman, XLV (April 1980), 68-74.

2962 National Hunt Racing Handbook. Haywards-Heath, Eng.: Vial-lupade, 1971--. v. 1--.

2963 National Hunt Trainer's Association. Report of the Subcom-mittee Appointed to Investigate the National Hunt Pro-gramme. Wellingborough, Eng.: Weatherby, 1971. 56p.

2964 National Steeplechase and Hunt Association. Steeplechasing in America. Elmont, NY, 1950--. v. 3--.

2965 O'Connor, Sally. "Everyone for Himself and the Devil Take the Hindmost." Horse Lover's National Magazine, XLIII (May 1978), 30-35.

2966 Pearn, Tony. The Secret of Successful Steeplechasing: Mostly

Chasing, Sometimes Hunting, and a Little Dressage. London: Pelham Books, 1972. 121p.

2967 Programmes of Steeplechases. Wellingborough, Eng.: Weatherby, 1971--. v. 1--.

2968 The Raceform Point-to-Point Annual. London: Raceform, Ltd., 1950--. v. 5--.

2969 The Racing Calendar: Steeple Chases Past. London: Weatherby, 1950--. v. 82--.

2970 Ratchus, A., comp. The Pointer Pocket Manual of Point-to-Pointers and Hunter-Chasers. London: S. V. Tachus, 1965. 80p.

2971 Sale, Geoffrey, comp. Hunter-Chasers and Point-to-Pointers. Newmarket, Eng.: Sale and MacKenzie, 1959--. v. 1--.

2972 Seth-Smith, Michael, et al. History of Steeplechasing. London: Joseph, 1969. 272p.

2973 Smith, Vian C. Point-to-Point. London: S. Paul, 1968. 168p.

2974 Watson, Sydney J. Between the Flags: A History of Irish Steeplechasing. Dublin: A. Figgis, 1969. 393p.

2975 Williams, Michael. The Continuing Story of Point-to-Point Racing. London: Pelham Books, 1970. 242p.

2976 Willoughby de Broke, John H. P., ed. Steeplechasing. Lonsdale Library, v. 32. Woodstock, VT: Countryman, 1956. 334p.

2 Specific Races

2977 Graham, Clive. The Grand National: An Illustrated History of the Greatest Steeplechase in the World. London: Barrie and Jenkins, 1972. 180p.

2978 Grand National Guide. Liverpool, Eng.: Kilburns, 1950--. v. 14--.

2979 Pye, J. K. A Grand National Commentary. London: J. A. Allen, 1971. 128p.

2980 Seth-Smith, Michael. "The Whitbread Gold Cup." In: Bill Kellaway, ed. Sports Spectacular. London: Queen Anne Press, 1972. passim.

2981 Smith, Vian C. The Grand National: A History of the World's Steeplechase. London: S. Paul, 1969. 207p.

2982 Welcome, John. The Cheltenham Gold Cup: The Story of a
Great Steeplechase. New and rev. ed. London: Pelham
Books, 1973. 213p.

2983 Wilding, Suzanne. "America's Grand National." Town and
Country, CXXXIII (May 1979), 143+.

G JOCKEYS

1 Collective Biography

2984 Ainslie, Tom. The Jockey Book: The Relationship of Jockeys
to the Winning and Losing of Horse Races. New York:
Simon and Schuster, 1967. 145p.

2985 Cleaver, Hylton. Their Greatest Rides. London: Hale, 1959.
158p.

2986 Fitzgeorge-Parker, Tim. Flat-Race Jockeys: The Great
Ones. London: Pelham Books, 1973. 256p.

2987 _____. Steeplechase Jockeys: The Great Ones. London:
Pelham Books, 1971. 128p.

2988 Luro, Horatio and A. G. Vanderbilt. "The Magic of Two
Great Jockeys as Seen by Two Experts." Classic, III
(August-September 1978), 84-87.
Steve Cauthen and Lester Piggott.

2989 McCann, Tom. "Can Girls Be Jockeys?" Horse and Horseman, III (October 1975), 26-30.

2990 Williams, Dorian. A Gallery of Riders. London: Burke,
1963. 128p.

2 Specific Individuals

Eddie Arcaro

2991 Arcaro, Eddie. I Ride to Win. New York: Greenberg, 1951.
273p.

2992 Frank, Steve. "Visit with Eddie Arcaro." In: Saturday
Evening Post, Editors of. Sport U. S. A. New York:
Nelson, 1961. pp. 441-447.

2993 Kahn, Robert. "Eddie Arcaro." In: Edward E. Fitzgerald,
ed. Heroes of Sport. New York: Bartholomew House,
1960. pp. 224-234.

2994 Lamparski, Richard. "Eddie Arcaro." In: his What Ever
Became Of.... New York: Crown, 1967. pp. 70-71.

2995   Morey, Charles. "Eddie Arcaro, King of the Stakes Riders."
In: Associated Press, Staff of. Sports Immortals. Englewood Cliffs, NJ: Prentice-Hall, 1974. pp. 202-208.

2996   Stump, Al J. "Eddie Arcaro." In: his Champions Against
Odds. Philadelphia: Macrae Smith, 1952. pp. 21-32.

2997   _____. "Heady Eddie." In: Esquire, Editors of. Great
Men and Moments in Sport. New York: Harper and Row,
1962. pp. 94-98.

Fred Archer

2998   Brennan, John. Fred Archer: His Life and Times. By John
Welcome, pseud. London: Faber and Faber, 1967. 208p.

Cecil H. Blacker

2999   Blacker, Cecil H. Soldier in the Saddle. London: Burke,
1963. 192p.

Edgar Britt

3000   Britt, Edgar. Post Haste. London: Muller, 1967. 175p.

Harry Carr

3001   Carr, Harry. Queen's Jockey. London: S. Paul, 1966.
190p.

Steve Cauthen

3002   Axthelm, Pete. The Kid. New York: Viking Press, 1978.
243p.

3003   Keely, Scott. Steve Cauthen. Mankato, MN: Creative Education, 1979. 32p. [juv.]

3004   Miklowitz, Gloria. Steve Cauthen. New York: Grosset and
Dunlap, 1979. 80p. [juv.]

3005   Meuser, Anne M. Picture Story of Jockey Steve Cauthen.
New York: Julian Messner, 1979. 64p. [juv.]

3006   Pitts, Don. "A Magnificent Bug." Horse and Rider, XVII
(April 1977), 46-49.

3007   Tuttle, Anthony. Steve Cauthen, Boy Jockey. New York:
G. P. Putnam, 1978. 47p. [juv.]

Joe Childs

3008   Childs, Joe. My Racing Reminiscences. London: Hutchinson, 1952. 180p.

Jim Coleman

3009   Coleman, Jim. A Hoofprint on My Heart. Toronto, Ont.:
McClelland and Stewart, 1971. 256p.

Dick Francis

3010   Francis, Dick. The Sport of Queens. Rev. ed. London:
Joseph, 1968. 245p.

Quintin Gilbey

3011   Gilbey, Quintin. Fun Was My Living. London: Hutchinson,
1970. 312p.

Lynn Haney

3012   Haney, Lynn. The Lady Is a Jock. New York: Dodd, Mead,
1973. 180p.

Anne Henderson

3013   Henderson, Anne. "The View from the Backstretch." Women
Sports, II (March 1975), 51-55.

Marie Irigary

3014   Halloran, Karen. "Lady Jockey at Sunland." Western Horseman, XLIV (April 1979), 33-34.

Julie Jewson

3015   Kweskin, Steve. "A Jockey Named Julie." Western Horseman, XLIII (September 1978), 23-24.

Rae Johnstone

3016   Johnstone, Rae. The R.J. Story. London: S. Paul, 1958. 202p.

George Lambton

3017   Lambton, George. Men and Horses I Have Known. New ed.
London: J. A. Allen, 1966. 208p.

Jack Leach

3018   Leach, Jack. A Rider on the Stand: Racing Reminiscences.
London: S. Paul, 1970. 128p.

3019   _____. Sods I Have Cut on the Turf. London: Gollancz,
1961. 192p.

John E. Longden

3020 Beckwith, Brainerd K. The Longden Legend. South Brunswick, NJ: A. S. Barnes, 1974. 235p.

3021 Stump, Al J. "John E. Longden." In: his Champions Against Odds. Philadelphia: Macrae Smith, 1952. pp. 91-102.

Jackie Martin

3022 Kweskin, Steve. "Jackie Martin, Quarter Horse Jockey." Western Horseman, XLV (March 1980), 60-64.

Joe O'Brien

3023 Hill, Marie. Gentleman Joe: The Story of Harness Driver Joe O'Brien. New York: Arco, 1975. 192p.

Lester Piggott

3024 Bailey, Ivor N. Lester Piggott, Champion Jockey. London: Barker, 1972. 156p.

3025 Duval, Claude. Lester: A Biography. London: S. Paul, 1972. 168p.

Gordon Richards

3026 Jackson, Robert. Gordon Richards. Windsor, Eng.: Day, Mason and Ford, 1952. 60p.

3027 Richards, Gordon. My Story. London: Hodder and Stoughton, 1955. 256p.

Bill Rickaby

3028 Rickaby, Bill. First to Finish. London: Souvenir Press, 1969. 154p.

Willie Shoemaker

3029 Morey, Charles. "Willie Shoemaker, Six Feet Tall in the Saddle." In: Associated Press, Staff of. Sports Immortals. Englewood Cliffs, NJ: Prentice Hall, 1974. pp. 266-271.

3030 Tower, Whitney. "How Cheerfully He Seems to Grin." Classic, IV (June-July 1979), 88-96.

3031 "Willie Shoemaker." In: Current Biography Yearbook, 1966. New York: H. W. Wilson, 1967. pp. 373-375.

Bob Sievier

3032 Brennan, John. Neck or Nothing: The Extraordinary Life of Bob Sievier. By John Welcome, pseud. London: Faber and Faber, 1970. 285p.

Charles Smirke

3033 Smirke, Charles. Finishing Post. London: Oldbourne, 1960. 184p.

Doug Smith

3034 Smith, Doug. Five Times Champion. London: Pelham Books, 1968. 191p.

Eph. Smith

3035 Smith, Eph. Riding to Win. London: S. Paul, 1968. 160p.

Robyn C. Smith

3036 Brown, Fern G. Racing Through the Odds: Robyn C. Smith. Milwaukee, WI: Raintree Editions, 1976. 47p. [juv.]

3037 Jacobs, Linda. Robyn Smith, In Silks. St. Paul, MN: E. M. C. Corp. , 1976. 38p. [juv.]

3038 "Robyn C. Smith." In: Current Biography Yearbook, 1976. New York: H. W. Wilson, 1977. pp. 383-385.

3039 Sports Illustrated, Editors of. "Robyn Smith." In: their Best of Sports Illustrated. Boston: Little, Brown, 1973. pp. 187-201.

3040 Stambler, Irwin. "Robyn Smith." In: his Women in Sports. Garden City, NY: Doubleday, 1975. pp. 60-70.

Tommy Smith

3041 McIlvaine, Jane. The Will to Win: The True Story of Tommy Smith and Jay Trump. London: J. A. Allen, 1967. 238p.

Pat Taafe

3042 Taafe, Pat. My Life and Arkle's. London: S. Paul, 1972. 84p.

Ron Turcotte

3043 "Ron Turcotte." In: Current Biography Yearbook, 1974. New York: H. W. Wilson, 1975. pp. 418-420.

Tommy Weston

3044 Weston, Tommy. <u>My Racing Life</u>. London: Hutchinson, 1952. 230p.

Fred Winter

3045 Hedges, David. <u>Mr. Grand National: The Story of Fred Winter, Jockey and Trainer</u>. London: Pelham Books, 1969. 176p.

<u>Further References</u>: See also Parts I: F and III above.

A HORSE SHOWS

3046 Abbey, Harlan C. Showing Your Horse: Blue Ribbon Horsemanship. South Brunswick, NJ: A. S. Barnes, 1970.
180p.

3047 Adams, Ruth. "Planning a Successful Horse Show." Western
Horseman, XLIII (November 1978), 16-20.

3048 American Horse Council. Horse Show Insurance. Washington,
D. C. , 1980. 7p.

3049 American Horse Shows Association. Rule Book. New York,
1950--. v. 33--.

3049a Augur, Helen. The Book of Fairs. Tower Books, 1971.
308p.
      Reprint of the 1939 edition.

3050 Austin, David W. "How to Put on a Playday." Western
Horseman, XXXVIII (February 1973), 23, 114-115.

3051 Baldwin, James. The Horse Fair. Great Neck, NY: Core
Collection Books, 1976. 418p.

3052 Batchelor, Vivien. The Observer's Book of Show Jumping and
Eventing. London: Warne, 1976. 192p.

3053 _____ and Julia Longland. Horse Trials Horses. London:
Pelham Books, 1970. 190p.

3054 Beard, Ronnie. "Horse Show Strategist." Practical Horseman, II (November-December 1973), passim.

3055 Bergen, Chan. "How to Suceed in Show Business: The Arizona Sun Country Circuit." Western Horseman, XXXIX
(April 1974), 60-62.

3056 Bloom, Lynda. "Grand Old Lady [Leila Havens] of the Show
Ring." Western Horseman, XLV (February 1980), 34-36.

3057 Burn, Barbara. The Horseless Rider: A Complete Guide to
      the Art of Riding, Showing, and Enjoying Other People's
      Horses. New York: St. Martin's Press, 1979. 233p.

3058 Burt, Don. "Not So Hot--Warm Ups." Horse and Rider,
      XVIII (July 1980), 24-26.

3059 Campbell, Judith. Pony Events. London: Batsford, 1969.
      128p.

3060 Carrithers, T. W. How to Put on a Horse Show. South
      Brunswick, NJ: A. S. Barnes, 1971. 199p.

3061 Childs, Marilyn C. Riding Show Horses. Princeton, NJ:
      Van Nostrand, 1963. 114p.

3062 Clarke, Margaret I. Riding, Jumping, and Showing. Adel-
      aide, Aust.: Rigby, 1971. 80p.

3063 Close, Pat. "Allen Ross: Horse Show Management." West-
      ern Horseman, XLIV (May 1979), 86-90.

3064 _____. "California Notes." Western Horseman, XXXIX
      (July 1974), 78-81+.

3065 _____. "Horses and Horsemen in California." Western
      Horseman, XLII (July 1977), 24-26, 101.

3066 _____. "Leonard Grotts, Horse Show Announcer." West-
      ern Horseman, XXXIX (September 1974), 7+.

3067 _____. "Tom McNair Discusses Showing the Arabian, Eng-
      lish and Western." Western Horseman, XXXVII (June 1972),
      55-58, 122-124.

3068 Coakes, Marion. Meet Stroller. London: Pelham Books,
      1967. 127p.

3069 Cooper, L. C. Horseshow Organizations. New ed. London:
      J. A. Allen, 1978.

3070 Eyestone, Cecil L. A Guide for 4-H Light Horse Shows and
      Events: Regulations, Scoring Procedures. Manhattan:
      Cooperative Extension Service, Kansas State University,
      1973. 15p.

3071 Fathing, T. E. "Show Promotion." Horseman, XXI (Novem-
      ber 1977), 63-67.

3072 Gray, Patricia C. Show and Tell. South Brunswick, NJ:
      A. S. Barnes, 1976. 85p.

3073 Griffith, Perry B. "Run a Safe Horse Show." Horse and
      Horseman, VII (September 1979), 14-17.

3074 Hanson, Christilot. Canadian Entry. Chicago: Follett Publishing Company, 1966. 140p.

3075 Harwood, Bill. "Showing." Horseman, XXII (December 1977), 20-25.

3076 Hinton, Phyllis. Showing Your Horse. Rev. ed. London: Country Life, 1964. 139p.

3077 Hogan, Chrystine J. "Course Analysis for Spectators." Practical Horseman, VIII (April 1980), 47-53.

3078 Holms, Edward. A Trip to the Horse Show. London: Nelson, 1973. 62p. [juv.]

3079 Hundt, Sheila W. Invitation to Riding. New York: Simon and Schuster, 1976. 334p.

3080 Hyde, Christopher. A Week Down in Devon: A History of the Devon [Pennsylvania] Horse Show. Philadelphia: Chilton, 1976. 145p.

3081 International Arabian Horse Association. Golden Book of Arabian Horse Showing. 48 pts. Burbank, CA, 1973-1979.

3082 Johnson, Pat. The Horse Show. Chicago: Rand McNally, 1963. 96p.

3083 Jones, Shirley M. "Junior Horse Shows: Yesterday and Today." Western Horseman, XXXVIII (December 1973), 22, 121-124.

3084 Kauffman, Sandra, comp. Rider's Digest: Showing and Combined Training. New York: Arco, 1977. 173p.

3085 King, Chuck. "Chowchilla: The Greatest." Western Horseman, XXXIX (June 1974), 74-77.

3086 McAulay, Sara. "Horse Show: All in a Day's Work." Classic, II (December 1976-January 1977), 52-61.

3087 _____. "Toronto's Royal: Love at First Sight." Classic, IV (October-November 1979), 44-49.

3088 Macgregor-Morris, Pamela. Champion Horses and Ponies of the Show Ring. London: Macdonald and Company, 1956. 223p.

3089 McKegg, Kathleen. "History of the American Horse Shows Association." Rapidan River Farm Digest, I (Winter 1975), 238-242.

3090 Murphy, Genevieve. Princess Anne and Mark Phillips Talking About Horses. London: S. Paul, 1976. 128p.

3091 National Horse and Pony Youth Activity Council. Fitting and Showing Horses. New York, 1979. 6p.

3092 _____. Horse Show Management Guidelines. New York, 1979. 19p.

3093 Oldham, William. "Let's Put the Show Back in Horse Shows." Appaloosa News, XXII (April 1967), 2-5.

3094 Pennsylvania. Department of Agriculture. Keystone International Livestock Exposition Catalog: Horse Division. Harrisburg, 1956--. v. 1--.

3095 Pinckney, Ed S., Jr. "Problems and Opportunities for the Horse Show Industry." Program/Proceedings of the National Horsemen's Seminar, II (1977), 28-31.

3096 Radlauer, Edward. Horsing Around. New York: Watts, 1972. 46p. [juv.]

3097 _____ and R. S. Horse Show Challenge. Chicago: Childrens Press, 1973. 79p. [juv.]

3098 Rhodes, Bob. "A Day at Devon." Horse of Course, IX (June 1980), 28-30.

3099 Richards, Ronnie. How to Show Your Horse and Win. Omaha, NE: Farnam Horse Library, 1978. 64p.

3100 Richter, Judy. "Preparing for a Horse Show." Practical Horseman, VII (January 1979), 8-15, 80-82.

3101 Rosner, Lynn. Let's Go to a Horse Show. New York: G. P. Putnam, 1975. 47p. [juv.]

3102 Self, Margaret C. American Horse Show, with the Official Rules and Regulations. New York: A. S. Barnes, 1958. 292p.

3103 _____. At the Horse Show with Margaret Cabell Self. New York: A. S. Barnes, 1966. 183p.

3104 Seth-Smith, Michael, ed. International Showjumping, Eventing and Dressage. London: New English Library, 1978. 128p.

3105 Sherred, Alison. Showing and Ringcraft Explained. New York: Arco, 1978. 96p.

3106 Skelton, Elizabeth. Ringcraft. London: Nelson, 1970. 102p.

3107 Spector, David. A Guide to American Horse Shows. New York: Arco, 1973. 128p.

3108 _____. So You're Showing Your Horse. New York: Arco, 1973. 120p.

3109 Spooner, Glenda. The Handbook of Showing. Rev. ed. London: J. A. Allen, 1977. 264p.

3110 Streeter, Carl B. Ready, Get Set, Show. South Brunswick, NJ: A. S. Barnes, 1979.

3111 "Study on the Economic Impact of Horse Shows." American Horse Council Newsletter, VII (February 1980), 3-6.

3112 Summerhays, Reginald S. and Charles E. G. Hope. Horse Shows: The Judges, Stewards, Organizers. London: Pelham Books, 1969. 160p.

3113 Thiffault, Mark. "A Day at the Horse Show." Horse and Horseman, VII (November 1979), 34-37.

3114 Tickner, John. Tickner's Show Piece. New York: Dial Press, 1960. 93p.

3115 Tristram, Dennis. "Green Horse--Black and Blue Rider." Horse and Rider, XVIII (March 1979), 16-19.

3116 Trozer, B. L. "The Horse Comes Back." Outdoor Indiana, XXXII (November 1966), 14-17.

3117 Warren, R. B. Nebraska 4-H Horse Show and Juding Guide. Lincoln: Cooperative Extension Service, University of Nebraska, n.d. 56p.

3118 Western Horseman, Editors of. Riding and Training for the Show Ring. Colorado Springs, CO, 1971. 48p.

3119 Wilding, Suzanne. "Horse Show, Italian Style." Town and Country, CXXIX (April 1975), 96+.

3120 Williams, Dorian. Horse of the Year: The Story of a Unique [British] Horse Show. New York: St. Martin's Press, 1976. 168p.

3121 _____. Showing Horse Sense. London: Barker, 1967. 128p.

B RODEO

3122 Allen, David. Official P.R.C.A. Pro-Rodeo Media Guide. Colorado Springs, CO: Professional Rodeo Cowboy's Association, 1979. 212p.

3123 _____. P.R.C.A. Pro-Rodeo: "The Cowboy Sport." Colorado Springs, CO: Professional Rodeo Cowboys' Association, 1979. 18p.

3124 Berry, Barbara J. Let'er Buck: The Rodeo. Indianapolis, IN: Bobbs-Merrill, 1971. 110p. [juv.]

3125 Boatright, Mody C. "The American Rodeo." American Quarterly, XVI (Summer 1964), 195-202.

3126 Clancy, Foghorn. My Fifty Years in Rodeo: Living with Cowboys, Horses, and Danger. San Antonio, TX: Naylor, 1952. 285p.

3127 Crenshaw, John. "Gallup-ing Rodeo." New Mexico Magazine, LVII (August 1979), 18+.

3128 _____. "Rodeo--a Spectator's Guide." New Mexico Magazine, LVIII (August 1979), 19+.

3129 Dane, Claudia. "Cowgirls Battle." Horse and Rider, XVII (January 1978), 19.

3130 Dayton, Jay. "The Confidence Man [Frank Craighead]." Horse and Rider, XVII (July 1978), 16-19, 51-52.

3131 Englander, Joseph B. They Ride the Rodeo: The Men and Women of the American Amateur Rodeo. New York: Macmillan, 1979. 126p.

3132 Fain, James. Rodeo: A Decade of Action. Logan, UT, 1976. 56p.

3133 Feague, Mildred H. Let's Find Out About Wild West Rodeos. New York: Watts, 1973. 47p. [juv.]

3134 _____. The True Book of Rodeos. Chicago: Childrens Press, 1972. 48p. [juv.]

3135 Fifty Years of Nebraska's Big Rodeo. Burwell, NE: J.J.J. Rodeo Books, 1975. 240p.

3136 Froome, George and Marie. Fifty Years of Rodeo: A Pictorial History of the Red Bluff [California] Round-Up. Red Bluff, CA, 1971. 150p.

3137 Girl's Rodeo Association. Reference Book. Pauls Valley, OK, 1950--. v. 2--.

3138 _____. Rule Book. Pauls Valley, OK, 1950--. v. 2--.

3139 Gray, Bob. Western Riding Games and Contests. 2nd ed. Cypress, TX: Cordovan Corp., 1964. 71p.

3140 Hall, Douglas K. Let'er Buck. New York: Saturday Review Press, 1973. 230p.

3141 _____. Rodeo. New York: Ballantine Books, 1976. 157p.

3142 Hanesworth, Robert D. Daddy of 'em All: The Story of Chey- enne Frontier Days. Cheyenne, WY: Flintlock Publishing Company, 1967. 168p.

3143 Haney, Lynn. Ride'em Cowgirl. New York: G. P. Putnam, 1975. 128p. [juv.]

3144 Hay, J. F. "Origins and Originality of Rodeo." Journal of the West, XVII (July 1978), 17-33.

3145 Helfrich, DeVere. Rodeo Pictures. Colorado Springs, CO: Western Horseman, 1966. 52p.

3146 Hill, Stub. "Brawley [California] Cattle-Call Rodeo." West- ern Horseman, XXXIX (November 1974), 39-40, 159-164.

3147 Howard, Robert W. Rodeo: The Last Frontier of the Old West. New York: New American Library, 1961. 144p.

3148 Hurley, Jimmie. "The Marvelous Marvels [Mike and Joe]." Western Horseman, XLI (November 1976), 38-41.

3149 _____. "The Rookie [Dee Pickett]." Horse and Rider, XVIII (June 1979), 30-33.

3150 "Inside the Arena." Horse Lover's National Magazine, XLIII (November 1978), 22-25.

3151 International Rodeo Association. A Humane Look at Profes- sional Rodeo. Rev. ed. Pauls Valley, OK, 1973. 21p.

3152 Josey, Martha and Jane Pattie. "A Winning Attitude." Horse and Rider, XIX (July 1980), 32-37.

3153 Justin Boot Company. Six Rodeo Greats Talk About Rodeo: The All-American Sport. Ft. Worth, TX, 1969. 16p.

3154 Karr, Lee and Lela. Rope Burns: A Fair Likeness of a Few Good Cowboys Who Know the Meaning of the Words. San Angelo, TX: Newsfoto Publishing Company, 1975. 112p.

3155 King, Chuck. "Unbelievable Augusta [Montana Rodeo]." West- ern Horseman, XLII (September 1977), 72-74.

3156 Lamb, Gene. Rodeo Back of the Chutes. Denver, CO: Bell Press, 1956. 279p.

3157 McGinnis, Vera. Rodeo Road: My Life as a Pioneer Cowgirl. New York: Hastings House, 1974. 225p.

3158 Nash, Archie L. "Thermopolis [Wyoming] Ranch Days."
Western Horseman, XLI (April 1976), 40-41, 122-124.

3159 N[ational] F[inals] R[odeo] in Action. Oklahoma City, OK,
1977. 56p.

3160 National Intercollegiate Rodeo Association. Yearbook. Huntsville, TX: Sam Houston State University, 1969--. v.
1--.

3161 O'Brien, Esse. The First Bulldogger. San Antonio, TX:
Naylor, 1961. 58p.

3162 Perry, Paul. The Rodeo. Mountain View, CA: Anderson-
World, Inc., 1980. 144p.

3163 Phipps, Gregory. "Corn Belt [Indiana] Cowboys." Western
Horseman, XLV (February 1980), 80-82.

3164 Poole, Peter N. "Australia's Own Cheyenne [Mount Isa Rodeo]."
Western Horseman, XXXVIII (November 1973), 62-64, 162-
165.

3165 Porter, Willard H. Roping and Riding: Fast Horses and
Short Ropes. South Brunswick, NJ: A. S. Barnes, 1975.
232p.

3166 Raley, Tom. Rodeo Fever. Phoenix, AZ: Latigo Press,
1979. 34p.

3167 Ramirez, Nora. The Southwestern International Livestock
Show and Rodeo. Southwestern Studies Monograph, no. 32.
El Paso, TX: Western Press, 1972. 40p.

3168 Ridgway, James L. and W. B. J. Lowden. Rodeo at Lang
Lang. Kilmore, Aust.: Lowden Publishing Company, 1976.
96p.

3169 Robertson, Mary S. Rodeo: Standard Guide to the Cowboy
Sport. Berkeley, California: Howell-North, 1961.
163p.

3170 Savitt, Sam. Rodeo: Cowboys, Bulls, and Broncos. Garden
City, NY: Doubleday, 1963. 99p.

3171 Schnell, Fred. Rodeo: The Suicide Circuit. Chicago: Rand
McNally, 1971. 127p.

3172 Sheldon, Jim and William Plummer. "Too Lazy to Work."
Quest, III (May 1979), 38-43.

3173 Shields, Bonnie. "Bishop [California] Mule Days." Western
Horseman, XLIV (January 1979), 56-58.

226 / Equestrian Studies

3174 Shields, Mitchell J. "Circuit in the Sun." Sandlapper, XII
(January 1979), 8-14.
Rodeo.

3175 Tippette, Giles. The Brave Men. New York: Macmillan,
1972. 393p.

3176 "Top Ten Rodeo Photos of 1971." Horse and Rider, XI (January 1972), 46-52.

3177 "Top Ten Rodeo Photos of 1972." Horse and Rider, XII (January 1973), 50-56.

3178 "Top Ten Rodeo Photos of 1973." Horse and Rider, XIII (January 1974), 50-55.

3179 "Top Ten Rodeo Photos of 1974." Horse and Rider, XIV (January 1975), 12-19.

3180 "Top Ten Rodeo Photos of 1975." Horse and Rider, XVI (January 1976), 26-32.

3181 "Top Ten Rodeo Photos of 1976." Horse and Rider, XVIII
(January 1977), 28-32.

3182 "Top Ten Rodeo Photos of 1977." Horse and Rider, XVII (January 1978), 38-43.

3183 "Top Ten Rodeo Photos of 1978." Horse and Rider, XVII
(January 1979), 18-22.

3184 "Top Ten Rodeo Photos of 1979." Horse and Rider, XIX (January 1980), 16-23.

3185 Treadwell, Sandy. "Hurry, Hurry, Step Right Up, America."
Classic, II (October-November 1977), 62-67.
Cheyenne Frontier Days Rodeo.

3186 Van Steenwyk, Elizabeth. Rodeo. New York: Harvey House,
1978. 78p. [juv.]

3187 Vorhes, Gary. "Bern [Gregory] Is the Name, Rodeo is the
Game." Western Horseman, XLI (December 1976), 94-96,
114-119.

3188 Western Horseman, Editors of. Rodeo Pictures. Colorado
Springs, CO, 1972. 48p.

3189 White, Randy. "They All Came Rejoicing, Bringing in the
Bucks." Western Horseman, XLV (July 1980), 38-43.

3190 Williams, Reg M. "Campdrafting in Australia." Western
Horseman, XXXVIII (January 1973), 37, 136-138.

3191 Winston Rodeo Awards Program. Winston's Pro-Rodeo. Winston-Salem, N.C.: R. J. Reynolds Tobacco Company, 1975. 48p.

3192 Witte, Randy. "Canada's All-Around Champion Cowboy, Mel Coleman." Western Horseman, XLIV (September 1979), 38-39.

3193 _____. "Copenhagen/Skoal Rodeo Superstars Championship." Western Horseman, XLIV (July 1979), 53-56.

3194 _____. "The Richest, Roughest Rodeo [National Finals]." Western Horseman, XLV (February 1980), 48-54, 96-97.

3195 _____. "What Ever Happened to Clyde [Vamvoras]?" Western Horseman, XLIII (January 1978), 62-65, 116.

3196 _____. "Who Is Tom Ferguson and How Does He Keep Winning All That Money?" Western Horseman, XLIV (August 1979), 28-32.

C COURSE DESIGN

3197 Ball, Alan. "Indoor Course Building Clinic." Practical Horseman, IV (August-September 1975), passim.

3198 Bloom, Lynda. "Raymond Gillen: Designing Trail Courses." Western Horseman, XLIII (May-June 1978), 38-40, 32-37.

3199 Carruthers, Pamela. "What Makes a Good Jumper Course?" Practical Horseman, II (April 1973), passim.

3200 Davis, Ray and Pat Close. "Controlling Dust in Indoor Arenas." Western Horseman, XXXVIII (April 1973), 33, 121-122.

3201 Haller, Roger. "Cross-Country Course Design." Practical Horseman, V (March 1977), 38-44, 51.

3202 Hogan, Chrystine J. "Designing Hunter Courses." Practical Horseman, VI (April 1978), 10-16, 74.

3203 Hough, Champ. "Hunter Course Design." Horse Lover's National Magazine, XLIII (April 1978), 19-26.

3204 Houston, Joan. Horse Show Hurdles. New York: Crowell, 1958. 243p.

3205 Langer, Larry. "Designing Jumping Courses for Small Shows." California Horse Review, XII (September 1975), 22-26.

3206 Shapiro, Neal. "An Approach to Analyzing Jumper Courses." Practical Horseman, IV (April 1976), passim.

3207 Thomson, Bill. Constructing Cross-Country Obstacles. London: J. A. Allen, 1972. 96p.

3208 Watts, Alan. Course Builder's Handbook for Horse Shows and Gymkhanas. New York: Arco, 1979. 119p.

3209 Wickes, Michael. "Build Your Own Jump Courses." Practical Horseman, VIII (May 1980), 54-55.

D JUDGING

3210 Abhau, Elliot. "More Than Looking Pretty." Horse Lover's National Magazine, XLV (April 1980), 46-48.

3211 Albaugh, Reuben. So You Want to be a Horse Judge. Leaflet, no. 2808. Rev. ed. Berkeley: Agricultural Extension Service, University of California, 1978. 7p.

3212 American Quarter Horse Association. Judging American Quarter Horses. Amarillo, TX, 1969. 9p.

3213 Arabian Horse Society. Guidelines for Organizing and Conducting a Youth Arabian Horse Judging Contest. Lebanon, OH, 1972. 16p.

3214 Barsaleau, Richard B. "The Veterinarian and Horse Show Judging." Veterinary Medicine, LCI (October 1966), 945-947.

3215 Blazer, Don. "Scandal in the Show Ring." Horse and Horseman, V (December 1977-January 1978), 30-33, 54-58.

3216 Bond, Marian. "How a Judge Sees You." Horseman, XXIII (February 1979), 48-52.

3217 _____. "The Human Element in Judging." Western Horseman, XXXVIII (November 1973), 44-46.

3218 Burt, Don. As the Judge Sees It: Arabian Showing. Covina, CA: Rich Publishing Company, 1973. 81p.

3219 _____. As the Judge Sees It: Western Division. Covina, CA: Rich Publishing Company, 1973. 75p.

3220 _____. "Judging Form and Function." Horse and Rider, XVII (September 1977), 32-34.

3221 _____. "The Qualities of a Judge." Horse Illustrated, XI (March-April 1979), 26-29.

3222 _____. "Rule Book Rhubarb." Horse and Rider, XIV (August 1975), 44, 69.

3223 _____. "Secrecy in Judging." Horse and Rider, IX (September 1970), 74.

3224 _____. "What Did I Do Wrong?" Horse and Rider, XI (June 1972), 70-73.

3225 Byford, Sharon. "Arabian Judges Seminar." Western Horseman, XXXVIII (August 1973), 90-91, 128.

3226 Clevenger, Barbara. "The Amateur vs. the Trainer." Horse and Rider, XIII (September 1974), 54-56.

3227 Close, Pat. "Hey, Judge." Western Horseman, XLV (April-May 1980), 102-103, 104-108.

3228 _____. "Judging, How It's Being Handled." Western Horseman, XLIII (May 1978), 34-36, 140-142.

3229 Cotterman, Dan and Don Burt. "Western Pleasure or Western Agony?" Horse and Rider, XII (April 1973), 36-40.

3230 DeSzinay, Andrew B. "Combined Training Judges." Dressage and CT, XIV (April 1978), 16-17.

3231 Forman, Alex. "Horse Show Judge in a Delicate Role: An Interview." Practical Horseman, V (August 1977), 22-25.

3232 Gallagher, James P. Arabian Youth Judging Guide. Burbank, CA: International Arabian Horse Association, 1978. 17p.

3233 Gibbons, Anne. "Guidelines for Judges." Dressage and CT, XIV (April 1978), 34-35.

3234 Haley, Neale. Judge Your Own Horsemanship. New York: Arco, 1974. 164p.

3235 Hatch, Eric. The Judge and the Junior Exhibition. New York: Duell, Sloan and Pearce, 1964. 89p. [juv.]

3236 Havill, Barbara. "Hunt Seat? Saddle Seat?" Horse and Rider, X (May 1971), 34-39.

3237 Hawkins, Steve. "What the Judges Like." Practical Horseman, III (May 1975), passim.

3238 Hipsley, Wayne G. Judging the Halter and Pleasure Horse in Individual and Team Competition. Boston: Cooperative Extension Service, University of Massachusetts, 1975. 49p.

3239 Hugo-Vidal, Victor. "How the Judge Marks His Card." Practical Horseman, IV (September 1976), passim.

3240 Hurley, Jimmie. "Judging the Saddle Bronc Event." Western Horseman, XL (March 1975), 60-62, 142-144.

3241 Jungherr, Carol. "The Mental Process of the Medal Judge." Practical Horseman, VI (September 1978), 8-13.

3242 King, Chuch. "The World a Pumpkin Roller: A Look at the A. Q. H. A. Judging." Western Horseman, XLIII (February 1978), 8-11.

3243 Morrison, Karen. "How Rodeo Events Are Judged." Horse of Course, VII (September 1978), 14-19.

3244 Plumb, Donna. "What Is the Dressage Judge Thinking?" Practical Horseman, VII (June 1980), 26-33.

3245 Rogalev, Georgii T. "The Competitor Through the Judge's Eyes." Dressage and CT, XVI (March 9, 1979), 6-9.

3246 Russell, Valerie. Judging Horses and Ponies. London: Pelham Books, 1978. 176p.

3247 Taggart, W. F. Horse Judging Guide for 4-H Club Members. Circular, no. E 746. Norman: Cooperative Extension Service, University of Oklahoma, 1963. 8p.

3248 Throgmorton, B. C. "The Competitive Trail Horse: How to Select a Champion." Western Horseman, XXXIX (May 1974), 110+.

3249 Timmons, Bill and Gail. "You Be the Judge." Horse and Rider, XVIII (February 1979), 36-38.

3250 Vasko, Kent A. Information for Veterinarians Officiating at CT and Dressage Events. Cleveland, OH: Dressage and CT, 1979.

3251 Wall, John F. and F. C. Jennings. Judging the Horse, for Running, Riding, and Recreation. New York: Funk and Wagnalls, 1955. 208p.

3252 "Walter Spencer Evaluates Horses." Western Horseman, XXXVII (January 1972), 64-66+.

3253 Weaver, Sue A. "A Judging Primer." Western Horseman, XLV (June 1980), 30-36.

3254 Winans, Peggy. "A Judge Talks Hunter Judging." Practical Horseman, II (March 1972), passim.

3255 Yenser, Karl. "Show Horse Abuse: An Interview." Equus, no. 33 (July 1980), 16-22.

3256 "You Be the Judge." Horse and Rider, IX (July 1970), 56-59.

E SPECIFIC EVENTS

1 Show Jumping

3257 Ansell, Michael P. Riding High: The Complete Guide to Show Jumping. South Brunswick, NJ: A. S. Barnes, 1978. 121p.

3258 Baker, Jerry. "Show Jumping: Where Is It Heading?" Practical Horseman, II (August 1973), passim.

3259 Barnes, Sheila. Sudden Success: The Story of a Show Jumping Team. New Rochelle, NY: Sportshelf, 1965. 116p.

3260 Blake, Neil F. The World of Show Jumping. London: Pelham Books, 1967. 192p.

3261 Blunt, Carlene. "C. B. Takes Her Time, Gets There First." Practical Horseman, VIII (June 1980), 6-10.

3262 Broome, David. Show Jumping Today. London: Barker, 1961. 127p.

3263 Bush, Doreen. "One for the Show." Horse and Rider, XIII (April 1974), 60-63.

3264 Butler, Patrick. "Show Jumping Successfully." Practical Horseman, III (January 1974), passim.

3265 Cargo, Brian and Judy, eds. Junior Show Jumping. New York: Crowell, 1977. 128p. [juv.]

3266 Chapot, Frank. "International Jumping." Practical Horseman, III (October 1974), passim.

3267 Clayton, Michael and William Steinkraus, eds. The Complete Book of Show Jumping. New York: Crown, 1975. 264p.

3268 Dawes, Alison. Showjumping for Horses and Riders. London: Macdonald and Janes, 1977. 152p.

3269 Dayton, Jay. "The Greatest Prix." Horse and Rider, XIII (December 1974), 52-56, 74-75.

3270 _____. "How Green Was Their Tally." Horse and Rider, XI (November 1972), 46-51.

3271 DeBolgar, Coloman. Showjumping. Wellington, New Zealand: Reed, 1968. 84p.

3272 D'Inzeo, Piero. More Than Victory Alone. Translated from the Italian. London: Pelham Books, 1970. 148p.

3273 D'Orgeix, Jean F. Horse in the Blood: A Show Jumper's Working Notebook. London: Kaye, 1951. 188p.

3274 Dwyer, Ted. Show Jumping Down Under. London: Hale, 1974. 120p.
Australia and New Zealand.

3275 Ffrench-Blake, Neil. The World of Show Jumping. Ft. Collins, CO: Caballus Publications, 1973. 190p.

3276 Fiedler, Andrew. Vibart and Friends. London: Pelham Books, 1970. 122p.

3277 Froud, Bill. Better Show Jumping. London: Kaye and Ward, 1975. 96p.

3278 Goodall, Daphne M. Successful Show Jumping. Rev. ed. New York: A. S. Barnes, 1964. 72p.

3279 Griffith, Perry B. "They Paid Their Dues." Horse and Rider, XI (January 1972), 40-45.

3280 Hallam-Gordon, C. , ed. International Show Jumping Book. London: Souvenir Press, 1968. 144p.

3281 Heath, Veronica. Come Show Jumping with Me. London: Muller, 1961. 156p. [juv.]

3282 Hugo-Vidal, Victor. "Rider the Breaker." Practical Horseman, VIII (May 1980), 8-15, 50-51.

3283 Longland, Julia. Clear Round: Interviews. New York: Mayflower Books, 1978. 192p.

3284 Macgregor-Morris, Pamela. Show Jumping: Officer's Hobby into International Sport. New York: St. Martin's Press, 1976. 128p.

3285 _____. Show Jumping on Five Continents. London: Heinemann, 1960. 244p.

3286 _____. The World's Show Jumpers. 2nd ed. , rev. London: Macdonald and Company, 1966. 191p.

3287 Marks, Jane and Joel. "Three of a Kind." Horse and Rider, XVII (May 1977), 46-49.

3288 Murphy, Genevieve. British Show Jumpers. London: S. Paul, 1968. 101p.

3289 O'Connor, Sally. "Practical Evening: The First Competition-- Stadium Jumping." Dressage and CT, XIV (January 1978), 26-28.

3290 _____. "Practical Eventing: Stadium Jumping." Dressage and CT, XV (December 1978), 18-19.

3291 Oliver, Alan. Show Jumping. London: S. Paul, 1957. 191p.

3292 "The Present and Future of Olympic Jumping." Horse and Horseman, I (March 1973), passim.

3293 Pullein-Thompson, Josephine. Show Jumping Secret. London: Collins, 1974. 126p.

3294 Sack, Kristine W., ed. North American Show Stoppers: North American Show Jumpers, 1971-1972. Lebanon, PA: Sowers Printing Co., 1973. 111p.

3295 Sherred, Alison P. "Winning Over Fences." Horse of Course, IX (June 1980), 42-49.

3296 The Show Jumping Year. London: Cassell, 1957--. v. 1--.

3297 Smith, Alan. The Daily Telegraph Book of Show Jumping. London: Collins, 1970. 160p.

3298 Smith, Harvey. Harvesting Success. London: Pelham Books, 1968. 160p.

3299 _____. V is for Victory. London: Kimber, 1972. 160p.

3300 Smith, Melanie. "Bringing the Best Out." Practical Horseman, VIII (April 1980), 8-11.

3301 Smyth, Patricia. Anatomy of a Show Jumper: Anneli Drummond-Hay. London: Barker, 1970. 153p.

3302 _____. Jump for Joy. London: Cassell, 1954. 211p.

3303 _____. Jumping Round the World. NY: Arco, 1964. 211p. American edition of the previous citation.

3304 _____. One Jump Ahead. London: Cassell, 1956. 256p.

3305 _____. Show Jumping. South Brunswick, NJ: A. S. Barnes, 1968. 177p.

3306 Steinkraus, William and Perry B. Griffith. "The Future of Jumping: Two Views." Horse and Horseman, III (October 1975), 58-60.

3307 Stratton, Charles. Encyclopedia of Show Jumping and Combined Training. London: Hale, 1973. 318p.

3308 Talbot-Ponsonby, John A. The Art of Show Jumping. New York: A. S. Barnes, 1960. 100p.

3309 Thomas, Graeme. "The Smart Asset." Horse and Rider, XVI
       (December 1976), 34-36.

3310 Toptani, Ilias. Modern Show Jumping. New, rev. ed. New
       York: Arco, 1973. 168p.

3311 Wachtel, Martha. "Around the Maclay Course with a Top Con-
       tender." Practical Horseman, VI (November 1978), 6-11.

3312 Webber, Geoffrey H. S. Show Jumping International. Prince-
       ton, NJ: Van Nostrand, 1969. 155p.

3313 Williams, Dorian. Clear Round: The Story of Show Jumping.
       London: Hodder and Stoughton, 1957. 192p.

3314 _____. Great Moments in Sport: Show Jumping. London:
       Pelham Books, 1973. 128p.

3315 _____. Show Jumper. South Brunswick, NJ: A. S. Barnes,
       1970. 162p.

3316 _____. Show Jumping. London: Faber and Faber, 1968.
       126p.

3317 _____. Show Jumping: The Great One. New York: Arco,
       1972. 142p.

3318 Williams, Michael. Show Jumping in Britain. London: Ian
       Allen, 1964. 72p.

2 Vaulting

3319 Gerber, Pat. "Vaulting." Western Horseman, XLIV (November
       1979), 44-50.

3320 "Hows and Whys of Vaulting." Horse and Horseman, I (May
       1973), passim.

3321 McCabe, Susan. "Flair of Flying." Classic, II (December
       1976-January 1977), 86-91.

3322 McCann, Tom. "Vaulting." Horse and Horseman, V (July
       1977), 38-43.

3323 Schram, Jolly. "Vaulting Needs Demonstration." Horseman,
       XXIV (January 1980), 60-62.

3324 Stedwell, Paki. "Gymnastics on Horseback." Horseman, XXII
       (July 1979), 48-51.

3325 _____. Vaulting: Gymnastics on Horseback. New York:
       Wanderer Books, 1979. 60p. [juv.]

3326 "Vaulting." Honolulu, X (January 1976), 42-43.

3 Dressage and Combined Training

3327 Bighia, Lucy. "Dressage." Horse Lover's National Magazine, XLIII (January 1979), 54-56.

3328 Blake, Neil F. The World of Dressage. Garden City, NY: Doubleday, 1969. 189p.

3329 Boylen, Christilot. Basic Dressage for North America. Sharon, Ont.: International Equestrian Sport Center, 1976. 102p.

3330 Burkhardt, Barbara. "The Dressage Seat Explained." Dressage and CT, XVI (March 23, 1979), 8-10.

3331 _____. "Introduction to Dressage." Western Horseman, XLIV (November 1979), 102-105.

3332 Burns, Joan S. "Music for Dressage." Dressage and CT, XV (December 1978), 20-21.

3333 DeCarpentry, Albert E. E. Piaffer and Passage. San Francisco, CA: Howell, 1961. 76p.

3334 DeKunffy, Charles. "Classical Equitation or Dressage: A Definition." Dressage and CT, XIII (December 1977), 16-17.

3335 Disston, Harry. Elementary Dressage. South Brunswick, NJ: A. S. Barnes, 1971. 125p.

3336 _____. "Combined Training: Brian Sabo, Talented Event Rider from California." Chronicle of the Horse, XLIII (April 4, 1980), 13-14.

3337 Eliscu, Lita. "Hilda Gurney, Dressage with the Thoroughbred: An Interview." Practical Horseman, V (September 1977), 11-14.

3338 Ffrench-Blake, Robert L. V. Dressage for Beginners. Boston: Houghton Mifflin, 1976. 78p.

3339 _____. Intermediate Dressage: Work at Second and Third Levels. Boston: Houghton Mifflin, 1977. 82p.

3340 _____. "What the Dressage Judge Thinks." Practical Horseman, V (October 1977), 53-56.

3341 Gomes, Carolyn. "The Gymnastic Art of Dressage." Horse and Horseman, V (December 1977), 24-29.

3342   Gosling, Nancy M.   "East Meets West at Michigan State."
        Western Horseman, XLV (March 1980), 102-116.

3343   Green, Carol.   Dressage Explained.   New York: Arco, 1977.
        96p.

3344   Griffith, Perry B.   "[Gwen] Stockebrand Style of Dressage."
        Horse and Horseman, VIII (June 1980), 22-25.

3345   Haas, Jewyl L.   "Dressage on Sidesaddle."   Dressage and CT,
        XII (June 1977), 20-22.

3346   Hall, Roger.   "The Fulmer Point-of-View."   Practical Horse-
        man, V (February 1977), 38-42.

3347   Hangen, Bodo.   "Conversations with Young Professionals."
        Dressage and CT, XIII (July 1977), 8-13.

3348   Hastings, J. C.   "Dressage in Nevada."   Nevada Horse Life,
        II (Winter 1978), 6-7.

3349   Jenkins, Margie P.   "Dressage: The Classic Art of Horseman-
        ship."   American Horseman, III (May 1973), 55-57, 64.

3350   Jousseaume, André.   Progressive Dressage.   Translated from
        the French.   London: J. A. Allen, 1977.   152p.

3351   Ladendorf, Janice M.   Practical Dressage for Amateur Train-
        ers.   South Brunswick, NJ: A. S. Barnes, 1973.

3352   Lewis, Elizabeth.   "Young Dressage Rider at the International
        Level: An Interview."   Practical Horseman, VI (July 1978),
        9-15.

3353   Ljungquist, Bengt.   Practical Dressage Manual.   Richmond,
        VA: Whittet and Shepperson, 1976.   166p.

3354   _____.   _____.   Abr., 2nd ed.   Potamac, MD, 1977.   157p.

3355   Maule, Tex.   "Mistress [Linda Mikolka] of the Happy Slaves."
        Classic, IV (February-March 1979), 66-68.

3356   Meredith, Kay.   "Dressage."   The Quarter Horse, I (July-
        August 1975), 8-9.

3357   Monkerud, Donald.   "The Keen Lady [Hilda Gurney]."   Horse
        and Rider, XVII (April 1977), 18-22.

3358   Necer, George.   "Le Dressage Cowboy."   Horse and Rider,
        XVI (September 1976), 22-25.

3359   O'Connor, Sally.   "Practical Evening: More Dressage."   Dres-
        sage and CT, XIV (May 1978), 20-23.

3360 Pearson, Penny. "Dressage: Elizabeth Lewis, International Competitor." Chronicle of the Horse, XLIII (April 4, 1980), 24-25.

3361 Podhajsky, Alois. The Art of Dressage: Basic Principles of Riding and Judging. Garden City, NY: Doubleday, 1976. 185p.

3362 Simmons, Diana C. "Dressage: The Awareness Connection." Horse and Rider, XVIII (November 1979), 28-33.

3363 Stainer, Sylvia. The Art of Long Reining. London: J. A. Allen, 1972. 32p.

3364 Stephens, M. D. "Elementary Dressage." Horse and Rider, XIX (July 1980), 48-52.

3365 Tavares, Nancee. "Arriving at the Seventh Departure." Horse and Rider, XVII (January 1978), 14-18, 43.

3366 _____. "Western (Pleasure) Dressage." Horse and Rider, XVI (January 1977), 14-19.

3367 Twelveponies, Mary. "The Dressage Connection." Horse and Horseman, VI (May 1978), 48-51.

3368 Van Schaik, H. L. M. "Dressage: Rider Position." Chronicle of the Horse, XLII (October 12, 1979), 11-12.

3369 Vasko, Kent A. "The Dressage Horse." Dressage and CT, XV (November 1978), 22-23.

3370 Wätjen, Richard L. Dressage Riding. Translated from the German. 3rd ed. London: J. A. Allen, 1966. 114p.

3371 Webb, Barbara. "On a Western Level." Horse and Rider, XVII (March 1978), 16-20.

3372 Wilde, Louise M. "The Classical Dressage Seat: Seat, Hands, and Aids." Western Horseman, XXXVIII (October-November 1973), 57-60, 185-187, 16-17, 165-170.

3373 Wilson, Terri. "Karl Mikolka on Advanced Dressage." Horse and Horseman, VII (June 1979), 28-33.

3374 Winter, Sally. "Diary of a Determined Dressage Addict." Classic, II (December 1976-January 1977), 76-84.

3375 Wynmalen, Henry. Dressage: A Study of the Finer Points of Riding. 2nd ed. London: Museum Press, 1958. 288p.

4 Three-Day Event

3376 Banks, Carolyn. "Problem A: 3-Day." Classic, IV (April-
      May 1979), 32-37.

3377 Beale, Jeremy J. Eventing in Focus. Philadelphia: Lippin-
      cott, 1976. 160p.

3378 Campbell, Judith. Eventing. London: Barker, 1976. 116p.

3379 Chew, Peter. "[Mike Plum] Better, Better, Best." Classic,
      III (August-September 1978), 66-72.

3380 Cooper, Barbara. Badminton: The Three-Day Event, 1949-
      1969. London: Threshold Books, 1969. 125p.

3381 "Eventing: An Old Equestrian Sport for New Hampshire."
      New Hampshire Profiles, XXVII (July 1975), 42-46.

3382 Freeman, G. W., ed. The Masters of Eventing. London:
      Eyre and Spottiswoode, 1978. 176p.

3383 Green, Carol. Eventing Explained. New York: Arco, 1977.
      96p.

3384 Mackay-Smith, Alexander. "Three Days at Ledyard." Western
      Horseman, XLIII (February 1978), 70-73.

3385 Marth, Marty and Del. "The Ultimate Test." Horse Illustrated,
      X (January-February 1979), 38-39.

3386 Maule, Tex. "Step 1 to the French Correction." Classic, IV
      (August-September 1979), 58-62.

3387 Miles, Hugh T. "Triplicate Trouble." Horse and Rider, XVI
      (May 1976), 42-46.

3388 O'Connor, Sally. "Eventing in the West." Dressage and CT,
      XVII (February 1980), 16-19.

3389 _____. "Practical Eventing." Dressage and CT, XIV (April
      1978), 22-24.

3390 _____. "Practical Eventing: On to Bigger Things." Dres-
      sage and CT, XV (October-November 1978), 22-25, 24-25.

3391 _____. "Practical Eventing: On to Preliminary." Dressage
      and CT, XVI (February 23, 1979), 11-13.

3392 _____. "Practical Eventing: Preparing for the First Com-
      petition." Dressage and CT, XIII (August 1977), 16-17.

3393 _____. "Practical Eventing: The First Three-Day Event."
      Dressage and CT, XVI (March 23, 1979), 14-17.

3394 Silver, Caroline. Eventing: The Book of the Three-Day Event. London: Collins, 1976. 176p.

3395 Smith, Charlotte. "Diary of a Groom at Burghley." Practical Horseman, VII (December 1979), 6-12, 49.

3396 Swallow, Rex. "Eventing in Northern Ireland." Dressage and CT; XIV (April 1978), 10-11.

3397 "The Tough Three-Day Event." Horse and Rider, IX (September 1970), passim.

3398 Treviranus, Caroline P. "The Burghley Cross-Country." Western Horseman, XL (March 1975), 28-32.

3399 _____. "One Way to Start Three Day." Classic, III (December 1977-January 1978), 130-136.

3400 _____. "Riding the Cross-Country, Fence-by-Fence." Practical Horseman, V (January 1977), 14-20.

3401 Vasko, Kent A. "The Event Horse." Dressage and CT, XVI (February 23, 1979), 16-18.

5 International and Olympic Competition

3402 Abbey, Harlan. "Jumpin' Joe [Fargis]." Horse and Rider, XVIII (September 1979), 38-41.

3403 Allhusen, Derek, et al. Riding the International Way. South Brunswick, NJ: A. S. Barnes, 1969. 120p.

3404 Dayton, Jay. "Will the World-Beaters Please Stand Out." Horse and Rider, XII (November 1973), 44-47.

3405 Eliscu, Lita. "Melle Van Bruggen: The New USET Dressage Coach." Dressage and CT, XVII (March 1980), 8-11.

3406 Griffith, Perry B. "Goodbye, Bengt [Ljungquist]--and Thanks." Horse and Horseman, VII (November 1979), 64-65.

3407 _____. "Preparing for Pan-Am." Horse and Horseman, VII (December 1979), 56-57, 60-61.

3408 _____. "USET Combined Training Trials." Horse and Horseman, V (October 1977), 14-18.

3409 _____. "USET Dressage Screening Trials." Horse and Horseman, V (August 1977), 14-18.

3410 _____. "USET Jumping Squad Screening Trials." Horse and Horseman, V (September 1977), 14-18.

3411 _____. "The USET Today and Tomorrow." Horse and
Horseman, VI (April 1978), 28-33.

3412 Gurney, Hilda. "A Study in Bronze." Horse and Horseman,
V (March 1977), 38-40.

3413 Harris, King. "Olympic Hopefuls." Horse and Rider, XVI
(July 1976), 56-59.

3414 Johnson, Elizabeth. International Riding. New York: Crowell,
1974. 91p.

3415 _____. Leisureguide's International Riding. New York:
Macmillan, 1973. 92p.

3416 Landsman, Bill. "Riding High." Olympian, IV (May 1978),
4-6.

3417 LeGoff, Jack. "Jack LeGoff Critiques U.S. Riders at the World
Championships." Practical Horseman, VI (December 1978),
6-14.

3418 Norrell, Michael G. and Pamela Davis. "Olympic Equestrian
Report." Western Horseman, XLI (November 1978), 54-58,
135.

3419 O'Connor, Sally. "Badminton: The Ultimate Event." Horse
Lover's National Magazine, XLIV (September 1979), 53-63.

3420 Price, Steven D. "Olympic Hopefuls." Horse Lover's National
Magazine, XLIII (July 1978), 55-61.

3421 Prior-Palmer, Lucinda. "Self Critique by an International
Riding Star." Practical Horseman, VI (August 1978), 8-12.

3422 Savitt, Sam. The Equestrian Olympic Sketchbook. South Brunswick, NJ: A. S. Barnes, 1970. 62p.

3423 Steinkraus, William. "High Spot [Pan American Games] on the
Road to Moscow." Classic, IV (October-November 1979),
32-35.

3424 _____, ed. The U.S. Equestrian Team Book of Riding: The
First Quarter Century of the U.S.E.T. New York: Simon
and Schuster, 1976. 287p.

3425 Talbot-Ponsonby, John A. Equestrian Olympic Games, Rome,
1960. London: Cassell, 1960. 39p.

3426 United States Equestrian Team. Questions and Answers About
the United States Equestrian Team. Gladstone, NJ, 1979.
8p.

6 Bronc-riding

3427 Brown, Barbara J. "Rookie Bronc Rider Cleve Loney." West-
      ern Horseman, XXXIX (July 1974), 68, 160-162.

3428 Davis, Ray. "Learning from Larry Mahan: Bareback Bronc
      Busting." Western Horseman, XXXVIII (April 1973), 74-
      75, 152-154.

3429 Hurley, Jimmie. "Joe Alexander's Ideal Bareback Bronc."
      Western Horseman, XXXIX (November 1974), 22-24.

3430 _____. "Saddle Bronc Champ: Monty Henson." Western
      Horseman, XLI (November 1976), 68, 145-149.

3431 _____. "Shawn Davis Describes the Ideal Saddle Bronc."
      Western Horseman, XXXVIII (August 1973), 30-32, 134.

3432 Rice, Lee. "Broncs and Bronc Riders." Western Horseman,
      XLII (May-June 1977), 14-15, 164-169, 10-13.

3433 Sankey, Ike and Lyle. "Stylish Bronc Riding." Horse and
      Rider, XVII (June 1978), 34-40.

3434 Thompson, Pauline. "Broncs and Brothers." Horse and Rider,
      IX (February 1970), 42-47, 70.

3435 Tippette, Giles. "The Harder They Fall." Texas Monthly,
      VII (October 1979), 118+.

3436 Witte, Randy. "Bill Smith on Saddle Bronc Riding." Western
      Horseman, XLIV (November 1979), 14-18.

7 Barrel Racing

3437 Davis, Ray. "Don't Fence Me In." Horse and Rider, XVII
      (June 1978), 62-66.

3438 _____. "Midwest Match Barrel Race." Western Horseman,
      XLI (January 1976), 122-124.

3439 Dickinson, Glory A. "Rich Little Poor Girl." Horse and Rider,
      XVII (January 1978), 34-35.

3440 Heath, Katty. "Winning the Hard Way." Western Horseman,
      XLIII (March 1978), 12-14, 102-105.

3441 Hurley, Jimmie. "Beauty [Joyce Shelley] and Her Beast."
      Horse and Rider, XIII (July 1974), 28-33.

3442 _____. "Just Joaking Around." Horse and Rider, XVII
      (July 1978), 28-33.

3443 _____. "On Top of Old Smokie." Horse and Rider, XVII (August 1978), 32-35.

3444 _____. "The Racey School Marm [Lynn McKenzie]." Horse and Rider, XVIII (July 1979), 32-35.

3445 _____. "Sammy Thurman Describes the Ideal Barrel Horse." Western Horseman, XXXVII (January 1972), 10-11+.

3446 _____. "They've Gotta Have Heart." Horse and Rider, XVII (April 1978), 30-34.

3447 Josey, Martha. "Barrel Racing." Horseman, XIV (April 1970), 76-81.

3448 _____. Fundamentals of Barrel Racing. Houston, TX: Cordovan Corp., 1969. 89p.

3449 _____. "The Winning Combination." Horse and Rider, XIV (April 1975), 17-23.

3450 McCann, Tom. "Rough Stock Dancers." Western Horseman, XLI (August 1976), 54-57.

3451 Markus, Kurt. "Becky Carson on Barrel Racing and Horse-manship." Western Horseman, XLIII (October-November 1978), 99-102, 97-100.

3452 Mayo, Jane. Championship Barrel Racing. 3rd ed. Houston, TX: Cordovan Corp., 1975. 85p.

3453 Simmons, Diana C. "A Gust [Danna Cogburn] from Guthrie [Oklahoma]." Horse and Rider, XVIII (April 1979), 24-29.

3454 Van Steenwyk, Elizabeth. Barrel Horse Racer. New York: Walker, 1977. 91p. [juv.]

8 Roping

3455 Conroy, Lonna J. Goat Tying. Colorado Springs, CO: West-ern Horseman, 1971. 32p.

3456 Davis, Ray. "Calf Ropers and Their Horses." Western Horse-man, XXXIX (November 1974), 50-52.

3457 _____. "Roping with Old-Timer Byrel Hittson." Western Horseman, XXXVI (September 1971), 86, 110-116.

3458 Hurley, Jimmie. "Walt Arnold's Ideal Steer Roping Horse." Western Horseman, XXXIX (November 1974), 66-68.

3459 Josey, Martha E. "Learnin' the Lariat: An Interview." Horse and Rider, XIV (January 1975), 46-51.

3460 _____. "Showing You the Ropes." Horse and Rider, X (September 1971), 36-42.

3461 King, Chuck. Team Roping and Team Tying. Colorado Springs, CO: Western Horseman, 1972. 32p.

3462 Livingston, Phil. "Team Roping Wild Horses." Western Horseman, XLI (March 1976), 14-15, 100-101.

3463 Mansfield, Toots. Calf Roping. Colorado Springs, CO: Western Horseman, 1971. 48p.

3464 Porter, Willard H. "Do Horses Like to Rope?" Western Horseman, XXXIX (July 1974), 40-42, 150.

3465 _____. "Fast Horses and Short Ropes." Horse and Rider, XIII (September 1974), 70-75.

3466 _____. "Roper's Log." Western Horseman, XLI (January 1976), 32, 126-129.

3467 _____. "Single Steer Roping." Horseman, XXI (March 1977), 30-35.

3468 Robertson, Anna. "The Camarillos Talk Team Roping." Western Horseman, XXXVIII (July-August 1973), 46-47, 166-167, 38-41, 179-183.

3469 Rooney, Liam. "You Can Learn Team Roping." Western Horseman, XLIV (August 1979), 38-41.

3470 Webster, Jane and Beryl M. Williams. "Team Ropin' at the Lazy Seven." Western Horseman, XXXIX (July 1974), 82, 168-170.

3471 Witte, Randy. "Ropin' Wide Open in West Texas." Western Horseman, XLV (January 1980), 34-38.

9 Charioteering

3472 Chariot Racing Annual. Idaho Falls, ID: Harris Publications, 1972--. v. 1--.

3473 Clement, D. Brent. "Female Chariot Drivers." Western Horseman, XXXVIII (September 1973), 80, 137-140.

3474 Harris, Darryl. "Ben Hurry." Horse and Rider, IX (March 1970), 42-46.

3475 Hurley, Jimmie. "Martha Lowe: A Female Ben Hur." Western Horseman, XLI (March 1976), 54-55, 131.

3476 Schorzman, Diane. "Training a Horse for Chariot Racing."
      Western Horseman, XLV (March 1980), 18-23.

3477 Simmons, Diane C. "The Chariot Challenge." Horse and
      Rider, XIX (March 1980), 34-39.

3478 Straub, Charles. "Charioteers." Farm Quarterly, XXI (Winter
      1966), 70-73.

3479 Williams, Beryl M. "Chariot Racing, Wyoming Style." West-
      ern Horseman, XLII (July 1977), 44.

3480 _____. "How to Build a Chariot." Western Horseman,
      XLIV (October 1979), 65-68.

3481 World's Champion Cutter and Chariot Racing Association.
      "Chariot Racing." Horseman, XVII (August 1972), 56-60.

10 Cutting

3482 Herring, Janet S. "The Cutting Edge." Equus, no. 25 (No-
      vember 1979), 30-36.

3483 National Cutting Horse Association. Annual Booklet. Ft.
      Worth, TX, 1974--. v. 1--.

3484 _____. Rulebook. Ft. Worth, TX, 1979. 30p.

3485 Reno, J. "Why Cutting Is Growing." Horseman, XXII (July
      1978), 45-48.

3486 Simmons, Diane C. "The Art of Cutting." Horse of Course,
      IX (July 1980), 20-28.

3487 Trent, Slim. "When Is a Cutting Horse Finished?" Horse
      and Rider, XI (January 1972), 34-39.

3488 Wilson, Sam. "My Favorite Cutting Horses." Horse and Rider,
      X (December 1971), 16-21, 60.

11 Halter

3489 Bond, Marian. "Aware and Square." Horse and Rider, XVII
      (January 1977), 38-41.

3490 Close, Pat. "Richard Shrake: Showmanship at Halter." West-
      ern Horseman, XLII (May 1977), 8-13.

3491 Gaines, David. "Halter Class for Athletes." Horseman, XXIII
      (May 1979), 24-30.

3492 Houk, Jerry. "Training and Showing at Halter." Horse and Rider, XIII (April 1974), 19-24, 73.

3493 Lemmon, Pat. "The Halter Horse: An Interview." Horse and Rider, XIV (June-July 1975), 16-23, 56-60.

3494 Opel, Sarah. "Introduction to the Halter Class." Horseman, XXIV (May 1980), 28-35.

12 Reining

3495 Connell, Ed. "Explaining Reining." Horse and Rider, XI (July 1972), 24-26.

3496 Horn, Bill. "Finesse Is the Name of the Game." Horse and Rider, XI (January 1972), 16-22.

3497 McHugh, Mac and Jim Alderson. "California-Style Reining." Horse and Rider, X (January 1971), 46-52.

3498 Meredith, Byron. "The Beauty of Mule Reining." Horse and Rider, XIV (July 1975), 50-55, 68.

13 Polo

3499 Abbott, Steve. "Polo: Class of the Field." Soldiers, XXXIV (July 1979), 41-43.

3500 "American Polo." Horse and Horseman, I (September-October 1973), passim.

3501 Barker, Ann. "Revival of a Dying Sport." Spur, XVI (May-June 1980), 72-79.

3502 Bartlett, Harry M. "The San Patricio Snake Killers." Western Horseman, XXXVI (December 1971), 36-37, 114-115.

3503 Bloom, Lynda. "Tough and Versatile." Horse and Rider, XVII (September-October 1977), 42-47, 28-33.

3504 Board, John. From Point-to-Point. London: C. Johnson, 1953. 176p.

3505 _____. Polo. Woodstock, NH: Countryman, 1957. 228p.

3506 British Horse Society and Pony Club. Polo for the Pony Club. Woodbury, NY: Barron's Educational Service, 1977. 93p.

3507 Callahan, Teresa. "College Polo for Women." Western Horseman, XLIII (September 1978), 48-49.

3508   Christopher, Renny. "Polo: Many Games." Horse Lover's
       National Magazine, XLIV (January 1979), 28-30.

3509   Colee, Donn, Jr. "A Capsule History of Polo." Western
       Horseman, XLIV (April 1979), 72-73.

3510   Davis, Lee. "Handling Polo Horses, with Lee Nelson." West-
       ern Horseman, XXXVIII (July 1973), 29-33, 134-135.

3511   Davis, Ray. "Bart Evans." Western Horseman, XLI (Septem-
       ber 1976), 50-51.

3512   Dean, Frank. "The Polo Pontentate." Western Horseman,
       XXXIX (December 1974), 46-50, 106-107.

3513   Disston, Harry. Beginning Polo. South Brunswick, NJ: A.
       S. Barnes, 1973.

3514   Donaldsen, Dana. "Some Things About Polo." Western Horse-
       man, XLII (April 1977), 116-121.

3515   Hobson, Richard. Polo and Ponies. London: J. A. Allen,
       1976. 96p.

3616   McMaster, R. K. Polo for Beginners and Spectators. New
       York: Exposition Press, 1954. 46p.

3517   Maule, Tex. "Brotherhood's Crowning Good." Classic, III
       (June-July 1978), 94-98.

3518   _____. "Gold in Those Polo Fields of Green." Classic,
       IV (June-July 1979), 50-56.

3519   _____. "No. 1 at Two is Working on Ten." Classic, II
       (December 1976-January 1977), 130-135.

3520   Mountbatten, Lord Louis. An Introduction to Polo. By Marco,
       pseud. 5th ed. London: Country Life, 1965. 175p.

3521   "Polo: It Really is for Everybody." Horse Lover's National
       Magazine. XLII (August 1977), 7-11.

3522   Robinson, Bruce W. "Square Peg and All-Around Horse."
       Horse and Rider, VII (August 1968), 14-18, 52.

3523   Runberg, C. Maybe. "Polo: Entering a New Golden Age."
       Equus, no. 30 (April 1980), 60-62.

3524   Shinitzky, Ami and Don Follmer. The Endless Chakker: 101
       Years of American Polo. Gaithersburg, MD: Polo Pub-
       lishers, 1978. 123p.

3525   Simmons, Diane C. "Polo's Western Heritage." Horse Lover's
       National Magazine, XLIII (January 1979), 37-44.

3526 Spencer, Herbert and Fred Mayer, eds. Chakkar: Polo Around
the World. Zurich, Switzerland: City-Druch, 1971. Unpaged.

3527 Staton, Gina M. "World Cup Polo." Horse Lover's National
Magazine, XLIV (September 1979), 46-52.

3528 Vickers, Wilmot G. H. Practical Polo. 3rd ed. London:
J. A. Allen, 1973. 78p.

3529 Vorhes, Gary. "Cowboy Polo." Western Horseman, XLI (November 1976), 104-107.

3530 Winkenwerder, Valerie. "Cholla: The Roping Polo Game."
Western Horseman, XLII (May 1977), 70-71.

14 Gymkhana

3531 Adderley, C. M. Pony Club Mounted Games and Gymkhanas.
Woodbury, NY: Barron's Educational Service, 1977. 112p.

3532 Bond, Marian. "[Johnny] Acosta Spells Action." Horse and
Rider, XIX (April 1980), 30-33, 49.

3533 Christopher, Renny. "Gymkhana." Horse Lover's National
Magazine, XLIII (August 1978), 26-30.

3534 "The Gist of Gymkhana." Horse and Rider, VIII (February
1969), passim.

3535 Grantz, Sherry. "Taming a Cyclone." Horse and Rider, XVI
(December 1977), 30-33.

3536 Holdsworth, Jean. The Small Gymkhana. London: H. F. and
G. Witherby, 1972. 62p.

3537 Josey, Martha. Riding the Gymkhana Winner. Omaha, NE:
Farnam Horse Library, 1978. 64p.

3538 Kenoyer, Natlee. Gymkhana Games. Hollywood, CA: Wilshire
Books, 1977. 128p.

3539 National Horse and Pony Youth Activity Council. Gymkhana
Guidelines. New York, 1979. 14p.

3540 Park, Don. "Gymkhana Becomes an Organized Sport." Horseman, XXIV (March 1980), 71-76.

3541 Thiffault, Mark. "The National Gymkhana Association." Horse
and Horseman, V (April 1977), 56-59.

3542 Thompson, Terry. "Gymkhana Horsemanship." Horse and
Rider, XVII (March 1978), 28-31.

15 Endurances and Competitive Trail-Riding

3543 Barsaleau, Richard B. "A Comparison Between Endurance
Riding and Competitive Trail Riding." Western Horseman,
XXXVIII (July 1973), 64-67.

3544 _____. "Wasatch Mountain Endurance Ride." Western
Horseman, XXXVIII (August 1973), 48-49.

3545 Bergen, Chan. "John Sumerlin: The Nation's Top Endurance
Rider Talks About the Sport." Western Horseman, XLII
(June 1977), 96-107.

3546 Bloom, Lynda. The Horse of Course: Guide to Winning at
Western Trail Riding. New York: Arco, 1979.

3547 Fitzgerald, C. "Pointers on Endurance Riding." Western
Horseman, XXXVIII (March 1973), 47-48, 157-160.

3548 Grogan, Liz. "The Making of a Competitive Trail Horse."
Western Horseman, XLIII (August 1978), 74, 132-133.

3549 Hayes, J. J. "Endurance Riding from a Veterinarian's Point
of View." Agricultural Technology, VIII (November 1977),
22-23.

3550 Hyland, Ann. Beginner's Guide to Endurance Riding. London:
Pelham Books, 1974. 128p.

3551 _____. "Britain's Top Endurance Ride." Western Horseman, XXXVIII (February 1973), 74-80.

3552 Ingram, Patricia. "Conditioning for the Long Run." Western
Horseman, XLV (March 1980), 40-46.

3553 "An Introduction to Competitive Trail Riding." Western Horseman, XXXIX (March 1974), 96-97+.

3554 Johnson, Virginia W. "The Early Days of Endurance Riding."
Western Horseman, XLIV (April 1979), 110-114.

3555 [No entry]

3556 Kelly, C. M. "Endurance Riding and 'Scoring' Endurance
Rides." New Zealand Veterinary Journal, XXV (December
1977), 393-394.

3557 Kydd, Rachael. Long Distance Riding Explained. New York:
Arco, 1979. 96p.

3558 Lewis, Cliff. "Training the Endurance Horse to Win." Horseman, XIV (April 1970), 48-55.

3559　McCaulley, LeMoyne. "Competition Calls." Horse Lover's National Magazine, XLIV (July 1979), 44-46.

3560　McKnight, Lenore. "An Ancient Endurance Ride [in Scotland]." Western Horseman, XXXVIII (November 1973), 48, 118-119.

3561　Marcucci, Areice. "Endurance Rx." Horse and Rider, XVIII (April-May 1979), 34-37, 24-27.

3562　O'Malley, Jeanne. "Long-Distance Equitation: Riding Strategy." Horse and Rider, XVI (May 1977), 33-35.

3563　Saare, Sharon, et al. Distance Riding Manual. Moscow, ID: Appaloosa Horse Club, 1974. 64p.

3564　_____. "Endurance and Competitive Riding." Horse and Rider, XVI (June 1976), 32-34.

3565　Schaefer, Jack W. The Great Endurance Horse Race: 600 Miles on a Single Mount, from Evanston, Wyoming, to Denver. Santa Fe, NM: Stagecoach Press, 1963. 60p.

3566　Sellnow, Les and Mary J. Nelson. "The Ups and Downs of Endurance Riding." Horse and Rider, XI (October 1972), 46-51, 56.

3567　Smith, Donna. "Some Brief Facts and Tips on Endurance Riding." Horse and Rider, X (August 1971), 75.

3568　Tellington, Wentworth J. Endurance and Competitive Trail Riding. Garden City, NY: Doubleday, 1979. 314p.

3569　Thomas, Heather S. "Selecting a Horse for Distance Riding." Chronicle of the Horse, XLIII (March 28, 1980), 36-37.

3570　Thorson, Juli S. "Preparing for Distance Riding." Horse and Horseman, VI (January 1979), 40-43.

3571　Wilding, Suzanne. "The World's Roughest Horse Ride: The 100-Mile Tevis Cup." Town and Country, CXXXIII (July 1979), 8+.

16　Buzhashi

3572　Graves, William. "Buzhashi." Western Horseman, XLV (February 1980), 20-21.

3573　Lincoln, Frederick B. "Buzhashi in Afghanistan." Western Horseman, XLI (April 1976), 4, 80.

17 Jousting

3574 Bloomfield, H. V. L. "The Ancient Art of Jousting [in Maryland]." Ford Times, LX (July 1967), 8-11.

3575 Dougall, Neil. "Jousting Returns in England." Western Horseman, XXXVIII (June 1973), 88-89, 185.

3576 "Joust Between You and Me: Ancient Battle Form, New Sport." Equus, no. 11 (September 1978), 15-18.

3577 Loeffelbein, Robert. "Jousting." Horseman, XXV (July 1980), 57-61.

3578 _____. Knight Life: Jousting in the United States. Lexington Park, MD: Golden Owl Publishers, 1978. 96p.

18 Trick Riding

3579 Dean, Frank. The Complete Book of Trick and Fancy Riding. Caldwell, ID: Caxton Printers, 1975. 259p.

3580 _____. Trick and Fancy Riding. Fresno, CA: Academy Guild Press, 1960. 262p.

3581 _____. Will Rogers Rope Tricks. Colorado Springs, CO: Western Horseman, 1970. 48p.

3582 Griffith, Connie. "Tricks in the Trade." Horse and Rider, X (March 1971), 28-32.

3583 Petitte, Edna. "Teach Your Horse Tricks." Horse Illustrated, XI (May-June 1979), 11-13.

3584 Scott, Rosemary. You Can Be a Trick Rider. Cisco, TX: Longhorn Press, 1973. 88p.

3585 Singer, Carl. "Trick Riding, with J. W. Stoker." Western Horseman, XXXVIII (January-February 1973), 60-61, 143-144, 42-44, 130-133.

3586 Smith, Helen. "Five Simple Tricks." Horse and Rider, X (May 1971), 40-44.

3587 Stinson, Jonnie. Teaching Your Horse Tricks. Springtown, TX, 1979. Unpaged.

19 Pulling Contests

3588 Kelly, Gerald R. "An Old Art with Brand New Interest: The Country Horse Pull." Yankee, XXXIX (July 1975), 28-36.

3589 Riddick, Peter. "Where [La Grange County, Indiana] Horses Vie with Tractors." Breeder's Gazette, CXXVII (September 1962), 8-10.

3590 Rosenkranz, Patrick. "Horse Plowing Contests." Western Horseman, XLIII (June 1978), 56-58.

3591 Telleen, Maurice. "Draft Horse Pulling Contests." Western Horseman, XLI (August 1976), 44-46.

Further References: See also Parts V and VI above, and IX below.

PART IX   NON-COMPETITIVE HORSEMANSHIP EVENTS

A   DRIVING

3592   Bergen, Chan.   "Buggy Nuts and Driving."   Western Horseman,
       XLIII (April 1978), 28-31.

3593   _____.   "Driving Events in Colorado."   Western Horseman,
       XLI (November 1976), 62-63.

3594   Bloom, Lynda.   "Drive 'em Wild."   Horse and Rider, XIV
       (March 1975), 50-55.

3595   _____.   "Pleasure Driving, with Dean Hodges."   Western
       Horseman, XLII (June 1977), 56-60.

3596   Burt, Don.   "Driving Ambition."   Horse and Rider, XIX (March
       1980), 10-12.

3597   Carey, Kathy.   "At Devon [Pennsylvania], They Go Buggy."
       Today, The [Philadelphia] Inquirer Magazine, (May 25, 1980),
       26-27.
       Antique Carriage Marathon at the Devon Horse Show.

3598   Cotterman, Dan.   "Forty-Horse Power."   Horse and Rider,
       XIII (March 1974), 30-34.
       Driving the 40-horse hitch.

3599   Dayton, Jay.   "The Wild World of Driving."   Horse and Rider,
       X (December 1971), 28-34.

3600   Dooley, D.   "Building the 40-Horse Hitch."   Western Horseman,
       XXXVII (March 1972), 92+.

3601   "The Fabulous Forty-Hitch."   Horse and Horseman, I (August
       1973), 80-83.

3602   Hamilton, Samantha.   "40 Horses 40."   Equus, no. 28 (Febru-
       ary 1980), 24-28.

3603   Hudgins, Sam.   "Heyday for Horses."   Horse and Rider, XIII
       (April 1974), 44-48.

3604 Joplin, Linda. "The Beauty of a Buggy." Western Horseman, XXXVIII (June 1973), 108, 175-176.

3605 Lincoln, Marshall. "Bill Cliff: Six-Horse Hitch Driver." Western Horseman, XXXVIII (December 1973), 76-77, 132-133.

3606 Ryder, Tom. On the Box Seat: A Manual of Driving. 3rd ed., rev. Macclesfield, Eng.: Horse Drawn Carriages, 1972. 180p.

3607 Timmis, Reginald S. Driving and Harness. London: J. A. Allen, 1975. 51p.

3608 Tollefson, Randi. "The Pleasure of Driving." Horse and Rider, XI (December 1972), 28-33.

3609 Walrond, Sallie. Encyclopedia of Driving. London: Horse Drawn Carriages, 1974. 293p.

3610 _____. A Guide to Driving Horses. London: Pelham Books, 1978. 136p.

3611 Watney, Marylian and William Kenward. Show Driving Explained. New York: Arco, 1978. 96p.

3612 Wilding, Suzanne. "He [Frank] Is the Impresario, She [Cynthia Hayden] Is the Star." Classic, II (June-July 1977), 116-124.

3613 Winship, Elizabeth. "The Second Annual Vermont Buggy Trip." Vermont Life, XXXII (Summer 1979), 58-60.

B TRAIL RIDING

3614 Albright, Vern. Horseback Across the Americas. Ft. Collins, CO: Printed Horse, 1974.

3615 Back, Joe. Horses, Hitches, and Rocky Trails. Denver, CO: Sage Books, 1959. 117p.

3616 Bailey, Gordon C. "Wildest Trail Ride." Horse and Rider, XIV (June 1975), 24-30. In South Africa.

3617 Barsaleau, Richard B. "Thoroughbred on the Long Trail." Western Horseman, XXXIX (September 1974), 24-26+.

3618 Bates, Ted. "First Trail Ride." Horse and Rider, XIV (April 1975), 52-56.

3619 Bauer, E. A. "This Summer, Put Yourself in the Saddle." National Wildlife, IV (June-July 1966), 41-46.

3620 Bergen, Chan. "Riding the Trails: Cavalier Riding Club."
Western Horseman, XLI (August 1976), 61-62, 125.

3621 Berry, Bob. "Spots on the Trail." Horse and Rider, XVI
(April 1976), 16-23.

3622 Bonython, C. W. "The Heysen Trail." Australian Parks and
Recreation, (February 1979), 14-16.

3623 Bowman, Edward. "Pleasure Horses in the Parks." National
Parks Magazine, XLI (November 1967), 4-6.

3624 Bradac, Judi and Frank. "Holidays on Horseback: Riding the
Wilderness Trails." Practical Horseman, VII (July 1979),
24-31.

3625 Brown, Alwin R. "Trail Riders in the Holy Land." Western
Horseman, XXXIX (November 1974), 76-78, 145-146.

3626 Cieplik, Watt. "A Horse Roundup of Riding Trails and Stables."
Los Angeles, XXI (December 1977), 152-160.

3627 Close, Pat. "Cynthia Cantteberry Talks About Trail Horses."
Western Horseman, XLIII (February 1978), 24-30.

3628 _____. "New Trend in Trail Courses." Western Horseman,
XLIV (September 1979), 100-103.

3629 Cochran, Max. "Horseback Outing in the Sierras." Western
Horseman, XLIV (October 1979), 52, 158.

3630 Conway, Larry. "Keep Those Tracks Close to Camp." Horseman, XXIII (April 1979), 70-71.

3631 Curtis, Lynne. "The Long Ride Home." Women Sports, II
(March 1975), 47-50.

3632 Dack, Sam. "Pack It In." Western Horseman, XLV (July
1980), 16-23.

3633 Davis, Bonnie. "Pleasure Trail Riding." Horse Lover's National Magazine, XLIII (May 1978), 10-12.

3634 Davis, Francis W. Horse Packing in Color. New York:
Scribners, 1975. 91p.

3635 Drakos, N. "Horse Trails in the Adirondacks." Conservationist, XXI (October-November 1966), 6-9.

3636 Ecuyere, Joli. "Horsing Around." San Francisco, XVII (June
1976), 44+.

3637 Foote, Nate and Elly. "Central American Horseback Tour."
Western Horseman, XXXIX (July 1974), 65-66, 158-160.

3638 _____. "South American Horseback Tour." Western Horseman, XXXVI (December 1971), 64-66, 140-142.

3639 Fox, Kathy. "Some Things to Know Before You Go." Western
Horseman, XLIV (December 1979), 28-32.

3640 Gerbino, Mary. "Yosemite National Park Horses for Hire."
Western Horseman, XLV (June 1980), 66-73.

3641 Gibbs, G. "Pack Trip Etiquette." Horseman, XXII (May 1978),
20-25.

3642 Grier, Bob. "Weekend in the Saddle." Nebraskaland, LIV
(May 1976), 8-12.

3643 Gumaer, Dorothy. "Wilderness Rides: Will They Become History or Remain a Reality?" Western Horseman, XXXVIII
(March 1973), 33, 122-123.

3644 Hart, Edward. Pony Trekking. London: David and Charles,
1976. 126p.

3645 Hatley, George B. "On the Trail of Chief Joseph." Western
Horseman, XLV (January 1980), 84-87.

3646 Huff, A. N. "Trail Riding." Program/Proceedings of the
National Horsemen's Seminar, II (1977), 93-97.

3647 Hunter, John K. Pony Trekking for All. London: Nelson,
1962. 120p.

3648 Kentucky. Department of Parks. Kentucky Trails Guide.
Frankfort, KY, 1976. 25p.

3649 Klein, Helen. "Outfitted for a Rocky High." Classic, II
(August-September 1977), 74-77.

3650 Kweskin, Steve. "Indiana's Brown County State Park." Western Horseman, XLI (September 1976), 86-87.

3651 LeBlanc, John C. "Planning the Horseback Pack Trip." Horseman, XXII (October 1978), 60-68.

3652 Lester, C. N. Trail Riding, 4-H Horse and Pony Project:
Guide for Adult Leaders. Blacksburg, VA: Cooperative
Extension Service, Virginia Polytechnic Institute and State
University, 1973. 6p.

3653 McHugh, Mac. "Sailing a True Trail Course." Horse and
Rider, VIII (November 1969), 16-21.

3654 Mann, Colin. "Lone Ride Across Australia." Western Horseman, XXXIX (January 1974), 42, 127-129.

3655 Markus, Kurt. "Hot Blood in the [Colorado] Mountains." Western Horseman, XLI (December 1976), 12-15.

3656 _____. "Six September Days in the Canadian Rockies." Western Horseman, XLIV (February 1979), 26-30.

3657 Merrill, William K. Vacationing with Saddle and Packhorse. New York: Arco, 1976. 302p.

3658 Murray, Barry. "Hitting the Trail--Softly." Horse and Rider, XII (June 1973), 44-47.

3659 Nelson, Mary J. "Trail Parks for Horseback Riding." American Horseman, III (May 1973), 32-35, 63.

3660 North Dakota. Travel Department. "Off the Beaten Path in North Dakota." Camp Guide, LVI (April 1968), 30-32.

3661 Ormond, Clyde. "Handling Horses and Horse Gear." In: his Outdoorsman's Handbook. New York: E. P. Dutton, 1971. pp. 253-296.

3662 Osmer, Virginia T. "The Two-Point Position for Trail Riding." Western Horseman, XXXIX (June 1974), 58.

3663 Pitts, Don. "Riding Away from It All." Horse Lover's National Magazine, XLIII (May 1978), 14-17.

3664 Pour, Anthony. "Back in the Saddle Again." Los Angeles, XXIV (June 1979), 199-201.

3665 Price, Steven D. Horseback Vacation Guide. Brattleboro, VT: Stephen Greene Press, 1975. 183p.

3666 Pritchett, Jane. "Grand Canyon Mule Boss [Gene Waldroup]." Western Horseman, XLI (December 1976), 60-65.

3667 Robertson, Anna. "Horsemen in the Wilderness." Western Horseman, XLII (July 1977), 54-57.

3668 Saare, Sharon. Know All About Trail Riding. Omaha, NE: Farnam Horse Library, 1979. 46p. 64p.

3669 Savitt, Sam. "The World's Most Demanding Horse Trail [Badminton, England]." Western Horseman, XXXVIII (April 1973), 26-29, 116-118.

3670 Shobalski, R. M. "Traveling by Horse." Western Horseman, XXXIX (September 1974), 73+.

3671 Spencer, Dick, 3rd. "The Outdoorsmen: A Trek to Yellow-Stone's Back Country." Western Horseman, XXXIX (March 1974), 6-8

3672 _____. "Packin' In Is for Everyone." Western Horseman, XLIV (December 1979), 52-56.

3673 Spooner, Glenda. Pony Trekking. Rev. ed. London: J. A. Allen, 1976. 150p.

3674 Tanner, Bob. "Tons of Mule Power." Horse and Rider, XVII (June 1978), 22-23, 47.

3675 Taylor, Judith. "No Room to Ride." Denver Magazine, VIII (March 1978), 40-43.

3676 "Thirty-First Annual Pikes Peak Range Ride: A Pictorial." Western Horseman, XLIV (November 1979), 51-53.

3677 Thompson, Terry. "A Better Trail Trip." Horse and Rider, XVII (February 1978), 24-27.

3678 "Trail Log: The Chief Joseph Trail." Appaloosa News, XX (September 1966), 2-4, 6-10.

3679 Trail Riders of the Wilderness. Annual. Washington, D.C., 1950--. v. 17--.

3680 Vogel, Charles. Trails Manual. Hollywood, CA: Equestrian Trails, Inc., 1971. Unpaged.

3681 Westbrook, Anne and P. D. Trail Horses and Trail Riding. New York: A. S. Barnes, 1963. 117p.

3682 Winnett, Thomas and Karl Schwenke. Sierra South: 100 Back-Country Trips in California's Sierra. 2nd ed. Berkeley, CA: Wilderness Press, 1975. 280p.

3683 Wood, Martha. "Carrying a Camera on Horseback." Western Horseman, XLIV (September 1979), 58-62.

C HUNTING

3684 Bailey's Hunting Directory. London: J. A. Allen, 1950--. v. 47--.

3685 Brander, Michael. Hunting and Shooting from the Earliest Times to the Present Day. New York: G. P. Putnam, 1971. 255p.

3686 Brent, Jeff. "Hunting Cats on Horseback." Western Horseman, XLI (April 1976), 64-66, 128-130.

3687 Carr, Raymond. English Fox Hunting: A History. London: Weidenfeld and Nicolson, 1976. 273p.

3688 Case, Walter O. , ed. Ninety Years of Horse and Hound.
London and New York: Hamlyn Publishing, 1977. 224p.

3689 Christopher, Renny. "History of Hunting." Horse Lover's
National Magazine, XLIII (December 1978), 30, 44.

3690 Dixon, William S. Fox Hunting in the Twentieth Century.
London: Hurst and Blackett, 1925. 312p.

3691 _____. Men, Horses, and Hunting. New York: W. F.
Payson, 1931. 333p.
Classics.

3692 Epperson, Glenn I. "Stag at Bay." Horse and Horseman, I
(January 1974), 28-32.

3693 Fine, Norman M. "The Bunratten Fox." Classic, III (February-March 1978), 82-87.

3694 Follmer, Don. "He [Melvin Poe] Gets It Honest, This Varmity
Man." Classic, III (June-July 1978), 136-140.

3695 Foxford, pseud. Horse and Hound Foxhunting Companion. London and New York: Hamlyn Publishing, 1978. 320p.

3696 Goeldner, Christian T. The Thoroughbred Field Hunter. South
Brunswick, NJ: A. S. Barnes, 1977. 127p.

3697 Hearst, Austine. "When Irish Dogs are Baying." Horse and
Rider, XVI (September 1976), 26-30.

3698 Herring, Jane S. "The Hunt Is On." California Horse Review,
XII (September 1975), 14-18.

3699 Hole, Christina. English Sports and Pastimes. Freeport, NY:
Books for Libraries, 1968. 182p.

3700 The Horse and Hound Yearbook. London: Odhams, 1950--.
v. 4--.

3701 "Horseback Hunting Techniques." Horse and Rider, VII (August
1968), passim.

3702 Hyams, Edward S. "Riding to Hounds." In: his New State-
manship: An Anthology. New York: Longmans, Greene,
1963. pp. 189-192.

3703 Koponen, Joan. "Hunting in Alaska." American Horseman,
IV (October 1974), 54-55, 62.

3704 Longrigg, Roger. The History of Fox Hunting. London and
New York: Macmillan, 1975. 272p.

3705 McIlvaine, Jane. To Win the Hunt: A Virginia Foxhunter in Ireland. Barre, MA: Barre Publishing Company, 1966. 100p.

3706 Meads, Jim. They Still Meet at Eleven. Gloucester, Eng.: Standfast Press, 1979. 140p.
Foxhunting.

3707 Price, Steven D. "Chris Howells: Huntsman." Horse Lover's National Magazine, XLIII (December 1978), 32-34.

3708 Self, Margaret C. The Hunter in Pictures. Philadelphia: Macrae Smith, 1972. 172p.

3709 _____. In Ireland. New York: Yoseloff, 1954. 220p.

3710 Simon, John. "Horses for Hunting." Horseman, XXIII (June 1979), 72-75, 78.

3711 Wadsworth, William P. Riding to Hounds: An Introduction for Foxhunters. Berryville, VA: Chronicle of the Horse, 1976. 47p.
First printed in 1962.

3712 Williams, John. An Introduction to Hunting. London: J. A. Allen, 1975. 61p.

D COWBOYS AND RANCH LIFE

3713 Adams, Ramon F. The Horse Wrangler and His Remuda. Austin, TX: Encino Press, 1971. 51p.

3714 _____. The Old-Time Cowhand. New York: Macmillan, 1961. 354p.

3715 Ainsworth, Katherine. "Los [Mexican] Charros." Westways, LXIX (October 1977), 44-47.

3716 Amaral, Anthony A. Will James: The Last Cowboy Legend. Reno: University of Nevada Press, 1979. 175p.

3717 Atherton, Lewis E. The Cattle Kings. Bloomington: Indiana University Press, 1961. 308p.

3718 Bauer, Helen. California Ranch Days. Garden City, NY: Doubleday, 1953. 128p.

3719 Bode, Winston. "Portrait of Pancho: Some Recollections of J. Frank Dobie." Texas Quarterly, VII (Winter 1964), 21-45.

3720 Bradfield, Byron. "Old-Style Roundup." Western Horseman, XLI (August 1976), 51-52, 130.

3721 Case, Leland D. "The Westerners: Twenty-Five Years of Riding the Range." Western Historical Quarterly I (January 1970), 63-76.

3722 Chadwick, Joseph. Cowboys and Cattle Drives. New York: Hawthorn Books, 1967. 127p.

3723 Davis, Ray. "Calf Working on the 7L." Western Horseman, XLV (January 1980), 11-14.

3724 _____. "Cow Work on the Running M." Western Horseman, XLI (August 1976), 116-118.

3725 Dobie, J. Frank. Cow People. Boston: Little, Brown, 1964. 305p.

3726 _____. Prefaces. Boston: Little, Brown, 1975. 204p.

3727 _____. Up the Trail from Texas. New York: Random House, 1955. 182p.

3728 Durham, Philip. The Adventures of the Negro Cowboys. New York: Dodd, Mead, 1966. 143p. [juv.]

3729 Eddy, Jerry. "Jum Shoulders, the Legend in a New Era." Western Horseman, XLV (April 1980), 28-32.

3730 Flanagan, Sue. Trailing the Longhorns: A Century Later. Austin, TX: Madrona Press, 1974. 209p.

3731 Forbis, William H. The Cowboys. New York: Time-Life, 1973. 240p.

3732 Frink, Maurice M. Cow Country Cavalcade: 80 Years of the Wyoming Stock Growers Association. Denver, CO: Old West Publishing Company, 1954. 243p.

3733 Glaubke, Robert. Ranching Around the World. Chicago: A. Whitman, 1964. 39p. [juv.]

3734 Green, Ben K. The Last Traildrive Through Downtown Dallas. Flagstaff, AZ: Northland Press, 1971. 73p.

3735 _____. Wild Cow Tales. New York: Ballantine Books, 1974. 306p.

3736 Greene, Carla. Cowboys: What Do They Do? New York: Harper and Row, 1972. 64p. [juv.]

3737 Hanes, Bailey C. Bill Pickett, Bulldogger: The Biography of a Black Cowboy. Norman: University of Oklahoma Press, 1977. 207p.

3738 Hardin, Floyd. "Stampede: Rangeland Terror." Montana Magazine of Western History, XIV (January 1964), 48-52.

3739 Hedgpeth, Don. The Texas Breed: A Cowboy Anthology. Flagstaff, AZ: Northland Press, 1978. 120p.

3740 Hendrix, John. If I Can Do It Horseback: A Cow Country Sketchbook. Austin: University of Texas Press, 1963. 355p.

3741 James, Will. Cowboys North and South. New York: Arno Press, 1975. 217p.
Reprint of the 1924 edition.

3742 Keating, Bern. Famous American Cowboys. Chicago: Rand McNally, 1977. 92p. [juv.]

3743 Kennon, Bob. From the Pecos to the Powder: A Cowboy's Autobiography. Norman: University of Oklahoma Press, 1965. 251p.

3744 King, Chuck. "Going Down the Road with Inflation." Western Horseman, XLV (July 1980), 44-48.
Difficulties faced by modern cowboys.

3745 Landin, Les. About Cowboys Around the World. Chicago: Melmont, 1963. 47p. [juv.]

3746 Langmore, Bank. The Cowboy. New York: Morrow, 1975. 251p.

3747 Lavender, David S. One Man's West. Garden City, NY: Doubleday, 1956. 316p. Rpr. 1977.

3748 McCauley, James E. A Stove-Up Cowboy's Story. Dallas: Southern Methodist University Press, 1965. 76p.

3749 McCoy, Tim. Tim McCoy Remembers the West. Garden City, NY: Doubleday, 1977. 274p.

3750 McCracken, Harold. The American Cowboy. Garden City, NY: Doubleday, 1973. 196p.

3751 McDowell, Bart. The American Cowboy in Life and Legend. Washington, D.C.: National Geographic Society, 1972. 211p.

3752 McKeen, Ona L. "The Cowhand." American Heritage, XIV (October 1963), 16-31.

3753 Moore, Daniel G. Log of a Twentieth Century Cowboy. Tucson: University of Arizona Press, 1965. 217p.

3754 Paul, Virginia. This was Cattle Ranching: Yesterday and Today. Seattle, WA: Superior Publishing Company, 1973. 192p.

3755 Perkins, Peter. Cowboys of the High Sierra. Flagstaff, AZ: Northland Press, 1979. 100p.

3756 Pirtle, Caleb. XIT: Being a New and Original Exploration, in Art and Words, Into the Life and Times of the American Cowboy. Birmingham, AL: Published for the Texas Cowboy Artists by Oxmoor House, 1975. 156p.

3757 Polk, Frank. F-F-F-Frank Polk: An Uncommonly Frank Autobiography. Flagstaff, AZ: Northland Press, 1978. 123p.

3758 Rennert, Vincent P. The Cowboy. New York: Crowell, 1966. 117p. [juv.]

3759 Reynolds, Robert. The Cowboy: A Contemporary Photographic Study. Portland, OR: Graphic Arts Center Publishing Company, 1975. 120p.

3760 Rogers, Anne. "Charro." Horse and Rider, X (February 1971), 46-50.

3761 Rojas, Arnold R. California Vaquero. Los Angeles, CA: Academy Publishers, 1953. 140p.

3762 _____. These Were the Vaqueros. Shafer, CA: Chuck Hitchcock, Distributor, 1975. 528p.

3763 _____. Vaqueros and Buckeroos. Shafer, CA: Chuck Hitchcock, Distributor, 1979. 312p.

3764 Rollins, Philip A. The Cowboy: An Unconventional History of Civilization on the Old-Time Range. Rev. and enl. ed. Albuquerque: University of New Mexico Press, 1979. 402p. Reprint of the 1936 Scribners edition.

3765 Rounds, Glen. The Cowboy Trade. New York: Holiday House, 1972. 95p. [juv.]

3766 Russell, Andy. Men of the Saddle: Working Cowboys of North America. New York: Van Nostrand-Reinhold, 1979. 192p.

3767 St. John, Bob. On Down the Road: The Life of the Rodeo Cowboy. Englewood Cliffs, NJ: Prentice-Hall, 1977. 256p.

3768 Sandoz, Mari. The Cattlemen. Lincoln: University of Nebraska Press, 1978. 527p.

3769 Santee, Ross. Cowboy. Lincoln: University of Nebraska Press,

1977.   257p.
Reprint of the 1928 edition.

3770 _____.   Men and Horses.   Lincoln: University of Nebraska
      Press, 1977.   268p.
      Reprint of the 1926 edition.

3771 Savage, William W., Jr.   The Cowboy Hero: His Image in
      American History and Culture.   Norman: University of
      Oklahoma Press, 1979.   179p.

3772 _____.   "The Cowboy Myth: A Comment."   Red River Valley
      Historical Review, II (Spring 1975), 162-171.

3773 _____., comp.   Cowboy Life: Reconstructing an American
      Myth.   Norman: University of Oklahoma Press, 1975.
      208p.

3774 Schmidt, James C.   Charro: Mexican Horseman.   New York:
      G. P. Putnam, 1969.   127p.

3775 Silcott, Philip B.   Cowboys.   Washington, D.C.:   National
      Geographic Society, 1975.   32p.   [juv.]

3776 Siringo, Charles A.   A Texas Cowboy, Including Addenda to the
      1886 Edition.   Lincoln: University of Nebraska Press, 1979.
      216p.

3777 Slade, James, 3rd.   "The Gauchos of Rio Grande do Sul
      [Brazil]."   Western Horseman, XLIII (May 1978), 8-12.

3778 Surface, William.   Roundup at the Double Diamond: The Amer-
      ican Cowboy Today.   Boston: Houghton Mifflin, 1974.
      237p.

3779 Tanner, Ogden.   The Ranchers.   New York: Time-Life, Inc.,
      1977.   230p.

3780 Thorp, Nathan H.   Pardner of the Wind: The Story of the
      Southwestern Cowboy.   Lincoln: University of Nebraska
      Press, 1977.   309p.
      Reprint of the 1945 Caxton edition.

3781 Ulph, O. C.   "Cowhands, Cow Horses, and Cows."   American
      West, III (Winter 1966), 64-71.

3782 Vanderbilt, Cornelius.   Ranches and Ranch Life in America.
      New York: Crown, 1968.   280p.

3783 Vernam, Glenn R.   The Rawhide Years: A History of the
      Cattlemen and the Cattle Country.   Garden City, NY:
      Doubleday, 1976.   227p.

3784   Waltrip, Lela.   Cowboys and Cattlemen.   New York: David
       McKay, 1967.   179p.

3785   Ward, Don.   Cowboys and Cattle Country.   Junior Library.
       New York: American Heritage, 1961.   153p.   [juv.]

3786   Ward, Fay E.   The Cowboy at Work.   New York: Hastings
       House, 1958.   278p.

3787   Wasson, Bryan.   Horses and Horsemen.   Abilene, TX: Cowboy
       Book Store, 1965.   122p.

3788   Westermeier, Clifford P.   Trailing the Cowboy: His Life and
       Lore as Told by Frontier Journalists.   Caldwell, ID: Cax-
       ton Printers, 1955.   414p.   Rpr. 1978.

3789   Whittemore, Loren R.   An Illustrated History of Ranching in
       the Pikes Peak Region.   Colorado Springs, CO: Dentan-
       Berkeland Printing Company, 1967.   81p.

3790   Zurhorst, Charles.   The First Cowboys and Those Who Followed.
       New York: Abelard-Schuman, 1973.   150p.

Further References: See also Parts V and VIII above, and X below.

PART X   THE HORSE IN HISTORY AND ENTERTAINMENT

A   NATURAL HISTORY OF THE HORSE

3791   Clabby, John. The Natural History of the Horse. New York:
       Taplinger, 1976. 116p.

3792   Colbert, Edwin H. "Perissodactyls." In: his Evolution of
       the Vertebrates. 2nd ed. New York: John Wiley, 1969.
       pp. 390-411.

3793   Cotterman, Dan. "Early Horse: Great Hoax on Equine World."
       Horse Illustrated, IX (September-October 1978), 42-45.

3794   Darling, Lois and Louise. Sixty Million Years of Horses.
       New York: Morrow, 1960. 64p. [juv.]

3795   DuPuy, William A. The History of the Horse. New York:
       Holt, Rinehart, and Winston, 1965. 29p. [juv.]

3796   Ehrenborg, Mrs. Cecil G. Horse Through the Ages. By Cecil
       G. Trew, pseud. New York: Roy Publisher, 1960. 75p.
       [juv.]

3797   Forsten, Ann-Marie. The Fossil Horses of the Texas Gulf
       Coastal Plain. Rev. ed. Austin: Texas Memorial Museum,
       1975. 86p.

3798   Haines, Francis. "Evolution and History of the Horse." Ra-
       pidan River Farm Digest, I (Winter 1975), 2-16.

3799   Ipcar, Dahlov. Horses of Long Ago. Garden City, NY:
       Doubleday, 1965. 59p. [juv.]

3800   Kitts, David B. American Hyracotherium (Perissodactyia Equi-
       dae). New York: American Museum of Natural History,
       1956. 60p.

3801   McLean, Malcolm D. Fine Texas Horses: Their Pedigrees
       and Performance, 1830-1845. Monograph in History and
       Culture, no. 1. Ft. Worth, TX: Texas Christian University
       Press, 1966. 153p.

3802 Mellin, Jeanne. <u>Horses Across the Ages</u>. New York: E. P. Dutton, 1954. 91p.

3803 Moscow, Henry. <u>Domestic Descendants</u>. New York: Time-Life, 1979. 128p.

3804 Posil, Elsa Z. <u>The True Book of Horses</u>. New York: Children's Press, 1961. 47p. [juv.]

3805 Quinn, J. H. "Miocene Equidae of the Texas Gulf Coastal Plain." <u>University of Texas Publications</u>, no. 55 (1955), 1-102.

3806 Romer, Alfred S. "Perissodactyls." In: his <u>Notes and Comments on Vertebrate Paleontology</u>. Chicago: University of Chicago Press, 1968. pp. 206-209.

3807 Simpson, George G. <u>Horses: The Story of the Horse Family in the Modern World and Though 60 Million Years of History</u>. Garden City, NY: Doubleday, 1961. 323p.

3808 Stock, Chester. <u>The Ascent of Equus: A Story of the Origin and Development of the Horse</u>. Paleontology Publication, no. 5. Los Angeles, CA: Los Angeles County Museum, 1944. 38p.

3809 Zappler, George. <u>From One Ancestor</u>. New York: Julian Messner, 1971. 54p. [juv.]

B   THE HORSE IN CIVILIZATION

1   General Works

3810 Afshar, Ahmad and Judith Lerner. "Horses of the Ancient Persian Empire at Persepolis." <u>Antiquity</u>, LIII (March and November 1979), 44-47, 218-219.

3811 Alexander, David. <u>The History and Romance of the Horse Told with Pictures</u>. New York: Cooper Square Publishers, 1962. 128p.

3812 Anderson, John K. <u>Ancient Greek Horsemanship</u>. Berkeley: University of California Press, 1961. 329p.

3813 Baker, Richard S. <u>Horse Sense: Horses in War and Peace</u>. London: S. Paul, 1962. 128p.

3814 Barloy, Jean J. <u>Man and Animals: 100 Centuries of Friendship</u>. Translated from the French. London and New York: Gordon and Cremonesi, 1978. 187p.

3815 Begnaud, Allen E. "Hoofbeats in Colonial Maryland." <u>Maryland Historical Magazine</u>, LXV (Fall 1970), 207-238.

3816 Bökönyl, Sandor. <u>Data on Iron Age Horses of Central and Eastern Europe.</u> Harvard University, American School of Prehistoric Research Bulletin, no. 25. Cambridge, MA: Peabody Museum of American Archaeology and Ethnology, 1968. 108p.

3817 Boyd, Mildred. <u>History in Harness: The Story of Horses.</u> New York: Criterion Books, 1965. 143p.

3818 Broderick, A. Houghton, ed. <u>Animals in Archaeology.</u> New York: Praeger, 1972. 180p.

3819 Chevevix-Trench, Charles P. <u>A History of Horsemanship.</u> Garden City, NY: Doubleday, 1970. 320p.

3820 _____. "Horsemanship in History." <u>History Today,</u> XX (November 1970), 771-781.

3821 Clifford, Timothy. <u>The Stable of Don Juan of Austria.</u> New York: Abaris Books, 1979.

3822 Csorba, J. J. <u>The Use of Horses and Mules on Farms.</u> Washington, D.C.: Agricultural Research Service, U.S. Department of Agriculture, 1959.

3823 Denhardt, Robert M. "The Horse in New Spain and the Borderlands." <u>Agriculture History,</u> XXV (October 1951), 145-150.

3824 Dent, Anthony. <u>The Horse, Through Fifty Centuries of Civilization.</u> New York: Holt, Rinehart and Winston, 1974. 288p.

3825 Downs, J. F. "Origin and Spread of Riding in the Near East and Central Asia." <u>American Anthropology,</u> LXIII (December 1961), 1193-1203.

3826 Evans, D. H. <u>Horses on Farms Today.</u> Loughborough, Eng.: University of Nottingham School of Agriculture, 1951. 22p.

3827 Fenton, Carrol L. <u>Animals That Help Us: The Story of Domestic Animals.</u> Rev. ed. New York: John Day, 1973. 128p. [juv.]

3828 Gianoli, Luigi, et al. <u>Horses and Horsemanship Through the Ages.</u> Translated from the Italian. New York: Crown, 1969. 441p.

3829 Golides, Clarence. "Hunting in the Old South." <u>Georgia Review,</u> XVIII (Fall-Winter 1964), 225-265, 463-478; XIX (Spring-Winter 1965), 93-120, 226-238, 350-359, 471-484; XX (Spring-Fall 1966), 99-107, 220-236, 352-369.

3830 Haddelsey, Vincent. <u>The Horse, Our [British] Heritage.</u> New York: Hastings House, 1972. 104p. [juv.]

3831 Haines, Francis. "Horses and the American Frontier." American West, VIII (March 1971), 10-15.

3832 Harrell, Laura D. S. "Jockey Clubs and Race Tracks in Antebellum Mississippi, 1795-1861." Journal of Mississippi History, XXVIII (November 1966), 304-318.

3833 Howard, Robert W. The Horse in America. New York: Follett, 1965. 298p.

3834 Hunt, Frazier. Horses and Heroes: The Story of the Horse in America for 450 Years. New York: Scribners, 1949. 306p.

3835 Hyams, Edward S. Animals in the Service of Man. Philadelphia: Lippincott, 1972. 209p.

3836 Irving, Robert M. Amity Agriculture. Geographical Series, no. 11. Vancouver, B.C.: British Columbia Geographical Series, 1969. 166p.

3837 Jankovich, Miklos. They Rode Into Europe: The Fruitful Exchange in the Arts of Horsemanship Between East and West. London: Harrap, 1971. 176p.

3838 Lewinson, Richard. Animals, Men, and Myths: An Informative and Entertaining History of Man and the Animals Around Him. Translated from the German. New York: Harper, 1954. 422p.

3839 McCoy, Joseph J. Animal Servants of Man. New York: Lothrop, 1963. 192p. [juv.]

3840 McLoughlin, Denis. Wild and Woolly: An Encyclopedia of the Old West. Garden City, NY: Doubleday, 1975. 570p.

3841 Mielsen, Lois C. "Work Horse Teams in Minneapolis [in the 1920's]." Western Horseman, XXXVIII (July 1973), 77-78.

3842 Pollard, Jack, ed. Horses and Horsemen: Wild Bush Horses, Thoroughbreds, and the Men Who Rode Them. Sydney, Aust.: A. H. and A. W. Reed, 1966. 315p.

3843 Russell, George B. Hoofprints in Time. South Brunswick, NJ: A. S. Barnes, 1967. 440p.

3844 Seth-Smith, Michael, ed. The Horse in Art and History. London: New English Library, 1978. 128p.

3845 Steffen, Randy. Horsemen Through Civilization. Colorado Springs, CO: Western Horseman, 1970. 48p.

3846 Stout, Joseph A. and Odie B. Frank. A Short History of the American West. New York: Harper and Row, 1974. 325p.

3847 Stream, John J. "Bronc Bustin' in the Big City [Chicago, 1910-1913]." Western Horseman, XLI (April 1976), 76, 124-125.

3848 Toynbee, Jocelyn M. C. Animals in Roman Life and Art. Ithaca, NY: Cornell University Press, 1973. 431p.

3849 Trippett, Frank. The First Horsemen. New York: Time-Life, 1974. 160p.

3850 Vernan, Glen R. Man on Horseback: The Story of the Mounted Men from the Scythians to the American Cowboy. New York: Harper and Row, 1966. 436p.

3851 Zeuner, Fredrich E. A History of Domesticated Animals. New York: Harper and Row, 1963. 560p.

2 Indians

3852 Berthrong, Donald J. The Southern Cheyennes. Norman: University of Oklahoma Press, 1963. 446p.

3853 Clark, LaVerne, H. They Sang for Horses: The Impact of the Horse on Navajo and Apache Folklore. Tucson: University of Arizona Press, 1966. 225p.

3854 Daniel, Forrest W. "Dismounting the Sioux." North Dakota Quarterly, XLI (Summer 1974), 9-13.

3855 Ewers, John C. "The Horse Complex in Plains Indian History." In: Roger C. Owen, James J. F. Deety, and Anthony D. Fisher, eds. The North American Indian: A Sourcebook. New York: Macmillan, 1967. pp. 494-503.

3856 _____. The Horse in Blackfoot Indian Culture. Bureau of American Ethnology Bulletin, no. 159. Washington, D.C.: Smithsonian Institution Press, 1969. 374p.

3857 Forbes, J. D. "Appearance of the Mounted Indian in Northern Mexico and the Southwest, to 1860." Southwest Journal of Anthropology, XV (Summer 1959), 189-212.

3858 Haines, Francis. "Horses of Western Indians." American West, III (Spring 1966), 4-15+.

3859 Harris, Freddie S. "How Indians Went from Dogs to Horses." In: Bob Grey, ed. Western Rider's Yearbook and Buyer's Guide for 1970. Houston, TX: Cordovan Corp., 1969. pp. 118-121.

3860 Hassrick, Royal B. The Sioux: Life and Customs of a Warrior Society. Norman: University of Oklahoma Press, 1964. 337p.

3861 Hofsinde, Robert. The Indian and His Horse. New York: Morrow, 1960. 96p. [juv.]

3862 Lavine, Sigmund A. The Horses the Indians Rode. New York: Dodd, Mead, 1974. 78p. [juv.]

3863 Mayhall, Mildred P. The Kiowas. Norman: University of Oklahoma Press, 1962. 315p.

3864 Miller, Alfred J. Braves and Buffalo: Plains Indian Life in 1837. Toronto, Ont.: University of Toronto Press, 1973. 176p.

3865 Roe, Franklin G. The Indian and the Horse. Norman: University of Oklahoma Press, 1955. 434p.

3866 Schmidlin, L. L. N. "The Role of the Horse in the Life of the Comanche." Journal of the West, XIII (January 1974), 47-66.

3867 Wilson, H. C. "Inquiry Into the Nature of Plains Indian Cultural Development." American Anthropology, LXV (April 1963), 355-369; LXVI (April 1964), 421-422.

3868 Winkenwerder, Valerie. "Plains Indian Horsemanship." Western Horseman, XLII (June 1977), 86-87.

3869 Wissler, Clark. "Influence of the Horse in the Development of Plains Culture." In: Edward A. Hoebel, Jesse D. Jennings, and Elmer R. Smith, eds. Readings in Anthropology. New York: McGraw-Hill, 1955. pp. 155-173.

3870 Worcester, Donald E. The Apaches: Eagles of the Southwest. Norman: University of Oklahoma Press, 1979. 389p.

3 Military and Cavalry

3871 Adcock, Frank E. The Greek and Macedonian Art of War. Berkeley: University of California Press, 1957. 109p.

3872 Anderson, John K. "Greek Chariot-Borne and Mounted Infantry." American Journal of Archaeology, LXXIX (July 1975), 175-187.

3873 Anderson, John Q., ed. Campaigning with Parson's Texas Cavalry, C.S.A.: The War Journal and Letters of the Four Orr Brothers, Twelfth Texas Cavalry Regiment. Hillsboro, TX: Hill Junior College Press, 1967. 173p.

3874 Anglesey, Marquess of. A History of the British Cavalry. 2 vols. Hamden, CT: Shoestring Press, 1973.

3875 Beeler, John. Warfare in England, 1066-1189. Ithaca, NY: Cornell University Press, 1966.

3876 Blacklock, Michael. The Royal Scots Greys: The 2nd Dragoons. London: Leo Cooper, 1971. 126p.

3877 Borden, Spencer. What Horse for the [U. S.] Cavalry? Fall River, MA: J. H. Franklin, 1912. 106p. A classic.

3878 Brackett, Albert G. History of the United States Cavalry, from the Formation of the Federal Government to 1st of June 1863. Freeport, NY: Books for Libraries, 1970. 337p. Reprint of the 1865 edition.

3879 Brander, Michael. The 10th Royal Hussars: Prince of Wales' Own. London: Leo Cooper, 1969. 137p.

3880 Brereton, John M. The Horse in War. New York: Arco, 1976. 160p.

3881 Brett-Smith, Richard. The 11th Hussars: Prince Albert's Own. London: Leo Cooper, 1969. 325p.

3882 Brown, Dee A. The Galvanized Yankees. Urbana: University of Illinois Press, 1963. 243p.

3883 _____. Grierson's [Civil War] Raid. Urbana: University of Illinois Press, 1954. 261p.

3884 Brown, Stuart E., Jr. The Horses of [the U. S. Army Remount Service at] Arlington. Berryville, VA: Chesapeake Book Company, 1964. 39p.

3885 Bukhari, Emir. Napoleon's Cavalry. San Rafael, CA: Presidio Press, 1979. 248p.

3886 Butterworth, William E. Soldiers on Horseback: The Story of the United States Cavalry. New York: W. W. Norton, 1967. 141p.

3887 Carter, Samuel. The Last Cavaliers: Confederate and Union Cavalry in the Civil War. NY: St. Martin's, 1979. 388p.

3888 Chandler, D. G. "The [Cavalry] Battle of Sahagun, 1808." History Today, XXIV (November 1974), 765-772.

3889 Chandler, Melbourne C. Of Gary Owen in Glory: The History of the Seventh United States Cavalry Regiment. Arlington, VA: United States Cavlary Association, 1960. 458p.

3890 Coddrington, Edwin B. The Gettysburg Campaign. New York: Scribners, 1968. 866p.

3891 Coffman, Edward M. "Army Life on the Frontier." Military Affairs, XX (Winter 1956), 193-201.

3892 Cottrell, Sue. Hoof Beats, North and South: Horses and Horsemen of the Civil War. New York: Exposition Press, 1975. 87p.

3893 Cunninghame, R. B. The Horses of the [Spanish] Conquest. Norman: University of Oklahoma Press, 1968. 145p.

3894 Dean, Frank. "The Roping Chinacos." Western Horseman, XXIX (January 1974), 38-39, 126-127.

3895 Denison, George T. A History of Cavalry from the Earliest Times, with Lessons for the Future. 2nd ed. London: Macmillan, 1913. 468p. Rpr. 1978.

3896 Dines, Glen. Long Knife: The Story of the Fighting U. S. Cavalry of the 1860 Frontier. New York: Macmillan, 1962. Unpaged. [juv.]

3897 Downey, Fairfax D. The Buffalo Soldiers in the Indian Wars. New York: McGraw-Hill, 1969. 127p.

3898 _____. Clash of Cavalry: The Baddle of Brandy Station, June 9, 1863. New York: David McKay, 1959. 238p.

3899 _____. Indian-Fighting Army. Ft. Collins, CO: Old Army Press, 1971. 319p. Reprint of the 1941 edition.

3900 Duanine, Carl L. The Dead Men Wore Boots: An Account of the 32nd Texas Volunteer Cavalry, 1862-1865. Austin, TX: San Felipe Press, 1966.

3901 Duke, Basil W. A History of [John H.] Morgan's Cavalry. Bloomington: Indiana University Press, 1960. 595p. Reprint of the 1867 edition.

3902 Dupuy, Trevor N. The Battle of Austerlitz. New York: Macmillan, 1968. 90p.

3903 Echohawk, Brummett. "Recollections of the Pawnee Scouts." Western Horseman, XXXVIII (January 1973), 26-28, 133-135.

3904 Ellis, John. Cavalry: The History of Mounted Warfare. New York: G. P. Putnam, 1978. 192p.

3905 Ffrench-Blake, R. L. V. The 17th/21st Lancers. London: Hamilton, 1968. 173p.

3906 Furneaux, Rupert. Invasion 1066. Englewood Cliffs, NJ: Prentice-Hall, 1967. 207p.

3907 Gibbs, Peter. Crimean Blunders. New York: Holt, Rinehart and Winston, 1960. 297p.

3908 Glaskow, Wasili G. History of the Cossacks. New York: Robert Speller, 1968.

3909 Glubok, Shirley. Knights in Armor. New York: Harper and Row, 1969. 48p. [juv.]

3910 Graham, S. S. "The Routine at Western Cavalry Posts, 1833-1861." Journal of the West, XV (July 1976), 49-59.

3911 Gray, John S. "The Pack Train on George A. Custer's Last Campaign." Nebraska History, LVII (Spring 1976), 53-68.

3912 Hamblin, Dora J. "Pomp, Pagentry and Pure Magic." Classic, III (April-May, 1978), 94-101.
      The Italian Carbinieri.

3913 Harris, John. The Gallant Six Hundred. New York: Mason and Lipscomb, 1973. 302p.

3914 Herd, James W. "Ancient Battle Horses." Western Horseman, XXXXIII (September 1973), 64, 169-172.

3915 Herner, Charles. The Arizona Rough Riders. Tucson: University of Arizona Press, 1970. 275p.

3916 Herr, John K. and Edward S. Wallace. The Story of the U.S. Cavalry, 1775-1942. Boston: Little, Brown, 1953. 275p.

3917 Hill, Donald R. "The Role of the Camel and the Horse in the Early Arab Conquests." In: Vernon J. Parry and M. E. Yapp, eds. War, Technology and Society in the Middle East. London and New York: Oxford University Press, 1975. pp. 32-43.

3918 Hills, R. J. T. The Life Guards. London: Leo Cooper, 1971. 128p.

3919 _____. The Royal Horse Guards: The Blues. London: Leo Cooper, 1970. 117p.

3920 Hindus, Maurice G. Cossacks: The Story of a Warrior People. Garden City, NY: Doubleday, Doran, 1945. 321p. Rpr. 1978.

3921 Hollister, C. Warren. The Military Organization of Norman England. Oxford, Eng.: at the Clarendon Press, 1965. 319p.

3922 Hooper, Frederick. The Military Horse. South Brunswick, NJ: A. S. Barnes, 1976. 105p.

3923 Howarth, David. Waterloo: Day of Battle. New York: Atheneum, 1968. 239p.

3924 Hughes, Willis B. "The First Dragoons on the Western Frontier." Arizona and the West, XII (Summer 1970), 115-138.

3925 Hutchins, James S. Boots and Saddles at the Little Big Horn: Weapons, Dress, Equipment, Horses and Flags of General Custer's 7th U.S. Cavalry. Ft. Collins, CO: Old Army Press, 1976. 82p.

3926 Jackson, Donald. Custer's Gold: The United States Cavalry Expedition of 1874. Lincoln: University of Nebraska Press, 1972. 152p.

3927 Johnson, David. Napoleon's Cavalry and Its Leaders. New York: Homes and Meier, 1978. 191p.

3928 Keliher, John G. History of the 4th United States Cavalry. Wahiaw, HI: Kemoo Stationers, 1960. 32p.

3929 Kellar, Allan. Morgan's Raid. Indianapolis, IN: Bobbs-Merrill, 1961. 272p.

3930 Knight, Oliver. Life and Manners in the Frontier Army. Norman: University of Oklahoma Press, 1978. 280p.

3931 Langhelle, Per Ivar. "Norwegian Army Pack Horses." Western Horseman, XXXVI (September 1971), 60-61, 124-126.

3932 Lawford, James ed. The Cavalry. Indianapolis, IN: Bobbs-Merrill, 1976.

3933 Leckie, William H. The Buffalo Soldiers: A Narrative of the Negro Cavalry in the West. Norman: University of Oklahoma Press, 1967. 290p.

3934 _____. The Military Conquest of the Southern Plains. Norman: University of Oklahoma Press, 1963. 269p.

3935 Legassick, Martin. "Firearms, Horses, and Samorian Army Organization, 1870-1898." Journal of African History, VI (Spring 1966), 95-115.

3936 Longstreet, Stephen. War Cries on Horseback: The Story of the Indian Wars of the Great Plains. Garden City, NY: Doubleday, 1970. 333p.

3937 Longworth, Philip. The Cossacks. New York: Holt, Rinehart and Winston, 1969. 409p.

3938 Lunt, James D. Charge [of British Cavalry] to Glory. New York: Harcourt, Brace, 1960. 248p.

3939 McConnell, H. H. Five Years a Cavalryman; or, Sketches of Regular Army Life on the Texas Frontier Twenty Years Ago. Freeport, NY: Books for Libraries, 1970. 319p. Reprint of the 1888 edition.

3940 Meals, Leona. "Horses of the [American] Civil War." Horse Lover's National Magazine, XXXI (August-September 1965), 24-26.

3941 Merrill, James M. Spurs to Glory: The Story of the U.S. Cavalry. Chicago: Rand McNally, 1966. 302p.

3942 Miller, E. B. "Veterinarian-Farriery Service in the Continental Army, April 1775-May 1977." American Veterinarian Medical Association Journal, CLXIX (July 1, 1976), 106-114.

3943 Mulford, Ami F. Fighting Indians in the 7th United States Cavalry: Custer's Favorite Regiment. New ed. Bellvue, NE: Old Army Press, 1970.

3944 Nicholson, J. B. R. The British Army of the Crimes. Reading, Eng.: Osprey Publications, 1974. 40p.

3945 Oakeshott, R. Edward. A Knight and His Horse. Philadelphia: Dufour, 1964. 96p.

3946 Oates, Stephen E. Confederate Cavalry West of the [Mississippi] River. Austin: University of Texas Press, 1961.

3947 Paget, Julian. The Story of the [British Horse] Guards. San Rafael, CA: Presidio Press, 1979. 304p.

3948 Patton Museum Society. United States Cavalry. Ft. Knox, KY, 1974. 60p.

3949 Phenix, W. Splendid Anachronism: British Horse Cavalry in the Victorian Age. Ann Arbor, MI: University Microfilms, 1975. 200p.

3950 Pierce, Lyman B. History of the Second Iowa Cavlary. Burlington, IA: Hawk-Eye Steam Book and Job Printing, 1965.

3951 Piggott, Stuart. "Chariots in the Caucasus and in China." Antiquity, XLVIII (March 1974), 16-24.

3952 Place, Marian. Rifles and War Bonnets. New York: Washburn, 1968. 151p. U.S. 10th Cavalry.

3953 Raskoff, Jack. "The Life of a Cavalryman." Western Horseman, XXXVIII (June-July 1973), 32-33, 158-162, 68-69, 174-176.

3954 "Reminiscences of Some Incidents in the Career of a United
States Dragoon Between 1819 and 1844." Texas Quarterly,
IX (Autumn 1966), 7-28.

3955 Rickey, Don. Forty Miles a Day on Beans and Hay: The En-
listed Soldier Fighting the Indian Wars. Norman: University of Oklahoma Press, 1963. 382p.

3956 Riggs, David F. East of Gettysburg: Stuart vs. Custer. Bel-
levue, NE: Old Army Press, 1970. 79p.

3957 Rogers, H. C. B. The Mounted Troops of the British Army.
London: Seeley Service, 1959. 256p.

3958 Roosevelt, Theodore. The Rough Riders. Williamstown, MA:
Corner House, 1971. 300p.
Reprint of the 1899 edition.

3959 _____. "The Big War [World War 1] Horse." Horse and
Rider, XII (May 1973), 60-63.

3960 Schuessler, Raymond. "The Horse in the [American] Revolution."
Cattleman, LXV (June 1978), 125-128.

3961 _____. "The War Chariot of the Hittites." Western Horseman, XXXVIII (April 1973), 96-98, 172-173.

3962 Selby, John. Balaclava: Gentlemen's Battle. New York:
Atheneum, 1970. 245p.

3963 _____. U.S. Cavalry. Man-at-Arms Series. New York:
Hippocrene Books, 1974. 40p.

3964 Seth-Smith, Michael, ed. The Horse in War. London: New
English Library, 1979. 128p.

3965 Simkins, Michael. The Roman Army from Caesar to Trajan.
Man-at-Arms Series. New York: Hippocrene Books, 1974.
40p.

3966 Smail, R. C. Crusading Warfare, 1097-1193. Cambridge,
Eng.: at the Clarendon Press, 1956. 272p.

3967 Smith, Gene. "Before the [British Cavalry's] Charing Stopped."
Classic, II (August-September 1977), 140-152.

3968 Smith, George W. and Charles Judah, eds. Chronicles of the
Gringos: The U.S. Army in the Mexican War, 1846-1848.
Albuquerque: University of New Mexico Press, 1968. 523p.

3969 Starr, S. Z. "Hawkeyes on Horseback: The Second Iowa Volunteer Cavalry." Civil War History, XXIII (September
1977), 212-227.

3970 Steffen, Randy. The Horse Soldier, 1776-1943: The U.S. Cavalryman--His Uniforms, Arms, Accoutrements, and Equipments. 4 vols. Norman: University of Oklahoma Press, 1977-1980.

3971 Stewart, Miller J. "From [U.S. Cavalry Horse] Recruit to Old Trooper." Horseman, XXI (January 1977), 48-52.

3972 Tate, James P. , ed. The American Military on the Frontier: Proceedings of the 7th Military History Symposium, United States Air Force Academy, 30 September-1 October 1976. Washington, D.C. : U.S. Government Printing Office, 1978. 194p.

3973 Tucker, John and Lewis S. Winstock, eds. The English Civil War: A Military Handbook. Harrisburg, PA: Stackpole Books, 1972. 80p.

3974 Tylden, Geoffrey. Horses and Saddlery: An Account of the Animals Used by the British and Commonwealth Armies from the 17th Century to the Present Day, with a Description of Their Equipment. London: Published in Association with the Army Museum Ogilby Trust, by J. A. Allen, 1966. 276p.

3975 United States. Army Ordnance Department. Horse Equipments and Cavalry Accoutrements, as Prescribed by G.O. 73, A.G.O. , 1885. Glendale, NY: Benchmark Publishing Company, 1970. 50p.
Reprint of the 1891 edition.

3976 _____ . _____ . _____ . Proceedings of the Board of Officers, Convened Under Special Orders Nos. 238 and 253 A.G.O. , 1873, on Horse Equipments, Cavalry Equipments and Accoutrements, Saddlers' and Smiths' Tools and Materials, and Standard Supply-Table for the Cavalry Service. Glendale, NY: Benchmark Publishing Company, 1970. 119p.
Reprint of the 1874 edition.

3977 Utley, Robert M. Frontier Regulars: The United States Army and the Indian, 1866-1890. New York: Macmillan, 1973. 462p.

3978 _____ . Frontiersmen in Blue: The United States Army and the Indian, 1848-1865. New York: Macmillan, 1967. 384p.

3979 Van Schmidt, Karl. Instructions for the Training, Employment and Leading of Cavalry. Translated from the German. New York: Greenwood Press, 1969. 232p.
Reprint of the 1881 edition.

3980 Walker, Henry P. "The Reluctant Corporal: The Autobiography of William Bladen Jett." Journal of Arizona History, XII (Spring-Summer 1971), 1-50, 112-144.

3981 Whitman, Sidney E. The Troopers: An Informal History of
the Plains Cavalry, 1865-1890. New York: Hastings House,
1962. 256p.

3982 Wormser, Richard C. The Yellowlegs: The Story of the United
States Cavalry. Garden City, NY: Doubleday, 1966. 468p.

3983 Young, Peter. The English Civil War Armies. Reading, Eng.:
Osprey Publications, 1973. 40p.

3984 _____ and Wilfred Emberton. The Cavalier Army. London:
Allen and Unwin, 1974. 189p.

4 Police, Parade and Fire Horses

3985 Abbott, Peter. "Playing with Fire." Horse and Rider, X
(December 1971), 46-53.

3986 Assaff, Edith. "Mounties of Motown." Horse and Rider, XIII
(April 1974), 40-42.
Mounted police in Detroit.

3987 Baillargen, J. A. "Seattle's Mounted Patrol." Western Horseman, XXXVIII (September 1973), 32, 50-51.

3988 Belmont, Pauline. Law, the Police Horse. Chicago: Reilly,
1962. Unpaged. [juv.]

3989 Campbell, Judith. Police Horses. Newton Abbot, Eng.:
David and Charles, 1967. 184p.

3990 Griffith, Perry B. "Form a Mounted Patrol." Horse and
Horseman, VII (March 1979), 26-29.

3991 Harris, Freddie S. "Fireman's Horse." Western Horseman,
XXXVIII (June 1973), 60-64, 190-195.

3992 Henry, John M. Mounted Drill Team. New York: A. S.
Barnes, 1954. 190p.

3993 Hewitt, Bob. "The Rurales of Mexico." Western Horseman,
XLII (June 1977), 120-122.

3994 Jackson, Paula S. "Indiana Horse Patrol." Western Horseman,
XLI (November 1976), 66, 157-161.

3995 Kenoyer, Natlee. The Fire Horses of San Francisco. Los
Angeles, CA: Westernlore Press, 1970. 94p.

3996 _____. "Our American Police Horses." Western Horseman,
XXXVI (November 1971), 56-58.

3997 Lilya, Barbara A. "How to Organize a Drill Team." Horse and Horseman, VI (March 1978), 38-47.

3998 Luciano, Peter. Training and Showing Your Parade Horse. Philadelphia, 1980.

3999 Narby, Mary. "[Police] Horses Are Back on the Street." Western Horseman, XLV (May 1980), 20.

4000 Nelson, Mary J. "R.C.M.P.: Accent on Mounted." Horse and Horseman, I (August 1973), 24-28, 84.

4001 Richardson, John. Gendarme, the Police Horse. Melbourne, Aust.: Lansdowne Press, 1971. 32p. [juv.]

4002 Rickell, Walt. "Cowboy Police Patrol." Horse and Rider, IX (August 1970), 36-40.

4003 Sassone, Rich. "Riot On, Baby." Horse and Rider, XI (February 1972), 46-50.
        Mounted members of the New York Police Department.

4004 Shulley, Z. "Fire Horses of Nevada." Nevada Horse Life, I (Summer 1977), 6-8.

4005 Simmons, Diane C. "Climbing the Parade Ladder." Horseman, XXIII (August 1979), 72-76.

4006 Slahor, Stephanie. "The Mountie Musical Ride." Horseman, XXIII (January 1979), 56-58.

4007 Tanner, Jean. "The Asphalt [Parade] Jungle." Horse and Rider, XVII (July 1977), 46-49, 56.

4008 Woodson, Weldon D. "Mounties: Centennial of Hard Riding." American Horseman, III (May 1973), 14-15, 52-53.

5 Transportation and Communication

4009 Bradley, George K. Fort Wayne's Trolleys. Chicago: O. Davies, 1963. 176p.

4010 Bradley, Glenn D. The Story of the Pony Express: An Account of the Most Remarkable Mail Service Ever in Existence and Its Place in History. Detroit, MI: Gale Research Company, 1974. 175p.
        Reprint of the 1913 edition.

4011 Buckley, R. J. A History of Tramways, from Horse to Rapid Transit. Newton Abbot, Eng.: David and Charles, 1975. 184p.

4012 Burford, A. "Heavy Transport in Classical Antiquity." Eco-
      nomic History Review, XIII (August 1960), 1-18.

4013 Clymer, Joseph F. American Horse-Drawn Vehicles. Los
      Angeles, CA: Westernlore Press, 1958. 106p.

4014 Collins, Dabney O. Great Western Rides. Denver, CA: Sage
      Books, 1961. 277p.

4015 Crofts, John E. V. Packhorse, Waggon and Post: Land Car-
      riage and Communications Under the Tudors and Stuarts.
      London: Routledge and Kegan Paul, 1967. 147p.

4016 Damase, Jacques. Carriages. Translated from the French.
      New York: G. P. Putnam, 1968. 120p.

4017 Dines, Glen. Bull Wagon--Strong Wheels for Rugged Men:
      The Frontier Freighters. New York: Macmillan, 1963.
      Unpaged.

4018 _____. The Overland Stage. New York: Macmillan, 1962.
      65p. [juv.]

4019 Dunlop, Richard. Wheels West, 1590-1900. Chicago: Rand
      McNally, 1977. 208p.

4020 East, Fred. Heroes on Horseback: The Story of the Pony
      Express. New York: Four Winds Press, 1969. 160p.
      [juv.]

4021 Farrell, Michael R. Who Made All Our Streetcars Go: The
      Story of Rail Transit in Baltimore. Baltimore, MD: N.R.
      H.S. Publication, 1973. 319p.

4022 Freelove, William F. An Assemblage of 19th Century Horses
      and Carriages. Farnham, Eng.: Perpetua Press, 1971.
      78p.

4023 Gardiner, Leslie. Stagecoach to John O'Groats. London:
      Hollis and Carter, 1961. 217p.

4024 Gordon, William J. The Horse World of London. Newton
      Abbot, Eng.: David and Charles, 1971. 190p.

4025 Gormley, William. "The Imps [Pony Express] of Satan." Horse
      and Rider, X (October 1971), 22-26.

4026 Gray, John S. "The Northern Overland Pony Express." Mon-
      tana, Magazine of Western History, XVI (October 1966),
      58-73.

4027 Hafen, LeRoy R. The Overland Mail, 1849-1869. New York:
      AMS Press, 1969. 361p.
      Reprint of the 1926 edition.

4028 Harris, Freddie S. "Jehus and Whips." Horseman, XV (June 1971), 58-64.

4029 _____. "What It Was Like to Travel by Horse." Horse Lover's Magazine, XXXIX (June-July 1974), 34-37.

4030 Higgs, Robert. "Horses or Tractors?: Some Basic Economics in the Pacific Northwest and Elsewhere." Agriculture History, XLIX (January 1975), 281-283.

4031 Howard, Robert W. Hoofbeats of Destiny. New York: New American Library, 1961. 191p. The Pony Express.

4032 _____. The Wagonmen. New York: G. P. Putnam, 1964. 220p.

4033 Jackson, W. T. "Wells Fargo Staging Over the Sierra." California Historical Quarterly, XLIX (June 1970), 99-113.

4034 _____. "Wells Fargo: Symbol of the Wild West." Western Historical Quarterly, III (April 1972), 169-196.

4035 _____. "Wells Fargo's Pony Express." Journal of the West, XI (July 1972), 405-436.

4036 Jensen, Lee L. The Pony Express. New York: Grosset and Dunlap, 1955. 154p.

4037 Johnston, Francis J. "Stagecoach Travel Through San Gorgonio Pass." Journal of the West, XI (October 1972), 616-635.

4038 Keith, T. B. "When Horses and Mules Pushed." Western Horseman, XXXIX (July 1974), 60-62.

4039 Kenoyer, Natlee. "Wells Fargo Express Horses." Western Horseman, XLII (April 1977), 58-60, 166-167.

4040 Kirkpatrick, Inez E. Stagecoach Trails in Iowa. Crete, NE: J. B. Publishing Company, 1976. 227p.

4041 Loeper, John J. The Flying Machine: A Stagecoach Journey [on the Old York Road] in 1774. New York: Atheneum, 1976. 62p. [juv.]

4042 Loomis, Noel M. Wells Fargo. New York: Crown, 1968. 340p.

4043 McCall, Edith S. Mail Riders: Paul Revere to the Pony Express. Chicago: Childrens Press, 1961. 125p. [juv.]

4044 Melvald, Maxine. "Evolution of the Carriage." Rapidan River Farm Digest, I (Winter 1975), 55-80.

4045 Middleton, William D. The Time of the Trolley. Milwaukee,
     WI: Kalmbach, 1967. 436p.

4046 Mitchell, Edwin V. The Horse and Buggy Era in New England.
     Ann Arbor, MI: Gryphon Books, 1971. 232p.

4047 Nathan, Mel C. The Pony Express. New York: Collector's
     Club, 1962. 108p.

4048 Outland, Charles F. Stagecoaching on El Camino Real, Los
     Angeles to San Francisco, 1861-1901. Glendale, CA: A.
     H. Clark Company, 1973. 339p.

4049 Palmer, Richard F. "The Old Time Mail": Stagecoach Days
     in Upstate New York." Lakemont, NY: North Country
     Books, 1977. 172p.

4050 Pfalser, I. L. "The Ancient Asian Pony Express [in Korea]."
     Western Horseman, XXXVIII (December 1973), 66-67, 149-
     153.

4051 Settle, Raymond W. Saddles and Spurs: The Pony Express
     Saga. Harrisburg, PA: Stackpole Books, 1955. 217p.

4052 _____. War Drums and Wagon Wheels: The Story of Rus-
     sell, Majors and Waddell. Lincoln: University of Nebraska
     Press, 1966. 268p.

4053 Shumway, George. Conestoga Wagon, 1750-1850: Freight Car-
     rier for 100 Years of America's Westward Expansion. 3rd
     ed. York, PA, 1968. 281p.

4054 Sparkes, Ivan. Stagecoaches and Carriages: An Illustrated
     History of Coaches and Coaching. Buckinghamshire, Eng.:
     Spurbooks, 1975. 160p.

4055 Spring, Agnes R. The Cheyenne and Black Hills Stage and
     Express Route. Lincoln: University of Nebraska Press,
     1965. 418p.
     Reprint of the 1948 edition.

4056 Stewart, George R. "Travellers by 'Overland.'" American
     West, V (July 1968), 4-12.

4057 Tarr, Laszlo. The History of the Carriage. Translated from
     the Hungarian. New York: Arco, 1969. 331p.

4058 Taylor, Morris F. First Mail West: Stagecoach Lines on the
     Santa Fe Trail. Albuquerque: University of New Mexico
     Press, 1971. 253p.

4059 Theobald, John and Lilian. Wells Fargo in Arizona Territory.
     Tempe: Arizona Historical Foundation, 1978. 210p.

4060 Vale, Edmund. The Mail-Coach Men of the Late Eighteenth
       Century. Newton Abbot, Eng.: David and Charles, 1967.
       300p.

4061 Vince, John. An Illustrated History of Carts and Wagons.
       Buckinghamshire, Eng.: Spurbooks, 1975. 160p.

4062 Voight, Virginia F. Stagecoach Days and Stagecoach Kings.
       Champagne, IL: Garrard, 1970. 95p. [juv.]

4063 Walker, Henry P. The Wagonmaster: High Plains Freighting
       from the Earliest Days of the Santa Fe Trail to 1880. Nor-
       man: University of Oklahoma Press, 1968.

4064 White, Joyce. "Pony Express Riders." Western Horseman,
       XLI (January 1976), 22-23, 115-117.

C THE HORSE IN ENTERTAINMENT

1 Circuses and Wild West Shows

4065 Cody, William F. Life and Adventures of Buffalo Bill. Free-
       port, NY: Books for Libraries, 1971. 352p.
       Reprint of the 1939 edition.

4066 Cotterman, Dan. "[Monte Montana] At the End of the Rope."
       Horse and Rider, XIV (March 1975), 26-31.

4067 Coup, William C. Sawdust and Spangles: Stories and Secrets
       of the Circus. Washington, D.C.: P. A. Ruddell, 1965.
       262p.
       Reprint of the 1901 edition.

4068 Deahl, William E., Jr. "Buffalo Bill's Wild West Show, 1885."
       Annals of Wyoming, XLVII (Fall 1975), 139-151.

4069 _____. "Buffalo Bill's Wild West Show in New Orleans."
       Louisiana History, XVI (Summer 1975), 289-298.

4070 Durant, John and Alice. Pictorial History of the American
       Circus. New York: A. S. Barnes, 1957. 328p.

4071 Fox, Charles P. A Pictorial History of the Performing Horse.
       Seattle, WA: Superior Publishing Company, 1960. 168p.

4072 _____. and Tom Parkinson. The Circus in America. Wau-
       kesha, WI: Country Beautiful, 1969. 289p.

4073 Freedman, Jill. Circus Days. New York: Harmony Books,
       1975. 128p.

4074 Frost, Thomas. Circus Life and Circus Celebrities [in Eng-
       land]. Detroit, MI: Singing Tree Press, 1970. 328p.

284 / Equestrian Studies

4075 Gollman, Robert H. My Father Owned a Circus. Caldwell, ID: Caxton Printers, 1965. 205p.

4076 Grant, H. Roger. "An Iowan with Buffalo Bill: Charles Eldridge Griffin in Europe, 1903-1906." Palimpsest, LIV (January-February 1973), 2-13.

4077 Hurley, Jimmie. "Buffalo Bill, Then and Now." Horse and Rider, XIV (July 1975), 30-35.

4078 Jensen, Dean. The Biggest, the Smallest, the Largest, the Shortest: A Chronicle of the American Circus from Its Heartland. Madison, WI: Wisconsin House Book Publishers, 1975. 205p.

4079 Long, Paul F. "Circuses Are Horses." Western Horseman, XLIV (April 1979), 94-97.

4080 Maeder, Marla C. "Wild Horse Show." Horse and Rider, XVI (September 1977), 60-63.

4081 Murray, Marian. Circus: From Rome to Ringling. Westport, CT: Greenwood Press, 1973. 353p.

4082 O'Brien, Esse F. Circus: Cinders to Sawdust. San Antonio, TX: Naylor, 1959. 268p.

4083 O'Connor, Richard. Buffalo Bill: The Noblest Whiteskin. New York: G. P. Putnam, 1973. 320p.

4084 Plowden, Gene. Singing Wheels and Circus Wagons. Caldwell, ID: Caxton Printers, 1977. 144p.

4085 _____. Those Amazing Ringlings and Their Circus. Caldwell, ID: Caxton Printers, 1967. 303p.

4086 Powledge, Fred. Born on the Circus. New York: Harcourt, Brace, 1976. 94p. [juv.]

4087 _____. Mud Show: A Circus Season. New York: Harcourt, Brace, 1975. 374p.

4088 Prelutsky, Jack. Circus. New York: Macmillan, 1974.

4089 Prideaux, Tom. "A Kid Who Thinks He Won't--and Other Circus Cuties." Classic, II (June-July 1977), 68-72.

4090 Reynolds, Chang. Pioneer Circuses of the West. Los Angeles, CA: Westernlore Press, 1966. 212p.

4091 Roth, Barbara W. "The 101 Ranch Wild West Show, 1904-1932." Chronicles of Oklahoma, XLIII (Winter 1965), 416-431.

4092 Russell, Don. The Wild West: or, A History of the Wild West
  Shows. Ft. Worth, TX: Amon Carter Museum of Western
  Art, 1970. 150p.

4093 Schwartz, Joseph. "The Wild West Show: 'Everything Genuine.' " Journal of Popular Culture, III (Spring 1970), 656-
  666.

4094 Shay, Arthur. What Happens at the Circus. Chicago: Reilly
  and Lee, 1972. Unpaged. [juv.]

4095 Shirley, Glenn. Pawnee Bill: A Biography of Major Gordon
  W. Lillie. Albuquerque: University of New Mexico Press,
  1958. 256p.

4096 Simon, Peter A. Big Apple Circus. New York: Penguin
  Books, 1978. 150p.

4097 Smith, Lewis. "Super Roper [Monte Montana]." Horse and
  Rider, XII (February 1973), 22-27.

4098 Speaight, George. "Some Comic [Trick Riding] Circus Entrees."
  Theater Notebook, XXXII (Spring 1978), 24-27.

4099 Spencer, Dick, 3rd. "101 Ranch and Rodeo Cowboys." Western Horseman, XLII (December 1977), 74-76.

4100 Sutton, Felix. The Big Show: A History of the Circus. Garden City, NY: Doubleday, 1971. 176p.

4101 [No entry]

4102 Tessalone, Tim. "Half Century of Show Biz: Monte Montana."
  Western Horseman, XLII (December 1977), 72.

4103 Tyler, Chuck. "A Tough [Circus] Act to Follow." Horse and
  Rider, X (February 1971), 52-56.

4104 Vernay, Peter. Here Comes the Circus. New York: Paddington Press, 1978. 287p.

4105 Westermeier, Clifford P. "Buffalo Bill's Cowboys Abroad."
  Colorado Magazine, LII (Fall 1975), 277-298.

4106 Yost, Nellie S. Buffalo Bill. Chicago: Swallow Press, 1979.
  500p.

2 Movies

4107 Adams, Les and Buck Rainey. Shoot-'em Ups: A Complete
  Reference Guide to Westerns of the Sound Era. New York:
  Arlington House, 1978. 633p.

4108 Amaral, Anthony J. Movie Horses: The Fascinating Techni-
      ques of Training. Hollywood, CA: Wilshire Books, 1978.
      152p.
      American edition of the following title.

4109 _____. Movie Horses: Their Treatment and Training. Lon-
      don: Dent, 1969. 152p.

4110 _____. "Trainer [Jack Lindell] of Hollywood Horses." West-
      ern Horseman, XXXVIII (April 1973), 77-78, 167-170.

4111 Boles, Chris. "Hollywood Stuntmen and Their Horses." West-
      ern Horseman, XXXIX (July 1974), 112-113, 182-185.

4112 Calder, Jenni. There Must Be a Lone Ranger: The American
      West in Film and in Reality. New York: McGraw-Hill,
      1974. 241p.

4113 Canutt, Yakima. Stunt Man: The Autobiography of Yakima
      Canutt. New York: Walker, 1979. 256p.

4114 Cary, Diana S. The Hollywood Posse: The Story of a Gallant
      Band of Horsemen who Made Movie History. Boston:
      Houghton Mifflin, 1975. 268p.

4115 Clint, Jack. "Western Movies: Myths and Images." Western
      Horseman, XLII (April 1977), 96-98, 152-154.

4116 Coldsmith, Don. "Hollywood Horses." Western Horseman,
      XXXVII (May 1972), 66+.

4117 Cotterman, Dan. "Murder at the Running W." Horse and
      Rider, XII (June 1973), 50-57.

4118 DeMarco, Mario. "Famous Western Movie Horses." Western
      Horseman, XLIV (August 1979), 66-70.

4119 Donovan, John. "The Scene Stealers." Horse and Rider, IX
      (March 1970), 60-64.

4120 Everett, Judy. "Ride 'em Down, Shoot 'em Up Horses."
      Western Horseman, XLIII (September 1978), 50-52.

4121 Everson, William K. A Pictorial History of the Western Film.
      New York: Citadel Press, 1969. 246p.

4122 Eyles, Allen. The Western: An Illustrated Guide. South
      Brunswick, NJ: A. S. Barnes, 1967. 183p.

4123 French, Philip. Westerns: Aspects of a Movie Genre. Rev.
      ed. New York and London: Oxford University Press, 1977.
      208p.

4124 Goode, James. The Story of "The Misfits." Indianapolis, IN: Bobbs-Merrill, 1963. 331p.

4125 Hintz, Harald F. Horses in the Movies. South Brunswick, NJ: A. S. Barnes, 1979. 146p.

4126 Hurley, Jimmie. "Custer Falls Again." Horse and Rider, XVI (November 1977), 38-43.

4127 _____. "Today's Singing Cowboys." Western Horseman, XLI (March 1976), 60-62, 118-120.

4128 Koehler, William K. The Wonderful World of Disney Animals. New York: Howell Book House, 1979. 252p.

4129 _____. "Ben Johnson: A Good Bad Guy." Horse and Horseman, VI (October 1978), 42-44, 65.

4130 Lewis, Jack. "Down Home with Dale Robertson." Horse and Horseman, VII (January 1980), 58-61.

4131 McAulay, Sarah. "Plain and Fancy Falls on Cue." Classic, III (October-November 1978), 70-77.

4132 Malder, Marla. "Gidget [Bosak] Goes to Hollywood." Horse and Rider, XVIII (August 1979), 44-49.

4133 Middleton, Marie. "International Velvet." Horse Lover's National Magazine, XLIII (December 1978), 14-17.

4134 Pattie, Jane. "Super Wrangler [Kenny Lee]." Horse and Rider, XIX (January 1980), 12, 32-35.

4135 Schuessler, Raymond. "Cowboy Hero of the Silent Screen: Tom Mix." Western Horseman, XXXVIII (November 1973), 102-103, 122.

4136 Smith, Helen M. "William S. Hart and 'Fritz.'" Western Horseman, XXXVIII (April 1973), 69-70, 154.

4137 Smith, Lewis. "The Lone Ranger Unmasked." Horse and Rider, XIII (January 1974), 36-39.

4138 _____. "Rudolph [Valentino] and 'Jadaan.'" Horse and Rider, XI (December 1972), 46-52.

4139 Thoene, Bodie. "Randall Ranch: 40 Years of Mounting the Movies." Western Horseman, XLII (September 1977), 32-34.

4140 Tuska, Jon. The Filming of the West. Garden City, NY: Doubleday, 1976. 628p.

PART XI HORSES AND HORSEMEN IN LITERATURE AND ART

A LITERATURE

1 General Works

4141 Boatright, Mody C. "The Beginnings of Cowboy Fiction."
Southwestern Review, LI (Winter 1966), 11-28.

4142 Cantwell, Robert. "A Novel [Emile Zola and Nana] Day at the
Races." Classic, III (February-March 1978), 124-131.

4143 Close, Pat. "Walter Farley and The Black Stallion." Western
Horseman, XXXVIII (December 1973), 38-39, 141-145.

4144 Cole, William, comp. The Poetry of Horses. New York:
Scribners, 1979. 180p.

4145 Corrigan, R. A. "Somewhere West of Laramie, on the Road
to West Egg: Automobiles, Fillies, and the West in The
Great Gatsby." Journal of Popular Culture, VII (Summer
1973), 152-158.

4146 Crew, Frederic. Devoted to Horses: A Book of Essays in
Miniature. London: Muller, 1956. 63p.

4147 Dent, Anthony. "Shakespeare's Horse-Borne England." History
Today, XXIII (July 1973), 455-461.

4148 Donaldson, Ian. "Adonis and His Horse." Notes and Queries,
XIX (April 1972), 123-125.

4149 Durham, Philip. "The Cowboy and the Myth Makers." Journal
of Popular Culture, I (Summer 1967), 58-62.

4150 Erisman, Fred. "Growing Up with the American West: The
Fiction of Jack Schaefer." Journal of Popular Culture, VII
(Winter 1974), 710-716.

4151 Etulain, Richard. "The Historical Development of the Western."
Journal of Popular Culture, VII (Winter 1974), 717-726.

4152 Fisher, J. H. "Chaucer's Horses." South Atlantic Quarterly, LX (Winter 1961), 71-79.

4153 French, Carol A. "Western Literature and the Myth-Makers." Montana, Magazine of Western History, XXII (April 1972), 76-81.

4154 Goble, Danney. "The Days That Were No More: A Look at Zane Grey's West." Journal of Arizona History, XIV (Spring 1973), 63+.

4155 Hamilton, Samantha. "Myths, Magic and the Horse: Man's Relationship with the Horse Through Literature." Equus, no. 13 (November 1978), 20-25, 72.

4156 Hopkins, Lee B., comp. My Mane Catches the Wind: Poems About the Horse. New York: Harcourt, Brace, 1979. 42p.

4157 Houghton, Donald E. "Two Heroes in One: Reflections on the Popularity of The Virginian." Journal of Popular Culture, IV (Fall 1970), 497-506.

4158 _____. "Whores and Horses in [William] Faulkner's Spotted Horses." Midwest Quarterly, XI (July 1970), 361-369.

4159 Johnson, L. P. "Lahelin and the Grail Horses." Modern Language Review, LXIII (July 1968), 612-617.

4160 Molen, Dayle H. "Andy Adams: Classic Novelist of the Western Cattle Drive." Montana, Magazine of Western History, XIX (January 1969), 24-35.

4161 Pivirotto, Peg. "The Author [Anna Sewell] of Black Beauty." American Horseman, III (March 1973), 19.

4162 Riddell, J. A. "Hasting's 'Foot-Cloth Horse' in Richard III." English Studies, LVI (February 1975), 29-31.

4163 Rowland, Beryl. Blind Beasts: Chaucer's Animal World. Kent, OH: Kent State University Press, 1971.

4164 Saxon, A. H. Enter Foot and Horse: A History of Hippodrama in England. New Haven, CT: Yale University Press, 1968. 249p.

4165 Sellars, Richard W. "The Interrelationship of Literature, History and Geography in Western Writing." Western Historical Quarterly, IV (April 1973), 171-185.

4166 Stegner, Wallace. "History, Myths, and the Western Writer." American West, IV (May 1967), 61-62.

4167 Thomas, Phillip D. "The Paperback West of Luke Short." Journal of Popular Culture, VII (Winter 1974), 701-708.

4168 Tinker, Edward L. The Horsemen of the Americas and the
      Literature They Inspired. 2nd, rev. ed. Austin: Univer-
      sity of Texas Press, 1967. 150p.

4169 Topping, Gary. "Zane Grey's West." Journal of Popular Cul-
      ture, VII (Winter 1974), 681-689.

4170 White, John I. "The Virginian." Montana, Magazine of West-
      ern History, XVI (October 1966), 2-11.

4171 Willett, Ralph. "The American Western: Myth and Anti-Myth."
      Journal of Popular Culture, IV (Fall 1970), 455-463.

2 Some Anthologies

4172 Adams, Andy. Andy Adam's Campfire Tales. Lincoln: Uni-
      versity of Nebraska Press, 1976. 296p.

4173 American Girl, Editors of. The American Girl Book of Horse
      Stories. New York; Random House, 1963. 183p. [juv.]

4174 Anderson, Clarence W. , comp. Clarence W. Anderson's Favor-
      ite Horse Stories, Collected and Illustrated. New York:
      E. P. Dutton, 1967. 192p.

4175 Arsenis, Mylda L. Horse and Rider Tales from Africa and
      Australia. London: Stockwell, 1960. 93p. [juv.]

4176 Braun, P. C. , ed. The Big Book of Favorite Horse Stories.
      New York: Platt and Munk, 1965. 336p. [juv.]

4177 Brennan, John, comp. The Welcome Collection: Fourteen
      Racing Stories. By John Welcome, pseud. London: Jo-
      seph, 1972. 254p.

4178 Brown, Beth, comp. The Wonderful World of Horses. New
      York: Harper and Row, 1967. 211p.

4179 Carruth, Jane, ed. Horse and Pony Stories. London: Octo-
      pus Books, 1978. 400p.

4180 Clarke, Francis E. , comp. High-Stepping Horses. New York:
      Macmillan, 1961. 210p.

4181 Collier, Ned, ed. Great Stories of "The West." Garden City,
      NY: Doubleday, 1971. 346p.

4182 Davidson, Margaret, ed. Seven True Horse Stories. New
      York: Hastings House, 1979. 96p. [juv.]

4183 Dobie, J. Frank, Mody C. Boatright, and Harry H. Ransom,
      eds. Mustangs and Cow Horses. Texas Folklore Society

Publications, no. 16. Dallas, TX: Southern Methodist
University Press, 1965. 429p.

4184 Dolch, Edward W. and Marguerite P. Horse Stories in Basic
Vocabulary. Champagne, IL: Garrard Press, 1958. 161p.

4185 Downey, Fairfax D., comp. My Kingdom for a Horse. Garden
City, NY: Doubleday, 1961. 325p.

4186 Edwards, Eleanor M., comp. Great Stories About Horses.
New York: Hart Publishing Company, 1963. 191p. [juv.]

4187 Evans, Pauline R., ed. Best Book of Horse Stories. Garden
City, NY: Doubleday, 1964. 279p. [juv.]

4188 Fenley, Florence. Heart Full of Horses. San Antonio, TX:
Naylor, 1975. 180p.

4189 Golden Prize and Other Stories About Horses. Racine, WI:
Whitman Publishing Company, 1965. 156p. [juv.]

4190 _____. Ben Green Tales. 4 vols. Flagstaff, AZ: Northland Press, 1974.

4191 Green, Ben K. Ben K. Green Back-to-Back. Austin, TX:
Encino Press, 1970. 51p.

4192 _____. Horse Tradin'. New York: Alfred A. Knopf, 1967.
304p.

4193 Isaak, W. Georg, ed. Of Horses and Men: An Anthology of
Horse Racing Stories. Garden City, NY: Doubleday, 1961.
353p.

4194 James, Will. Cow Country. Lincoln: University of Nebraska
Press, 1973. 240p.

4195 Kays, Donald J. Horseman's Scrapbook in Verse and Prose.
Columbus, OH: Long's College Book Company, 1954. 221p.

4196 Macgregor-Morris, Pamela, comp. Great Horse Stories. New
York: Hill and Wang, 1961. 223p.

4197 Murphy, Genevieve, ed. The Horse Lover's Treasury: An
Illustrated Anthology of Verse and Prose. Garden City,
NY: Doubleday, 1964. 320p.

4198 Orchard, Vincent K., comp. Best Racing Stories. London:
Faber and Faber, 1952. 304p.

4199 Runnquist, Ake, ed. Horses in Fact and Fiction: An Anthology.
London: Cape, 1957. 224p.

4200 Savitt, Sam. <u>Sam Savitt's True Horse Stories.</u> New York: Dodd, Mead, 1970. 90p. [juv.]

4201 Self, Margaret C., ed. <u>A World of Horses: An Anthology.</u> New York: McGraw-Hill, 1961. 384p.

4202 Smith, Vian. <u>Horses in the Green Valley.</u> Garden City, NY: Doubleday, 1971. 149p.

4203 <u>Tales of the Horse from Blackwood.</u> Edinburgh, Scotland: Blackwood, 1969. 281p.

4204 Watson, J. N. P., ed. <u>The World's Greatest Horse Stories.</u> New York: Paddington House, 1979. 336p.

4205 Western Writers of America. <u>Wild Horse Roundup: A Collection of Stories.</u> New York: Arno Press, 1978.

4206 Wilding, Suzanne, ed. <u>Horse Tales.</u> New York: St. Martin's Press, 1977. 201p.

4207 _____. <u>Horses, Horses, Horses: A Collection of Stories.</u> Princeton, NJ: Van Nostrand, 1970. 184p. [juv.]

3 And a Few Novels

4208 Aldridge, James. <u>The Marvelous Mongolian.</u> Boston: Little, Brown, 1974. 183p.
       A captured Mongolian horse and a Shetland pony escape England and through a series of adventures return to China.

4209 Bagnold, Enid. <u>National Velvet.</u> New York: Morrow, 1949. 306p.
       The classic tale in which a girl wins a horse in a lottery and later rides it to victory in the Grand National Steeplechase.

4210 Bailey, Jean. <u>Cherokee Bill.</u> New York: Abingdon House, 1952. 190p.
       A stray horse is trained by a 12-year-old boy before his family participated in the 1893 Cherokee Strip Run.

4211 Bechko, P. A. <u>Hawke's Indians.</u> Garden City, NY: Doubleday, 1979. 192p.
       Unconvinced by new-fangled motorcycles, outlaw Rawlins saves his gang's horses, which come in handy for the climactic escape.

4212 Benedict, Dorothy P. <u>Fabulous.</u> New York: Pantheon, 1961. 220p.
       Youngsters race an Appaloosa colt on a Montana ranch.

4213 Bulla, Clyde R. Take Care of Dexter. New York: Scholastic
      Book Service, 1973. 71p.
         A lad fights to save an old horse from extermination.

4214 Farley, Walter. The Black Stallion. New York: Random
      House, 1977. 275p.
         A youth and a colt, returned to civilization after a ship-
      wreck, meet a retired jockey; the three combine into a
      winning race team. Reprint of the 1941 edition, the first
      in a Black Stallion series.

4215 Francis, Dick. Blood Sport. New York: Harper and Row,
      1968. 241p.
         A British intelligence agent seeks a world-famous, but
      kidnapped, thoroughbred.

4216 _____. Bonecrack. New York: Harper and Row, 1972.
      201p.
         A father pressures a stable to insure that his son races
      the favorite horse in an important handicap.

4217 _____. Enquiry. New York: Harper and Row, 1970. 219p.
         A British jockey is framed for throwing a race and fights
      to overturn his disbarment from the turf.

4218 _____. Flying Finish. New York: Harper and Row, 1967.
      249p.
         An air transport pilot and amateur steeplechase jockey
      ferries horses out of England.

4219 _____. For Kicks. New York: Harper and Row, 1965.
      244p.
         An Australian breeder poses as a stable lad to uncover
      the identity of someone who is fixing certain British horse
      races.

4220 _____. Forfeit. New York: Harper and Row, 1969. 247p.
         A British journalist becomes involved in the seamy side
      of racing while a temporary writer for a sports journal.

4221 _____. High Stakes. New York: Harper and Row, 1976.
      201p.
         An unemployed jockey enters into a contest with his for-
      mer employer over a prize race horse.

4222 _____. In the Frame. New York: Harper and Row, 1977.
      230p.
         A young horse painter encounters art fraud in Australia.

4223 _____. Knockdown. New York: Harper and Row, 1975.
      217p.
         An ex-jockey encounters many mysterious problems after
      purchasing a thoroughbred.

4224 _____. Nerve. New York: Harper and Row, 1964. 273p.
Skullduggery in a group of English steeplechase jockeys,
including suicide, creates high tensions around the track.

4225 _____. Odds Against. New York: Harper and Row, 1966.
280p.
Sid Halley, a crippled ex-jockey, turns private eye to
frustrate shady racetrack purchasers.

4226 _____. Rat Race. New York: Harper and Row, 1971.
214p.
A pilot and a jockey seek answers to a mysterious plane
crash.

4227 _____. Risk. New York: Harper and Row, 1977. 240p.
An English steeplechase jockey is kidnapped.

4228 _____. Slayride. New York: Harper and Row, 1974.
219p.
An investigator from the English Racing Club seeks a
missing British jockey in Norway.

4229 _____. Smokescreen. New York: Harper and Row, 1972.
213p.
An English actor seeks answers to a mysterious illness
in South African race horses.

4230 _____. Trial Run. New York: Harper and Row, 1979.
246p.
A British steeplechase jockey looks into potential scandal at the Moscow Olympics.

4231 _____. Whip Hand. New York: Harper and Row, 1980.
320p.
Detective Sid Halley investigates mysterious illnesses
suffered by his client's race horses.

4232 Frick, Marlena. The Homecoming. New York: McKay,
1965. 79p.
An old man refuses to deliver his employer's horse to
the bull ring where it is slated to serve as a picador's
mount.

4233 Giles, Janice H. Six-Horse Hitch. Boston: Houghton Mif-
flin, 1969. 436p.
Joe Fowler drives a coach for the 1860's Overland
Stage.

4234 Hawkes, John. The Lime Twig. Norfolk, CT: New Directions, 1961. 175p.
A man and a couple steal a race horse and run it under
a false name in the Golden Bowl race.

4235 Heimer, Melvin A. <u>Penniless Blues.</u> New York: G. P. Putnam, 1955. 311p.
A race horse survives the differences in five owners over a period of years.

4236 Henry, Marguerite. <u>Brighty of the Grand Canyon.</u> Chicago: Rand McNally, 1953. 222p.
A prospector discovers a little lone burro living in the Grand Canyon of Arizona.

4237 _____. <u>Justin Morgan Had a Horse.</u> Chicago: Rand McNally, 1954. 169p.
A lad rescues a horse from a cruel owner and finally has the pleasure of seeing it ridden by President James Monroe.

4238 _____. <u>White Stallion of Lipizza.</u> Chicago: Rand McNally, 1964. 116p.
An Austrian youth is admitted to the Spanish Riding School and focuses his attention on a famous old horse.

4239 Henry, Will. <u>The Bear Paw Horses.</u> Philadelphia: Lippincott, 1973. 214p.
An old brave and a squaw steal horses for the Nez Percé.

4240 Holland, Barbara. <u>The Pony Problem.</u> New York: Scholastic Book Service, 1977. 122p.
A young girl must save her pony from the S. P. C. A.

4241 Huffacker, Clair. <u>The Cowboy and the Cossack.</u> New York: Trident Press, 1973. 253p.
Cowboys and Cossacks herd cattle to 1890's Vladivostok.

4242 Kalnay, Francis. <u>Chucaro: Wild Pony of the Pampa.</u> New York: Harcourt, Brace, 1958. 126p.
An Argentine gaucho lassos a wild pony for a young friend to tame.

4243 Kessel, Joseph. <u>The Horsemen.</u> Translated from the German. New York: Farrar, Straus, 1968. 469p.
A tale of horsemen and buykhashi in Afghanistan.

4244 Kosinski, Jerzy. <u>Passion Play.</u> New York: St. Martin's Press, 1979. 271p.
A middle-aged horseman seeks one-on-one polo games.

4245 Lea, Tom. <u>The Hands of Cantu.</u> Boston: Little, Brown, 1965. 244p.
Rustlers sell Spanish horses to the Indians in the 16th Century Southwest.

4246 Lehmann, Arthur H. <u>Noble Stallion.</u> Translated from the

German. New York: Holt, 1955. 208p.
An ex-Austrian cavalry officer raises a Lipizzaner colt
after World War I.

4247 McClarey, Jane I. A Portion for Foxes. New York: Simon
and Schuster, 1972. 607p.
A modern tale of divided loyalties set against a background of foxhunting and horses in Virginia.

4248 McMeekin, Clark. The Fairbrothers. New York: G. P.
Putnam, 1962. 288p.
A family of Kentucky horse breeders are involved in
the first running of the Kentucky Derby.

4249 O'Hara, Mary. My Friend Flicka. New York: Dell, 1973.
349p.
A youngster's parents give him a colt on their Wyoming
ranch; reprint of the 1941 edition.

4250 _____. Thunderhead. New York: Dell, 1969. 320p.
Sequel to the previous title and reprint of the 1943 edition in which Flicka's albino foal fails to become a famous
racehorse.

4251 Ottley, Reginald. Brumbie Dust. New York: Harcourt, 1969.
143p.
A modern tale of horses and horsemen in Australia.

4252 Peyton, K. M. Flambards. Cleveland, OH: World Publishing Company, 1968. 206p.
A girl learns to love riding on the estate of her egocen-
tric English uncle.

4253 Rock, Gail. The Thanksgiving Treasure. New York: Bantam Books, 1976. 92p.
With the aid of her horse, a girl teachers her unkindly
uncle the true meaning of Thanksgiving.

4254 Sandberg, Helga. Gingerbread. New York: Dial Press,
1964. 192p.
A Michigan farm girl trains a blind horse.

4255 Savitt, Sam. The Brown Mare. Middletown, CT: Xerox
Education Publications, 1976. 157p.
A girl and her young jumping horse; originally published
as Vickie and the Brown Horse.

4256 Sewell, Anna. Black Beauty. New York: Grosset and Dunlap, 1978. 256p.
The classic tale of a beautiful black horse.

4257 Sinclair, Harold. The Horse Soldiers. New York: Harper,
1956. 336p.

Recreates Grierson's Civil War cavalry raid in the Vicksburg area.

4258 Smith, Vian. Pride of the Moor. Garden City, NY: Doubleday, 1962. 284p.
A lad recues an old mare from an English moor; the colt of this horse becomes a famous racing animal.

4259 Stander, Siegfried. The Horse. Cleveland, OH: World Publishing Company, 1969. 134p.
An abandoned white horse in South Africa is adopted into a herd of zebras.

4260 Stein, Daniel M. Wall of Noise. New York: Crown, 1961. 383p.
A compassionate trainer becomes owner of a renegade racing horse.

4261 Stewart, Mary. Airs Above the Ground. New York: Morrow, 1965. 286p.
What secret involving a famous Lipizzaner stallion is to be found in a small Austrian circus?

4262 Stranger, Joyce. Breed of Giants. New York: Viking Press, 1967. 209p.
Hard luck surrounds an English owner of Shire horses until rich buyers come on the scene.

4263 Villarreal, José A. The Fifth Horseman. Garden City, NY: Doubleday, 1974. 398p.
Mexican cowboy Heraclio attempts to match the horsemanship skills of his four brothers.

4264 Wellman, Manly W. Gray Riders. New York: Aladdin, 1954.
Looks at the Civil War cavalry exploits of J. E. B. Stuart.

4265 Wister, Owen. The Virginian: A Horseman of the Plains. New York: Macmillan, 1902. 504p. Rpr. 1979.
The classic tale of an anonymous cowboy who combats evil.

4266 Wojciechowska, Maia. A Kingdom in a Horse. New York: Harper and Row, 1965. 143p.
A youngster secretly rides a horse in a rodeo and feels badly when it is injured.

B   ART

1 General Works

4267 Anderson, Clarence W. Bred to Run: A Portfolio. New York: Harper, 1960. 12p.

4268 _____. Deep Thru the Heart: Profiles [Lithographs] of Twenty Valiant Horses. New York: Macmillan, 1947. 104p.

4269 Behrens, June. Looking at Horses. Chicago: Children's Press, 1976. 36p. [juv.]

4270 Board, John. A Year With Horses: A Sketchbook. London: Hodder and Stoughton, 1954. 40p.

4271 Cushion, John P. Animals in Poetry and Porcelain. New York: Crown, 1974. 224p.

4272 Dennis, Wesley. Portfolio of Horses. Chicago: Rand McNally, 1964. 36p.

4273 Fox, Charles P., ed. American Circus Posters in Full Color. New York: Dover Publications, 1978. 43p.

4274 Horse and Rider: Eight Centuries of Equestrian Paintings. London: Thames and Hudson, 1950. 96p.

4275 The Horse in Art. Master Draughtsman Series. Alhambra, CA: Borden Publishing Company, 1966. Unpaged.

4276 Klein, Fred. "Life-Sized Fruit [by John Skeaping] of a Life-Long Affair." Classic, II (August-September 1977), 100-103.

4277 Kuhn, Bob. The Animal Art of Bob Kuhn: A Lifetime of Drawing and Painting. Westport, CT: North Light Publishers, 1973. 128p.

4278 Linn, Phyliss. "Ageless Art of the Ice Ages." Classic, III (October-November 1978), 148-151.

4279 _____. "Came the Colorful Revolution." Classic, II (June-July 1977), 100-103.

4280 _____. "Clean Cut [Posters] to Tell a Tale." Classic, IV (June-July 1979), 58-61.

4281 _____. "Finally Freeing Form." Classic, III (August-September 1978), 80-83.

4282 Livingstone-Learmouth, David. The Horse in Art. New York: Studio Publications, 1958. 48p.

4283 McCabe, Susan. "Two Arts [of Kyra Downton] That Beat as One." Classic, IV (June-July 1979), 44-48.

4284 McLeod, Juliet. A Hundred Horses. London: Seeley Service, 1960. 87p.

4285 Meyjes, Nicholas. The Field Book of the Horse. London: Seeley Service, 1960. 87p.

4286 Morris, George F. Portraiture of Horses. Shrewsbury, NJ: Fordacre Studios, 1952. 280p.

4287 Neiman, LeRoy. Horses. New York: Abrams, 1979. 349p.

4288 Rice, Don, ed. Animals, a Picture Sourcebook. New York: Van Nostrand-Reinhold, 1979. Unpaged.

4289 Savitt, Sam. America's Horses. Garden City, NY: Doubleday, 1966. 93p.

4290 Schmalenbach, Werner. The Noble Horse: A Journey Through the History of Art. Translated from the German. London: J. A. Allen, 1963. 148p.

4291 Seton, Ernest T. Studies in the Art Anatomy of Animals. Philadelphia: Running Press, 1977. 96p. Reprint of 1896 edition.

4292 Skeaping, John R. Horses. London: Studio Books, 1961. 55p.

4293 Suares, Jean C. The Illustrated Horse. New York: Crown, 1979. 64p.

4294 Virginia. Museum of Fine Art. Sport and the Horse: A Catalogue of the Exhibition of Paintings Established at the Museum, April 1-May 15, 1960. Richmond, 1960. 87p.

4295 Wetmore, Ruth Y. Horses on Stamps. Topical Handbook, no. 52. Milwaukee, WI: American Topical Association, 1966. 59p.

4296 Zuelke, Ruth. The Horse in Art. Minneapolis, MN: Lerner Publications Company, 1965. 64p. [juv.]

2 Specific Artists and Schools of Art

a Chinese

1 General

4297 Linn, Phyllis. "Heavenly Horses." Classic, III (December 1977-January 1978), 100-103.

2 Han Kan

4298 Lee, J. J. "Tu Fu's Art Criticism and Han Kan's Horse

Paintings." American Oriental Society Journal, XC (July 1970), 449-461.

b Egyptian

4299 Schulman, A. R. "Egyptian Representations of Horsemen and Riding in the New Kingdom." Journal of Near Eastern Studies, XVI (October 1957), 263-271.

c Greek

1 General

4300 Benson, Jack L. Horse, Buck, and Man: The Origins of Greek Paintings. Amherst: University of Massachusetts Press, 1970. 182p.

4301 Houser, Caroline. "Is It from the Parthenon?" American Journal of Archaeology, LXXVI (April 1972), 127-137.

4302 Markman, Sidney G. The Horse in Greek Art. Baltimore, MD: Johns Hopkins University Press, 1943. 211p.
      The classic on the subject.

4303 Root, M. C. "Etruscan Horse Race from Poggio Civitate." American Journal of Archaeology, LXXVII (April 1973), 122-137.

2 Exekias

4304 Moore, M. B. "Horses by Exekias." American Journal of Archaeology, LXXII (October 1968), 357-368.

d Great Britain

1 General

4305 Cadfryn-Roberts, John, ed. British Sporting Prints. London: Ariel Press, 1955. 12p.

4306 Coombs, David. Sport and the Countryside in English Paintings, Watercolours, and Prints. Oxford, Eng.: Phaidon Press, 1978. 192p.

4307 Laver, James. English Sporting Prints. London: Ward, Lock, 1970. 96p.

4308 Linn, Phyllis. "Painters to the Country Gentry." Classic, III (June-July 1978), 132-135.

4309 Nevill, Ralph. Old Sporting Prints. London: Spring Books, 1970. 92p.

4310 Orchard, Vincent R. The British Thoroughbred: Reproducing 16 Original Paintings by the Masters of Horse Portraiture, with Detailed Biographical Commentaries on the Horses. New York: Taplinger, 1966. Unpaged.

4311 Walker, Stella A. Sporting Art, England, 1700-1900. London: Studio Vista, 1972. 200p.

2 Henry Alken

4312 Noakes, Aubrey. The World of Henry Alken. London: Wetherby, 1952. 184p.

3 John Board

4313 Board, John. Horse and Pencil. London: Christopher Johnson, 1950. 160p.

4 Alfred Munnings

4314 Munnings, Alfred. An Artist's Life, the Second Burst, and the Finish. 3 vols. London: Museum Press, 1950-1952.

4315 Pound, Reginald. The Englishman: A Biography of Sir Alfred Munnings. London: Hutchinson, 1962. 244p.

5 James Pollard

4316 Selway, N. C. The Golden Age of Coaching and Sports, as Depicted by James Pollard. Leigh-on-the-Sea, Eng.: F. Lewis, 1972. 61p.

6 George Stubbs

4317 Stubbs, George. The Anatomy of the Horse. London: J. A. Allen, 1966. 147p.
       Reprint of the 1766 edition.

4318 Taylor, Basil. Stubbs. New York: Harper & Row, 1971. 220p.

e Western Art of the United States

1 General

4319 Ainsworth, Edward M. The Cowboy in Art. Cleveland, OH: World Publishing Company, 1968. 242p.

4320 Bergen, Chan. "Cowboy Artists of America Exhibition." Western Horseman, XLV (February 1980), 46-47, 62.

4321 _____. "On the Trail with Cowboy Artists." Western Horseman, XLIV (December 1979), 80-86.

4322 Broder, Patricia J. 50 Great Paintings of the Old American West. New York: Brown, 1979. Unpaged.

4323 _____. Great Paintings of the Old American West. New York: Published for the Thomas Gilcrease Institute of American History and Art, Tulsa, Oklahoma, by Abbeville Press, 1979. Unpaged.

4324 _____. Hopi Painting. New York: E. P. Dutton, 1978. 319p.

4325 Curry, Larry. The American West: Painters from Callin to Russell. New York: Viking Press, 1972. 198p.

4326 Davis, Ray. "Texas Cowboy Artists Meet on the Triangle Ranch." Western Horseman, XXXIX (February 1974), 70-71, 147-148.

4327 Dockstader, Frederick J. Indian Art in America. Greenwich, CT: New York Graphic Society, 1961. 224p.

4328 Edens, Lettye P. "Women Western Artists." Western Horseman, XXXVIII (July 1973), 40, 153-154.

4329 Ewers, John C. Artists of the Old West. Enl. ed. Garden City, NY: Doubleday, 1973. 240p.

4330 _____. Plains Indian Painting. New York: AMS Press, 1979. 84p.

4331 Feder, Norman. North American Indian Painting. New York: New York Graphic Society, 1967. Unpaged.

4332 Garbutt, Bernard. The Day of the Horse. Flagstaff, AZ: Northland Press, 1976. 82p.

4333 Harman, Fred. The Great West in Paintings. Chicago: Sage, 1969. 185p.

4334 Harmsen, Dorothy. American Western Art. Denver, CO, 1977. 256p.

4335 _____. Harmsen's Western Americana: A Collection of One Hundred Western Paintings, with Biographical Profiles of the Artists. Flagstaff, AZ: Northland Press, 1971. 213p.

4336 Hassrick, Peter. The Way West. New York: Harry Abrams, 1977. 240p.

4337 Hassrick, Royal B. Western Painting Today: Painters of the Contemporary American West. New York: Watson-Guptill, 1975. 128p.

4338 Hogarth, Paul. Artists on Horseback: The Old West in Illustrated Journalism, 1857-1900. New York: Watson-Guptill, 1972. 288p.

4339 Hollmann, Clide A. Five Artists of the Old West: George Kallin, Karl Bodmer, Alfred Jacob Miller, Charles M. Russell, and Frederic Remington. New York: Hastings House, 1965. 128p.

4340 Howard, James K. Ten Years with the Cowboy Artists of America: A Complete History and Exhibition Record. Flagstaff, AZ: Northland Press, 1977. 214p.

4341 Joe, Eugene B. Navajo Sandpainting Art. Tucson, AZ: Treasure Chest Publications, 1978. 32p.

4342 Krakel, Dean. Adventures in Western Art. Kansas City, MO: Lowell Press, 1977. 377p.

4343 Linn, Phyllis. "Bronze Rush Back to the Golden West." Classic, IV (February-March 1979), 72-75.

4344 Samuels, Peggy and Harold. The Illustrated Biographical Encyclopedia of Artists of the American West. Garden City, NY: Doubleday, 1977. 549p.

4345 Taft, Robert. Artists and Illustrators of the Old West. New York: Scribners, 1971. 400p.

2 Charles P. Adams

4346 Barbour, Ann C. "Charles Partridge Adams: Painter of the West." Denver Westerners' Roundup, XXXII (January-February 1976), 3-17.

3 James Bama

4347 Bama, James. The Western Art of James Bama. New York: Peacock Press, 1975. 44p.

4 Joseph Beeler

4348 Beeler, Joe. "Joe Beeler and the State of the Art: An Interview." Western Horseman, XLIV (April 1979), 46-47, 141-142.

4349 Hedgpeth, Don. Cowboy Artist: The Joe Beeler Story. Flagstaff, AZ: Northland Press, 1979. 115p.

4350 Jarrett, Walter. "Joe Beeler: Artist of the American West."
      Mankind, III (December 1971), 40-49.

5 Albert Bierstadt

4351 Hendricks, Gordon. Albert Bierstadt: Painter of the Ameri-
      can West. New York: Henry Abrams, 1974. 360p.

6 Edward Borein

4352 Davidson, Harold G. Edward Borein, Cowboy Artist. Garden
      City, NY: Doubleday, 1974. 189p.

7 Harold Bryant

4353 Look, Al. Harold Bryant: Colorado's Maverick with a Paint
      Brush. Denver, CO: Golden Bell Press, 1962. 115p.

8 Cyd Chambers

4354 Bergen, Chan. "Cyd Chambers: Artist with a Torch."
      Western Horseman, XXXIX (February 1974), 22-24,
      92-96.

9 John Clymer

4355 Reed, Walt. John Clymer: An Artist's Rendezvous with the
      Frontier West. Flagstaff, AZ: Northland Press, 1977.
      141p.

10 William Chappell

4356 Ward, Nancy. "Western Artist Bill Chappell." Western
      Horseman, XXXVI (September 1971), 46-47, 121-123.

11 Darol Dickerson

4357 Dickerson, Darol. "Adding Animation to Horse Photos."
      Horseman, XXIII (July 1979), 28-30, 32.

4358 _____. "Better Horse Photos." Horseman, XXIII (May
      1979), 40-44.

4359 _____. "Horse Photography." Horse Illustrated, XII (June
      1980), 9-10.

4360 _____. Photographing Livestock: The Complete Guide.
      Flagstaff, AZ: Northland Press, 1978. 88p.

4361 Mette, John. "The Darol Dickerson Approach: Photographing
      Horses." Western Horseman, XLV (May 1980), 90-93.

12 Richard Greeves

4362 Carson, Will. "A Genuine Greeves: Bronzes by Dick Greeves."
Western Horseman, XXXVI (June 1971), 52-54, 132-134.

13 Vincent Haddelsey

4363 Haddelsey, Vincent. Haddelsey's Horses: Paintings. New
York: St. Martin's Press, 1978. 62p.

14 W. H. D. Koerner

4364 Hutchinson, William H. The World, the Work and the West
of W. H. D. Koerner. Norman: University of Oklahoma
Press, 1978. 243p.

15 David S. Lavender

4365 Lavender, David S. One Man's West. Lincoln: University
of Nebraska Press, 1956. 316p. Rpr. 1977.

16 W. R. Leigh

4366 DuBois, June. W. R. Leigh: The Definitive Illustrated Biography. Kansas City, MO: Lowell Press, 1978. 209p.

17 Frank C. McCarthy

4367 McCarthy, Frank C. The Western Paintings of Frank C. Mc-
Carthy. New York: Ballantine Books, 1974. 50p.

18 Alfred J. Miller

4368 Miller, Alfred J. The West of Alfred J. Miller (1837), from
the Notes and Water Colors in the Wallers Art Gallery.
Rev. enl. ed. Norman: University of Oklahoma Press,
1967. 208p.

19 William Nebeher

4369 Wells, Sally H. "Bill Nebeher: Capturing the West in Bronze."
Western Horseman, XLV (March 1980), 76-77.

20 Thomas Phillips

4370 Phillips, Tom. The Sketches of Tom Phillips. Kansas City,
MO: Lowell Press, 1971. 188p.

21 Ace Reid

4371 Stowers, Carlton. "Cartoonist Ace Reid." Western Horseman, XLIII (May 1978), 124-125, 148.

22 Frederic Remington

4372 Anderson, LaVere. Frederic Remington, Artist on Horseback.
      Champaign, IL: Garrard Press, 1971. 152p. [juv.]

4373 Baker, Donna. Frederic Remington. Chicago: Children's
      Press, 1977. 62p. [juv.]

4374 Broder, Patricia. " 'The Buffalo Signal': The Lost Reming-
      ton Bronze." Southwest Art. VIII (May 1979), 68-71.

4375 Dary, David A. "Frederic Remington in Kansas." Persim-
      mon Hill, VI (Spring 1976), 29-35.

4376 DeMarco, Mario. "Remington." Horseman, XXII (December
      1977), 38-44.

4377 Dodd, Loring H. "Frederic Remington." In: his Golden
      Moments in American Sculpture. New York: Dresser,
      1967. pp. 98-101.

4378 Gregg, R. N. "The Art of Frederic Remington." Connois-
      seur, CLXV (August 1967), 269-273.

4379 Hassrick, Peter H. "Remington and Russell." American
      West, XIV (November 1977), 16-29.

4380 Jackson, Marta, ed. Illustrations of Frederic Remington.
      New York: Bounty Books, 1970. 192p.

4381 McCracken, Harold. Frederic Remington Book. Garden City,
      NY: Doubleday, 1966. 284p.

4382 _____. The Frederic Remington Studio Collection. Cody,
      WY: Whitney Gallery of Western Art, 1959. 12p.

4383 McKown, Robin. Painter of the Wild West: Frederic Reming-
      ton. New York: Julian Messner, 1959. 192p.

4384 Naylor, M. "Frederic Remington." Connoisseur, CLXXV
      (February 1974), 138-146.

4385 Peter, Adeline and Ernest Raboff. Frederic Remington. Gar-
      den City, NY: Doubleday, 1973. 32p. [juv.]

4386 Pitz, Henry C. , comp. Frederic Remington: 173 Drawings
      and Illustrations. New York: Dover Publications, 1972.
      140p.

4387 Remington, Frederic. Frederic Remington's Own Outdoors.
      New York: Dial Press, 1964. 190p.

4388 _____. "Horses of the Plains." In: Thomas C. Jones,

ed. Shaping the Spirit of America. New York: J. G.
Ferguson, 1964. pp. 157-167.

4389 _____. Remington's Frontier Sketches. New York: Burt
Franklin, 1969. 22p.

4390 Vorpahl, Ben M. Frederic Remington and the West, with an
Eye to the Mind. Austin: University of Texas Press,
1978. 294p.

23 Charles M. Russell

4391 Adams, Ramon F. Charles M. Russell: The Cowboy Artist.
Pasadena, CA: Trails End Publishing Company, 1948.
350p.

4392 Conrad, Bernard. "Charles M. Russell and the Buckskin
Paradise of the West." Horizon, XXII (May 1979), 42-49.

4393 Dodd, Loring H. "Charles M. Russell." In: his Great Moments in American Sculpture. New York: Dresser, 1967.
pp. 105-108.

4394 Ellsberg, William. "Charles, Thou Art a Rare Blade." American West, VI (March and May, 1969), 4-9, 40-43+.

4395 Garst, Doris S. Cowboy Artist: Charles M. Russell. New
York: Julian Messner, 1960. 192p.

4396 Laycock, George. "Charles M. Russell." Farm Quarterly,
XIII (Autumn 1958), 52-55+.

4397 Linderman, Frank B., ed. Recollections of Charly Russell.
Norman: University of Oklahoma Press, 1963. 148p.

4398 Linn, Phyllis. "Faithful Lover of a Vanishing Era." Classic, II (October-November 1977), 130-133.

4399 McCracken, Harold. "Charles M. Russell." In: his Portrait
of the Old West. New York: McGraw-Hill, 1952. pp.
187-194.

4400 _____. Charles M. Russell Book: The Life and Work of
the Cowboy Artist. Garden City, NY: Doubleday, 1957.
236p.

4401 Renner, Frederic G. Charles M. Russell Paintings, Draw-
ings, and Sculpture in the Amon G. Carver Collection:
A Descriptive Catalog. Rev. ed. Austin: University of
Texas Press, 1966. 160p.

4402 _____. Charles Marion Russell: Greatest of All Western
Artists. New York: The Westerners, 1968. 24p.

4403 Russell, Austin. C. M. R. : Charles M. Russell, Cowboy Artist--a Biography. New York: Twayne, 1957. 247p.

4404 Russell, Charles M. Charles M. Russell Paintings of the Old American West. New York: Crown, 1979. 104p.

4405 _____. Good Medicine: Memories of the Real West. Garden City, NY: Garden City Publishing Company, 1941. 152p. Rpr. 1966.

4406 _____. The Western Art of Charles M. Russell. Edited by Lanning Aldrich. New York: Ballantine Books, 1975. Unpaged.

4407 Skelton, Lola. Charles Marion Russell: Cowboy, Artist, Friend. New York: Dodd, Mead, 1962. 230p.

24 John K. Schnurrenberger

4408 Bergen, Chan. "Canadian Artist John Ralph Schnurrenberger." Western Horseman, XLII (April 1977), 30-31.

25 Conrad Schwiering

4409 Wakefield, Robert. Schwiering and the West. Aberdeen, SD: North Plains Press, 1973. 207p.

26 Robert Scriver

4410 Clark, Helen. "The Western Art of Bob Scriver." Horse and Rider, IX (April 1970), 38-42.

27 Gus Shafer

4411 Shafer, Gus. Gus Shafer's West. Kansas City, MO: Trail West Publishers, 1974. 150p.

28 Cecil Smith

4412 Weedon, M. V. "Western Artist Cecil Smith: Last of a Rare Breed." Western Horseman, XLII (January 1977), 6-8.

29 Gordon Snidow

4413 Snidow, Gordon. Gordon Snidow: Chronicler of the Contemporary West. Flagstaff, AZ: Northland Press, 1973. 70p.

30 Grant Speed

4414 Bergen, Chan. "Grant Speed: From Working Cowboy to Working Artist." Western Horseman, XLV (April 1980), 86-88.

4415 Hedgpeth, Don. From Broncs to Bronzes: The Life and Work of Grant Speed. Flagstaff, AZ: Northland Press, 1980. 110p.

31 Harold von Schmidt

4416 Reed, Walt. Harold von Schmidt Draws and Paints the Old West. Flagstaff, AZ: Northland Press, 1972. 230p.

4417 Von Schmidt, Harold. The Western Art of Harold Von Schmidt. New York: Peacock Press, 1976. 52p.

3 How to Draw the Horse

4418 Adams, Norman and Joe Singer. Drawing Animals. New York: Watson-Guptill, 1979. 159p.

4419 Bolognese, Don. Drawing Horses and Foals. New York: Franklin Watts, 1977. 68p. [juv.]

4420 Calder, Alexander. Animal Sketching. New York: Sterling, 1972. 63p.

4421 Caldron, W. Frank. Animal Painting and Anatomy. New York: Dover Publications, 1975. 336p.

4422 Coldsmith, Don. "Painting." Horseman, XXII (December 1977), 26-37.

4423 Cook, Gladys E. and Victor Perard. Drawing Horses. Pitman Art Series, no. 16. New York: Grosset and Dunlap, 1966. 60p.

4424 Cowell, Cyril. Your Book of Animal Drawing. 2nd ed. London: Faber and Faber, 1963. 64p. [juv.]

4425 Davidow-Goodman, Ann. Let's Draw Animals. New York: Grosset and Dunlap, 1960. 80p. [juv.]

4426 Dember, Sol. Drawing and Painting the World of Animals. 2 vols. Indianapolis, IN: H. W. Sams, 1977.

4427 Foster, Walter T. How to Draw Horses: A Simple Way to Draw Horses. How to Draw Book, no. 11. Tustin, CA: Foster Art Service, 196?. 40p.

4428 Gray, Arlie. Drawing and Painting Horses. Lexington, KY, 1959. 75p.

4429 Kirberger, Roberta. Draw Classic Arabian Horses. Blanchard, OK, 1980.

4430   Rickell, Walt. "How to Draw the Horse." Horse and Rider,
       X (March-May, 1971), 67-70, 68-71, 68-71.

4431   Savitt, Sam. "Draw Horses with Sam Savitt." Practical
       Horseman, VII (December 1979), 64-69.

4432   Thelwell, Norman. Drawing Ponies. New York: Watson-
       Guptill, 1966. 56p. [juv.]

4433   Tollefson, Randi. "Drawing the Individual Horse." Western
       Horseman, XXXVII (January-February 1972), 106+, 84+.

4434   _____. "Pencil Equitation." Horse and Rider, XI (October
       1972), 22-26.

4435   Zaidenberg, Arthur. How to Draw Dogs, Cats, and Horses.
       New York: Abelard-Schuman, 1959. 63p. [juv.]

4436   _____. How to Draw the Wild West. New York: Abelard-
       Schuman, 1972. 64p. [juv.]

PART XII   THE HORSE ON FILM:

A Guide to 16mm Educational Motion Pictures

Introduction:

Students and educators have long recognized the use of 16mm films as a learning tool. To that end, the following 208 titles are listed in this section. The references were drawn from various sources and publications, including:

> Diffor, John C. , comp. Educators Guide to Free Films.
> 40th ed. Randolph, WI: Educators Progress Service,
> Inc. , 1980. 790p.

> United States. General Services Administration, National
> Archives and Records Service, National Audiovisual
> Center. A Reference List of Audiovisual Materials
> Produced by the United States Government. Washing-
> ton, D.C. , 1978. 354p.

> _____. Library of Congress. Catalog Publication Di-
> vision. Library of Congress Catalogs: Audiovisual
> Materials. Washington, D.C.: U.S. Government Print-
> ing Office, 1950--.

> Film catalogs of the following universities: Kent State
> University, University of California, University of Wis-
> consin, Southern Illinois University, University of Iowa,
> West Virginia University.

Addresses for the above materials may be found within their texts.

A number of independent film producers have made equestrian products. Some of these are noted in the above catalogs while others are not. Should you be unable to locate an address for a given citation, consult the latest edition of the R. R. Bowker Company's Audiovisual Market Place: A Multimedia Guide.

4437 A. J. Q. H. A. , the Now Thing. 16mm, color, sound, 22 min.
      American Quarter Horse Association, 1973.

Depicts the 1973 American Junior Quarter Horse Association Convention and National Finals Show.

4438 About Horses. 16mm, b & w, sound, 11 min. Australian Department of the Interior, 1950.
Looks at various breeds of Australian horses.

4439 After Four Thousand Years--a Solution. 16mm, color, sound, 13 min. Association Films, n. d.
Treatments for lameness.

4440 The All-American Horse for Show and Pleasure. 16mm, color, sound, 27 min. American Horse Shows Association, 1977.
Examines the versatility of the American Saddlebred horse.

4441 Ambassadors on Horseback. 16mm, color, sound, 22 min. E. K. Edwards and Son, n. d.
The U.S. Equestrian Team in action.

4442 The American Horse. 16mm, color, sound, 17 min. Extension Service, University of California, 1942.
A history.

4443 America's New No. 1 Sport. 16mm, b & w, wound, 28 min. Time, 1953.
Horseracing.

4444 Appaloosa. 16mm, color, sound, 30 min. DeAtley Film Productions, n. d.
A history of the breed, narrated by Dale Robertson.

4445 Arabian English Pleasure. 16mm, color, sound, 45 min. International Arabian Horse Association, 1976.
Training, attire, and riding the Arabian English-style.

4446 Arabian Horses. 16mm, color, sound, 23 min. International Arabian Horse Association, 1976.
A history of the breed.

4447 Argentina--Horsemen of the Pampas. 16mm, b & w, sound, 20 min. United World, 1948.
Gauchos and their horses.

4448 The Argentine Gaucho Today. 16mm, color, sound, 30 min. Tinker Foundation, 1964.
A comparison of cowboys in North and South America, with emphasis on the Gaucho.

4449 Barrel Racing-Cutting. 16mm, color, sound, 28 min. American Quarter Horse Association, 1974.
Examines the techniques of barrel racing and cutting.

4450 Basic Grooming. 16mm, color, sound, 10 min. Marshall
      Faber Film Productions, n. d.
      How to groom a horse properly.

4451 Basic Nutritional Requirements of the Horse. 16mm, color,
      sound, 16 min. Kerr-Gray Enterprises, 1974.
      What goes into feeding the equine.

4452 The Basic Principles of Hunter Seat Equitation. 16mm, color,
      sound, 27 min. American Horse Shows Association, 197?.
      What the judge looks for.

4453 The Basic Principles of Saddle Seat Equitation. 16mm, color,
      sound, 27 min. American Horse Shows Association, 1978.
      Horsemanship, attire, appointments, etc. , are examined.

4454 The Basic Principles of Stock Seat Equitation. 16mm, color,
      sound, 27 min. American Horse Shows Association, 1978.
      Pros and cons in Stock Seat judging.

4455 Beginning. 16mm, color, sound, 4 min. Insight Productions,
      1973.
      The world of the young thoroughbred.

4456 A Better Way. 16mm, color, sound, 8 min. National Labor-
      atories, n. d.
      The importance of horse worming.

4457 The Big A. 35mm, color, sound, 10 min. Paramount Pic-
      tures, 1960.
      Examines horse breeding on Kentucky farms.

4458 Birth of a Colt. 16mm, color, sound, 3 min. Thorne Films,
      1972.
      Looks at the behavior associated with a mare's giving
      birth.

4459 Birth of a Foal. 16mm, b & w, sound, University of Cali-
      fornia, Davis, 1968.
      The process from preparation of the mare until the
      colt first stands.

4460 Calgary Cowboy Stampede. 16mm, b & w, sound, 10 min.
      Castle Films, 1949.
      The annual Canadian rodeo.

4461 Call Me Skinny. 35mm, b & w, sound, 11 min. Paramount
      Pictures, 1953.
      Training and size requirements of jockeys.

4462 Canadian Stampede. 35mm, b & w, sound, 8 min. RKO-
      Pathé, 1954.
      A visit to the annual rodeo at Calgary, Alberta.

4463 Centaur. 16mm, color, sound, 10 min. National Film Board
of Canada, 1973.
The nature, movement, and grace of the horse in shown.

4464 Challenge of Champions. 16mm, color, sound, 14-1/2 min.
Florida Department of Commerce, 1972.
Racing at Gulfstream Park.

4465 Champion Irish Thoroughbreds. 35mm, b & w, sound, 9 min.
Paramount Pictures, 1955.
Examines various aspects of Irish interest in horses,
especially racing.

4466 Cheyenne Days. 35mm, color, sound, 10 min. Vitaphone
Corp. , 1953.
The annual Wyoming rodeo.

4467 Cheyenne Frontier Days. 16mm, color, sound, 19 min.
Cheyenne Chamber of Commerce and Wild Life Films,
1948.
The annual Wyoming rodeo.

4468 Chuckwagon. 16mm, color, sound, 10 min. National Film
Board of Canada, 1965.
Chuckwagon racing at the Calgary Stampede.

4469 Circle of Champions. 16mm, color, sound, 14-1/2 min.
Florida Department of Commerce, 1973.
Racing at Gulfstream Racetrack.

4470 Citation--First Horse. 16mm, b & w, sound, 3 min. Official
Films, 1960.
Looks at the 1948 Triple Crown winner.

4471 The Color of Gold. 16mm, color, sound, 27 min. Palomino
Horse Breeders of America, 1976.
Breeding, training, and exhibiting the Palomino.

4472 Common Hoof Problems. 16mm, color, sound, 21 min. Cambridge Films, n. d.
Examines fourteen different problems.

4473 Conquista. 16mm, color, sound, 20 min. Alan Landsburg
Production, 1974.
Indians first view the horses of the Spaniards.

4474 Corrective Shoeing. 16mm, color, sound, 21 min. Cambridge Films, n. d.
How to correct gait problems.

4475 The Cowboy. 16mm, b & w, sound, 11 min. Arthur Barr
Productions, 1949.

4476   The Cowboy. 16mm, color, sound, 54 min. Time-Life,
          1970.

4477   Cowboy and Indian. 16mm, color, sound, 45 min. National
          Film Board of Canada, 1972.
          Three films depicting history, life-styles, and attire
          of cowboys and their mounts, with some attention in the
          latter to Indians.

4478   Cowboys and Indians. 16mm, color, sound, 27 min. Pony
          of America Club, Inc., 1977.
          History and activities of the Pony of America.

4479   Dapples and Bays, Pintos and Greys. 16mm, color, sound,
          17 min. Modern Talking Picture Service, n. d.
          Shows wild horses of the American West.

4480   The Day of the Horse. 16mm, color, sound, 10 min. Land-
          mark Production, 1974.
          The role of the horse in 1890's America is examined.

4481   A Diamond in the Rough. 16mm, color, sound, 16 min.
          E. K. Edwards and Son, n. d.
          The preparation of a rough Shetland Pony.

4482   Donald Pierce. 16mm, color, sound, 22 min. Tele-Sports,
          1973.
          Depicts the life and work of a California jockey.

4483   Donkeys. 16mm, color, sound, 11 min. Coronet Instructional
          Media, 1974.
          Donkey activities in various moods.

4484   Down the Straightway. 16mm, color, sound, 13-1/2 min.
          American Quarter Horse Association, 1968.
          Quarter Horse racing in four major contests.

4485   Easy in the Saddle. 16mm, color, sound, 18 min. Portia
          Mansfield Motion Pictures, 1955.
          Horse care and riding techniques.

4486   Eddie Arcaro. 16mm, b & w, sound, 25 min. Conselor,
          n. d.
          An interview with the famous jockey.

4487   Elegia. 16mm, color, sound, 20 min. United World Films,
          1969.
          Looks at horses on the plains of Hungary.

4488   Every Child's Dream. 16mm, color, sound, 15 min. E. K.
          Edwards and Son, n. d.
          A promotional piece concerning Shetland Ponies.

4489 Faces in the Crowd. 16mm, color, sound, 4 min. Communicaet Film Productions, 1973.
A quick look at one boy's day at a racecourse.

4490 Finale. 16mm, color, sound, 3 min. Insight Productions, 1974.
A brief look at horseracing.

4491 Fire Away, the Story of a Trotter. 35mm, color, sound, 19 min. Paramount Pictures, 1962.
From foaling to the first big race.

4492 Five Hundred Horses. 35mm, b & w, sound, 10 min. Paramount Pictures, 1955.
Harness race training at Florida's Ben White Raceway.

4493 For the Love of a Horse. 16mm, color, sound, 14 min. Film Arts (Toronto), 1973.
A girl learns to ride.

4494 From the Cradle to the Crown. 16mm, color, sound, 30 min. Tennessee Walking Horse Breeders and Exhibitors Association, 1976.
Follows the life of a walker foal through the Celebration stage.

4495 Gauchos Down Uruguay Way. 35mm, b & w, sound, 11 min. Columbia Pictures, 1954.
Daily life of a South American cowboy.

4496 Gentling. 16mm, color, sound, 12 min. Marshall Faber Film Productions, n. d.
How to gain a horse's confidence.

4497 Goin' Down the Road. 16mm, color, sound, 25 min. R. J. Reynolds Tobacco Company, 1975.
A look at rodeos and champion cowboy Jim Shoulders.

4498 The Good Servant. 16mm, color, sound, 19 min. Campbell Harper Films, 1964.
The Clydesdale.

4499 Grand Prix Dressage, 1932 Olympic Games. 16mm, b & w, sound, 15 min. American Horse Shows Association, 1936.
An older film with still-excellent coverage.

4500 Gulfstream '75. 16mm, color, sound, 14 min. Florida Department of Commerce, 1976.
Racing at Gulfstream racecourse in 1975.

4501 The Gulfstream Story. 16mm, color, sound, 15 min. Tel-Air Interests, 1962.
A history of the race course and 1961 racing at it.

4502 Gulfstream--the Home of Champions. 16mm, color, sound,
      15 min. Tel-Air Interests, 1963.
      Racing at the Florida Track in 1962.

4503 Hackneys, the Aristocrats of the Show Ring. 16mm, color,
      sound, 27 min. American Horse Shows Association, 1978.
      A history of the breed and a look at its ring activities.

4504 Harness Champions. 16mm, b & w, sound, 10 min. Castle
      Films, 1950.
      The story of the Hambletonian Cup race.

4505 High Country. 16mm, color, sound, 12 min. A.C.I. Pro-
      ductions, 1962.
      Another look at the annual Calgary Stampede.

4506 Highlights of the I.F.R. 16mm, color, sound, 26 min. In-
      ternational Rodeo Association, 1976.
      Action at the rodeo.

4507 History of the Turf. 16mm, color, sound, 13 min. Film
      Arts (Toronto), 1973.
      A brief history of thoroughbred racing.

4508 Horse. 16mm, color, sound, 12 min. A.B.C. Media Con-
      cepts, 1972.
      Horses and language.

4509 Horse. 16mm, color, sound, 22 min. A.B.C. Media Guild,
      1976.
      Evolution and domestication.

4510 The Horse and Its Relatives. 16mm, b & w, sound, 10 min.
      Coronet Films, 1942.
      Examines various members of the horse family from
      thoroughbreds to zebras.

4511 Horse Farm. 16mm, color, sound, 15 min. Grover-Jennings,
      1960.
      Looks at a farm where horses are raised for pleasure
      riding.

4512 Horse Feeds and Horse Feeding. 16mm, color, sound, 27
      min. Cambridge Films, n.d.
      What to feed the horse and how.

4513 The Horse in North America. 16mm, color, sound, 24 min.
      UCLA, 1942.
      From fossils through importation and development.

4514 Horse in the Limelight. 16mm, b & w, sound, 17 min. Sol
      Films, 1956.
      Views the 1956 Equestrian Olympics in Stockholm, Sweden.

4515 Horse Management and Stock Seat Equitation. 35mm, color,
      sound, 26 min. Carnation Albers Company, 1970.
           Care and riding technique.

4516 Horse Sense. 16mm, color, sound, 23 min. U.S. Dept. of
      Agriculture, 1953.
           Mounting, riding, and care.

4517 Horse Shoeing. 16mm, b & w, sound, 19 min. U.S. Office
      of Education, 1944.
           Employs a "how to do it" approach.

4518 The Horse with the Flying Tail. 16mm, color, sound, 47
      min. Disney, 1960.
           How a Palomino cow horse becomes a member of the
      U.S. Equestrian Team.

4519 Horsemanship--Aids and Gaits. 16mm, b & w, sound, 40
      min. U.S. Army, 1942.
           Movements and controls.

4520 Horsemanship--Judging and Cross Country Riding. 16mm,
      b & w, sound, 33 min. U.S. Army, 1942.
           The principles involved.

4521 Horsemanship--Mr. Decathlon. 16mm, color, sound, 28 min.
      American Quarter Horse Association, 1966.
           The use of the quarter horse in riding, racing, and
      rodeo.

4522 Horsemanship--Mounting at Military Saddle. 16mm, b & w,
      sound, 32 min. U.S. Army, 1942.
           Getting aboard.

4523 Horsemanship--the Quarter Horse at Halter, Roping, Cutting,
      Reining. 16mm, color, sound, 45 min. American Quarter
      Horse Association, 1965.
           Employment of the quarter horse in those various events.

4524 Horsemanship--Ride, Cowboy, Ride: Parts I and II. 16mm,
      color, sound, 60 min. American Quarter Horse Associa-
      tion, 1965.
           Versatility in work, sport, and pleasure.

4525 Horsemanship--Saddling and Bridling. 16mm, b & w, sound,
      24 min. U.S. Army, 1942.
           The proper methods.

4526 Horsemanship--Supplying Exercises. 16mm, b & w, sound,
      17 min. U.S. Army, 1942.
           Exercises for the horse.

4527 Horsemanship--They're Off and Running. 16mm, color, sound,

45 min. American Quarter Horse Association, 1965.
Reviews Quarter Horse racing.

4528 Horsemanship--Youth and the Quarter Horse. 16mm, color,
sound, 52 min. American Quarter Horse Association,
1965.
Racing and training the Quarter Horse.

4529 Horsemen of the Western Trails. 16mm, b & w, sound, 11
min. Encyclopaedia Britannica Films, 1949.
Cowboys and cowgirls work their horses.

4530 Horsepower. 16mm, color, sound, 9 min. Memphitis Productions, 1973.
Horses vs. machines in the logging industry.

4531 Horses. 16mm, b & w, sound, 30 min. KQED, 1957.
Japanese equine paintings.

4532 Horses and Their Ancestors. 16mm, color, sound, 12 min.
McGraw-Hill, 1963.
Developmental history.

4533 Horses Can Take It. 16mm, color, sound, 26 min. Contemporary Films, 1941.
Pictures a two-day trail ride.

4534 Horseshoers. 16mm, b & w, sound, 14 min. Norwood Studios, 1960.
Farriers and their craft.

4535 How to Rope a Calf. 16mm, color, sound, 27 min. Cambridge Films, 1977.
Instructions from R. E. Josey.

4536 How to Run the Barrels and Win. 16mm, color, sound, 25
min. Cambridge Films, 1978.
Explained and demonstrated by Martha Josey.

4537 How to Spot Horse Health Problems by Observation. 16mm,
color, sound, 20 min. Cambridge Films, 1976.
Shows how, through daily observation, horse health
problems can be spotted.

4538 The Hunt Seat Horse. 16mm, color, sound, 15 min. American Quarter Horse Association, 1971.
Training for the Bridle Path Hack class.

4539 If Wishes Were Horses. 16mm, color, sound, 25 min. Pyramid Films, 1978.
Views the world of the thoroughbred.

4540 An Introduction to Conformation. 16mm, color, sound, 18

min. E. K. Edwards and Son, n. d.
As applicable to Shetland Ponies.

4541 An Introduction to Endurance Riding. 16mm, color, sound,
15 min. DeAtley Film Productions, 1977.
Conditioning tips for distance contests.

4542 Fanie Sue and Tugaloo. 16mm, color, sound, 10 min. Cen-
tron, 1971.
A young girl lives on a horse farm.

4543 Judging Mares at Halter. 16mm, color, sound, 28 min.
Texas Agricultural Extension Service, 1973.
A "how to do it" guide.

4544 Junior Bronc Busters. 16mm, b & w, sound, 10 min. Castle
Films, 1952.
Boys and girls compete in a junior rodeo.

4545 Leather and Lather. 35mm, b & w, sound, 8 min. RKO-
Pathé, 1954.
Examines cowboy and Gaucho pastimes.

4546 Lure of the Turf. 35mm, b & w, sound, 8 min. RKO-Pathé,
1952.
The history and romance of Saratoga racetrack.

4547 Man on Horseback. 16mm, b & w, sound, 10 min. General
Motors Corp. , 1940.
Selecting and training police horses.

4548 Mighty Biscuit Triumphs Again. 16mm, b & w, sound, 3
min. Official Films, 1961.
Seabiscuit's racing victories in the late 1930's.

4549 Mr. Decathlon. 16mm, color, sound, 33 min. American
Quarter Horse Association, 1977.
Reviews the basic importance of good conformation.

4550 Mother [Marjorie Kessler] Was a Champ. 35mm, b & w,
sound, 9 min. Paramount Pictures, 1953.
Portrait of a riding champion.

4551 Move 'em Out. 16mm, color, sound, 30 min. WMVS-TV, 1973.
Looks at Iowa farmer Dick Sparrow's 40-horse hitch.

4552 Nashua Sold for Record Price, December 14, 1955. 16mm,
b & w, sound, 5 min. Official Films, 1960.
A brief review of the thoroughbred's victories.

4553 New Era of a Champion. 16mm, color, sound, 14-1/2 min.
Florida Department of Commerce, 1972.
Derby Day at Gulfstream racetrack.

4554 New Zealand Thoroughbred. 16mm, color, sound, 18 min.
      New Zealand Government, 1951.
         Horses are seen on New Zealand stud farms.

4555 The 1959 Hambletonian and Little Brown Jug. 16mm, color,
      sound, 29 min. U.S. Trotting Association, 1960.
         Important harness races in Illinois and Ohio.

4556 No Hoof--No Horse. 16mm, color, sound, 19 min. Alberta
      Department of Agriculture, 1973.
         Hoof maintenance through skilled farriery.

4557 Nowhere to Run. 16mm, color, sound, 20 min. Phoenix
      Films, 1976.
         The plight of the Mustang.

4558 Of Horses and Men. 16mm, color, sound, 10 min. Disney,
      1968.
         A history.

4559 The Olympics of Racing. 16mm, color, sound, 13 min.
      Florida Department of Commerce, 1974.
         Famous race horses are seen at Gulfstream Park.

4560 On the Fifth Day. 16mm, color, sound, 29 min. American
      Quarter Horse Association, 1973.
         Examines the evolution of the Quarter Horse.

4561 1/4 Horse, 3/4 Dynamite. 16mm, color, sound, 23 min.
      American Quarter Horse Association, 1970.
         Training and conditioning at Los Almitos racetrack.

4562 Orthopedic Problems in Horses Relative to Specific Activities.
      16mm, color, sound, 21 min. Cambridge Films, 1979.
         Shows how the effects of physical performance can be
      minimized through good conformation, feeding, and shoeing.

4563 Palio. 16mm, color, sound, 30 min. Phoenix Films, 1976.
         Horse racing in Italy.

4564 Palomino, the Golden Horse. 16mm, color, sound, 11 min.
      Simmel-Meservey, 1946.
         Horse care and fundamentals.

4565 Parasites in Horses. 16mm, color, sound, 25 min. Asso-
      ciation Films, n.d.
         What they are and how to control them.

4566 Philip and the White Colt. 16mm, color, sound, 23 min.
      Columbia Pictures, 1973.
         Looks at the problems of a silent boy and his only
      friend.

4567 Pinto--Ride with Color. 16mm, color, sound, 17 min. Pinto
Horse Association, 1975.
Pinto color patterns and horse show activities are viewed.

4568 Ponies. 16mm, color, sound, 14 min. Moreland-Latchford,
1972.
An artistic portrayal of Welsh Ponies.

4569 The Pony. 16mm, b & w, sound, 29 min. McGraw-Hill,
1958.
Children raise a pony on a Canadian farm.

4570 The Pony Express in America's Growth. 16mm, b & w,
sound, 10 min. Coronet, 1960.
A history.

4571 The Pony Farm. 16mm, color, sound, 11 min. Frith Films,
1957.
Raising and keeping Shetland Ponies.

4572 The Pony Trail. 16mm, b & w, sound, 29 min. WOI-TV,
1958.
A history of the Pony Express.

4573 Portrait of a Horse. 16mm, color, sound, 28 min. Pyramid
Films, 1967.
Impressions based on animated views of oil paintings.

4574 The Portuguese Horse. 16mm, color, sound, 9 min. Modern
Talking Picture Service, n. d.
Horse training and riding in Portugal.

4575 Prelude. 16mm, color, sound, 5 min. Insight Productions,
1973.
Autumn on a horse farm.

4576 Pre-Natal and Post-Natal Care of Mares and Foals. 16mm,
color, sound, 21 min. Cambridge Films, 1976.
Explains various aspects of the conception-birth process.

4577 Pride of the Blue Grass. 35mm, color, sound, 71 min.
Allied Artists, 1954.
Focuses on the rehabilitation of a lame race horse.

4578 Pride, the Saddle Horse. 16mm, b & w, sound, 11 min.
Encyclopaedia Britannica Films, 1941.
Development and training of a pleasure horse.

4579 The Proud Breed. 16mm, color, sound, 26-1/2 min. Au-
dience Planners, n. d.
Uses of the Arabian Horse.

4580 The Quarter Horse. 16mm, color, sound, 33 min. Carnation-

Albers, 1964.
Care, feeding, training, and uses of the breed.

4581 Quarter Horse Barrel Racing. 16mm, color, sound, 10 min.
American Quarter Horse Association, 1974.
A look at this timed rodeo event.

4582 Quarter Horse Cutting. 16mm, color, sound, 20 min. American Quarter Horse Association, 1975.
Points out what to look for in judging this event.

4583 Quarter Horse--the Horse America Made. 16mm, color,
sound, 39 min. American Quarter Horse Association,
1970.
Versatility and history of the breed.

4584 The Queen's Plate. 16mm, color, sound, 21 min. National
Film Board of Canada, 1959.
A review of Canada's premier race.

4585 A Race of Horses. 16mm, color, sound, 10 min. Film
Australia, 1974.
Looks at the thoroughbred in Australia.

4586 Racing Tradition. 16mm, color, sound, 14-1/2 min. Florida
Department of Commerce, 1973.
Racing at Miami's Hialeah racetrack.

4587 Railbird's Album. 35mm, b & w, sound, 8 min. RKO-Pathé,
1954.
Looks at the training of a thoroughbred from foaling
through his first race.

4588 Reining the Horse. 16mm, color, sound, 27 min. American
Quarter Horse Association, n.d.
Examines the techniques involved.

4589 Reward of Champions. 16mm, color, sound, 14-1/2 min.
Florida Department of Commerce, 1973.
Another look at racing at Gulfstream Park.

4590 Ride a White Horse. 35mm, color, sound, 10 min. Vitaphone
Corp., 1953.
How girls learn to ride on a Nebraska ranch.

4591 A Ride in the Country. 16mm, color, sound, 20 min. H. K.
Edwards and Son, n.d.
Explains the 3-day event.

4592 Ride to Win. 16mm, color, sound, 26 min. Fraser W.
Smith, 1973.
Action at the Prince Philip Cup mounted games in
Canada.

4593 Riders of the Pony Express. 16mm, b & w, sound, 30 min.
       Sovereign Productions, 1953.
       A history.

4594 Riding High. 16mm, color, sound, 18 min. Davart Produc-
       tions, 1953.
       Views trail riding in the Canadian Rockies.

4595 Ridin', Ropin', Rodeo. 16mm, color, sound, 11 min. New
       Mexico State Tourist Bureau, 1947.
       Rodeos in New Mexico.

4596 Rodeo Cowboy. 16mm, color, sound, 27 min. Rick Fried-
       berg Productions, 1974.
       Examines the lives and techniques of rodeo riders.

4597 Rodeo Daredevils. 35mm, b & w, sound, 10 min. Columbia
       Pictures, 1956.
       Focuses on bronc bustin', calf roping, and trick riding.

4598 Rodeo Educational Film. 16mm, color, sound, 13 min. In-
       ternational Rodeo Association, 1976.
       Examines the basics of this contest form.

4599 The Rodeo Goes to Town. 16mm, b & w, sound, 10 min.
       20th Century Fox, 1941.
       Looks at the behind-the-scenes events at a rodeo.

4600 Rodeo Roundup. 35mm, color, sound, 10 min. Vitaphone
       Corp., 1954.
       Various rodeo contests are featured.

4601 Roses on the River. 16mm, color, sound, 28 min. Kentucky
       Department of Public Information, 1973.
       Reviews events of the 1972 Kentucky Derby.

4602 Rough Ridin' Youngsters. 35mm, b & w, sound, 9 min.
       Paramount Pictures, 1953.
       Looks at the annual La Junta, Colorado, Kids' Rodeo.

4603 Rough Riding. 35mm, color, sound, 10 min. MGM, 1954.
       Rules and requirements of bronc busting and calf roping.

4604 Rumble of the Wheels, Jingle of the Chains. 16mm, color,
       sound, 14 min. Modern Talking Picture Service, n.d.
       Clydesdales in action.

4605 Run, Appaloosa, Run. 16mm, color, sound, 48 min. Disney,
       1966.
       An Indian horse wins racing fame.

4606 The Saddlemaker. 16mm, color, sound, 17 min. National
       Film Board of Canada, 1961.
       The making of a saddle from cowhide is explained.

4607   San Fernando Saddle Champs.   35mm, b & w, sound, 10 min.
        Paramount Pictures, 1955.
            Equestrian sports in the San Fernando Valley are viewed.

4608   Saturday.   16mm, color, sound, 15 min.   Communicaet Film
        Productions, 1972.
            What one boy's day at a racetrack is like.

4609   Secretariat, Big Red's Last Race.   16mm, color, sound, 25
        min.   Viking Films, 1975.
            The Canadian International of 1973.

4610   Shetlands at Home Anywhere.   16mm, color, sound, 16 min.
        E. K. Edwards and Son, n. d.
            Housing and stabling for the Shetland Pony.

4611   Shoemaker Wins Record 485 Races, December 31, 1953.   16-
        mm, b & w, sound, 5 min.   Richard B. Morros, 1960.
            A review.

4612   Shoes and Smiths.   16mm, b & w, sound, 15 min.   KQED-
        TV, 1957.
            Fitting horseshoes.

4613   Showcase of Champions.   16mm, color, sound, 14-1/2 min.
        Florida Department of Commerce, 1974.
            Gulfstream racetrack.

4614   Showing and Judging Hunters.   16mm, color, sound, 27 min.
        American Horse Shows Association, 1978.
            Presents a detailed look at ring showing.

4615   Showtime for Saddlebreds.   16mm, color, sound, 13 min.
        Venard Films, n. d.
            Treats of a variety of ring events.

4616   The Spanish Riding School of Vienna.   16mm, color, sound,
        16 min.   Austrian Institute, 1975.
            A demonstration and review of the school's history.

4617   Spike--the Montana Horseman.   16mm, color, sound, 12 min.
        Learning Corp. of America, 1976.
            Discusses the lifestyle of a cowboy.

4618   Stable Stakes.   35mm, b & w, sound, 10 min.   Columbia Pic-
        tures, 1955.
            Thoroughbred training at Hasty Horse Farms for racing
        at Hialeah.

4619   Stampede.   16mm, b & w, sound, 29 min.   National Film
        Board of Canada, 1963.
            Follows cowboy Kenny Parsons at the 1962 Calgary
        Stampede.

4620 Stampede Stopover. 16mm, color, sound, 13 min. Imperial
Oil (Toronto), 1961.
A girl visits the Calgary events.

4621 The Superlative Horse--an Ancient Fable. 16mm, color,
sound, 36 min. Phoenix Films, 1975.
Horse judging in old China.

4622 Survival of the Fittest. 16mm, color, sound, 48 min. American Quarter Horse Association, 1978.
Focuses on the work of veterinarian Dr. Marvin Beeman.

4623 Team Roping. 16mm, color, sound, 28 min. American
Quarter Horse Association, 1978.
Looks at a fast-rising equestrian sport.

4624 Teasing and Breeding Procedures. 16mm, color, sound, 21
min. Cambridge Films, 1977.
A complete short course for horsemen.

4625 Therapeutic Shoeing. 16mm, color, sound, 23 min. Cambridge Films, 1977.
How to increase the usefulness of horses with hoof
problems.

4626 This Is a Horse Show. 16mm, color, sound, 15 min. De-
Atley Film Productions, n. d.
What to look for at such an event.

4627 This Is Harness Racing. 16mm, color, sound, 15 min. MAR-
CHUCK, 1975.
A survey of the sport.

4628 Thoroughbred. 16mm, color, sound, 21 min. Insight Productions, 1972.
Examines the life of a racehorse from birth to competition.

4629 Trail Ride. 16mm, color, sound, 20 min. National Film
Board of Canada, 1964.
A summer event in Alberta's Blood Indian Reserve.

4630 Training Colts. 16mm, b & w, sound, 15 min. KQED-TV,
1957.
Both a history of the American horse and a view of
training techniques.

4631 Training Police Horses. 16mm, b & w, sound, 10 min.
20th Century-Fox, 1942.
For the New York City Police Department.

4632 Training the Dressage Horse. 16mm, b & w, sound, 20 min.

American Horse Shows Association, n. d.
A German film with English subtitles.

4633 Trooping the Colour. 16mm, color, sound, 10 min. British
Central Office of Information, 1950.
Looks at the Horse Guards' parade.

4634 Trotting Top Notchers. 35mm, b & w, sound, 9 min. Columbia Pictures, 1956.
The grooming and training of a trotter.

4635 Twin Riding Champs. 35mm, b & w, sound, 10 min. Paramount Pictures, 1954.
Californians display training and performing abilities.

4636 Two Bolts of Lightning. 16mm, color, sound, 15 min. American Quarter Horse Association, 1977.
Views the World Championship Cutter and Chariot Racing finals.

4637 Vaquero. 16mm, color, sound, 15 min. Garrett Productions,
1974.
A history of the Mexican cowboy.

4638 Venezuelan Equine Encephalomyelitis (VVE): A National Emergency. 16mm, color, sound, 11 min. U. S. Department
of Agriculture, 1972.
Combating horse sleeping sickness.

4639 The Welsh Pony, a Source of Pleasure to Sportsmen of All
Ages. 16mm, color, sound, 27 min. American Horse
Shows Association, 1976.
History and movement of the breed.

4640 Why Appaloosas? 16mm, color, sound, 30 min. DeAtley
Film Productions, n. d.
A history, narrated by Burt Reynolds with scenes from
his ranch.

4641 Win, Place, or Show. 16mm, b & w, sound, 30 min. National Film Board of Canada, 1955.
Describes thoroughbred horse-racing in Canada.

4642 With Flying Colours. 16mm, color, sound, 55 min. Insight
Productions, 1974.
Highlights of Canada's 1973 racing season.

4643 World Championships. 16mm, b & w, sound, 59 min. Marshall Faber Film Productions, n. d.
Views the Appaloosa horse show in Lincoln, Nebraska.

4644 The World's Most Versatile Horse. 16mm, color, sound,
13 min. American Quarter Horse Association, 1969.
The Quarter Horse.

4645 <u>The Working Hunter and Jumper.</u> 16mm, color, sound, 15 min. American Quarter Horse Association, 1976. Selecting, schooling, and showing.

PERIODICALS CITED

The articles in Parts I-XI were taken from the following list of periodicals. Complete details on particular journals, periodicals, or magazines may be found in: Union List of Serials in Libraries of the United States and Canada, 5 vols. (New York: H. W. Wilson co., 1965); New Serial Titles, 1950-1960, 2 vols. (Washington, D. C.: Library of Congress, 1961); New Serial Titles, 1961-1965, 3 vols. (New York: R. R. Bowker Co., 1967); New Serial Titles, 1966--. (Washington, D. C.: Library of Congress, 1967--); Ulrich's International Periodical Directory, 18th ed. (New York: R. R. Bowker, Co., 1978); and Ayer Directory of Publications, 112th ed. (Bala Cynwyd, PA.: Ayer Press, 1980).

Agriculture History
Agricultural Technology
American Anthropology
American Cattle Producer
American Education
American Farriers Journal
American Horseman
American Journal of Archaeology
American Journal of Veterinary
　Research
American Notes and Queries
American Oriental Society Journal
American Quarterly
American Speech
American Veterinary Medical As-
　sociation Journal
American West
Animal Industry Today
Annals of Wyoming
Antiquity
Appaloosa News
Argosy
Arizona and the West
Arizona Highways
Australian Parks and Recreation

The Backstretch
Breeder's Gazette
Breeder's Reference Guide

British Veterinary Journal
Brown's Guide

California Historical Quarterly
California Horse Review
Canadian Business Management
Canadian Horse
Chicago
Chronicle of the Horse
Chronicles of Oklahoma
Classic
Colorado Magazine
Connecticut
Connoisseur
Conservationist
Cornell Veterinarian
Cosmopolitan
Country Gentleman
Country Journal

Denver Magazine
Denver Westerners' Roundup
Desert
Disabled U. S. A.
Dressage and CT

Economic History Review
Empire State Report
English Studies

Equine Veterinary Journal
Equus
Extension Service Review

Farm Journal
Farm Quarterly
Farmer's Bulletin
Feedstuffs
Frontier and True West

Genetics

Heavy Horse Driving
History Today
Honolulu
Horizon
Horse Action
Horse and Horseman
Horse and Rider
Horse Illustrated
Horse Lover's Magazine
Horse Lover's National Magazine
Horse of Course
Horseman

Isis

Journal of African History
Journal of Agriculture (Mel-
  bourne)
Journal of Animal Science
Journal of Arizona History
Journal of Finance
Journal of Heredity
Journal of Mississippi History
Journal of Near Eastern Studies
Journal of Physiology
Journal of Popular Culture
Journal of Range Management
Journal of the [British] Minis-
  try of Agriculture
Journal of the West

Los Angeles
Louisiana History

Maryland Historical Magazine
Midwest Quarterly
Military Affairs
Minnesota History
Modern Language Review
Money

Montana Magazine of Western
  History
The Morgan Horse

Nature Magazine
Nebraska History
Nebraskaland
Nevada Horse Life
Nevada Magazine
New Hampshire Profiles
New Orleans
New Mexico Magazine
New West
New Zealand Journal of Agri-
  culture
North Dakota Quarterly

Occupational Outlook Quarterly
Olympian Outdoor Indiana

The Paint Horse Journal
Palimpsest
Parade Magazine
Persimmon Hill
Phoenix
Practical Horseman

Quarter Horse Journal
Quarter Horse World
Quest

Rangeman's Journal
Rapidan River Farm Digest
Red River Valley Historical Re-
  view

Sandlapper
Soldiers
South Atlantic Quarterly
Southwest Art
Southwest Journal of Anthropo-
  logy
Southwestern Review
The Spot-Lighter
Spur
Synergist

Texana
Texas Monthly
Texas Quarterly
Theater Notebook
Town and Country

Turf and Sport Digest

Utah Science

Vermont Life
Veterinary Medicine
Veterinary Record

Western Historical Quarterly
Western Horseman
Westways
Women Sports
World Review of Animal Pro-
duction.

Yankee

INDEX

The citations in this index are keyed by entry to the references in Parts I-XI of the bibliography. Included herein are authors, editors, joint-authors and joint editors. Cross references are made between pseudonyms and real names.

tion, 833-834, 3877
American Paso Fino Horse
Association 719
American Quarter Horse Asso-
ciation 860-864, 3212
American Saddle Horse Breeders'
Association 697-700
American Shetland Pony Club
1031
Ammann, Max E. 139
Anderson, C. William 430, 611,
1200, 2273, 2449, 4174, 4267-
4268
Anderson, G. Kent 1633
Anderson, James D. 914
Anderson, John K. 3812, 3872
Anderson, John Q. 3873
Anderson, LaVere 4372
Anderson, M. M. 720, 956,
2005
Andrist, Friedrich 551
Anglesey, Marquess of 3874
Ansell, Michael P. 1887, 3257
Appaloosa Data, Inc. 728
Arab Horse Society 742-743
Arabian Horse Association
International 744
Arabian Horse Registry of
America 745
Arabian Horse Society 3213
Arbuckle, Helen 1824
Arcaro, Eddie 2922, 2991
Arkansas, State Racing Com-
mission 2757
Arlandson, Lee 731
Armstrong, Kathleen 592
Arnold, Jobie 431, 701, 1722,
2851
Arnold, Oren 594, 1858
Arquette, Carol 746
Arsenis, Mylda L. 4175
Ashland, Linda 2848
Assaff, Edith 3986
Atherton, Lewis E. 3717
Atkinson, Ted 2669
Austin, David W. 3050
Australian Information Service
185
Australian Jockey Club 915
Avis, Frederick C. 65
Axthelm, Pete 3002
Ayres, Michael 2879, 2948

Babcock, Gil 1589

Back, Joe 3615
Baerlein, Richard 1204
Bagley, Kathryn N. 1383
Bagnold, Enid 4209
Bailey, Gordon C. 3616
Bailey, Ivor N. 3024
Bailey, Jean 4210
Bailey, Nevajec 309
Baillargen, J. A. 3987
Baird, Eric 1236, 2274
Baker, Donna 4373
Baker, F. H. 2599
Baker, Jerry 2097-2099, 3258
Baker, John P. 1341
Baker, Richard S. 3813
Balch, Glenn 612-613, 732
Baldwin, James 3050
Ball, Alan 3197
Ball, Charles E. 2408
Ballantine, Derek 2670
Ballantine, William 2275
Bama, James 4347
Banks, Carolyn 3376
Banner, Susan 1460
Baranowski, Zdzislaw 66
Barbalace, Roberta C. 1032
Barber, Ted. 1077
Barbour, Ann C. 4346
Barker, Ann 3501
Barker, Herbert M. 2650
Barloy, Jean J. 3814
Barnard, Patty 733
Barnes, P. K. 1414
Barnes, Sheila 3259
Barnes, Sid 1205
Barnes, Sisley 1044
Barnett, Mike 2450
Barr, David 2949
Barrett, John L. M. 2276
Barrie, Douglas M. 916, 2671
Barsaleau, Richard B. 3214,
3543-3544, 3617
Bartel, D. L. 291
Bartlett, Harry M. 3502
Barton, Frank T. 702, 2277
Batchelor, Denzil 2880
Batchelor, Vivien 3052-3053
Bates, Ted 3618
Battersby, M. E. 1807
Bauer, Dan 2950
Bauer, E. A. 3619
Bauer, Helen 3718
Bauer, Joseph J. 2611
Bayens, Cheri 2228

Borden, Spencer 749, 3877
Boren, Jon 2453
Born, Marjorie 1021
Borwick, Robin 1046
Botlorff, Robert M. 12
Boucaut, James 750
Boulat, Annie 2849
Bourassa, Jean 388
Bower, A. 1723
Bowman, Edward 3623
Bowmar, Dan M. 160
Boyd, Mildred 3817
Boylen, Christilot 3329
Brackett, Albert G. 3878
Bradac, Juli 3624
Bradbury, Peggy 1287, 1385,
1724
Bradfield, Byron 3720
Bradley, George K. 4009
Bradley, Glenn D. 4010
Bradley, Melvin 2282
Brady, Irene 615
Brainard, Jack 2205
Brander, Michael 69, 100, 3685,
3879
Brandl, Albert 292, 2454
Brann, Donald R. 1416-1417
Braun, P. C. 4176
Brendt, Jeff 3686
Brennan, John 2673, 2683,
2982, 2998, 3032, 4177
Brett-Smith, Richard 3881
Breuer, Les H., Jr. 1288-
1289
British Bloodstock Agency 515
British Horse Society and Pony
Club 1725, 2455, 3506
British Horse Society and Sports
Council Steering Committee
2283
Britt, Edgar 3000
Broadhead, W. S. 703
Brock, Paul 751
Broder, Patricia J. 4322-
4324, 4374
Broderick, A. Houghton 3818
Brooke, Geoffrey F. H. 1787,
2283a-2285
Brookshire, Frank 1047
Broome, David 3262
Brotchie, J. F., Jr. 2575
Broun, Heywood H. 2882-2883
Brown, Alwin R. 3625

Brown, Barbara J. 3427
Brown, Beth 4178
Brown, Bud 1463
Brown, Dee A. 3882-3883
Brown, Fern G. 3036
Brown, Frank A. 2071
Brown, Stephanie 2660
Brown, Stuart E., Jr. 3884
Brown, William R. 752
Browne, Edwin H. C. 2795
Brush, Peter 2951
Brusha, Mary A. 957
Bryans, J. T. 389
Buchanan, Buck 1898
Buchanan, Lamont 2924
Buck, Susan 434
Buckley, Amelia K. 14
Buckley, R. J. 4011
Bud Brown, F. V. 2642
Bukhari, Emir 3885
Bulla, Clyde R. 4213
Bullard, T. L. 1290
Bullen, Anne 997
Burch, Preston M. 2072-2073
Burford, A. 4012
Burke, John G. 15
Burkhardt, Barbara A. 16,
2008, 3330-3331
Burks, Katherine S. 1394
Burn, Barbara 3057
Burns, Joan S. 3332
Burns, Robert H. 1826
Burns, Ursula 998, 1023
Burt, Don 1395, 1557, 2388,
3058, 3218-3224, 3229, 3596
Bush, Doreen 1827, 3263
Buske, Randy 851
Butler, Doug 1464-1465
Butler, Patrick 3264
Butterworth, William E. 3886
Byers, Marjorie 2555
Byford, Sharon 2456, 3225
Byrne, Judith M. 2286

Cadfryn-Roberts, John 4305
Cady, Steve 1216
Calder, Alexander 4420
Calder, Jinni 4112
Caldron, W. Frank 4421
Caley, Homer K. 1292
California, Horse Racing Board
2758
Callahan, Teresa 3507

Wright, Gordon 2381-2382,
  2539-2540
Wright, Graeme 98
Wright, Howard 1175
Wright, W. 1783
Wyland, E. E. 2430
Wyman, Walter D. 1134
Wynmalen, Henry 305, 504,
  2383, 3375

Xenophon 2384

Yates, Elizabeth 386
Yenser, Karl 3255
Yost, Nellie S. 4106

Young, John R. 803, 1531,
  1632, 1677, 1803, 1971-
  1972, 2032
Young, Peter 3983-3984
Younghusband, Jimmy 2385
Youree, Dale 2174

Zaidenberg, Arthur 4435-4436
Zappler, George 3809
Zeuner, Frederick E. 3851
Zimmerman, Mrs. James M.
  2807
Zoll, Don 1784, 2431
Zuelke, Ruth 4296
Zurhorst, Charles 3790
Zwarun, Suzanne 1857